Planters, Merchants, and Slaves

Planters, Merchants, and Slaves

Plantation Societies in British America, 1650–1820

TREVOR BURNARD

The University of Chicago Press   Chicago and London

The University of Chicago Press, Chicago 60637
The University of Chicago Press, Ltd., London
© 2015 by The University of Chicago
All rights reserved. No part of this book may be used or reproduced in any
manner whatsoever without written permission, except in the case of brief
quotations in critical articles and reviews. For more information, contact
the University of Chicago Press, 1427 E. 60th St., Chicago, IL 60637.
Published 2015
Paperback edition 2019

28 27 26 25 24 23 22 21 20 19   1 2 3 4 5

ISBN-13: 978-0-226-28610-5 (cloth)
ISBN-13: 978-0-226-63924-6 (paper)
ISBN-13: 978-0-226-28624-2 (e-book)
DOI: https://doi.org/10.7208/chicago/9780226286242.001.0001

Library of Congress Cataloging-in-Publication Data

Burnard, Trevor G. (Trevor Graeme), author.
  Planters, merchants, and slaves : plantation societies in British
America, 1650–1820 / Trevor Burnard.
        pages : illustrations, maps ; cm.—(American beginnings, 1500–1900)
    Includes bibliographical references and index.
    ISBN 978-0-226-28610-5 (cloth : alk. paper)—ISBN 978-0-226-28624-2
(ebook) 1. Plantations—North America—History. 2. Plantations—
Jamaican—History. 3. Slavery North America—History. 4. North
America—History—Colonial period, ca. 1600–1775. I. Title. II. Series:
American beginnings, 1500–1900.
    HD1471.N7B87 2015
    306.3'49—dc23
                                                                                        2015001142

Contents

Illustrations

Abbreviations

AHR   American Historical Review
BL   British Library
CO   Colonial Office Papers, National Archives, Kew, London
CSP   *Calendar of State Papers,* Colonial Series, 34 vols. W. Noel Sainsbury et al. (London: His Majesty's Stationery Office), 1860–1994
IRO   Island Record Office, Twickenham, Jamaica
JA   Jamaica Archives, Spanishtown
NA   National Archives, Kew, London
T   Treasury Papers, National Archives, Kew London
TSTD   Trans-Atlantic Slave Trade Database, http://slavevoyages .org/tast/index.faces
WMQ   *William and Mary Quarterly*

Introduction: Plantation Worlds

An Argument

This book is about the origins and implementation of the large integrated plantation and the plantation system based on chattel black African slavery in British America between the mid-seventeenth century and the early nineteenth century. In this period the system was at its height and was as yet unchallenged by attacks on slavery emanating from Europe and by slave revolts, such as the Haitian Revolution of 1791–1804, which showed that planters and plantations were not invulnerable. But for most of the century preceding that revolt, the plantation system was a primary means whereby empire could be made to pay and bring profit to the homeland.

I put forward two major claims in this book. First, while the basic forms of the plantation system changed little over a very long period of time, it was also an institution with a history. As Russell Menard lamented, "The history of the integrated plantation and the gang system are treated as if they had no history but simply emerged fully developed as soon as commercial sugar cultivation on a large scale appeared in Barbados."[1] I stress both the longue durée and *conjonctures* and events, to use Fernand Braudel's distinction between kinds of historical time. For most of its duration, the plantation system was relatively unchanging. On occasion, however, it changed very quickly in fundamental ways and in ways related to external events. For example, it

FIGURE 1. Thomas Jefferys, *Map of the West Indies* in Jefferys, *The West Indies Atlas, or a General Description of the West Indies* (London, 1780). Private collection.

is not coincidental that the shift to the large integrated plantation system in seventeenth-century British American societies occurred at the same time as massive mobilizations of soldiers in the War of the Three Kingdoms in Britain in the 1640s and 1650s, and Britain's participation in the Nine Years' War and the War of the Spanish Succession between 1688 and 1713.

Secondly, the rise and consolidation of the plantation complex in British America should be seen alternately through Atlantic, British American, and imperial perspectives. We might conceive of the plantation system of eighteenth-century British America as a Venn diagram: if the plantation system is the middle circle, then the other two circles are the imperial system and British American societies. The plantation world was part, but not the entirety, of the imperial world. It was also part, but not the entirety, of the British American world. Alternative models to the plantation model existed, some of which had advantages over the plantation system that planters never recognized. Imperial policy makers' knowledge of the plantation system and how it worked was very limited. Indeed, the model that influenced many imperial officials in their thinking about America after the end of the Seven Years' War was India as ruled through the East India Company. I examine the plantation world of the eighteenth century not solely through the eyes of self-interested and narrowly focused planter elites, but also through the perspective of the rulers of the British empire. They saw the plantation system not just as a means of enhancing English (and then British) wealth, but also as an element within a larger geopolitical context in which Europe, Asia, and Africa also competed for imperial attention.[2] I examine the plantation world through the eyes of enslaved Africans; they are not the primary subjects of this book, but they were the means through which plantation wealth was created. Understanding how they were treated, exploited, and governed, and working out how they responded to such poor treatment, is central to grasping the plantation process. Indeed, their experiences are the most vital experiences associated with plantations, as they were the primary actors in this institution, at least in the Americas.

Similarly, the circle in our imaginary Venn diagram that represents America contains plantation and nonplantation worlds. To a large extent, these worlds were complementary. Without the wealth of the plantations to sustain them, those parts of British North America not devoted to plantation agriculture were poor and unimportant: eighteenth-century Connecticut, a poor colony with a stagnant economy and a provincial ruling class, is a good example of how the Americas might have looked had a plantation economy not existed.[3] But over time well-placed ideologues in a demographically thriving American north began to resent the pretensions of planters and their assumption that their interests were the interests of the British Atlantic world. James Otis, from Massachusetts, for example, fulminated that, unlike settlers in the Caribbean, who were a "compound mongrel mixture of English, Indian and Negro" (implying, using the parlance of the day, that they were like Spanish Americans), northern colonists were "free born British white subjects," as truly British as Britons themselves.[4] At the very height of their economic power, in the early 1770s, planters faced unanticipated opposition from people who did not live in slave societies.

Several assumptions animate this book. First and most important, the large integrated plantation was an extraordinary mechanism for generating wealth and prosperity. The large integrated plantation had dozens and perhaps hundreds of enslaved laborers. It was a self-contained unit on which all elements of production were combined in one place, and it generated wealth for its owners to a greater extent than any other American or British institution prior to the Industrial Revolution. The particular economic vitality of the plantation was realized only when its economies of scale became apparent. The large integrated plantation developed as a result of a confluence of factors, but the most significant was the solving of intractable problems of discipline over enslaved Africans. The solution to the problem of discipline did not come about quickly. It took some time to convince ordinary white men that working on a plantation and disciplining slaves was a job that offered many rewards, notably financial ones. Once the economic success of the large integrated plantation became well-known, as it did by the second quarter of the eighteenth century, many places quickly adopted it. Not all societies in British America that might have become plantation societies managed to do so, but those that did flourished. By the middle of the eighteenth century, and well into the nineteenth—at least in those parts of America that had access to fresh inputs of slave labor to replace slaves who died—the mature plantation system worked very effectively for the great majority of white people.

On a global scale, the plantation colonies of British America were minor players, not comparable with the great Asian empires of India and China, which produced tropical crops such as cotton and sugar primarily for domestic consumption.[5] But plantations were highly productive and profitable enterprises. The plantation colonies performed strongly not just in comparison to plantation colonies elsewhere, notably Brazil, but also with emerging industrial nations. Per capita product in Jamaica, for example, went from £8 in 1750 to £13.2 in 1770 to £29.2 in 1800, while per capita product in England and Wales in 1770 was £10. The choices made in the late seventeenth century to specialize in the large integrated plantation to produce tropical crops for export were vindicated in the third quarter of the eighteenth century, when planters benefited from economies of scale possible on some of the largest private enterprises in the early modern world. The principal features of the plantation complex were large-scale landholdings and slave-based labor forces; hierarchical and race-based management systems; export orientation; high-value per-capita output; and the application of scientific techniques of management to improve productivity.

This type of semi-industrial organization, which was present on large integrated plantations, was invented in Barbados in the mid-1640s almost from whole cloth, although there some antecedents in the start of the sugar industry in the Mediterranean and Atlantic islands in the late Middle Ages. It developed after the move toward widespread African slavery in the mid-1640s. Initially Barbadian planters used the dispersed plantation method to grow sugar, as was customary in Brazil. In this system small planters grew sugarcane using a few laborers and then took the cane to a mill owned by a large farmer for processing. Not until the 1660s was it clear that the integrated large plantation in which cane was grown and processed in the same unit offered considerable economies of scale, and not until the 1680s did the integrated plantation became dominant in Barbados. Even at that date the dispersed system did not disappear. David Eltis has shown that small farmers who grew sugar for export but who did not own their own mills were interspersed with the large planters who had adopted the integrated system. The dispersed system always had advantages, such as a more even distribution of costs and risks and, most important, significantly lower entry costs. The integrated plantation, the first example of which in Barbados, in operation by 1654, seems to have been the plantation of James Drax and his two hundred slaves, was much more amenable to managerial control over the factors of production, especially labor discipline. It also became closely connected with gang labor in which slaves worked in closely supervised, regimented formations.[6]

Second, the plantation system was dynamic, and the people who profited most from it were forward-thinking entrepreneurial risk takers who did a lot to make British America in their own image. The plantation system was not separate from and incidental to British and British American life between 1650 and 1820. In particular, the plantation system was modern rather than backward. It was an intrinsic part of merchant capitalism and was not inimical to industrial capitalism. Moreover, planters were quick to adapt to new situations and new problems. The plantation system was not a system that was going to fail owing to intrinsic problems in how it was constructed or because slavery—the institution that sustained it—was an outmoded institution that eventually would be replaced as the world became more modern. Indeed, the limits to the growth and flourishing of the plantation system did not come from internal constraints or from the danger that large numbers of enslaved Africans and African Americans posed to the rule of planters: they came from outside opposition, such as an increasingly powerful abolitionist movement in Britain and then the United States. There is no reason we should see in the plantation system a teleology of inevitable decline. In fact, the plantation system was internally coherent, economically adaptive, politically and socially acceptable, and beneficial for most white people. It was, of course, terrible for black people, even free ones.

Poor and middling whites, most of whom did not initially own many slaves, were important in making possible the transition to the large integrated plantation system in the late seventeenth and early eighteenth centuries. Keeping them satisfied was a major political and social imperative, and it required more than a shared commitment to white supremacy.[7] This is not to deny that an ideology of white supremacy was growing in plantation societies in the eighteenth century. The increasing stress laid upon the racial superiority of white people in plantation societies in the eighteenth and nineteenth centuries was undeniable. But ordinary white people had many reasons to support the plantation system. The economic benefits of the plantation system flowed mostly to merchants and planters, but enough benefits went to other white people to make the whole system palatable on economic grounds alone. Nevertheless, even though ordinary whites were generally content with living in plantation systems, they were very sensitive to their class and racial position. Managing ordinary whites was as important as controlling large enslaved populations.[8]

Violence, War, and Revolution

Third, understanding how the plantation system was born, how it grew, and how it maintained itself over time requires appreciating the importance of violence. Planters were violent people, and their underlings were usually even more violent. They employed violence mostly against slaves. By the nineteenth century some planters had convinced themselves that slavery in plantation settings could be maintained with minimal recourse to violence. Such thoughts did not occur to the men (and, occasionally, women) who perfected the plantation system in the late seventeenth and early eighteenth centuries and who participated enthusiastically in the Atlantic slave trade. The large integrated plantation (an agricultural estate with dozens to hundreds of slaves on which all aspects of the production of tropical goods for European markets were performed) was born in violence. It was sustained by the willingness of men experienced in warfare or the Atlantic slave trade to employ extreme violence against adult African men. Moreover, planters were absolutely certain that the state supported their right to command the labor and persons of enslaved people. In this respect, the plantation system manifested Hobbes's *Leviathan*.[9] Relentless violence at all levels of the system meant resistance of any serious or sustained kind from enslaved people was very difficult and ensured that successful resistance was impossible.

Wars had a great impact on plantation societies and were often the sources of changes in plantation organization. Thus, a lot of attention will be paid here to major Atlantic wars, from the Wars of the Three Kingdoms in the 1640s and 1650s; to the wars between England/Britain and France and Spain from 1688 to 1713; to the Seven Years' War, the American Revolution, and the French revolutionary wars of the second half of the eighteenth century and the first two decades of the nineteenth century. The plantation system was part of a global tectonic shift in the eighteenth century that spawned merchant capitalism, increasingly integrated global markets and systems, and a diverse world of production and consumption. This book places particular emphasis on the American Revolution as an event that had major consequences not only for the plantation system but also for our understanding of this event in global as opposed to American terms. The American Revolution led to an artificial division (for trivial reasons, in the larger context of things) between two sections of the plantation world. This division hinders us from viewing the plantation system encompassing the southern parts of North America, the Caribbean, and the northern parts of South America as a coherent whole, with close connections and structural similarities over a sustained period of time. The center of that large system changed over time, at least in British America. In the seventeenth century the center was Barbados; in the eighteenth it moved westward to Jamaica; and in the nineteenth the center moved both northward and southward, to Louisiana in the United States and to British Guiana in the British empire.

The American Revolution split the plantation world of English-speaking peoples into two. As a result, the Revolution looks very different depending on the vantage point from which one views it. We need to regard it from the perspective of a colonial plantation world that encompassed the West Indies and Florida as well as from the perspective of those plantation areas of the thirteen colonies that declared for independence in 1776. We also need to take into consideration the views of Britons from southern England. In that part of Britain, the main result of the American Revolution was that it made people wonder whether American protestations that they were fighting for liberty should change how slavery was viewed. The ideological tumults of the American Revolution and the separation of the largest body of slaveholders from British America into the new United States of America gave an impetus to a small group of abolitionists to press ahead to weaken slavery in the British empire.

If the plantation world had not split, abolitionists' task would have been more difficult. The long-term result of the American Revolution was to severely weaken the commitment of the British empire to the slave trade, the life force that kept slavery going, and then to slavery itself. From the viewpoint of the southern colonies of British America, the short-term hardships brought about by war were compensated by the long-term advantages of creating a proslavery constitution that allowed slavery to thrive and be protected for seventy-five years—two full generations longer than in the British empire.[10]

What were the worlds of plantation British America? There were three: the tobacco coast, comprising eastern Maryland, Tidewater Virginia, and the North Carolina coastal plain; the Lowcountry South, consisting of South Carolina, Cape Fear in North Carolina, and coastal Georgia and East Florida; and the British West Indies. We will look at each region in turn from around the time of the Seven Years' War and then during and after the American Revolution.

The Tobacco Coast

The Chesapeake was always meant to be a plantation society, in the sense of a plantation as a profit-making agricultural enterprise, oriented toward exports rather than subsistence farming. Early Virginia, settled first by the English under the auspices of a commercial company based in London, was intended to be a commercial outpost, on the Iberian model, in which precious metals would be mined, furs and other goods obtained from trade from Native Americans processed, easily gathered tropical crops brought together, and a few other export commodities, like naval stores, cultivated. The idea was that a small group of settlers living mostly in bounded towns would send goods for sale to England. The plan foundered on the absence of gold and silver, the hostility of Native Americans, and, most important, the unwillingness of settlers to be constrained by the rules and regulations of the Virginia Company. It took a long time for the plantation economy to succeed. It took even longer for the characteristic patterns of the plantation system of the eighteenth century to emerge. By 1612 Virginia had discovered a crop— tobacco—that served as an export commodity, and the first Africans had begun to trickle into the colony to supplement the growing numbers of English indentured servants.[11] How the Chesapeake became transformed in the late seventeenth century into a region with a substantial plantation regime and a confident ruling class will be discussed below. What is important to note here is that until the last decades of the seventeenth century, large plantations in the Chesapeake were very few in number and limited in importance. From the 1630s to the 1670s the Chesapeake remained, as Lorena Walsh notes, "a good 'poor man's country' where men and women possessed of modest capital or who were willing to finance migration through a labor contract might, if they survived the hostile Chesapeake disease environment, achieve a greater competency than they would have if they remained home."[12] As befitted a good "poor man's country," there were very few large planters—men with land and labor well above the norm—during most of the seventeenth century. There were probably no more than a dozen or more men in the 1640s with thousands of acres and labor forces numbering more than thirty slaves. Although wealthy planters started to buy slaves as a matter of deliberate choice by the late 1630s and early 1640s, substantial numbers of Africans entered the Chesapeake labor force only in the 1670s, with heavy migration beginning in the 1690s and peaking at 15,700 in the 1730s. Until 1700 only 6 percent of non-office-holding Virginia householders owned a slave. The Chesapeake thus had slaves and an export economy, but until the first or second decade of the eighteenth century it was neither a slave society nor a plantation economy similar to that established in Barbados in the mid-seventeenth century. As Philip Morgan comments, "By the late seventeenth century, Virginia had a plantation economy in search of a labor force." As late as 1700, blacks were only a sixth of the population of the Chesapeake, and just 10 percent of slaves lived in units of twenty-one or more individuals.[13]

By the middle of the eighteenth century, however, the Tobacco Coast was a substantial plantation region of British America as well as a major farming area, although average wealth per free white person and per capita remained modest. In the American South, however, the Tobacco Coast was disproportionately economically and politically powerful. It accounted for 82 percent of southern wealth outside of the Lowcountry, as seen in table 1.1. Its wealth was due to its large population of enslaved people, who formed the great majority of the wealth-producing

Table 1.1 Wealth by Region: Britain and British America, 1774

Region	Total Physical Wealth (£'000stg.)	Per Free White (£stg.)	Per Capita (£stg.)
England/Wales	278,000	42.1	42.3
British America	161,946	89.6	57.5
Thirteen colonies	109,570	60.2	46.5
Northern colonies	49,052	42.2	39.3
Southern colonies	60,518	92.7	54.7
West Indies	51,926	1,042.5	114.1

Sources: Trevor Burnard, "'Prodigious Riches': The Wealth of Jamaica before the American Revolution," *Economic History Review* 54 (2001): 520; B. R. Mitchell, *British Historical Statistics* (Cambridge: Cambridge University Press, 2011), 864; Alice Hanson Jones, *Wealth of a Nation to Be: The American Colonies on the Eve of Revolution* (New York: Columbia University Press, 1980), 54, 58; E. A. Wrigley and Roger Schofield, *The Population History of England, 1541–1871* (Cambridge: Cambridge University Press, 1981), 534.

Table 1.2 Wealth in Plantation America, 1774

Region	Wealth (£'000stg.)	No. of Whites	No. of Blacks	Population	Per White (£stg.)	Per Black (£stg.)	Per Capita (£stg.)
Plantations	104,358	519,301	799,534	1,321,335	201.0	130.5	79.0
Tobacco Coast	37,588	438,600	295,100	734,400	85.7	127.4	51.2
Lowcountry	14,844	35,300	92,500	129,600	420.5	160.5	114.5
West Indies	51,926	45,401	411,934	457,335	1143.7	126.1	113.5

Sources: See table 1.1. For population figures, see John J. McCusker and Russell R. Menard, *The Economy of British America, 1607–1789* (Chapel Hill: University of North Carolina Press, 1985); Russell R. Menard, "Economic and Social Development of the South," in *The Cambridge Economic History of the United States: The Colonial Era*, ed. Stanley L. Engerman and Robert E. Gallman (New York: Cambridge University Press, 1996).

part of the population. If wealth is divided by the number of blacks in the population, then average wealth was, at £127.4, slightly higher than in the West Indies and 3.2 times higher than per capita wealth in the northern farm colonies. Nevertheless, the comparatively large number of whites in nonplantation areas of the Tobacco Coast reduced overall wealth levels. Many of these whites were poor and landless.

By the middle of the eighteenth century the Tobacco Coast was economically diversified, with a core plantation area that produced tobacco for European markets and a farming area that produced corn and wheat. The biggest change in the region came early in the eighteenth century with the transition to a naturally increasing slave population.[14] Virginia planter Henry Fitzhugh spelled out the economic implications of this fundamental demographic shift. In 1766 he gloated that "my negroes increase yearly by which I am enabled to settle new quarters and consequently my exports must increase."[15] Unlike in other plantation regions in British America, the Atlantic slave trade dwindled into unimportance by the time of the American Revolution. Indeed, by the early nineteenth century the Chesapeake had become a slave-exporting region.[16] The transition to a naturally reproducing enslaved population led to a dramatic reorientation of slave-management policies. Planters became agricultural managers rather than entrepreneurs with a diverse portfolio of interests. In particular, planters moved away from active involvement in commercial life, with a firm division opening up between merchants and planters.[17]

This move made sense for most native-born planters with substantial inheritances and established positions in society, but it also had significant and mostly negative collective consequences. Great planters in the core tobacco-growing region of Tidewater southern Virginia found it hard to adapt to rapid economic change. The American Revolution was a political triumph for Virginia planters, with a Virginian dynasty firmly implanted in the presidency, but it was an economic disaster. The only area that prospered in this period was Baltimore, which had connections to Pennsylvania and the Middle Colonies that insulated it from troubles in the tobacco economy.[18]

Chesapeake planters remained efficient managers of diminishing resources after the American Revolution, but some actions proved counterproductive, as modernization yielded short-term profits at the expense of long-term environmental trouble. By 1816–17 parts of the Chesapeake faced a fully fledged subsistence crisis, while poverty was endemic and increasing. Even planters were not immune, and as they forced their enslaved people to work harder and screwed more and more out of tenants, white employees, and the poor of the region, class tensions multiplied.[19] Decline was registered in a static or declining population as poorer whites, sometimes accompanied by their slaves, dealt with economic downturn by migrating out of the region, especially Virginia, to places such as Kentucky.[20]

What differentiated the Tobacco Coast from the other two plantation regions was, first, the development by the second quarter of the eighteenth century of a diversity of plantation and nonplantation crops and, second, overall lower wealth of whites and noticeable white poverty. By the 1770s, for example, more than half of the free families in Prince George's County, Maryland, a rich planting parish, were landless tenants. Everywhere in the Upper South the number of poor people increased after 1760. By the late 1760s nearly one in seven householders in Anne Arundel County, Maryland, depended on charity. Colonial governments were busy multiplying poorhouses. Allan Kulikoff estimates that on the eve of the Revolution as many as one-third of white families in the Tidewater Chesapeake were poor.[21]

One reason for increased poverty within the tobacco economy was that planters were unable to increase productivity through effective use of new technologies. Indeed, soil exhaustion meant that in the 1750s productivity declined to 1690 levels. Productivity gains were made possible in the cultivation of grains, especially maize, and through replacing hoes with plows. Large planters were able to do this; smaller planters without slaves were not. Scholars have argued that there was some trickle-down of wealth to free workers, tenants, and small planters owing to greater success in grain production. Certainly, the wealth of tenant estates in Maryland increased by nearly 30 percent between 1740 and 1759, and declining consumer prices for goods meant even poor people enjoyed modest gains in living standards.[22]

It is unclear, however, whether many small farmers or agricultural laborers were aware of their improving situation. The rise of inequality made such small improvements seem somewhat derisory. Poor people fell behind richer people in their share of overall wealth. Between the 1730s and the 1760s the share of total wealth owned by the poorest 50 percent of Virginia planters fell from 7 percent to 4 percent. Householders who did not own slaves were especially disadvantaged, as they could not adopt new methods of husbandry and were forced to keep to older, unprofitable ways of farming. Tenant farmers were worse off than small planters as their rents rose, and the landless suffered most of all.[23] This plantation region, therefore, saw uneven benefits for whites, mainly because increasing white population and the Malthusian problems that resulted meant that many whites were shut out of the plantation system.

The Lowcountry

The second region of plantation British America, the Lowcountry of the Carolinas and Georgia, did much better overall from plantation agriculture in the eighteenth century. It was slow to develop, even though slavery was established as a principal feature of the labor force from the beginning of settlement in 1670, and despite the presence of sizable and very influential numbers of planters from Barbados arriving in the 1670s and 1680s, bringing with them a specific template for the creation of a plantation society. But if these Barbadians wanted to remake Carolina in the image of Barbados, this undermined the visionary, but somewhat impractical, schemes of the eight Lords Proprietors of Carolina, men of high rank and extensive commercial experience in England. What Anthony Ashley Cooper—Lord Ashley and later Earl of Shaftesbury—wanted was for Carolina to be a place that would plant a self-perpetuating English community, with definable social hierarchies and an agricultural system that drew on the region's obvious natural bounty, to develop individual prosperity within a constrained and controlled social structure. It did not work. Early planters, drawn mostly from England and Barbados, with some Irish and French Huguenots among them, quickly undermined, through highly individualistic settlement practices, any notion of the plantation as a collective enterprise. They replaced this vision with a more mundane, if realistic, idea of the plantation as an independent English household, producing not wheat or vegetable gardens as intended, but maize and beans as taught them by Native Americans, as well as livestock farms. Settlement increased rapidly, so that the 200 settlers of 1670 had increased to 6,000 by 1700, including 2,600 African and Indian slaves. Nevertheless, the abundant land of the region was barely touched, with plantations clustered along a few rivers near Charleston. And the colony had not moved very far toward becoming a plantation society on the Barbadian model. As Philip Morgan acutely notes, the South Carolina Lowcountry had "a labor force in search of a plantation economy." Most planters were not much more than subsistence farmers and exported provisions and wood products to the Caribbean and deerskins from the interior to Britain.[24]

It was only after rice was established as the principal commodity crop in the first decades of the eighteenth century that the region started to take on the lineaments of the large integrated plantation system. Hardly any rice was planted before the mid-1690s, but initial plantings in coastal swamplands proved highly successful. By 1710 1.5 million pounds of rice was being produced for export, and by 1720 around 6 million pounds was exported. Rice was not the only new commodity to be started in this period. Between 1705 and 1729 parliamentary legislation encouraged the production of naval stores, peaking at nearly 60,000 barrels in 1725. By 1739 naval stores had declined to just 11,000 barrels. When it was profitable, however, it contributed to a remarkable export boom. With naval stores, especially rice, and then indigo, the labor force had a crop that it could be used to cultivate. How South Carolina came to plant rice and who the prime movers were in its introduction is highly contested, but the effects of planters taking the risk of moving from the highlands to the swamps were clear.[25] It brought some, but not all, of the demographic characteristics of the West Indies to the Lowcountry. The population of blacks rose dramatically to 22,700 in 1730, with 56 percent of slaves working on slave units of 30 or more enslaved people.[26]

Nevertheless, South Carolina was different from the West Indies, even after rice had transformed settlement and culture by the 1720s. It was neither as wealthy nor as obviously dominated by blacks as Barbados, Jamaica, or Antigua. How one views the Lowcountry depends, of course, on whether we take an American or an Atlantic approach. By American standards the Lowcountry was easily the richest region of British North America. Indeed, in its wealth, its commitment to plantation agriculture, and its largely black population, the Lowcountry was an American outlier. Alice Hanson Jones made careful estimates of wealth in the thirteen colonies in 1774 and showed that the productive resources held in the Lowcountry were of a different order from other British America assets. The Lowcountry was easily the richest region in the American South: probated decedents in the Charleston area were worth four times as much as white residents of a prosperous region of the Tobacco Coast and nearly ten times as much as people living in the established areas of the interior.[27]

If we take an Atlantic approach, however, the Lowcountry's wealth was moderate, the number of black people compared to whites was not extraordinary, and the economy was surprisingly diverse for a society seemingly committed to monoculture. Only 25 percent of plantations in South Carolina between 1730 and 1776 primarily produced rice, and a further 11 percent were mainly devoted to indigo. By contrast, 60 percent of farmers produced corn, potatoes, or peas.[28] Large plantations overwhelmingly grew rice, with a minority producing indigo. Unlike planters elsewhere, Lowcountry planters were uninterested in diversification. Over time the Lowcountry became less, rather than more, agriculturally diverse. Naval stores and lumber production were pushed to the Lowcountry's periphery, such as the Cape Fear region of North Carolina, and rice became ever more predominant, with rice exports per capita rising from 70 pounds in 1700 to 380 in 1720, 1,000 in 1740, and over 2,000 by the mid-1770s.[29]

One way of dramatically emphasizing the differences in wealth between the three regions of plantation British America is to compare the cost of setting up a plantation. The costs were highest in the old West Indian plantation colonies. Various estimates suggest that a moderate sugar plantation with 146 slaves in the rapidly developing northwest of Jamaica cost £17,249, at £119 per slave, in 1775. A plantation with 167 enslaved people in the older part of Jamaica cost £18,089 to establish, or £108 per slave. A very large plantation with 300 slaves producing 300 hogsheads per annum was estimated by planter historian Edward Long in 1774 to cost £28,039, or £93 per slave. Even more expensive was a small sugar plantation in St. Kitts, where the average cost per slave in 1775 for a plantation with 47 slaves was £146: the major expense was land, which, at £3,200 for 110 acres was £29.1 per acre compared to £9.45 per acre in northside Jamaica. By comparison, plantations in South Carolina were smaller, with fewer than 50 slaves on initial founding, and were less expensive to set up. Russell Menard has collected six estimates of plantation set-up costs in the Carolinas from the 1710s to the 1770s. In 1710 a rice plantation with 1,000 acres and 40 slaves cost £1,000, or £25 per slave. In 1755 a careful estimate of a 1,000-acre plantation with 40 slaves suggests the cost had doubled to £2,000, or £50 per slave. By the 1770s a forty-hand rice plantation on 200 acres cost £2,500, or £62.50 per slave.[30]

South Carolina and Georgia were rice-planting colonies, and planters devoted as much resources as they could to expanding land for production of these crops. The 1740s saw a dramatic collapse in rice prices, which put many rice plantations in severe jeopardy. But recovery was swift. The rice industry proved very profitable from the Seven Years' War until well into the period of the early republic, except during the American Revolution. A census for the central inland parish of St. James Goose Creek in 1745 gives a guide to the structure of landownership, slave ownership, and staple production in the heart of the Lowcountry large plantation area. It may have been the richest locality in British North America with 70 percent of slaves living on plantations with more than fifty slaves. The median land holding was 908 acres, with 41 percent of properties over 1,000 acres. By the 1770s the whole of the Lowcountry was increasingly similar to St. James Goose Creek, with 52 percent of enslaved people living in units of more than fifty slaves. These slaves produced more than 3,000 pounds of rice per acre, up from 1,000 pounds in the early eighteenth century.[31]

As these figures suggest, a rice plantation was a large undertaking in an age of often limited agricultural enterprises. A rice plantation was at least five hundred acres, often over a thousand acres, at a time when some Massachusetts colonists were struggling to maintain farms of just thirty acres and English yeomen farmed holdings of fifty acres.[32] Rice planters extensively transformed these lands using up-to-date agricultural techniques, especially tidal-swamp rice fields. These fields, irrigated and improved, were a wonder of the Enlightenment age of agricultural experimentation.[33] But although rice lands were the most important part of a plantation, the rice plantation was also a diverse operation. It contained a mixture of fields under cultivation, drained forests, uncultivated swamps and woods, and makeshift pastures. These diverse locations gave lots of opportunities for enslaved people to follow their own impulses: to work on their own behalf or to hunt and fish.[34]

The improvements to rice plantations made them more productive, and more valuable. The organization of the rice trade became ever more efficient over time. The prices of both land and slaves kept advancing,[35] and significant fortunes began to be made. Joseph Allston, for example, started in the 1760s as a small planter with about 5 slaves. In the early 1770s he owned 500 slaves on five plantations with a net income of about £5,000–6,000. He was probably worth around £100,000. Henry Laurens, the most prominent planter-merchant in the mid-eighteenth-century

Lowcountry, was richer still. He made just under £7,860 sterling per annum in addition to his mercantile activities in 1772 from the labor of 325 slaves on four plantations, a spectacular return on capital of 18.3 percent in 1771–72. That was the highest rate of return he ever made, but between 1766 and 1773 his profits matched those made in any other plantation system. He averaged over 10 percent rate of return per annum in these years.[36] Laurens and other Lowcountry merchant and planter magnates were devoted to Enlightenment tenets of agricultural improvement within a slaveholding culture. Rice was central to this ethos of 'constant improvement,' as the contemporary historian David Ramsay noted at the time.[37]

By 1775 the Lowcountry was profitable and growing. The region had 129,600 people, of whom 92,500 were enslaved blacks. What differentiated the region most from the West Indies was that it bordered a massively expanding interior, which by 1775 had 73,100 people in South Carolina and Georgia, with a further 111,000 in the North Carolina Piedmont. Of these, 148,100 were white, mostly of non-English heritage. The black population was also changing, becoming a majority creole population by the 1740s, and self-sustaining without the Atlantic slave trade by the 1760s. The plantation economy moved northward into the Cape Fear region of North Carolina and southward into Georgia and even into eastern Florida. A boom in indigo exports from small levels in the 1750s to over £150,000 per annum in the 1770s made planters in the region very optimistic. Lowcountry exports around 1770 reached around £4 per capita, three times those from the rest of British North America, even if well below those from the West Indies.[38]

The War for Independence profoundly affected this upward trajectory, as will be discussed in chapter 5. Henry Laurens was captured by the British in 1780 en route to a diplomatic post in the Netherlands and held prisoner in the Tower of London for the next year, during which time his plantations faced unprecedented destruction. His son, John, George Washington's favorite officer and perhaps the only South Carolinian of distinction who might have moderated Carolinian commitment to chattel slavery, died in battle in a minor and pointless skirmish on 27 August 1782. When Laurens returned to South Carolina in 1785, it was to reduced circumstances—"the shattered remains of a once great Estate"—and a changed world. Honored as a great patriot, he reflected on the gap between his public persona and his private distress, noting in 1786 that "once I was engaged in a very large and extensive Commerce [but] at present I export the Produce of my own Plantation." But South Carolina eventually recovered, especially after

FIGURE 2. This print was one of several made around 1766 by an anonymous painter and engraved in England by John Boydell in 1770. Several were dedicated to leading Jamaican planters, in this case the Hon. John Palmer. See also figure 8 and the jacket illustration. *A View of the Town and Harbor of MONTEGO BAY, in the Parish of ST JAMES, JAMAICA, taken from the Road leading to ST ANNS* (1770). Private collection.

the introduction of the cotton gin in the 1790s, which allowed the interior to become as much a plantation economy as the rice-producing Lowcountry. Political alignment between the two regions followed in 1808, and by the early nineteenth century the region as a whole was prospering as much as in the 1760s. Some of its wealthiest men—such as Joshua John Ward, with 1,121 slaves, and Nathaniel Heyward, with 2,340 slaves—were as rich as West Indian magnates. By this time South Carolina and Georgia were no longer part of the West Indies, as London had envisioned them before the Revolution, but were a vibrant area of the growing American South.[39]

The West Indies

The final region of plantation America was the wealthiest one: the islands owned by the British in the Lesser Antilles, and Jamaica in the

Greater Antilles. By the early nineteenth century Britain had also established a beachhead on the tip of South America, taking over Demerara, Berbice, and Essequibo from the Dutch. By 1830 the total area of the British West Indies was 105,295 square miles, of which British Guiana accounted for 78.8 percent. There were 684,995 slaves in the region by this date, up from 316,891 in 1750. In the earlier period Jamaica had easily the most slaves, with 127,881; Barbados had 63,410, and Antigua had 31,123. In 1830 Trinidad, British Guiana, St. Vincent, and Grenada had joined the older colonies of Jamaica, Barbados, and the Leeward Islands as colonies with major concentrations of slaves.[40] Its early development is covered extensively in chapters 2 and 3.

The West Indies looks on the surface to be the least diverse region of plantation America. It was dominated by a single crop—sugar—and was more reliant on external trade than the other regions. Yet it was not a uniform economy, even if it had a mostly uniform climate, ideal for the production of tropical crops, including cacao in the seventeenth century and indigo, cotton, and especially coffee in the eighteenth century. The plantation was more dominant in the West Indies than anywhere else in British America. Some West Indian colonies, such as the Bahamas, Anguilla, Barbuda, and the Cayman Islands, were never plantation societies. Other colonies produced only minor amounts of sugar, such as Dominica, where suitable land was limited, given its mountainous terrain and wet climate. In marginal plantation colonies such as British Honduras, the principal economic activity was cutting down mahogany trees; most male slaves were woodcutters and most female slaves, domestics. The most diverse colony was Jamaica, where sugar was the most important crop; but only 52 percent of slaves worked in that crop, compared to over 75 percent in Barbados and in the Leeward Islands. Other slaves worked in coffee, tended livestock, or worked in Jamaica's towns. Jamaica's commitment to sugar was strong, but it was accompanied by lots of other kinds of tropical production occasioned by its varied physical environment and the relatively slow movement of the frontier settlement.[41]

With a white population that never reached 50,000 before the American Revolution and was just over 2 percent of the total white population in British America, the West Indies produced just under a third of the total wealth of British America in 1774. Average wealth was £1,043 per white person, over ten times as much as the average wealth of white people in other parts of British America. The only outlier was Barbados, where a relatively large white population had average wealth a fifth of that of Jamaica. In Barbados average wealth was closer to South Carolina

Table 1.3 Wealth of Jamaicans and South Carolinians, 1774: Total Physical Wealth (includes slaves; excludes realty and financial assets and liabilities)

Name	Wealth (£stg.)	Name	Wealth (£stg.)
Jamaica:		Carolina:	
William Beckford	81,621	Peter Manigault	27,960
John Bryan	41,959	Elijah Postele	15,561
John Nixon	32,218	John Ainslie	11,796
John McLeod	31,882	Richard Capers	8,785
Ennis Read	22,498	Benj. Williamson	8,225
Peter McKenzie	16,448	John Cottell	8,128
Benjamin Pereira	14,129	Arch. McNeill	8,064
Gilbert Mathison	13,950	Thomas Jones	7,960
George Williams	12,435	Christopher Jenkins	7,680
Archibald Sinclair	11,614	John Tonge	5,845

Source: Inventories, JA, IB1/11/3/55–6; Jones, *Wealth of a Nation to Be*, 180.

levels. One sign of West Indian prosperity was that per capita wealth, even including very poor black slaves, was nearly twice as much as in British America as a whole. What this meant at an individual level can be seen in table 1.3, where the ten wealthiest people inventoried in 1774 in Jamaica are compared to the ten wealthiest people in South Carolina. Total wealth, excluding real estate and financial assets, of the richest Jamaicans was £246,872, compared to £101,308 for South Carolina. There were four Jamaicans wealthier than Peter Manigault, easily the wealthiest man who died in British North America in that year, and eighteen Jamaicans wealthier than the tenth wealthiest South Carolinian.[42]

Some parts of the West Indies were not as wealthy as Jamaica. Places without extensive commitment to sugar, like Dominica, the Virgin Islands, some of the very small islands, and the marginal plantation colony of British Honduras, were not especially rich. It was sugar that brought riches. The wealth that sugar brought was well recognized and led planters to move out of all other crops. By the late eighteenth and early nineteenth centuries, sugar and its by-products made up nearly 100 percent of the value of exports of some islands, like Barbados and the Leeward Islands, and 90 percent in Trinidad. Coffee was important in Jamaica, mainly because much of its topography was unsuited to sugar, but even there, by the early nineteenth century sugar made up 72 percent of exports. Only a few late-settled colonies, such as Dominica, kept producing minor staple crops. In short, the economic trend in much of the West Indies was the opposite of the Chesapeake's: away from diversification and toward monoculture. The result of this push was a dramatic increase in the amount of sugar produced, though the leading producers changed over time. Barbados was dominant until the 1730s, then the Leewards until the 1740s, and Jamaica from the 1740s until the second decade of the nineteenth century. Production peaked in Jamaica in 1805, when exports reached 100,000 tons, nine times more than Barbados a century previously. After the abolition of the slave trade in 1807, Jamaican sugar production declined and stagnated, while Barbados saw a late burst. The real growth occurred in Demerara-Essequibo and Berbice between 1810 and 1827, where productivity expanded at a phenomenal rate, with the amount of sugar produced per slave increasing from 0.20 ton between 1815 and 1819 to 0.65 ton between 1830 and 1834.[43]

The West Indies differed from the other plantation areas of British America in having enslaved populations that never experienced a natural population increase (except in Barbados, and there only very late in the slavery period). The slave population of the West Indies climbed to 776,105 by 1807 but then fell by 14 percent to 664,970 in 1834. If Barbados is excluded, the reduction was 17 percent. The reasons the West Indies was unable to have a self-sustaining slave population are complex, but sugar was a big culprit. The labor regime was harsh in sugar cultivation, especially for women of childbearing age, and fertility rates remained very low. In the West Indies slavery killed, and sugar killed most of all. The push to sugar monoculture was thus disastrous for long-term population growth. Nevertheless, few planters were concerned about this as long as the Atlantic slave trade flourished. The slave trade allowed the black population of the West Indies to increase from 98,000 in 1690 to 434,000 in 1770 to 700,000 by 1800, and it enabled slave productivity to increase by over 50 percent in the same period.[44]

The plantation complex in the West Indies was expansive, flexible, and innovative. It was not scientifically backward or resistant to the Enlightenment spirit of improvement. The region saw numerous patents for inventions for improved milling and processing machinery. In 1768, for example, Jamaica became the first place in the Americas to apply steam power to a manufacturing process. Boulton and Watt found a multitude of takers for their steam engines throughout the Caribbean. Just as important as technological advances was planters' relentless quest for agricultural improvement in the tools used by slaves to make tropical staples, in the allocation of various types of labor to different plantation activities, in training enslaved men in particular to become skilled slaves, and in the increasing sophistication of managerial techniques of control and coercion. Planters were entrepreneurial and were always looking for ways to maximize production. In Jamaica one means was the development of the provision ground system, in which slaves grew their own food. In Carolina planters moved away from producing rice by gangs to having enslaved people make rice through "task" work—in other words, assigning a daily amount of work that had to be done and letting slaves work on their own grounds once they had completed their tasks.

What the provision ground system also did, however, was to accentuate West Indian planters' dependence on outside forces. The West Indies was richer than the other regions of plantation America; it was also markedly less self-sufficient. The West Indies was part of an integrated world in which labor was principally obtained from Africa by means of British mercantile investment, and provisions and food were sourced from the northern colonies of British America. Profitability and productivity were therefore always more subject in the West Indies than elsewhere to disruption and more vulnerable to the influence of outside events, as planters found to their cost after the abolition of the slave trade.[45]

Organization of the Argument

The organization of this book is simple. The first two chapters examine how the large integrated plantation arose and explore why it arose quickly in Barbados but slowly in other places, even though people knew that it was likely to lead to considerable personal and collective economic success. The key issue leading to the emergence of the large integrated plantation and the means by which it could be made to work was solving the problem of controlling large numbers of brutalized and traumatized enslaved people. Chapter 3 outlines that success as it was manifested in a variety of plantation settings throughout British America. Chapter 4 is an in-depth exploration of the plantation system in late seventeenth- and eighteenth-century Jamaica, the most important and the wealthiest plantation society in this period. The final chapter looks at how the plantation system coped during the major eighteenth-century conflict affecting plantation societies, the American Revolution. So let's plunge straight in, with that great early eighteenth-century writer, Daniel Defoe, for our guide to English thinking about the plantation system, and black chattel slavery, as the large integrated plantation showed its effectiveness as a wealth-creating system of labor organization.

ONE

The Rise of the Large Integrated Plantation

Daniel Defoe and the Plantation System

Daniel Defoe never set foot in the Americas, but he was a prescient observer of the fast-developing plantation societies of the American South and the British West Indies around the turn of the eighteenth century. His most famous novel, *Robinson Crusoe* (1719), is a foundational text about European imperialism and race relations in the Americas. *Moll Flanders* (1722), a picaresque novel in which the heroine gains redemption for a wicked life in the form of marriage to a wealthy Virginia planter, is also revealing about British impressions of early eighteenth-century America. His less celebrated novel *Colonel Jack* (1722) is interesting as a guide to important transitions in plantation societies in the late seventeenth and early eighteenth centuries. It deals with the adventures of an English thief who was taken to the Chesapeake in the early years of the eighteenth century to be a servant, was promoted to be an overseer of slaves, and eventually found fame and fortune in armed service.[1] One way of reading *Colonel Jack* is to see it as a commentary on slave-management practices, especially about the difficulty of forcing ethnically alien (to the English, at least) African enslaved men to do what those men did not want to do.

Defoe's hero was present, fictively at least, at a major transformation in American life. It involved two interrelated developments: the invention of the large integrated plantation and the rise of great planters. Both developments occurred at a particularly difficult period in British American history. Historians have long recognized that the calamitous decades on either side of the eighteenth century saw the evolution of important institutions. For people living through the years between the Glorious Revolution of 1688 and the 1720s, America seemed to have lost its way. In retrospect, however, we can see this period as ushering in a new period of sustained prosperity. It initiated a new, rich ruling elite whose wealth was derived from successful exploitation of slave labor in large integrated plantations.[2] Most important, the developing planter elite found an effective means whereby slavery could be made to work. It was on the large plantations of the American South, and even more in the British West Indies, that slavery was most efficient. The fortunate planters who oversaw these developments became immensely powerful. Their slaves, on the other hand, experienced the worst degradation slaves faced in any period in American history.[3] The advent of the large integrated plantation was crucial in creating both wealthy planters and also traumatized, degraded enslaved people.

Slow Growth of the Integrated Plantation

But moving to the large integrated plantation took time. The problem, simply stated, is that the emergence of the large integrated plantation in other places of British America besides Barbados, where hundreds of slaves labored and where all the processes of staple production were carried out in a single enterprise, occurred later than one would have expected given the widespread establishment of slavery everywhere in English America by the mid-seventeenth century. Why did the movement to a plantation model based on large-scale African chattel slavery presided over by a wealthy planter class take so long to occur in societies such as Jamaica and Virginia, which were ideally suited to it? Why did it take nearly a hundred years for Virginia to become a plantation society on the Barbadian model? Why did Jamaica, an island larger than Barbados, populated to a large extent by people with experience in Barbados, with land well suited to the production of sugar, and with a populace anxious to make quick and large fortunes, not become a proper plantation society for over thirty years? The obvious counterfactual to what happened in the American South and the British West Indies in the last quarter of the seventeenth century is that canny colonists, aware of what had happened in Barbados, moved as soon as they could to the fully fledged plantation system. The shift should have occurred in the Chesapeake in the 1660s, in the Leeward Islands and Jamaica in the 1670s, and in South Carolina in the 1680s, rather than in the 1700s and 1710s. In each of these societies the preconditions for plantation development were in place decades before the actual shift occurred.

The move to a plantation system was not revolutionary in its speed and implications; rather, the shift to plantation agriculture in British America was surprisingly slow, except in Barbados. Even there the shift to sugar in the 1640s and 1650s was a gradual process that merely sped up and intensified a process already under way. It was not a revolution, but an evolutionary process.[4] The introduction of slavery, the move to sugar, and the rise of the large integrated plantation did not produce a "big bang" or a "sugar revolution"—a transformative event in which a previously failed society suddenly became very successful. We used to think that sugar was introduced after the failure of other crops, that Dutch financiers with no previous involvement in Barbados brought knowledge about sugar from Brazil, that the sugar revolution led to the importation of African slaves who displaced white servants, and that small farmers were driven out by avaricious large planters who quickly amassed all available land.[5] But the rise of the large integrated plantation occurred when Barbados was enjoying an export boom, and when the planting of tobacco, cotton, and indigo was very profitable. It was not financed by the Dutch, but by London merchants, who had been involved in Barbados for some years before investing directly in the island, and who later transformed regular trade with Barbados into the commission system, which brought planters directly into the Atlantic financial system. Moreover, slaves were there in large numbers before sugar became a principal crop, and the shift occurred while Barbados was still a society of small farmers. These small farmers did not disappear as large planters grew more important, but adjusted themselves to sugar's growing importance.[6]

But why was the move to the large integrated plantation so slow elsewhere when it was so quick in Barbados and when poorer whites were not immediately displaced by the rise of a great planter class? Planters in other places were aware of the transformations that had occurred in Barbados. As early as 1649 the London merchant William Bullock alerted Virginia planters to Barbadian success. Barbados, he asserted, five years previously "lay languishing of the disease Virginia now groans under." Now it was a flourishing place with a hundred ships going there in 1648 and land raised from "almost nothing to be as dear or dearer than in England." This transformation was due to sugar production, "for their

Government is not so good that any wise man should be in love with, nor is this Island so extraordinary pleasant to entice men above other places."[7]

One answer for slow transformations elsewhere is farm building: it took a long time everywhere except Barbados to transform semitropical and tropical landscapes into plantation grounds.[8] Barbados was exceptional because most of the hard work clearing and cultivating land had been done before sugar production started in earnest. And it was hard work, even in Barbados. When the first settlers arrived in the 1620s and 1630s the land was covered by rain forest, and it took a great deal of work for settlers to cut down the massive trees, many over a hundred feet tall. Richard Ligon's map of around 1650 shows that the only thoroughly cleared area was along the leeward coast, and the interior was largely uncleared.[9] Yet it was easier to develop land in Barbados than in mountainous Jamaica or in Virginia outside the immediate vicinity of the Tidewater. The amount of land that needed to be cleared for a tobacco plantation in Virginia was larger than for a sugar or cotton plantation in Barbados. Settlers were confined for much of the seventeenth century to the fertile and relatively easily cleared land adjacent to the great rivers of the Chesapeake Bay. The hardest land to clear was the swamplands of the Carolinas, which were perfect for growing rice but which needed draining, damming, ditching, and developing. The process was costly, took up the time of a large labor force, and was also technologically complicated.[10] Barbados, on the other hand, was by the 1670s as settled as southern England. Governor Jonathan Atkins declared that "there was not a foot of land in Barbados that is not employed even to the very seaside," and visitors thought that it looked like one continuous green garden.[11] By contrast, Jamaica in this period looked barely inhabited. Most of the population was concentrated in a small area of the southeast around the towns of Port Royal and St. Jago de la Vega. The mountainous interior was occupied, to the extent that it was occupied at all, by runaway slaves who were forming Maroon societies.[12]

Geography was also important. David Eltis argues that transportation costs for shipping sugar from Jamaica and transporting slaves there slowed its move to fully developed plantation agriculture in the late seventeenth century. He claims that Jamaica, and also Saint-Domingue, were beyond the western limits of large-scale sugar production in the last quarter of the eighteenth century. Between 1673 and 1690 the price of slaves in Jamaica was higher than in Barbados by more than the cost of transporting slaves between the two islands. Location was thus a problem, especially when Barbados was rich, able to buy almost all the slaves that could be supplied by British traders, and had great comparative advantages for shippers and slave traders. It made sense for the Royal African Company to concentrate its attention on supplying that market. The Chesapeake was similarly disadvantaged in the slave trade before a dramatic expansion in numbers shipped to Virginia in the early eighteenth century. In 1664 the Maryland legislature, enthused by the prospects of widespread slavery in the colony, sought to have the Royal African Company bring a shipment of Africans every year. Only one is known to have come. Maryland planters could not afford the purchase prices, and opportunities for sales of African captives were far better in Barbados. The level of slave imports into the Chesapeake was minimal for several decades after slavery had become well established in the region: only two or three ships came to Virginia in the 1660s and not many more in the 1670s. Shipments slowly increased but were still only 2,000 in the 1680s and 4,000 in the 1690s.[13]

Nevertheless, Eltis overestimates the difficulties of Jamaica's location. Jamaica may not have received all of the slaves it wanted from the places it wanted to get them from and at prices it could afford. But Eltis shows that while the different price of prime male slaves in Jamaica compared to that in Barbados was uncompetitively high between 1671 and 1675, at £4.6 per slave, the difference in prices dropped to under £1 a decade later. By the 1690s the price of slaves in Jamaica was actually lower than in Barbados, and it stayed lower until 1707. The majority of slaves going to Jamaica between 1673 and 1700 arrived in the late 1670s and 1680s, when the price differential between slaves sold in the two islands was most pronounced.[14]

The Problem of Disciplining Slaves

The supply of slaves thus was not that terrible, and the prices of captive Africans were not so high that planters in Jamaica could not buy slaves. The number of planters who bought slaves in the last quarter of the seventeenth century in Jamaica was substantial, and not all buyers were rich. Poorer buyers were able to participate in the market for slaves because slaves were relatively abundant: Jamaica received almost as many slaves in Barbados. In addition, sugar exports grew appreciably, doubling between 1682–83 and 1689–91 before stagnating in the 1690s as Jamaica suffered from natural disasters, yellow fever, and French invasion.[15] Moreover, Jamaica had other methods of moneymaking that compensated for Barbados's early start in plantation agriculture. The wealth obtained from piracy in the 1660s through to the 1680s, and the sizable entrepôt trade with Spanish America could have been employed in planting. But not enough Jamaicans wanted to move from these commercial activities into planting, causing considerable political tension in a society divided between a pro-planting faction and those who saw Jamaica's future as trading with Spanish America.[16]

The main reason Jamaica and Virginia were so slow in developing the large integrated plantation was that the logistics of managing large numbers of slaves constrained planters from increasing their slave forces past a certain size. Managing a gang of fifty traumatized, hostile, and potentially violent African slaves was a different proposition from controlling a smaller group. Maintaining discipline over labor forces of hundreds of slaves, as was increasingly the case in the British West Indies by the second decade of the eighteenth century, was more difficult still. That the most problematic concern for large planters was keeping slaves in check leaps out from the admittedly limited literature on master-slave relations in the early days of the large integrated plantation. The shift from small-scale to large-scale slave plantations came about once planters solved the problem of discipline through the application of terror. To terrify slaves, they needed people willing to inflict terror. These people were ordinary white men acting as overseers and bookkeepers on slave plantations: subalterns, using the proper definition of subaltern as a junior officer or a noncommissioned soldier.[17]

Much of the evidence for this statement is scanty and inconclusive because the records are silent or opaque about the crucial issues that led to the fundamental changes outlined above. There is sufficient circumstantial evidence about the development of the large integrated plantation emerged to argue that this new subaltern class emerged in the last decade of the seventeenth century in such places as Jamaica as a result of three simultaneous developments: the decline in opportunities outside the plantation economy for ordinary white men; the increased presence in plantation America of men who experienced very brutal treatment as soldiers and noncommissioned officers; and the increasingly racialized disposition of labor on large plantations, where white men were promoted out of indentured servitude into managerial positions. What planters needed were men prepared to do whatever it took to control enslaved men and women working in dreadful work and living environments. They found such men among poorer whites, men accustomed to violence, men who were prepared to put up with the hardships of supervising recalcitrant slaves and growing perishable crops in return for good wages and the rewards of white privilege.

Colonel Jack

In making this argument, the plot of Defoe's *Colonel Jack* serves a useful purpose. The hero of *Colonel Jack* is born a gentleman but through a variety of circumstances becomes a pickpocket in London. The internal logic of the novel suggests that Colonel Jack was born in the 1680s and came to the Chesapeake area sometime around 1710 or perhaps a few years earlier, by which date the large integrated plantation was well established. In the novel Jack was kidnapped, sent to Virginia, sold to a rich planter, and consigned to hard labor and rough treatment on a tobacco plantation with fifty servants and two hundred slaves. Before long, however, he had been promoted to overseer. He was given a horse "to ride up and down the Plantation to see the Servants and the Negroes" and a horsewhip "to correct and lash the Slaves or Servants when they proved negligent or quarrelsome, or, in Short, were guilty of any offense."[18]

Readings of *Colonel Jack* usually focus on Jack's pursuit of gentility.[19] It can also be read, however, as a guide to the problem of slave management on large plantations. Defoe confines his discussion of punishment almost entirely to the slave rather than the servant population. He mentions servants mainly to highlight the protosentimentalist theme whereby Jack finds it difficult to overcome the natural empathy he has with other people in bondage, given that he "was but Yesterday a Servant or Slave like them and under the authority of the same Lash."[20] But in *Colonel Jack* only slaves face punishment. By the time Defoe was writing white indentured servitude was less important than in the seventeenth century. No large plantation in the Chesapeake had a mixture of fifty servants and two hundred slaves—a more likely breakdown was five or ten servants and two hundred slaves if the plantation was in Jamaica, and one or two servants and fifty slaves if the plantation was in Virginia.[21] Nevertheless, the modal experience for whites on the plantation might have mirrored Jack's. Jack was a servant indentured for his passage across the Atlantic who very soon after arrival was moved into wage labor as a plantation operative. Jack's career path was not uncommon. The situation was more complicated in the Chesapeake, where large importations of convicts meant that there was a sizable body of coerced white laborers in plantation workforces until after midcentury.[22] By the early eighteenth century the numbers of white indentured servants had plummeted from previous levels. The explanation is that white men were promoted out of servitude into overseerships. The labor force became almost entirely black, while whites became part of the managerial class.[23]

How whites moved out of servitude into management is one theme in *Colonel Jack*. But a more powerful theme is that the only way to control slaves is use extreme violence. Defoe devotes no attention to the ways in which his hero devised stratagems for more effective planting. He moves directly from recounting how Jack was promoted to a long discussion of the how overseers kept their slaves in check. At first Jack was apprehensive about whipping slaves because of his empathy with his fellow laborers. But his empathy was misplaced because it led to increased insubordination "insomuch, that the Negroes perceiv'd it, and I had soon so much Contempt upon my Authority, that we were all in disorder." One slave he lashed even laughed at his softness, having "the Impudence to say behind my Back, that if he had the Whipping of me, he would shew me better how to whip a Negroe."[24]

That terror alone was the only way in which slaves could be controlled was tempered in Defoe's telling by a subdiscourse wherein the threat of terror against miscreants was accompanied by the promise of mercy. As Boulukos suggests, "Defoe narrates what could be called the invention of slave-owner paternalism, the moment in which a policy of unashamed cruelty is abandoned from the suspicion that gentler ways might produce more efficacious results."[25] Through the exercise of mercy by all-powerful but merciful disciplinarians, gratitude toward masters could be inculcated in people whose "brutality and obstinate Temper" made them naturally ungrateful.[26]

Defoe thus shrank from the implications of his argument that Africans could be controlled only by a "rod of iron." He wanted to dispel suspicions that the English were cruel tyrants. The abrupt and disconcerting shift halfway through his treatment of African character from seeing African "temper" as arising from environment to arguing that it could be changed through good treatment may be indicative of a characteristic eighteenth-century failure to take seriously the difference between culture and essence. It is just as likely to be a narrative strategy that shrinks from the implications inherent in an argument that actively presupposes the English to be as naturally cruel as Africans are naturally barbarous.[27]

Defoe acknowledges that his ingenious argument for slaveowner paternalism was unrealistic and naïve. Jack himself adopts the idea of inculcating slaves' gratitude through terror after transforming himself from an apathetic whipper of Negroes into a man who was willing have a slave "scourg'd . . . to Death," rather than being slaves' "jest [rather] than their Terror." Jack concedes also that his new policy would have no chance of succeeding in the West Indies because there "the Overseers really know no such thing as mercy."[28] Here Defoe follows the many statements of Jamaican writers that the essence of slavery was terror, from Edmond Hickeringill in 1661 to James Knight and Charles Leslie writing in the 1730s and 1740s, when life for black Jamaicans was at its nadir. Knight argued that extreme violence was necessary against a people who were so "sullen, deceitful, [with a] Refractory Temper." Leslie was certain that "No country excels [Jamaica] in a barbarous Treatment of Slaves, or in the cruel Methods they put them to death." Leslie insisted, however, that such harsh usage was acceptable owing to the nature of African character. Slavery in Jamaica was brutal "given how impossible it were to live amongst such Numbers of Slaves, without observing their Conduct with the greatest Niceness and punishing their Faults with the utmost Severity."[29]

The Advantages of the Plantation System

By the time *Colonel Jack* was written, the path for success for young European migrants with little money and few connections was in the plantation economy. Yet until the last decades of the seventeenth century, ordinary white men could do other jobs. As Peter Thompson argues, "In post-Restoration Virginia, as rates of mortality declined and the number of women in the colony increased, little commonwealths, or family units of production, became more common than they had been at any time previously, and Virginia's taxpayers were increasingly likely to be married. The very factors that restricted access to marriage in the third generation of settlement, chief among them a growing scarcity of land, only heightened the potential political power of the poor to middling laborer who had managed to acquire a household."[30] Thompson points to an important alternative history, namely that in places such as Jamaica, Barbados, and the Carolinas the dominant social and economic form would have been small labor forces of white families, servants, and some slaves. They would have produced food mainly for themselves, with a small surplus for local and overseas markets. Larger estates would have been few and exceptional. In short, the kind of social patterns that existed in the farm-building stage of settlement might have continued into the eighteenth century.

The slow and contested transition to a fully developed plantation regime was not confined to Virginia. What Ira Berlin calls "the plantation revolution" came late to most parts of British America. Large numbers of enslaved Africans were present from the 1640s in Barbados; the 1660s in the Chesapeake, Jamaica, and the Leeward Islands; and from the 1680s in the Carolinas.[31] One reason it is surprising that the transition to "the plantation revolution" was delayed is that a crucial feature allowing for the revolution to occur was in place early on:[32] African slavery in British America was heritable and perpetual. The majority of slaves worked in agriculture producing staple crops such as sugar, tobacco, and rice. They were subjected to extremely harsh discipline under the almost total control of their masters.[33]

A template for controlling and disciplining slaves was established in the Barbados slave code of 1661, copied in most of its essentials by lawmakers in all the main slaveholding societies in British America. It gave masters immense latitude in how they treated slaves and set in stone a harsh disciplinary regime.[34] In addition, with the forming of the Royal African Company in 1672, British American planters were offered a steady and guaranteed flow of enslaved Africans. In short, all the preconditions for the large integrated plantation were present by the middle decades of the seventeenth century. One indication of how complete the acceptance of lifetime hereditary African slavery had become by the 1660s was that in 1669 John Locke's "Fundamental Constitutions" for Carolina legitimated the right to hold property in the form of slaves, making Carolina the only British American colony where racially based slavery was present from the start of colonization.[35]

Moving to a plantation involved making a choice. Having all the conditions in place for the plantation system to develop was not enough. There were several places in the larger Atlantic world ideally suited for large-scale plantation agriculture that did not immediately become plantation societies after the introduction of slavery and tropical agriculture. The obvious example is Cuba, which in the nineteenth century became the premier sugar-producing society in the world. It languished in the economic and social doldrums, however, for most of the seventeenth and eighteenth centuries. Its relative backwardness in that period came despite the fact that it had produced high-quality sugar since the sixteenth century, in competition with other crops, notably tobacco, wood, and hides. Yet it did not have plantations with large concentrations of slaves until the early nineteenth century.[36]

It is important to stress that the transition to plantation societies was not preordained because the advantages of plantations for white people living in tropical regions are retrospectively obvious. The benefits of moving to a fully fledged plantation system were clear well before the transition took place. Late seventeenth-century British American colonists saw how successful the transition had been in Barbados. William

Bullock knew it in 1649. Entrepreneurial men in the Chesapeake, the Leeward Islands, and Jamaica were conscious about Barbados in the middle of the seventeenth century because they drew closely on what Barbadian planters had done in their codification of slave laws in 1661.[37] They emulated these laws because they wanted to emulate Barbados. Barbados was a counterpoint to imperial disappointment about the future prospects of late seventeenth-century British America; Adam Smith made this clear when celebrating American growth and expansion on the eve of the American Revolution. As he stated, in 1776 "the island of Jamaica was an unwholesome desert; little inhabited and less cultivated. . . . The island of Antigua, the two Carolinas, Pen[n]sylvania, Georgia, and Nova Scotia were not planted. Virginia, Maryland and New England were planted; and although they were very thriving colonies, yet there was not . . . a single person who foresaw . . . the rapid progress which they have since made. . . . The island of Barbados, in short, was the only British colony of any consequence of which the condition at the time bore any resemblance to what it is at present."[38]

Richard Ligon explained in his encomium to Barbados in 1657 that through "the sweet negotiations of sugar," Barbadians had "in a short time . . . [grown] very considerable," both in "Reputation and Wealth." The most "Industrious and painful" settlers, men who had the most "percing sights and profound judgments," had established "very great and vast estates" that were sufficiently large to enable them to buy English estates that produced £10,000 per annum. Their wealth was so great that "they economise on nothing," as one French visitor explained. They paid outrageous sums for clothes, furnished their houses "sumptuously," went "well-mounted on very handsome horses . . . covered with rich saddle-cloths," and they ate very well and drank "the best wines from more than six areas in Europe."[39]

By the early 1650s Barbados was more densely populated than anywhere in the British empire save London. White population began to fall from this time, but white prosperity did not diminish. By 1680, Richard Dunn writes, Barbados was "the richest, most highly developed, most populous, and most congested English colony in America, with a thriving sugar industry and 50,000 inhabitants, including 30,000 slaves."[40] The socioeconomic model first articulated in Barbados—with its exploitative and materialistic orientation, its concentration upon sugar production, its slave-powered plantation system, its highly stratified social structure, its great disparities in wealth and styles of living, and its high ratio of blacks to whites—had its problems (heavy white mortality, philistinism, and worries about slave revolts, for example), but it was a highly appealing model for aspiring gentlemen in the American South and the Caribbean. The cultural hearth established in Barbados spread to the Leeward Islands, Jamaica, South Carolina, Cape Fear, Georgia, and eastern and western Florida in the eighteenth century and, crossing national boundaries, to Guadeloupe and Martinique in the seventeenth century, to Saint-Domingue in the eighteenth century, and to Cuba and Puerto Rico by the nineteenth century.[41]

There was not much difference between what happened in Barbados and what happened in Jamaica or Virginia except that peculiar conditions in Barbados in the 1640s and 1650s made what was actually a gradual movement from a diversified economy appear to be a sudden and discontinuous punctuation. If sugar prices had been as high in the 1670s as they were in the 1640s and 1650s, for example, then Jamaican planters may have been able to acquire the high profits from sugar that their predecessors in Barbados had gained. They would have spent that money both in acquiring African slaves at premium prices and also in raising the price of lands suitable for sugar cultivation to ridiculous prices. Such strategies might have forced out smaller producers, as happened in mid-seventeenth-century Barbados, leading to the rapid rather than the slow development of the large integrated plantation.[42]

What Was Special about Barbados?

The shift to the large integrated plantation in Barbados was accomplished with little opposition from poor whites, but there were three key considerations that made Barbados special. First, the move happened during an export boom, rather than during a depression, as happened in the Chesapeake and Jamaica. It dated from the 1640s and 1650s, when other exports, notably cotton, sold for good prices in England and small farmers had lots of opportunities outside sugar to make money. During this period small farmers increased their labor forces rapidly, from 4.3 workers per estate in 1640–41 to 25.5 workers in the mid-1650s.[43]

Secondly, the shift to the large integrated plantation occurred during the biggest crisis in British history: the mid-seventeenth-century civil wars in England, Scotland, and Ireland, when Britain mobilized its population into fighting forces on an unprecedented scale. The result was that a very large percentage of men aged between fifteen and thirty—the modal ages for migrants, voluntary and involuntary—were likely to have had military experience, including participation in especially harrowing wars. Thirdly, the move to sugar and the large integrated plantation took place when migration into the island was increasing rather than declining. The peak years of British migration into Barbados came in the 1640s and 1650s, especially the former decade, when 55,900 migrants (82 percent of all migration into British America) came to the English Caribbean, almost all to Barbados. The next decade saw nearly 40,000 migrants coming to the English Caribbean before the numbers declined precipitously in the 1660s and 1670s.[44]

The biggest transformation that occurred in Barbados in the mid-seventeenth century was the replacement of indentured servants with slaves, and a consequent escalation in the scale of plantations so that they became factories in the field as opposed to small farms. The ways in which Africans came to Barbados and were made slaves has been well explored, and we know that Africans, when they got to Barbados, were made to labor in the fields and forced to work harder and with less possibility of changing their status than previously.[45] We know a good deal less about what happened to white servants. We do not know what planters used them for or what else happened to them after the integrated plantation became properly established sometime in the 1660s and 1670s. What we need to know is whether by the mid-seventeenth century Barbados was the worst poor man's country, a land of misery for ordinary whites as much as for enslaved Africans, or a place of growing opportunity where rising wealth was sufficiently well distributed as to satisfy whites.

Let's look at white servants first. One important point is that whites who were not landholders in mid-seventeenth-century Barbados had a more varied experience than most African slaves. Slaves were workers, pure and simple. Whites, however, were needed not only to work, but also to fight. They formed part of a militia that would be useful in securing the island both against external threats and against the internal enemy: enslaved Africans. This policy worked for the most part, but it could be problematic when servants rebelled against white authority. Richard Ligon argued that this happened in 1647, just before he arrived in the island. A group of servants ("their sufferings grown to great heights") conspired to "fall upon their Masters, and cut all their throats, and by that means to make themselves [not] only freemen but Masters of the island." The conspiracy was discovered, and eighteen ringleaders were executed "for example to the rest," because they were "so haughty in their resolutions, and so incorrigible."[46]

Some white servants fared badly in mid-seventeenth-century Barbados. The conditions of indentured servitude were different than in Britain, and over time those differences resulted in many servants being increasingly ill-treated.[47] Masters treated servants as commodities, buying and selling them as they did other property and combining them with slaves as part of their workforce. Ligon even claimed that servants were treated worse than slaves. He argued that slaves "are kept and preserv'd with greater care than the servants . . . [who] have the worse lives, for they are put to very hard labor, ill lodging, and their diet very sleight." He noted that "they are beaten by the Overseer; if they resist, their time is doubled." In addition, he stated that he had "seen an Overseer beat a Servant with a cane about the head, till the blood has followed, for a fault that is not worthy the speaking of."[48]

This cruelty shocked Ligon, not because it was cruel per se, but because it was done by one Christian to another. He expected Africans to be badly treated, but he thought that white servants deserved better. It is significant that he followed these comments by commending one of his favorite planters, Colonel Walrond, for an act of kindness in sending for England for special gowns, "such as poor people wear in Hospitals," when he discovered that his servants came home from work "wet through with their sweating," so as to preserve white servants' health. By contrast, later in his history, he related a gruesome tale about how the same Colonel Walrond, "having lost three or four of his best *Negroes*" through suicide cut off the head of an African who had killed himself, and "caused all his *Negroes* to come forth, and march around this head" so that they realized they would not return to their own country if they killed themselves because it was impossible for "the body could go without a head."[49]

Slaves had to put up with scandalous treatment in ways that white servants did not. The worst-treated servants were those who came to the island involuntarily, especially those taken duplicitously by "spirits" working in Bristol and London; those who were convicts; and those who were prisoners of war. Many of the last group, amounting to several thousand people, were Irish prisoners of war from Cromwell's invasion of southern Ireland. This group was especially feared by planters as heretics, potential rebels, and traitors. But even those servants who came from better backgrounds found it difficult to cope in the booming Barbadian economy of the 1640s. Unlike servants arriving in the 1630s, who often were able to acquire land and set up as independent small farmers, servants arriving after the mid-1640s found it impossible to buy increasingly expensive land. Land prices in Barbados catapulted from £1.20 per acre in 1638 to £5.50 per acre in 1650. Consequently, many of the servants arriving in this latter period became landless proletariats. The names of only fifty-nine of nearly two thousand servants who left Bristol for Barbados between 1654 and 1675 appear on the list of landholding freemen in a census made in 1679. As Simon Newman argues, "The high proportion of vagrants, convicts and prisoners of war amongst the bound white work force of mid-seventeenth to mid-eighteenth century Barbados created a group of workers whose lives were forfeit, and even those who survived a decade of plantation labor would find themselves excluded from virtually all paying work and the object of distrust and even hatred by planters."[50]

Nevertheless, not all servants were losers in the transition from small farming to large plantations in mid-seventeenth-century Barbados. Servants could come voluntarily to the Americas and were often able to drive bargains about where they would go and how much they would be paid. As Russell Menard argues, "Servants were not simply passive victims of a process beyond their control."[51] David Galenson has shown that older, literate, and skilled servants were able to sign contracts that had significantly shorter terms than less well-placed servants. Christopher Tomlins argues that historians have overemphasized the malign characteristics of indentured servitude and notes that for most people it was a temporary rather than permanent condition. One way that we have been fooled in thinking indentured servitude more important than it in fact was is that seventeenth-century colonials seldom distinguished between indentured servants serving out their time and wage-earning employees. But as Tomlins stresses, there were sharp differences between servants and slaves. In Barbados the less privileged servants, especially those who came involuntarily to the island as Irish prisoners of war or as convicts, may have been treated in ways that were similar to some African slaves, but that ill-treatment was more a function of ethnicity than equivalence between two categories of bound labor. Members of the militia in the late seventeenth century, for example, tended to be English rather than Irish, even though the Irish may have made up a substantial minority of white inhabitants.[52]

Servants in Barbados

What did Barbadian servants do when they finished their indenture? After the 1630s only a few became landholders. Many left the island to seek their fortune, like the 3,500 men who left in 1655 for the Western design in Hispaniola and then Jamaica; the 700–1,000 who accompanied Sir Thomas Modyford to Jamaica in 1664; and the 1,300 that left for the Carolinas before 1690. However, the only empirical evidence we have about people leaving the island is from 1679, when a list of travelers was created for presentation to the Committee on Trade to Plantations. Of the 593 people leaving the island in 1679, of whom 73 percent had served out their time and thus were ex-servants, the most popular destinations were Boston (68 travelers), Antigua (65), Virginia (62), London (51), Bristol (39), Jamaica (35), and New York (32).[53] Ex-servants leaving Barbados in the second half of the seventeenth century were part of a hugely significant outflow of what Thomas Modyford called "experienced planters" who brought knowledge about the distinctive Barbadian way of doing agriculture to other potential plantation areas. The total number that left is hard to establish with precision, but Richard Dunn's figure of 10,000 departures by midcentury seems plausible.[54]A much larger number probably died before they had a chance to move. We don't have data on mortality good enough to work out life expectancy rates, but there was undoubtedly a surplus of white deaths over births in a population that sustained itself only through high levels of immigration. Most of these immigrants, however, probably stayed on the island, even though it was increasingly difficult to get land. The white population of Barbados remained high by West Indian standards, dropping slowly from a high of around 30,000 in 1650, despite a major yellow fever epidemic in the crucial years of transition between 1647 and 1652, when around 6,000 people may have died and in which time Richard Ligon claims that "the living could hardly bury the dead." It fell to 22,400 in 1670 before declining more rapidly in the 1690s and 1700s to about 17,900, when yellow fever returned to devastating effect.[55]

Some servants were "reduced" to working alongside slaves in cane fields even after they had served their time. Hilary Beckles describes two such men, Robert Frument and Othoniell Hughes, and records their outrage at the parlous state they were reduced to; their indignity at being treated as if they were black men was a particular grievance.[56] The poor prospects for white servants out of their indentures concerned at least one Barbadian governor a great deal, partly because he shared Frument's and Hughes's disgust at being treated as black men in white skins, and even more because such poor prospects increased white emigration and reduced the number of men available to serve in militias. Governor Francis Russell was explicit about the poor treatment of white ex-servants. In 1695 he wrote:

There is no encouragement given to white servants when their time is expired, for they have only about forty shillings given to them for all their services, and no other inducement to stay in the Island. The other Colonies offer so much encouragement that servants leave Barbados as soon as their term is ended. I dare say that there are hundreds of white servants in the Island who have been out of their time for many years, and who have never a bit of fresh meat bestowed on them nor a dram of rum. They are domineered over and used like dogs, and this in time will undoubtedly drive away all the commonalty of the white people and leave the Island in a deplorable condition, to be murdered by negroes or vanquished by an enemy, unless some means be taken to prevent it. Nor can we depend upon these people to fight for the defense of the Island when, let who will be master, they cannot be more miserable than their countrymen and fellow-subjects make them here.[57]

Russell argued that Barbados needed an Act of Parliament and proposed an ambitious scheme in which planters provided land to ex-servants and a properly equipped and paid militia. He argued that England had to force this issue because "I am sure that the people will never do it for themselves." He was right: the Barbadian assembly refused to pass such an act. So did the English Parliament.[58] Planters did, however, recruit 2,000 former soldiers, presumably stranded in the island during the wars of the late seventeenth and early eighteenth centuries, to act as militia tenants and probably slave overseers in 1700.[59]

How we consider the conditions of ordinary white life in this period depends on how seriously we take the issue of class. Certainly class tensions between poor and rich whites intensified in the mid-seventeenth century. Dispossessed white ex-servants became more violent toward cruel and avaricious masters as the condition of the former declined. The rich also became openly contemptuous of the poor: comments from visitors to the island from near the end of slavery describe the typical poor white man as a feckless welfare recipient who, though "proud as Lucifer himself" on account of a "freckled ditchwater face," was part of "as degenerate and useless a race as can be imagined."[60] Nevertheless, a larger number of whites were small landholders and farmers. They made a decent competency from subsistence farming, the production of crops, including rum and occasionally sugar for export, and (though this is not usually mentioned) wage earning as plantation managers. There were also a considerable number of white men who moved to Bridgetown, where they made a decent living. The French priest Père Jean-Baptiste Labat exclaimed upon visiting Bridgetown in 1700 that "the largest trade in the New World is carried on here." Simon Smith's reconstructions of the mercantile activities of the youthful Quaker merchant Richard Poor, Jr., shows that a middling trader—Poor had turnover of £1,000 per annum on average between 1709 and 1712, which, if he made 15 percent a year, suggests an income of £150—could do very well. Population pressure and geographical expansion meant that there was increasing demand for houses and warehouses, placing upward pressure on rents. Bridgetown proved an important adjunct to the plantation economy.[61]

David Eltis insists that in Barbados in the late seventeenth century "the export sector was broadly based . . . and poverty in the old world sense of the term scarcely existed." His careful analysis of Barbadian custom-house records in the mid-1660s shows that nearly one in four men in the island produced goods for export. The rum that the poorest of these men produced was below the rates allowed in Bridgetown for indigents as poor relief. In 1665 and 1666 only thirty-three adults got poor relief in the town, suggesting that in Bridgetown poverty was nonexistent, countering claims that Barbados was especially miserable for white people, and supporting governors' claims in the 1670s that begging for alms in Barbados did not exist. But poorer Barbadians probably got money from elsewhere, perhaps through working for wages as plantation overseers. In addition, they produced subsistence crops on their smallholdings. Eltis concludes "that the rise of a plantocracy did not necessarily mean the impoverishment of smallholders."[62]

Evidence to support or contradict Eltis is sparse, however, with Henry Drax's instructions to servants the only hint that white men customarily worked in the plantation economy. Sources are unhelpful because when servants were enumerated they were seldom named. Landless plantation employees rarely left wills or inventories. What contemporaries meant by the term "servant" is also unclear. In the seventeenth century a variety of conditions were denoted by that term, including people whom we would consider waged employees. It is hard to know how many servants were overseers in the seventeenth century, especially if we assume that planters used slave drivers in place of white men.[63]

But we do have some guides through the thicket of speculation. First, we know that from the 1660s on Barbadian legislators went out of their way to legally differentiate between white servants and black slaves—in part for racial reasons, in part because servants were Christian and slaves were not, but also in part because servants were as much soldiers as workers. Barbadian leaders saw servants as bulwarks against a growing enslaved population that was becoming more restless as the large integrated plantation became more dominant. There was no actual revolt in Barbados before 1816, but rumors of slave insurrection disturbed Barbadian planters every few years between the 1670s and 1690s: planned uprisings were discovered in 1675, 1683, 1686, and 1692. The putative rebels were put to death with maximum violence and much torture.[64]

Governors were perpetually concerned about threats to security both from foreign invaders and from African slaves. After becoming governor in the 1660s Lord Willoughby wrote to Lord Clarendon, "I feare our negros will growe to hard for us." The solution was to make ordinary white men better soldiers, and more committed to the interests of fellow whites than to fellow black workers. The role of servants within the Barbadian militia was a perpetual concern for seventeenth-century governors and island politicians. When the supply of servants began to dry up in the 1670s and 1680s, Barbadians were mostly concerned with the number of men the militia was losing. A planter lamented in the mid-1680s that there were fewer "Christian servants which are the nerves and sinews of a plantacon" arriving; this was a problem, as they had been "excellent planters and good souldiers" who "kept the Colonies in soe formidable a posture that they neither feared ye insurreccons of theire Slaves nor a forreinge invasion of forreine enemies." The decline of servants cost planters money, because under a 1652 militia law planters were required to supply one man for every 20 acres they owned and a man and a horse for every 100 acres. We can translate this legal requirement to discover how many servants short large planters with 60 or more slaves were, based on the 1679 census. These 175 planters owned 20,289 acres and should have had 2,339 servants able to serve in the militia and a further 468 men in the militia with horses. If we discount the second requirement as hard to determine, then the shortage of servants among the labor forces of large planters was 1,775.[65]

Governors might have thought that the militia was not very effective, and London bureaucrats may have been upset that the numbers of men in the militia were much lower than they had been led to believe, but Barbadians took militia service seriously. Most men able to bear arms did so. In 1684, of 6,761 men considered able to bear arms, 5,911 did. In 1679 the 5,588 militiamen were divided into eight regiments. Barbados was thus a highly militarized society. The correlation between military rank and political status was very close, and most councilors were high-ranking militia officers. The militia was generally very effective, with regular drills and musters and with militiamen being good marksmen and dutiful militia attendees.[66]

In making careful distinctions between African slaves, who were described in the 1661 consolidation of laws about servants and slaves as a "heathenish, brutish and an uncertaine, dangerous kind of people," and white servants, legislators were influenced by Barbados's need for white soldiers. Servants were treated as Englishmen entitled to the protection of English law and entitled to minimum allotments of food and clothing. Their movements were strictly controlled, and they were punished severely and physically if they ran away. The most significant item in the code that distinguished servants from slaves, however, was a license given to *all* whites to give runaway blacks a "moderate whipping." By contrast, any slave offering "any Violence to any Christian" was to be severely whipped for a first offense and then physically mutilated for a second one. What this clause suggests is that it had become customary by the Restoration for whites of any description to be placed in positions of authority over blacks. White violence against blacks was assumed, customary, and indeed welcomed.

Whites in Barbados after the Transition to Plantations

By the time the integrated plantation was fully in place in the last quarter of the seventeenth century, white servants expected to be treated better than slaves, and to do different work. It is noticeable that a particular feature of their claims that they were badly treated was that they were worse off than slaves.[67] But while there may have been equivalence between how slaves and servants who had been prisoners of war were treated in the transition period to slavery during the Wars of the Three Kingdoms in the 1640s and 1650s, that had ended by the 1680s. The failed Monmouth Rebellion saw 600 rebels sent to Barbados, where it seems they were employed in relatively privileged positions as tradesmen and overseers. They were also employed as militia tenants (people allowed to squat on a planter's land in order to satisfy the militia requirements of owners of large acreages). Governor James Kendall noted of them that planters had "taught them to be boilers, distillers and refiners," all of which were skilled jobs.[68]

Most white people did not leave the island but stayed and worked within, or around, the plantation system. The decline in white population in late seventeenth-century Barbados was occasioned by high white mortality rather than by large-scale desertion of the island by white people squeezed out of employment by the land engrossment and massive wealth of large planters. On the contrary, the introduction of the plantation complex increased the wealth of most but not all of the white population, including small landholders, urban residents, and waged employees. It also may have contributed to a degree of social harmony absent in the mid-seventeenth century that Barbadians later thought a distinctive characteristic of their society. By the middle of the eighteenth century Barbadians prided themselves on being the "civilized island," a claim made in implicit condemnation of the aggressive and combustible planter populations of Jamaica and Antigua. They considered their society to be the most successful replication of English society in eighteenth-century British America and hailed harmony between classes of white people as indicative of this successful process of Anglicization.[69]

The introduction of large-scale slavery into mid-seventeenth-century Barbados and the subsequent rise of the integrated plantation did not force large numbers of white indentured servants to leave the island, leaving behind a group of impoverished peasants lacking the resources to join the planter elite.[70] Rather, the start of the integrated plantation complex lifted most economic boats among the free population, while doing very much the opposite for the black population, who became in Barbados and elsewhere the poorest people in the Americas.[71] Average wealth increased, if unequally, and opportunities for employment and wealth making within the plantation system were plentiful.

In eighteenth- and early nineteenth-century Barbados, ordinary whites became so entrenched within the plantation system they became its greatest supporters. They also supported, with reservations, the ruling class of large planters, at least while the ruling class did not undermine their privileged position in Barbados by being overly generous to free "coloreds" (the group of people they most despised) or too accommodationist to British humanitarians (next on the list). Thus, in the 1810s ordinary white freeholders, or Barbadian yeomen, united in a group called the Salmagundis against the great planter-supported group called the Pumpkins. The former resisted any reform of the plantation system, including efforts to improve the condition of enslaved people, and insisted on protecting white supremacy at any cost. The Salmagundis thought that the 1816 slave rebellion in Barbados, in which between 400 and 1,000 slaves were killed in battle or executed, was proof positive of the folly of indulging the ambitions of free blacks and enslaved people. Enough white Barbadians agreed for the Salmagundis to win a landslide victory in the Assembly elections of 1819, a victory that reminded the ruling elite that they violated ordinary whites' sense of their economic and cultural place at their peril. The principal advocate for the rights of poor whites, John Poyer, insisted that white supremacy was not enough. Rich planters had to boost the economic prospects of poor whites by keeping free coloreds in a subordinate place and privileging poor whites in poor relief and in employment. By this means, the "superfluous wealth of the opulent" could be used to provide "homes for the poor, and employment for the industrious." In short, if Barbados "furnish[ed] employment and subsistence for her numerous sons at home," then the island would be made more secure and "the community would enjoy the advantages of a general circulation of the wages of industry."[72]

Notions of white supremacy were always associated with economic prosperity. When in 1708 John Oldmixon praised ordinary white men in Barbados for their fighting qualities, he declared that the so-called *Creoleans* were "as brave Men as any in the World, for they would certainly fight resolutely for so rich and so pleasant a Country."[73] They might not have fought so hard if Barbados had been pleasant but not rich. By the early nineteenth century white Barbadians of all social standing agreed that the plantation system was a good thing. Ordinary white Barbadians knew, however, that running a plantation or being involved in controlling slaves was not easy, even if it promised pleasing amounts of wealth. The revolt of 1816 showed them that they needed to treat slaves with the utmost severity. To do otherwise was unwise because, as Daniel Defoe argued, "*Negroes* cannot be mannag'd by Kindness, and Courtisy; but must be rul'd with a Rod of Iron, [and] beaten with *Scorpions*."[74]

Alternatives to Plantation Employment

A closer look at how the transition to the large integrated plantation system in Barbados occured demonstrates that it was an evolutionary rather than a revolutionary process and that it was fraught with problems for poorer people, even in the place where conditions were most propitious for the transition. Elsewhere the risks in moving from smallholding to large-scale sugar planting were especially pronounced. The dangers involved in creating a plantation were considerable. A remarkable set of records from a Jamaican planter in the 1670s details the frustration. Cary Helyar was an aspiring but impecunious younger son from a genteel background. He came to Jamaica in the early 1660s, made some money in slave trading, and developed good connections to leading politicians. His political connections brought him money and influence, and he used both to buy land in roughly the same region where Francis Price set up planting. The land he cleared was prime sugar land. By 1674, he boasted to his brother, his Bybrook plantation of 1,236 acres was "almost square, of as good land and as well-watered as any in the island." Yet planting on Bybrook was far from plain sailing. It required a large capital investment in slaves, equipment, and livestock. Even before Helyar started planting, he had spent nearly £2,000 in buying 55 slaves, 14 white servants, a mill, and livestock. The cost of his land, however, was minimal. He did not buy his land on the open market, but acquired it as "new land" through patent at minimal cost from the Jamaican government.[75]

Helyar died suddenly in July 1672, and his place was taken by his young assistant, William Whaley. Whaley kept spending the money given him by Helyar's brother in England—on boiling and curing houses and on skilled workmen. Whaley began to produce good sugar, worth £400 per annum, but spent all the proceeds in expanding his property. By Whaley's death in 1676, Bybrook was probably the premier sugar property in Jamaica. But no money from this increasingly valuable property came to the person financing the estate's expansion. It wasn't until the late 1680s that Bybrook started producing the sorts of profits that the Helyars' investment warranted. The good times did not last long. The decade of the 1690s was a rough one in Jamaican history and even worse in the history of Bybrook, which reverted, catastrophically, to absentee management after 1691. Production of sugar dropped, slaves died and were not replaced, equipment wore out, and the Helyars could not find honest and skilled attorneys to supervise the work of overseers. By the time the Helyars sold out in 1713, the property was worn out and close to worthless. As Helyar and Whaley's experience suggests, sugar planting was a tricky business. It also required close supervision by resident planters: the only time this plantation really made money was between 1687 and 1691, when the Helyars were personally in charge. [76]

Large-scale tobacco planting was similarly tricky. Tobacco was an ideal beginner's crop because it could be grown on a small scale and required little capital investment, except for labor. There were a number of barriers to large plantations. Most planters could manage only four or five workers by themselves, because tobacco growing required close supervision of labor. To get more labor, moreover, a tobacco planter had to go into debt. The wealthier and more politically well-connected planters used what money they had to buy slaves. Wealthy planters bought slaves as soon as they could and bought as many as they could afford or get credit for. They would have bought more if the supply from Africa had not been disrupted by the Wars of the Three Kingdoms and if the Navigation Act of 1660, which made it hard to get slaves from the Dutch, had not been passed.[77] The result was that plantations stayed small until very late in the seventeenth century. The modal kind of enterprise in seventeenth-century Virginia and Maryland was a small owner-operated farm worked by a family with the help of a few servants, most of whom were white, and with the support of hired hands. Until the early 1660s land was relatively cheap, costs of entry low, tobacco prices high, and labor difficult to come by and expensive to maintain. Small planters flourished; large planters languished.[78]

The former group enjoyed a spartan but relatively comfortable existence. The fortuitous survival of a set of accounts made between 1662 and 1673 for the plantation of Robert Cole, a middling planter of St. Mary's County, enable us to evaluate the way of life of a small Chesapeake planter in the mid-seventeenth century. Cole was hardworking, prudent, and a cautious spender, His accounts show that a small planter could live reasonably well if he combined subsistence farming with the production of a few staple crops for export. He plowed whatever small profits arose from plantation agriculture back into the purchase of additional inputs of labor. He succeeded, although the process was not always comfortable, and the profits, at least after the initial boom scaled down, were not spectacular. He and his family made do without amenities that could not be grown or raised locally. As a result, over the course of eleven years his estate grew from £208 to £360. There was little reason for him to take the huge risk that borrowing money to buy slaves entailed (if he could find both money to borrow and also slaves to buy). The financial rewards of his system were sufficient in a place where very few people had much money, and there were few goods to buy. The social rewards were even better. Small planters tended to be appointed to local offices, like justice of the peace, and that, plus the increasingly comfortable, if frugal, standard of living, made emigration to the colony and the rigor of farm building worthwhile.[79]

Nor did poorer men in other places try to become large planters. As luck has it, one of the very few records we have from late seventeenth-century Jamaica that give us insight into how propertyless white men thought about different career prospects in the plantation world connects us directly to the Helyar plantation. William Dampier, the buccaneer and global circumnavigator, first left England for the West Indies in 1673, at the age of twenty-two, in order to manage a plantation for "a neighboring gentleman, Colonel Hellier, of East Coker in Somersetshire." Managing a plantation proved disagreeable: Dampier left Helyar's employ within a few weeks after an argument and tartly declared after an unfortunate experience as an overseer to "captain Heming" at his northside plantation that "I was clearly out of my element." Abandoning Heming's service, he returned to the sea, first entering into business in the coastal trade, then loading logwood in the Bay of Campeachy, and by 1678 crewing with buccaneers on the Spanish Main.[80]

Dampier's career choices were not unusual for ordinary white men in Jamaica in the 1670s. Privateering was an attractive option when Henry Morgan was plundering the Spanish possessions in the Caribbean, and when Port Royal was at its height as the buccaneer's capital. John Taylor, an adventurer in the mid-1680s, has left a vivid portrait of this rollicking town in a fascinating account of Jamaica in 1687. It suggests that for ordinary white men, an enjoyable life could be made roistering in the narrow streets of Port Royal, seeking fame and fortune through plundering expeditions against the Spanish, and supplementing income and ensuring a measure of landed independence through growing small quantities of crops on a few acres of land in nearby parishes. It was not only Port Royal "merchants and gentrey" who "live here to the hights of splendor," but "all sorts of mechanicks and tradesmen . . . all of which live here verey well, earning thrice the wages given in England, by which means they are enabled to maintain their famallies much better than in England, by which tradesmen 'tis much advanced both in strength and wealth, still becoming more formidable." Residents of Port Royal ate exceedingly well and drank even better. They could find all the entertainment they needed in an "aboundance of punch houses, or rather more fitly called brothel houses," enjoying "all sorts of debauchery" with a "crue of vile strumpets and common prostratures" that "infected" a place "more rude and anticque than ere was Sodom." Living in such a manner was more agreeable than subjecting oneself to disciplining "pore slaves" and suffering from the "incursions and outrages of runaway vassals and Negroas."[81]

The career of Lawrence Prince, Morgan's lieutenant in Panama, exemplifies the decisions of ordinary white men that took them away from the plantation economy. Prince was a modest landowner in St. Andrews in the 1670s with thirty-five acres of land, on which he grew indigo. He owned a few slaves. Between 1675 and 1678 he bought ten slaves in three shipments sent to Jamaica by the Royal African Company. He went off privateering with Morgan several times but does not seem to have made a great deal of money. He died in 1683 and bequeathed his land and his by now dozen slaves to his son, also named Lawrence, while providing well for his other son and two daughters. Nevertheless, his oldest son was unable to replicate his father and become a small slave owner and landowner. Lawrence Jr. sold his land in 1700, three years before he died. His son Charles died in 1728, owning five slaves but no land. How Charles maintained himself without land is unclear, but he may have become an operative within the plantation economy. Certainly that is what happened in other cases. Humphrey Seaward, for example, was the son of a late seventeenth-century smallholder in St. Andrew. Unlike Lawrence Prince, Jr., he held onto his small acreage, but by the 1730s he was supplementing his income by serving as an overseer commanding 150 slaves on Mary Elbridge's sugar plantation.[82]

Dreams of Independence

It was not foreordained that Jamaica be a premier sugar-producing colony, nor that sugar would be mainly grown on large integrated estates. Settlers planted a variety of crops, such as indigo, an easy crop to plant that received a good price in England. Cotton was also grown, as were allspice and ginger. For many small slave owners, either ranching or planting provision crops offered more potential than producing sugar. For Richard Blome, writing about Jamaica in 1670, the most promising crop was cacao. It was not cheap to set up a cacao walk, even though Jamaican planters had the advantage of being able to take over preexisting Spanish walks. But once the trees started to produce cacao beans, five years after being planted, the likely return per annum might be as high as £840. Blome was enthusiastic about the prospects. The crop, he stated was "the principal, and most beneficial *Commodity* of the *Isle*." He envisioned Jamaica becoming a profitable, well-settled island in which small landowners could establish families and make money from a range of plantation crops, all of which, like cacao, would involve relatively small labor forces. Blome thought one could clear above £500 from cacao with four servants and about sixteen slaves. Unfortunately, however, blight in 1671 on the southside cacao plantations halted the cacao industry before it really began to develop.[83]

Taylor's and Blome's accounts suggest that it was not the dream of every settler to become the owner of a large sugar estate. It was not that men did not aspire to great wealth and influence, but that the risks involved in planting were considerable and could jeopardize other ambitions. Two pamphlets printed in South Carolina in the early eighteenth century, by Thomas Nairne in 1710 and by John Norris in 1712, give us a guide as to what factors animated settlers to remove to embryonic plantation societies. Nairne and Norris both referred to South Carolina as an "American Canaan," a land that "flows with milk and honey," stressing in particular the astonishing ease by which ordinary men could live and accumulate wealth and provide for their families in an environment overflowing with abundance. They portrayed South Carolina as a paradise for yeomen farmers: it had cheap land, fertile soil, and easy access to the slaves that made living on cheap land worthwhile. Norris contended that one good laboring man could clear enough land in one year to "easily maintain a Wife and Ten Children, sufficient with *Corn, Pease, Rice, Flesh, Fish and Fowl.*" If, moreover, he had £100 sterling to invest, he could buy three slaves and 150 acres, allowing himself and his family to settle with "Comfort and Decency." Eventually he could get "a competent estate and live very handsom[e]ly." Even servants working for wages, Nairne thought, could "in a few Years" become "Masters and Owners of Plantations, Stocks and Slaves." Everyone, they argued, could obtain wealth without having to work too hard. But material betterment was only one part of the equation. It was merely a means to a larger ambition: that of becoming independent, masterless men who had controllable dependents.[84]

Norris argued that free people wanted their own land rather than to work for others. "How much better," he declaimed in biblical fashion, it was "for Man to improve their own Lands, for the rise of themselves and Posterity, to sit under their own Vine, and eat the Fruits of their Labour." But Norris and Nairne thought that great estates and small farms could coexist together. Indeed, implicit in their arguments was an expectation that South Carolina provided opportunity for all conditions of whites—those with substantial sums to invest, who became great planters; those with smaller sums who became family farmers; and those without money who were able to save to become landowners by working for high wages as slave overseers.[85]

Persuading poorer whites to work within the plantation system was vital but difficult, as the vignette from William Dampier's life suggests. White men in a slave society expected to be masters and wanted to be independent. For most of the seventeenth century this combination of wealth and independence was best attained within a semisubsistence frontier economy. Until the late 1680s white immigrants to the plantation American South and the British West Indies were easily able to become independent smallholders. Lorena Walsh has described the social mobility available to ordinary white men and women with great care and detail for the mid-seventeenth-century Chesapeake and makes a strong case for this period strongly fostering the growth and consolidation into power of a considerable small planter class. Middling to small planters (men with estates of no more than £200, and usually much less) had neither the money nor the mercantile connections to buy slaves, each worth around £23 in the mid-seventeenth century. They nonetheless lived well by their own lights, producing tobacco and some grain for export, raising livestock, and growing subsistence crops, and managing to live without excessive consumer goods. Their wealth grew slowly but impressively: nonhuman physical wealth on Maryland's lower western shore rose by about 2.7 percent per annum between the 1650s and the 1680s. A considerable number of men were able to become independent landowners, managed to support families while they were alive and pass down an inheritance to them when they were dead, enjoyed some public recognition as members of a flourishing militia and as jurymen and perhaps justices of the peace, and had enough leisure time to hunt and to cultivate family and friends. Most small planters had little reason to risk becoming large planters, with lots of slaves and lots of debt (if credit had somehow magically become available), rather than relying on farm building and the assiduous cultivation of assets that allowed them to achieve the aim of becoming an independent yeoman on the English model.[86]

Jamaica before the Transition

Jamaica provides an important case study into how vital the nonplantation sector was before the transitions of the late seventeenth century. Jamaica also shows how a society of independent small slaveholders, white indentured servants, and small gangs of slaves was transformed into the classic plantation society of large planters, white managers, and black slaves. Until the mid-1670s any immigrant was able to get land given to him virtually free via the patent system. Without much effort, a man could acquire livestock and a few slaves necessary to cultivate small acreages of land. Even after most available land had been patented, land was still comparatively cheap, at least by Barbadian standards, especially if a settler was willing to farm land in the hills and mountains that was not ideal for sugar cultivation. A comprehensive study of deeds for St. Andrew Parish in the 1660s and 1670s shows not only that the amount of patentable land was considerable, but also that most land sales involved small amounts of money. One could buy fifty acres for a few pounds. The average price per acre of land sold was well under £1. If the land available through patent is added to land sales, then the average price of land fell to under 10 shillings an acre. Moreover, most of it was on the Liguanea Plain, ideal land for sugar cultivation.[87] If a man needed money, he could easily acquire it either as a buccaneer or by producing goods for the Spanish American trade. If farming did not appeal, then a decent income could be gained as a tradesman or within the commercial world of booming Port Royal. Relatively few men upon their death in this period left large estates, on the Bybrook model, with significant slave forces able to produce sugar and other sugar by-products on the scale by then common in Barbados.[88]

The extent to which small slaveholders dominated the economy can be seen in an analysis of inventories taken in the 1670s and 1680s. Between 1674 and 1689, 554 individuals in Jamaica left inventories of their estates. Of these, 381 were slave owners who possessed 5,979 enslaved workers (most of whom were African, though there were about 50 slaves noted as "Indian") and 299 indentured servants. A further 17 people owned servants but not slaves. The average size of the owned workforce was 11 slaves and 1 servant. The 29 men who owned over 50 slaves apiece owned 48 percent of enslaved people, meaning that an appreciable percentage of enslaved people lived in small to medium slaveholdings. There were 102 slave owners who owned 2,146 slaves (36 percent of the total) in slaveholdings that contained between 11 and 50 enslaved people. The very large slaveholdings characteristic of eighteenth-century Jamaican slavery were rare. Four men owned more than 130 slaves: Samuel Long had 288 slaves and 12 servants, Charles Modyford had 242 slaves and 8 servants, Daniel Hickes had 173 slaves and seven servants, and Sir Henry Morgan had 131 slaves and 7 servants. Significantly, each of these men was not only rich, but politically well connected, allowing greater access than normal to large numbers of African imports. Morgan was a governor, Modyford was the son of a governor, Long was chief justice, and Hickes was the leading merchant in Port Royal.[89]

We can also see the relatively widespread distribution of slave property in Jamaica in a comprehensive census made for the inland parish of St. John in 1680. Analyzing this document, Richard Dunn concluded that "the biggest planters in St. John completely dominated the scene." They owned 77 percent of slaves and 61 percent of servants, held the best land, and were the major sugar producers. Yet the largest slaveholdings were still relatively small. Only Colonel John Cope, with 180 slaves and 15 servants, owned what would be considered a fully stocked sugar estate by the standards of the mid-eighteenth century. Just 5 men owned more than 50 slaves. Big planters (50 or more slaves) owned 56 percent of slaves, and middling planters (10–50 slaves) owned 261 slaves and 26 servants, or over a third of the bound labor force. At least 10 of these middling planters produced sugar.[90]

These small landholdings were surprisingly productive. Sugar production was not necessarily synonymous with large plantations in the seventeenth century. A considerable amount of sugar was made by small planters during the 1660s. As David Eltis states for Babados, "while a large proportion of the island's free white male population had some involvement with export produce, most of them must have had a major commitment to the domestic or subsistence economy as well." Both small proprietors and great planters grew sugar.[91] Similar patterns were true in Jamaica, although the levels of indentured servitude were never as high as in mid-seventeenth-century Barbados. Sugar production in Jamaica leapt between 1671 and 1689 from 1,000 to 12,000 hogsheads per annum. While the number of plantations producing sugar also grew, from 60 in 1674–75 to 151 in 1686–96, the average number of slaves on these plantations was small by eighteenth-century standards. In 1674–75 the average plantation had 20 slaves; only 2 plantations had more than 50. By 1686–96 the average number of slaves per plantation had crept up to 27, and 16 of 151 plantations held 50 or more slaves. As is clear from these figures, the modal experience for planters, and for a good proportion of slaves, was working on small to medium plantations.[92]

The fortuitous survival of a census for Port Royal in 1680 shows other slave-owning patterns. The average number of slaves per white family was 1.67, compared to 3.55 in a census conducted in Bridgetown in the same year. A few men, notably Sir Henry Morgan, who had 10 white servants and 14 black slaves, had large labor forces, but most men did not. The average number of slaves owned by Port Royal residents who were inventoried was 8; the merchant Daniel Hickes had the most slaves, with 173 enslaved people in his inventory when he died in 1689. Hickes, like Robert Phillips (d. 1689) with 59 slaves, William Slaughter (d. 1700) with 69 slaves, and John Wilmot (d. 1694), with 54 slaves, were the progenitors of an important breed, urban merchants who used their wealth to buy estates in the countryside that they stocked with slaves out of their urban slave-trading activities.[93]

Port Royal in 1680 was an affluent and highly militarized town, with 1,181 militiamen, one-third of them seamen.[94] It had strong connections to Spanish America and to economic activities it generated internally. One of its most important sources of income was that it was an entrepôt for the sale and distribution of manufactured goods from England. White Jamaicans in the late seventeenth century had money and lived well, as John Taylor chronicled in his account of the town in 1688. They especially loved to spend money on consumer goods. Governor William Beeston rather censoriously commented in 1700 that Jamaican "people are not very sparing, neither in their clothing, diet or any way of using [goods]." Trade data bears out his statement. White Jamaicans imported goods from London worth £30,974 in 1686 and £48,232 in 1697, meaning that a white population of around 8,000 in the earlier year and about 7,000 in

1697 imported £3.87 per white capita in 1686 (somewhat higher than in Barbados in the same year) and £6.89 per white capita in 1697—probably around ten times as much per head as was imported by the residents of the Chesapeake. Jamaica imported 1.7 times as much English goods as the Chesapeake Bay area did in 1697, despite having a white population of 7,000 compared to the Chesapeake's white population of 85,000.[95]

Some of these goods were immediately resold into Spanish America. The trade with Spanish America was substantial. In 1679 Jamaica's naval officer reported that the island's ships had traded around £20,000 with Spanish America in the previous sixteen months. English merchants began to use Jamaica as a base for direct trade with Spanish America instead of the Spanish port of Cadiz. The most important goods traded to Spanish America were, increasingly, enslaved Americans. In the late seventeenth century perhaps one-third of all Africans coming to Port Royal were transshipped to Spanish America. James Castillo, agent for the Spanish *asiento*, was the single largest slave purchaser from the Royal African Company in Port Royal in the 1680s. Port Royal merchants preferred to sell to Spaniards, as they paid higher prices than locals and, more important, paid in cash. In addition, Port Royal was the buccaneer's home, and piracy created a financial bonanza for the town and island. Henry Morgan was reported to have taken as much as £100,000 from his spectacular raid on Portobello in 1668. Jamaican contraband commerce amounted to more than £100,000 per year in the 1680s, two-thirds of the total amount of plantation produce sent to London in 1686. Ordinary white men could easily avoid the plantation sector given how much wealth could be gained elsewhere.[96]

Whites in many places were reluctant to move from societies based on small farming to ones based on plantation agriculture. But after the shift took place, most whites quickly reconciled themselves to the large integrated plantation because of the advantages it brought to the great majority of them.[97] Their main challenge was in reconciling themselves and their societies to the violence that lay at the heart of the success of the large integrated plantation system.

TWO

Violence, White Solidarity, and the Rise of Planter Elites

Benefits of Working in the Plantation System

Why was an economy based on the large integrated plantation that brought great benefits to all white residents not
adopted immediately everywhere that plantation agriculture was feasible? Ordinary white men hesitated to work in
a system where they needed to work closely with enslaved
black people. Their hesitation was due not to any fellow-
feeling for black people as men and women trapped in a relentless machine, but to their satisfaction with the rewards
they already had. Ordinary white men doubted whether the
unpleasant life of an overseer on a large integrated plantation would improve their lives. What was especially unpleasant about this profession was controlling by brute force hostile, traumatized, and potentially violent enslaved men and
women.

The essential contours of this question were laid out
in Edmund Morgan's magnificent exploration, published
forty years ago, of the world of early Virginia. He argued
that the transition from one system of economic organization to another was neither peaceful nor uncontested. This
chapter explores the violent confrontations out of which
the large integrated plantation emerged. For Morgan, what
was significant was the violence that occurred between different groups of white people: class-related violence. This

chapter focuses on the violence that white people exercised against Africans. The transition to the large integrated plantation system was very slow because white people had to learn the particular kinds of violence that kept a "brutish" and "dangerous" people in check. Learning to use that violence did not come naturally, but arose out of the particular historical context of the Atlantic slave trade and large-scale European warfare.

The specific kind of violence useful to control enslaved Africans was not inherent in the violence that characterized the barbarous years of early settlement. Disciplining angry, alienated, and aggressively hostile African slaves was a tough business. Most people shrank from the challenge. Those willing to mete out brutal treatment to enslaved Africans and who did so once the large plantation was established were prepared by their previous experiences as soldiers in European wars or as sailors on slave ships. Not only was the world of the plantations a world of warfare, but its essential features were determined during periods of social crisis. Its utility as an economic system was so great that it may have been a system that would have developed anyway. But it developed as it did in Barbados, and then in Virginia, Jamaica, and the Leeward Islands, because it accompanied or followed periods when large numbers of British men were mobilized into large European armies. These armies, the product of a far-reaching military revolution in Britain in the mid- to late seventeenth century, were financially complex organizations that functioned through utilizing a degree of harsh discipline and lockstep training unknown elsewhere. They employed methods of organization remarkably similar to the discipline and rational organization that marked the organization of labor on the large integrated plantation. The demands of war in Britain and Europe gave rise to the fiscal-military state, a development that allowed Britain to reshape its empire in the eighteenth center. One little-appreciated manifestation of these complex changes was their contribution to the development of the large integrated plantation, an institution staffed by men who were, in a literal sense, the foot soldiers of empire.[1]

Outside Barbados the plantation system evolved slowly. Jamaica, for example, had almost everything necessary to become a plantation society on the Barbadian model by the early 1670s. What it lacked was the means to marshal its increasingly large slave population into sugar-producing gangs. The truly revolutionary aspect of the plantation system was not that it was based upon the labor of captive Africans, for unfree labor was customary in all forms of agriculture throughout the seventeenth century; it was the way in which slaves were worked. As

Gabriel Debien commented, "The making of sugar, even the simplest raw sugar, requires, if undertaken on any scale, the rotation of numerous disciplined work teams, a regime of punishing toil, closely supervised by day and by night. This was a new type of work, an element of social revolution."[2]

The Gang System

The employment of gang labor allowed planters to be more productive than when making crops using dispersed systems of mixed farming. Once the gang system emerged, first in Barbados in the 1660s, its productivity advantages were so great that the sugar industry was reorganized around it. Its efficacy was recognized early on. The first description of gang labor was a series of instructions given by a leading Barbadian sugar planter, Henry Drax, to his overseer in a book first published in the mid-eighteenth century but probably written around 1670. Drax believed that the "best way to prevent Idleness is constantly to Gang all the Negroes in the Plantations in the Time of Planting." He advised his overseer to put "All the Men Negroes into two gangs, the ablest and best by themselves for Holeing and the stronger Work, and the more ordinary Negroes in a Gang for Dunging." Women and "lesser Negroes" were also to be divided into two gangs.[3]

It took some time for planters to work out and implement its hallmark characteristic, its lockstep discipline and liberal use of the whip.[4] There was nothing intrinsically complicated about putting slaves to work in this way. Any careful observer of how sugar, tobacco, and rice were produced would see that the best way to make such commodities was to break down the various activities of making these crops into distinct steps and have each of those steps performed by controlled gangs of laborers. Moreover, other early modern institutions existed, most notably the massive European armies in which many planters would have served, in which crucial aspects of the gang system were replicated.[5]

Forcing bonded laborers to do this arduous and boring kind of work— work outside the experience of most workers in seventeenth-century Africa, Europe, or America—was difficult. Gang labor was highly productive, but it was so psychologically oppressive and physically demanding that it was never consistently employed with free laborers. Workers hated gang labor and would not undertake it freely. As a seventeenth-century Barbadian slave was quoted saying bitterly, "The devil was in the Englishman that he makes everything work; he makes the Negro work, he makes the horse work, the ass work, the wood work, the water work and the wind work."[6] Violence was necessary to make people work in gangs.

Violence was intrinsic to the plantation system from the start. We can see this in Richard Ligon's account of the island in the 1640s, just as Barbados adopted the large integrated plantation system and as enslaved Africans outnumbered whites. Ligon explored how English colonists created a harmonious social structure even though Barbados, the most profitable colony England owned, was a "tinderbox of oppressive servitudes," with "the most brutal labor regime in the Atlantic basin." It was a place of extreme social disorder and inequality. It might be a model commonwealth, Ligon thought, but only if the violence of the masters was controlled. Barbados had a diverse population, including rich planters; white indentured servants; political prisoners, including Irish refugees from Cromwell's massacre of the Irish at Drogheda in 1649; and around 6,000 to 7,000 African slaves. It hovered always on the edge of blowing up: it was a combustible society. He used metaphors of fire to stress its flammable and explosive nature. After describing the natural beauty of the island and its useful vegetation and lamenting that death stalked the population, he expostulated, "Truly, I have seen such cruelty there done to Servants, as I did not think one Christian could do to another." Servants responded through arson so that "whole lands of Canes and Houses too, are burnt down and consumed, to the utter ruine and undoing of their Masters." Ligon argued that the ill-treatment of servants explained and justified their violent reactions. But African violence against white masters was a different matter. They used fire maliciously. He talked not just of a plot by slaves to set fire to a boiling house and claim it was an accident, but also of how "an excellent Negroe" was burned to death when the candle he was holding got too close to a hogshead of liquor, setting the hogshead and him alight. As Susan Scott Parrish concludes, Ligon saw "that the Caribbean was not only a geographic but also a political burning zone, wherein the fire that was used to turn cane into casks of market-ready sugar could be used by its laborers to destroy the crops." Fire, Ligon thought, was a legitimate form of resistance that white servants might use against a tyrannical master. If enslaved people resorted to fire, Ligon believed that it was an act of treason because slaves lay outside the boundaries of civil society.[7]

Planters could not persuade or force white servants to work in gangs. They accepted that there were certain levels of freedom that could not be taken away from Europeans.[8] They were far less constrained in how they treated black slaves. Gender assumptions played a part in the move

FIGURE 3. There are few visual depictions of white colonists in seventeenth-century Barbados. Although this engraving, seemingly made in the Netherlands, does not realistically depict the Barbados landscape, it does have background details of enslaved Africans, trade goods, and shipping that would have conveyed to a European audience what Barbados was like. Copperplate engraving, "Englese Quakers en Tabak Planters aen de Barbados," in Carel Allard, *Orbis Habitatus Oppida et Vestitus* (Amsterdam, [1680?]). Details of this engraving's history are derived from www.slaveryimages.org, compiled by Jerome S. Handler and Michael Tuite.

to harsher and more coercive work regimes. White planters hesitated to use white women as field laborers. They drew on traditions in Europe where women's work was distinguished sharply from that of men.[9] Determining what Barbadian planters thought about having white bound labor is difficult. Many planters, especially those who themselves worked alongside small slave forces, preferred white servants to black slaves.[10] But larger planters, the men orchestrating the shift to the large integrated plantation, were ambivalent at best about keeping white servants. Henry Drax advised his manager, "I shall Not leave you many White Servants the fewer the better were itt not Incumbent duty on all to keepe the Number the Act of militia requiers for the Countreys Service." He found white servants troublesome owing to their propensity for "drunknese," which he thought "the vice the Whits are much addicted to." It is possible that the wealthiest Barbadian planters were like their Virginian counterparts a decade or so later in being eager and early adopters of slave labor. [11]

Planters needed men willing to apply substantial physical force to make large gangs of enslaved people work. This task was not for the thin-skinned, as discussions of what overseers had to do to slaves makes clear. Antoine Biet, a French priest who visited the island in 1654, was shocked at the "severity" of slavery and the frequent use of the lash by overseers on slaves. The law of 1652 that allowed whites to beat slaves found on the roads without passes was, he believed, a sanction for sadistic violence: slaves "are given fifty blows with a cudgel; these often bruise them severely." He described some sadistic crimes against slaves, such as a master cutting off an ear, roasting it, and forcing the earless slave to eat it, and lamented that "it is inhuman to treat [slaves] with so much harshness." Isaac Berkenhead, who visited a year after Biet, added that planters were happy to kill their slaves, "doggs and they being in one ranke with each other." Significantly, however, Biet thought that some violence against slaves was justified, as planters "must keep these kinds of people obedient."[12]

Violence and Overseers

Ira Berlin summarizes well the violence toward slaves that happened in the Chesapeake as the plantation regime took hold. His summary applies even more forcefully to Jamaica, Barbados, and South Carolina. As Berlin notes, the plantation regime needed raw power to sustain it. Slavery had always been brutal in British America, but the level of violence increased dramatically as the size of slave labor forces increased. After 1700, Berlin explains, "Chesapeake slaves faced the pillory, whipping post, and gallows far more frequently and in far larger numbers than before." Moreover, the punishments meted out to slaves were both cruel and increasingly ingenious. Humiliating punishments were invented, such as William Byrd II forcing a bedwetting slave to drink a "pint of piss." In addition, grotesque mutilations for criminal infractions and gruesome tortures leading to executions for those slaves caught after daring to rebel were employed frequently.[13]

An example from Barbados shows the inherent violence of the system. A failed revolt in 1675 resulted in six rebels burned alive; eleven others beheaded and dragged through the streets, after which their heads were stuck on poles; and dozens of slaves castrated.[14] Indeed, just as more horrific kinds of capital punishment gradually fell out of favor in seventeenth-century England, new kinds of tortures, such as hanging slaves in gibbets and burning rebels over a slow fire, were introduced into the southern and island colonies. The overseer on the Helyar Estate in Jamaica described in 1677 a rebel being tortured and killed by a slow fire: "His legs and armes was first broken in peeces with stakes, after which he was fasten'd upon his back to the Ground—a fire was made first to his feete and burn'd uppe by degrees; I heard him speake severall words when the fire consum'd all his lower parts as far as his Navill. The fire was upon his breast (he was burning near three houres) before he dy'd." The British American colonies reverted to medieval forms of punishment (castration had long been absent from the British criminal code, for example) while dramatically increasing the frequency of punishments.[15]

Of course, enslaved drivers did some of the hard disciplinary work. Drivers were specially chosen for their "activeness, diligence and honesty." They occupied a curious position. On the one hand, they were the leaders in slave communities. On the other, they were planters' agents in terrorizing slaves. They customarily carried out whippings. Planters, too, were involved in disciplining slaves, though usually at a distance. The state-sponsored tortures and executions of slaves were under their control. But, as is made clear in *Colonel Jack* and in plantation-management manuals from the late seventeenth century, generously recompensed white servants did the other major disciplinary tasks.[16] They did not work as laborers alongside slaves, as was the practice for indentured servants on small estates, but were managers involved in controlling, cajoling, and punishing slaves.[17]

The trouble with using drivers as managers was that whites could not entirely trust them. Skilled and privileged slaves tended to lead revolts, the most famous example being, of course, Toussaint Louverture.[18] Reverend Robert Robertson, a staunch conservative and astute observer of plantation life, insisted that "in all their Plots and Conspiracies . . . the *Creole-Negroes* . . . and some of those from Africa that were most favour'd . . . have been found deepest in the Design, and the prime Directors and Actors of all the mischief."[19] Keith Mason describes a privileged, or key, slave called Frank who bears out Robertson's claim. Frank lived in Nevis in the Leeward Islands, a colony with significant social unrest from ordinary whites. They felt discriminated against, as absentees "breed up their negroes to all manner of trades and make overseers of them."[20] Frank was one such privileged slave, owned by Sir William Stapleton, an absentee planter and proprietor in 1724 of a large sugar estate with 138 slaves.[21] He was an experienced, acculturated, and well-respected slave, favored by whites, and with authority among enslaved people. He replaced an elderly black driver during a period of plantation instability when the white managerial workers were involved in internecine conflict. Frank established himself firmly in the favor of the manager and his absentee owner. As a result, he received considerable privileges: his own house, livestock, and better clothing and food. Indeed, he was seen as an individual rather than a number, which was a rare accomplishment for a slave in early eighteenth-century records. He was so highly valued ("an extraordinary good negro") that when he was imprisoned as a result of a reported slave conspiracy in Nevis in 1725, his employers spirited him away to England so that he would escape retribution from angry whites.[22]

Nevis whites were not impressed. They thought Stapleton overly indulgent to a traitorous rebel. They threatened Frank's life and resented how he been able to leave the island. His return in 1729 caused consternation. The white manager, a resident planter called Joseph Herbert, told Stapleton, "There are several p[e]r[s]ons here that has laid themselves under the strongest obligations to destroy him whenever they shall see him." They probably felt justified in their hatred of Frank when he ran away soon after returning to Nevis in 1729. Stapleton's white employees told him, in language resembling Daniel Defoe's, that Frank's "treachery" was inevitable given the lack of gratitude inherent in the African character: they argued that he was "a very ungratefull rogue." Herbert concluded that his "extraordinary privileges . . . induce some negroes to think they are above their fellow slaves and consequently puts 'em upon subtle attempts."[23]

What Frank's story demonstrates is how reducing the distance between slave drivers and white managers, and muddling the responsibilities that each group of plantation workers had, was counterproductive for smooth management. Stapleton and Herbert went well beyond normal solicitousness when they supported him against white employees. Herbert did so because he was using Frank as a conduit for selling estate property that rightly belonged to Stapleton. The Stapleton Estate was in disarray, which is one reason Frank made himself so indispensable to the manager that he was prepared to move heaven and earth to have Frank returned to the plantation. Herbert trusted Frank more than his fellow whites. He wrote to Stapleton when Frank was in England that "I ever had a good opinion of him but never so great as since I have known the want of him." He may have liked Frank because other slaves did not accept his own rule and approached the estate's attorney, Stapleton's cousin, Timothy Tyrell, soon after Herbert was selected manager to object to his appointment. They engaged in various acts of recalcitrance, to which Herbert responded weakly. Stapleton soon came to distrust Herbert, using an indentured servant to spy on his manager. He replaced him as manager in 1730. Unfortunately for Stapleton, the new manager was an unmitigated disaster. The ensuing dissension among white servants encouraged Frank to insinuate himself into the management of the plantation and undermine it from within.[24]

Planters believed that the plantation work could not proceed without competent white middle managers because, as Henry Drax argued in his 1670s Barbadian slave-management manual, "Many Negroes will be apt to Lurk and Meech from their Work, without great Care be taken to prevent it." White overseers had to make "every Negro doth his Part, according to his ability, the weak hands must not be pressed, nor the Strong suffered to shrink from their Work." They needed to constantly monitor slave activities: "your under-Overseer must constantly have a List of the gang under his particular Care, that he may be able to give a Particular Account of everyone, whether Sick or how employed." Punishment should be immediate and exemplary: "If att any time you take Notice of a fault that you design to punish lett itt bee Emediately Executed Espetially on Negroes: Many of them being of the houmer for awoyding punishments when threatened."[25]

The Plantation System's Effect on White Servants

The plantation system did not necessarily drive away whites. The Barbadian white population maintained its numbers in the last quarter of the seventeenth century, and many whites participated in the plantation economy as producers of rum and occasionally sugar. In the Chesapeake, the white population grew appreciably just as the plantation system was taking root in the early eighteenth century. Between 1700 and 1720 the white population of Virginia and Maryland jumped from 85,000 to 128,000, following stagnation in the economic recession of 1680–1700. The Jamaican white population went into precipitous decline as the plantation system evolved, but most of that decline can be accounted for by outbreaks of epidemic disease in the 1690s.[26]

Certainly planters did not need white indentured servants as laborers once they had an appreciable number of slaves. White servants became overseers and bookkeepers whose principal task was the management and punishment of slaves. A planter with a labor force of 100 to 200 slaves needed at least 5 white functionaries. The Barbados census of 1715 gives us some rough idea of the number of landowners and servants. There were 16,888 white people in the island. Between 2,600 and 2,900 lived in Bridgetown, and another 1,167 lived nearby in the Parish of St. Michael. The remaining 12,776 lived in the countryside, where there were 995 plantations, of which 627 could be considered large integrated plantations producing sugar, with between one and three mills each. Simon Smith estimates that there were 5,826 adults working on these plantations. Of these, perhaps 3,000 or 4,000 were servants. There were 5.9 whites per household on plantations, 4.4 in Bridgetown, and 3.2 in rural smallholdings.[27]

West Indian whites experienced a much worse demographic regime than whites in the Chesapeake.[28] The amount of white immigration into the late seventeenth-century Caribbean was considerable, but it would have needed to remain at the enormous levels of the first half of the seventeenth century for white numbers to be maintained, given white mortality rates. David Galenson used figures compiled by Henry Gemery to estimate that the number of people who emigrated from England into the islands dropped from 40,000 in the 1640s to 15,000 in the 1670s (of whom almost 10,000 went to Barbados and most of the rest to Jamaica) before increasing to 19,000 in the 1690s and precipitously falling to under 10,000 in the 1700s. These figures are probably too low, if extrapolations from Jamaica are correct, but they give some idea of magnitude. Immigration into the British West Indies was greater than European immigration into the northern colonies of British America, which was no more than 5,000 in the 1640s and 1670s and was negative between 1690 and 1710. It was probably equal to immigration into the American South, which Galenson estimates at 14,000 in the 1640s, 18,000 in the 1670s, 3,000 in the 1690s, and 25,000 in the 1700s. High mortality rates, however, meant that the West Indian white population declined from around 47,000 in 1660 to about 30,000 in 1710. Meanwhile, the natural (non-immigrant) white population increase in Virginia and Maryland led to a threefold increase in population between 1670 and 1720.[29]

In the West Indies mortality rates varied greatly. White mortality was not as bad in Barbados in the eighteenth century. Rates of death per 1,000 people in the Parish of St. Michael, including Bridgetown, were 128 in 1683 (as compared to between 37 and 42 per 1,000 in colonial Boston and New York), but fell to 66 per 1,000 in the first decade of the eighteenth century and to 49.4 per 1,000 between 1749 and 1762. By contrast, mortality rates in Jamaica remained very high throughout the seventeenth and eighteenth centuries and reached epidemic rates, especially in Kingston, between the 1690s and 1740s. Jamaica was at the high end of exposure to epidemiological regimes, with mortality rates in its most salubrious parish around 70 deaths per 1,000 people per annum in the late seventeenth century, and in rural parishes between 80 and 90 deaths per 1,000 people. Kingston was notoriously unhealthy, with mortality rates reaching over 200 deaths per 1,000 people in the second quarter of the eighteenth century. By contrast, death rates in eighteenth-century Britain averaged between 25 and 30 per 1,000 people and were even lower, at between 15 and 20 deaths per 1,000 people, in New England. In British North America death rates were 28 per 1,000 in the eighteenth century. The only region that even came close to matching West Indian mortality rates was South Carolina, where infant mortality was over 250 per 1,000, and where half the population died before the age of twenty. Mortality levels in Jamaica, however, were virtually in another league. Life expectancy was appalling, most immigrants died soon after arrival, and horrific infant and child mortality rates made the island virtually child-free: 587 out of every 1,000 children died before their tenth birthday.[30]

Barbados, and certainly Virginia, probably had enough whites to cater to the plantations' need for white supervisors. In Jamaica, however, where the slave population was rapidly increasing around the turn of the eighteenth century and where large estates of 100 or more slaves were increasingly common, attracting sufficiently large numbers of whites to work in plantations was hard. Planters were probably unable to attract white overseers in sufficient volume before the turn of the century to make the transition to the large integrated plantation. It took a particular combination of circumstances for this situation to change and for whites to enter willingly into plantation service.

In Jamaica legislators were extremely concerned about the low numbers of whites in the island, especially as the plantation system matured. Beginning in the 1690s, when white population decline became obvious, the Jamaican Assembly repeatedly tried to increase white immigration into Jamaica by sponsoring migration schemes (none of them successful) from 1719 to 1750.[31] They also tried to limit the numbers of nonresident landowners by making them pay larger quit rents and by imposing fines for uncultivated land. Most important, beginning in 1703 laws were passed that placed a tax on planters if they did not maintain a ratio of one white man on their properties for every twenty slaves owned. Between 1703 and 1713 deficiency laws took the form of quartering acts, by which planters who did not have enough white servants could be required to billet regular troops. In 1716 a fully formed deficiency act specifying the numbers of white servants needed per slave force and the fines assessed when such numbers were not met was passed by the Assembly. Although the Board of Trade initially disallowed the act because of who was to administer it, it was passed properly by 1720 and was the forerunner of many later deficiency acts. Initially this act was intended to encourage white immigration rather than to be a penalty on planters who failed to hire sufficient servants. But from 1720, when the act was amended to levy a fine on planters without a ratio of one white man to every thirty slaves, the tax became a considerable imposition on most planters, few of whom kept the required number of white employees. By 1750 the tax revenue gained from the deficiency laws was an important source of government monies.[32] The deficiency law is a rare example of legislators implementing a law bound to cost them considerable amounts of money. Taken together, these laws show a desperate need for white employees.

Jamaica needed white immigrants because they needed plantation managers and militia soldiers. This may be the reason we have a surprising amount of information about the size of Jamaica's white population, especially in the years when yellow fever epidemics were most virulent, between 1692 and 1730, and when fears of French invasion and Maroon war were most pronounced. The figures produced are not consistent, but overall patterns are clear. White population fell in the 1690s, a decline that was not reversed until after 1730. For Jamaican governors, what was more significant than population decline was that the number of men able to bear arms declined precipitously after the Port Royal earthquake of 1692 and the first and most virulent attack of yellow fever in 1694. There were 4,050 men able to bear arms in the white population in 1673 but only 2,465 in 1698. The result was a weakened militia. In 1694 there were only 1,774 men in the militia, in 1706 there were 2,641, and in 1710 and 1715 the numbers were 2,722 and 2,679 respectively. Numbers, in short, plateaued in the first decades of the eighteenth century. Governor Robert Hunter ordered a survey of the white population in 1730. The number of men able to bear arms was just 2,500, of whom 60 percent were indentured servants, most of whom he believed to be Irish and therefore unreliable. Hunter may have underestimated these numbers, as his estimate of the total number of freeholders and servants was around 4,500. Of most use is Hunter's division of the white population. He noted there were 1,650 freeholders and 3,993 servants in 1730, of whom 2,190 were indentured servants and another 1,790 were hired servants. Of these, 990 were women, making the number of white male servants probably able to bear arms about 3,000. Jamaica had around

75,000 slaves, of whom about 70 percent worked on sugar plantations. If a similar ratio of white male servants was assigned to sugar plantations, this means a ratio of servants to slaves of 1 to 25. Such a ratio met the demands, just, of the deficiency law; but one imagines that many plantations ran short of whites, especially because it is likely that many servants worked in towns rather than the countryside.[33]

Fear of Slave Revolts

White Jamaicans believed that a larger white population was needed to ensure their safety against a growing slave population, their implacable enemies. The geography of Jamaica accentuated planter problems because the mountainous interior provided slaves with chances of escape impossible on small cleared islands like Barbados and Antigua. The willingness of seventeenth-century Maroons to give escaped slaves haven also encouraged runaways. A prime factor influencing slave decisions to rebel was also the size of the plantation on which a slave lived. Slaves were more unruly in seventeenth-century Jamaica than anywhere else in the British Atlantic world. The island did not face an island-wide revolt, but slave revolts were more frequent in the last third of the seventeenth century than at any time in Jamaica's history. Between 1673 and 1694 Jamaica experienced six slave revolts, with two smaller conspiracies to revolt in 1702 and 1704. The first two revolts, in 1673 and 1675, occurred on isolated plantations on the north side, each with over 50 slaves. The next revolt occurred on the large plantation of Captain Edmond Duck, near Spanish Town. Duck owned nearly 100 slaves, of whom 30 escaped after killing Duck's wife and several other whites. They met slaves from two other large estates, those of Sir Thomas Modyford and William Helyar, and caused considerable damage, alarming terrified whites. Whites remained scared until most of the slaves were captured and subjected to horrific tortures and painful deaths. The most serious revolt occurred in 1685–86, when 150 slaves on the north side and 105 from Widow Guy's sugar plantation in St. John seized arms, killed whites, and burned and plundered for months before the uprising was put down. Guy's slaves took account of white weaknesses: John Helyar wrote on 27 March 1686 that the revolt came about "through the faults of the white servants, who were gotten drunk and therefore unable to Quell them."[34]

John Taylor gave a detailed description of four revolts that occurred between 1682 and 1686, three at large plantations: the revolt of Madam

Guy's slaves, an abortive rebellion by 180 slaves of Colonel Ivy in Vere in 1683, and the 1684 rebellion at the Duck plantation. The fourth revolt was a planned rebellion of Port Royal slaves.[35] Taylor dwelt lovingly on the barbaric tortures that planters forced on slaves caught in these rebellions, pondering little the morality of such treatment. He was convinced Africans could be controlled only through terror. He related how "Collonel Ivey" discovered a plot, cornered his slaves, and read out from Jamaica's slave code (a book that "is hated by those slaves, and they still say 'tis the divile's book"). Ivey acted as judge and jury of his frightened slaves:

[He] caused all his slaves to be bound and fetter'd with irons, . . . and then caus'd them to be severely whip't, caused some to be roasted alive, and others to be torn to peices with dogs, others he cutt off their ears, feets and codds, and caused them to eat 'em; then he putt them all in iron feters, and soe with severe whipping every day forced them to work, and soe in time they became obedient and quiet, and have never since offer'd to rebel. Thus did God bring to nothing their damnable disigne, and prevent the horrid rebellion and murther they intended.[36]

Even at this stage of Jamaican history the divisions between blacks and whites were entrenched.[37] White servants did not join with black slaves. Moreover, Africans did not hesitate to kill their fellow white laborers. The slaves of Widow Guy "murther'd fifteen Christian souls, all that belonged to the plantation but two, as the overseer which was then at the Port about his mistrise's negotiations, and Madam Greg herself whom a Negro woman . . . hid amongst old Negro cloaths." The slaves of Edmond Duck "murther'd him and about twenty more of his family, and sadly abused and wounded his wife whom they left for dead in the plantation."[38] Security from slave attack was achieved only when individual plantations had sufficient white employees to keep slaves in order.

The Move to Large Plantations: Jamaica

Why were whites willing to work in the plantation economy in the last decades of the seventeenth century, when they had not been willing to do so previously? And to what extent did whites have the skills and fortitude necessary to control slaves? Evidence is very limited, but we can make some guesses. John Taylor, for example, noted how unpleasant the life of a white servant was, claiming that "the wealthy planter" was "verey severe to his English servants, for alltho' they are not putt to worke att the hough as the Negroa slaves are, yet they are kept verey hard to their labor att felling of timber, hewing staves for casks, sugar boyling and other labors, soe that they are little better than slaves." Indeed, in some respects they were worse off than slaves, because if a servant was a pretty female domestic "to be sure hir master cloathes her well and hir mistris bestows many curses on hir and blowes to the bargain." Servants were cheaper and more dispensable than slaves, meaning that "there is not half that car taken of 'em as over their Negros, and when dead noe more ceremony at their funerale than if they were to berey a dogg."[39]

Servants, therefore, had every reason to "repent their rash adventures in comming from England, to be slaves in America." They could escape their travails by becoming overseers, just as Defoe's Jack did. In the last page of his book Taylor argued that servants who accepted their lot as servants and did not increase their time of servitude by running away could "advance their fortune, for those manservants which come hither come commonly (if of a cappacity) employed in shops and to be supervisors of storehouses and in plantations." He noted also that "Negroa slaves" were "committed to the government of the overseer, who has other whit servants under him, as drivers to keep them to their labor, soe that one whit servant commands some twenty of 'em, under the overseers." The implication is clear: these servants had taken managerial positions. Taylor does not explicitly describe how slaves worked, whether in gangs or at task work, but the way he describes their work patterns suggests working in gangs: "all hands turn outt to labor both men and women together, where they all work at the hough etc., and are followed on by their drivers, which if they loiter sone quickens their pace with the whip."[40]

Taylor focused in particular on how slaves were controlled, observing that positive incentives encouraged slaves to work, and that male slaves were given wives, "without which they will not be contented, or worke." But it was pointless to provide slaves with more than "a linnen arsclout" for clothing because "they differ only from bruite beast only by their shape and speech." They were in addition "ignorant pore souls" who responded only to violence. He described how, if they "have committed robbery, prove sullen, refuse to work or the like," they were whipped "till their backs are covered with blood; then he rubs them with salt brine, and soe forces them to their work again." Further infractions led to whippings and overseers' rubbing their raw backs with molasses "for the wasps, merrywings and other insects to torment." Englishmen might think such treatment "hard" but Africans needed it "for if you should be kinder to 'em they would soner cutt your throat than obay you, for they are soe stubborn that with all this whiping, missery, or torment, they shall seldom be seen to shead a tear, but rather at first laugh, and then afterwards stand scilent."[41]

It was on large plantations that the hierarchy of white overseers, bookkeepers, and drivers was needed. Their work was unpleasant and the possibility that slaves would rise up and kill them was always strong. The relatively low number of large plantations extant before 1700 suggests that planters found it difficult to get enough white laborers to do this job. But things changed rapidly between the 1690s and the 1720s. In these decades Jamaica was transformed in several ways. There were some local particularities to Jamaica (notably much worse white demography), but the process there resembled what happened elsewhere. In addition, the transition in Jamaica is worth telling in itself, as it has not been told before, and it also involves the origins of what was by many measures Britain's most economically successful eighteenth-century colony.

What changes occurred? First, the population of Jamaica became considerably blacker. The white population decreased from a high point in the mid-1680s, while the black population catapulted from being relatively equal to the white population to being much greater. As early as 1700, therefore, Jamaica was a country populated mainly by black slaves ruled by a small minority of whites. Secondly, the size of slaveholdings increased dramatically. By the 1720s most Jamaican slaves were found in labor forces of 100 or more. This structure persisted virtually unchanged until the end of slavery. Thirdly, white servitude declined dramatically. Until the 1680s most planters with medium to large slave forces owned white servants. Beginning in the 1690s the number of inventoried white servants faded away until by the 1720s they were rare. Fourthly, land prices soared as farm building was completed, as most patentable land had been distributed (over a million acres had already been patented by 1683, with the 88 largest patentees owning more than 2,000 acres each), and as fertile land in the best areas became highly desirable sugar-cane land. These four interrelated developments explain the rise of the large integrated plantation in Jamaica in the first twenty-five years of the eighteenth century.

Let's deal first with changes in Jamaica's population. In 1662 the total population was 4,207: 3,653 whites and 554 black slaves. By 1673 enslaved Africans had increased to 7,768, exactly equal to the number of whites. By 1693 the estimated population of whites had slipped to 7,365, its lowest point between 1670 and 1834, while the number of enslaved

Africans rocketed to over 40,000. In the next century whites increased slowly to 12,737 in 1774 and 18,347 in 1788. Black numbers continued their upward climb, reaching 110,000 by 1752 and 210,894 by 1788, by which time there were 7,610 freed people of African descent.[42]

Of course, some of the things that big planters did to shore up their economic and political position affected poorer whites adversely. Their desire for land, as well as their suppression of privateering, made life harder for landless white men. But planters did not want to force poor whites away. The Jamaican Assembly was desperate for new white settlers, if only to serve in the militia in order to protect Jamaica from rebellious slaves and increasingly disruptive bands of Maroons.[43] No large exodus of whites went from Jamaica to other plantation areas in the late seventeenth century. Nor did many people return to England. Indeed, it became harder to leave Jamaica in the 1690s as warfare ravaged the island, forcing its lawmakers to declare martial law and refuse to let any soldiers leave. Moreover, the effects of the Glorious Revolution and the death in 1688 of the forceful but reckless Jamaican governor the duke of Albemarle ended a two-decade struggle between buccaneers and small farmers on the one hand and sugar planters on the other. Big planters conclusively won this power struggle. One consequence was the suppression of buccaneering. Buccaneers, increasingly marginalized and then criminalized as pirates, were forced to move north to Tortuga and the Bahamas. It was no longer possible, therefore, for small planters to get money through legal plundering raids against Spanish colonies.[44]

White numbers declined as rapidly as they did mostly owing to disease. White mortality rates were always high, but they became catastrophic in the 1690s. The earthquake of Port Royal started a serious decline. Not only were over 1,000 people killed in one of the greatest natural disasters in the history of the Americas, but also 1,000 or so more people perished in the subsequent period of famine and fever that swept Jamaica's southern parishes.[45] Between 1692 and 1695, moreover, malaria became epidemic. War and the slave trade accentuated white mortality problems. Africans brought with them malaria and yellow fever. The latter disease was the greatest killer of Europeans in the early modern Caribbean. Yellow fever is a devastating disease, killing perhaps 10 to 20 percent of the nonimmune population when it first strikes. An outbreak of yellow fever, however, requires extremely specific conditions. Jamaica was a perfect storm for the spread of yellow fever, especially after 1694, when an expeditionary force sent to Jamaica provided the island with a large body of young nonimmune Europeans living in close proximity to each other and as the development of the sugar industry provided stagnant water and abundant clay-bottomed water vessels for mosquitoes to breed in. The result was epidemic mortality at levels virtually never reached in any place that Britons lived save West Africa.[46]

At the same time black numbers skyrocketed. White Jamaicans had an insatiable appetite for African slaves. Indeed, it has been assumed to be so insatiable that there has never been any serious historical inquiry into the introduction of slavery into Jamaica. Slavery was already established when the English conquered the island in 1655. As planters became established in the island after 1660, any excess of income over expenditure was usually parlayed into purchasing slaves. It was not just large planters who bought slaves: the records of the Royal African Company between 1674 and 1708 shows that purchasers came from every sector of Jamaican society, with Africans generally sold to individuals in relatively small parcels of between one and five slaves.[47] Initially Jamaicans did not get as many slaves as they wanted. Barbados was an easier place for ships from Africa to reach, and Barbadian planters had a greater market presence. By the 1680s, however, the Royal African Company was transporting nearly as many Africans to the island as planters wanted. Slave imports jumped from 14,383 in the 1670s to 33,458 in the 1680s. Slave arrivals fell in the 1690s to 29,475, but from the end of Queen Anne's War in 1702 and after the ending of the Royal African Company monopoly over the slave trade in 1707, slave imports jumped to 53,725 in the 1710s and 77,952 in the 1720s.[48] These levels of slave importation allowed for the rapid transformation of Jamaica into a society where nearly 90 percent of the population was enslaved Africans.

More slaves eventually meant larger slave forces. But increases in the average size of slave forces occurred gradually, even glacially. Of 538 inventories recorded between 1690 and 1706, just 11 contained 100 or more slaves. The average slaveholding for 385 slaveholders was 20 slaves. The absentee planter Sir Thomas Modyford owned 527 slaves at his death in 1704, but the size of his slave force was exceptional.[49] In the next twenty years, however, a qualitative shift in the size of slave forces occurred. An analysis of 5,047 inventories with slaves made between 1722 and 1786 lists 182,583 slaves, or 36 per inventory. Most important, the number of large slave forces of 100 or more slaves increased dramatically, to 440 slaveholdings containing 110,365 slaves. The percentage of slaves in these forces increased to 60 percent, with three-quarters of slaves held in forces of 50 or more. By the 1720s 5 inventories per annum listed more than 100 slaves, and 9 inventories per annum noted 50 or more slaves. In 1727 Jonathan Gale died with 727 slaves; John Foster died four years later owning 766 enslaved people; in 1737 Sir James Campbell left 921 slaves in his inventory; and in 1738 Peter Beckford died with a personal estate over £200,000 that included 1,669 slaves. The presence of these enormous slave forces made Jamaican slavery different in size and scale from slavery anywhere else in seventeenth-century British America.[50]

The Fate of Indentured Servants

By the 1720s the coerced labor force on plantations was larger and blacker than it has been thirty years earlier. One finds an occasional indentured servant listed in inventories after 1720, but the numbers noted are extraordinarily small. Only 25 servants are listed in 7,152 inventories made between 1722 and 1784. The shift to a coerced labor force that was entirely black preceded the move to larger slave forces by two decades. Until the 1690s a good proportion of bound laborers were indentured servants. Between 1674 and 1689, 299 indentured servants were noted in 136 inventories or 4.9 percent of a coerced labor force of 6,278. The number of servants in inventories, moreover, did not decline even when the numbers of slaves increased during these years by something like four- or fivefold. Beginning in the 1690s, however, indentured servitude rapidly declined. There were only 53 servants listed in 26 inventories from a total of 538 taken between 1690 and 1705, amounting to just 0.7 percent of a total bound labor force of 7,866. Within a few years Jamaica had virtually stopped practicing a form of labor organization that had been customary in the British Atlantic from the founding of Jamestown in 1607. The disappearance of indentured servants is especially apparent in large slaveholdings. Just 3 of 11 estates inventoried in the 1690s and 1700s where there were more than 100 slaves had indentured servants, and only Sir Thomas Modyford owned more than one indentured servant: he had four indentured servants out of a workforce of 531.

A similar movement happened at the same time in the Chesapeake, and it occurred in ways very similar to the Barbadian experience. In Barbados the number of servants per estate with bound labor increased from an average of 4.3 to 9.1 between 1640–41 and 1650–57. Numbers increased in a period when the average number of slaves per estate with bound labor jumped from none to 16.4, demonstrating how servant numbers were maintained after slaves had been well established as the dominant labor force. In Virginia indentured servants in wealthy Virginia counties on the lower Tidewater disappeared in bound labor forces between the mid-1680s and the mid-1690s. It was a remarkable and rapid transformation of the labor system.[51]

Or at least, people designated as indentured servants stopped being recorded in inventories. There is a gap that must be explained between the very low numbers of indentured servants listed in inventories, and comments by well-informed commentators such as Governor Robert Hunter in Jamaica, who suggested in the 1730s that the numbers of indentured servants in the labor force were quite high. The explanation is pretty simple. Men coming as indentured servants from Britain to Jamaica in the second and third quarters of the eighteenth century were not treated as indentured servants, working in the fields alongside slaves, nor were they thought of as items of property whose labor could be bought and sold. They became, like Defoe's Colonel Jack, hired employees. They stopped being thought of as being kinds of property (in the sense that their time of indenture could be sold), even though some servants may have remained bonded until the cost of their passage had been worked off.

We have very little evidence about what servants thought about the multiple transitions accompanying the establishment of a plantation regime in either Jamaica or the Chesapeake, but some tantalizing hints emerge from a curious episode in Maryland between 1704 and 1708 that led to the hanging for rebellion of Richard Clarke, a down-on-his-luck planter from Ann Arundel County. Clarke was suspected to have burned down the statehouse in Annapolis in 1704. Maryland's governor, John Seymour, used rumors against Clarke to characterize him as "the greatest of villains" and the ringleader of a plot to create mayhem in the province. The plot, Seymour argued, involved discontented servants and possibly Seneca Indians and raised for the governor concerns over lower-class petty crime at a time of considerable change in Maryland's economic orientation and imperial governance. Most Maryland planters recognized that Seymour used Clarke for his own purposes in order to develop a panic over threats to imperial rule that could be used to buttress his and his council's authority. The local population could not be manipulated into believing the more lurid attempts by the governor to turn Clarke into an object of fear, guilty of "divers heinous offences . . . agt which He stands out riding armed to the Terrour of the Sherriffe." They were rightly suspicious of the governor's motives and resisted his attempts to use Clarke's "treason" to cement support for imperial power. Seymour lamented that his officials could not locate Clarke because his many friends and relatives thought him "a stout fellow," and thus they were "very backward, if not altogether unwilling to bring him in."

Indeed, when Clarke was apprehended early in 1705, the Anne Arundel sheriff allowed him to escape. Even when the governor pressured the assembly to make him an outlaw, based on a made-up rumor that he was fomenting Indian attack, Clarke remained at large in the county until deciding, for reasons unknown, to surrender in March 1708. He was hanged on 9 April 1708.[52]

Clarke was an unconvincing standard-bearer for servant discontent. Born in 1670, Clarke, like many young men from established but not wealthy families, was forced to make important decisions about how to advance investment in inherited estates at a very difficult time. Maryland faced tough times in the 1690s owing to a prolonged depression in tobacco prices as well as persistent war overseas and in the province. Only planters willing to plunge heavily into a booming slave market realized the economies of scale necessary to make substantial money. Clarke, however, did not buy slaves, but stuck with servant labor. It was not a wise choice in a country where the enslaved population increased by 60 percent between 1704 and 1710, and when white population in the same period fell by 20 percent. Clarke borrowed heavily to buy an extra 1,000 acres of land but never bought more than two slaves. He seems to have wanted to use his servants as his fellow planters used slaves. He was hauled up before the county court in May 1704 for beating a servant to death and again a few months later for the mistreatment of another servant. Clarke was not alone in his harsh treatment of servants: lots of servants in this year ran away from masters, according to court reports, and several accused their masters of working them too hard. Clark was found not guilty of any crime by a planter-dominated court. But he was a man in trouble. Heavily in debt, he mortgaged his land to a major Annapolis moneylender, Charles Carroll, and liquidated land. He got so desperate that he may have forged £600 in exchange bills, a crime punishable by whipping and having an ear cut off. Marylanders may have found it hard to believe that such a person could inspire servants to revolt against elected authority.[53]

By the end of 1706, however, servants and poorer planters may have been more receptive to the allure of a brave and uncaptured outlaw. Broader economic changes affected rich and poor alike, especially as the rise of planter elites accentuated the gap between rich men and poorer white men, like Clarke, who had missed out on prosperity. Servants, realizing that they had fewer opportunities than in previous generations, were especially disgruntled. They testified to being lured from service by promises of wealth from privateering and by chances of gaining new land on the frontier. A special assembly committee arrested some of them who lived around Annapolis and who were suspected of being sympathetic to Clarke. These were artisans and the laboring poor of the new town of Annapolis, a group of people Seymour found especially hostile to his centralizing instincts, even while he recognized that they were justified to an extent in their disquiet by widespread hardship. Rumors about Clarke were mostly hearsay, but the reality of arrest frightened many servants into confessing to things that helped confirm Seymour's suspicions of a plot against his authority. They claimed Clarke had recruited them to escape to North Carolina and there join a privateer to the Spanish West Indies. The accused were called before the provincial court in May 1707. Most were whipped, although Thomas Peacock, who was convicted of an additional offense of burglary, was hanged.[54]

Clarkes's conspiracy, if it actually existed, never became real. It never moved from mere rumor to something planters had to take seriously. Servants did not rise up against the merging slaveholding planter elite, even though servants were always comparatively rambunctious in the province, with a suspected revolt in 1721, and more frequent examples of servants running away than was the case for slaves.[55] It is possible that some servants and small planters supported dissent against planter rule. One source thought that 300 men were "scouring up their rusty pistols" at protest at Clarke's hanging.[56] We know too little about the episode to be more certain. Perhaps what this curious incident shows is that poorer whites, just like rich planters and imperial officials, made choices about what they were going to do as massive African importations transformed Chesapeake plantation societies. Some turned to opportunities as artisans in the new urban center of Annapolis. Others thought of running away to North Carolina or to sea as a pirate. Others probably accommodated themselves to the new realities of a plantation economy dominated by large planters, who by the 1720s were using their control of legal processes to force plantation employees to accept wages rather than, as was previously common, a share of tobacco or corn crops, thus making them work harder for less reward.[57]

Indentured Servants in Jamaica

If we know only a little about servants in the Chesapeake, we know even less directly about servants in Jamaica. What happened to indentured servants in Jamaica after 1690? Possibly the numbers of indentured servants coming from England dried up, as may have also been true in Virginia.[58] That the surviving indenture records from Middlesex and Bristol both end in 1685 supports that proposition. Nevertheless, indentured servants continued to be sent to Jamaica after 1685. Up to 800 servants were transported to Jamaica and Barbados following the suppression of the Monmouth Rebellion in 1686. More significant, records exist for servants going to Jamaica from London between 1719 and 1759. There were 1,780 people who left London to be bound in Jamaica for terms of service of four or five years.[59] Most arrived in the 1720s and 1730s, but only 3 men from these indenture records are listed in inventories as indentured servants. What these records suggest is that indentured servitude operated throughout the seventeenth and eighteenth centuries, but that most people bound in Jamaica served only a little time as servants. Most of these servants were probably promoted, like Defoe's Jack, to overseerships soon after they came over. One example arrived on Sir William Stapleton's Nevis estate in 1724. Stapleton was dissatisfied with the performance of his manager, a resident planter called Joseph Herbert. He sent David Stalker as an indentured servant to work on the estate and report back to him on the manager's performance. Unsurprisingly, the report was negative, leading Stapleton to dismiss Herbert and replace him with Stalker.[60]

Do these interrelated developments—a declining white population, the sudden end of white indentured servitude, and the growth in large integrated plantations—mean a concomitant decline in the numbers of whites working within the Jamaican plantation economy? Given that the records are virtually silent about ordinary white people who were neither landowners nor slave owners, it is difficult to prove that after 1690 the growth of a subaltern class of white plantation managers emerged, who formed the disciplining class that enabled slave forces to expand until they reached their eighteenth-century norm. But considerable circumstantial evidence suggests that by the 1690s there existed a pool of landless men with few alternatives outside plantation employment who could serve as plantation overseers.

The numbers of such men probably increased considerably in the 1680s and 1690s. First, the growth of the Atlantic slave trade increased the number of seamen arriving in Jamaica's ports. It was customary for slave ships to release sailors after the Africa-to-Jamaica part of the voyage because the heavy crewing needs necessary to keep captive Africans subdued at sea ended once the captives had been unloaded. Ships returning across the Atlantic did not require more than a skeleton crew to care for cargoes of produce, Spanish bullion, and bills of exchange. Some sailors deposited in Jamaica ended up on plantations. Captains often encouraged seamen to desert in Jamaica so that they did not have to take them back to Britain. They actively banished sick sailors from their ships. Poor and sick sailors then became beggars on the Kingston docks.[61] Secondly, thousands of soldiers arrived in the island from English expeditionary forces sent to Jamaica from 1694. Most soldiers perished from disease, and some died in battle. If they survived, however, soldiers were unlikely to get passage home and had to survive through working on plantations. Thirdly, indentured white servants out of their service needed to work. Many found jobs in Port Royal as tradesmen or in merchant houses. A number of ex-servants also joined privateering expeditions. The destruction of Port Royal in 1692 threw tradesmen and merchants' clerks out of employment. They found it difficult to get new positions in Kingston, the town that replaced Port Royal as the commercial capital of Jamaica. Kingston did not become the commercial center that Port Royal had been until sometime in the 1710s or 1720s. The suppression of privateering also limited options available to landless white men outside of the plantation sector.[62]

Thus, circumstantial evidence indicates that there was a sizable body of landless white men in Jamaica in the decades from the 1690s with few options outside plantation employment. The surviving militia lists for 1694 and 1700 mention 1,774 men, of whom 274 were not private soldiers, in 1694; and 3,156 men, 373 officers, sergeants, or corporals, in 1700. Most men without positions of authority in civil society were people who were not officers. One particular problem is that it is hard to find information about these marginal men. They hardly exist in any records relating to property, presumably because they had few assets that were worth distributing to heirs and therefore did not leave wills or inventories, the major sources of the period. It is highly likely that it was from among these men that planters chose the plantation subaltern class.[63]

Landless white men could not opt out of the plantation system as they had done previously because the range of options available to them had narrowed. In particular, they found it hard to own land. Until the 1680s it was relatively easy for most white men to become landowners. Patentable land was abundant (and in the first days of settlement was given out as a reward for military service), and the price of land for sale was minimal. An analysis of deeds for St. Andrew Parish shows that the average price of land sold in the 1670s was 34 pence an acre, rising to 42 pence an acre during the 1680s. Given that St. Andrew was a settled parish where a good proportion of land was cultivated early, land in parishes distant from the southern region where population was most dense was cheaper still.[64]

During the 1690s, however, the price of land in Jamaica skyrocketed. The price increases are somewhat evident in the average price per acre, which increased to 68 pence per acre in St. Andrew in the 1690s, 73 pence per acre in the 1700s, 95 pence per acre in the 1710s, and, most dramatically, £1.89 per acre in the 1720s. The rise in average price per acre is misleading, however, because these prices include mountainous land, which was difficult to cultivate and thus very cheap. Land on the settled area of the Liguanea plains was considerably more expensive. Cleared land became very expensive and well out of reach for all except big planters. In 1695, for example, a parcel of 40 acres sold for £133, while in 1697 a sugar plantation of 126 acres fetched £333. The early years of the eighteenth century saw prices increase further. In 1700 60 acres went for £300, while in 1701 28 acres of prime land was sold for £206. The following year saw a fully developed sugar plantation of 300 acres sold for £1,000. That plantation was sold again six years later at a whopping profit, with the price for 300 acres now at £2,500. In 1713 another prime sugar property of 262 acres was sold for £2,200, while 80 acres of cane land sold for £800. Such prices were out of reach for ordinary whites with inventoried wealth of under £200 and annual incomes of around £20. Despite these constraints, landownership was not completely out of reach for ordinary white men. Small plantations never disappeared completely from the parish. As late as 1754 there were 128 small estates in St. Andrew producing provisions, coffee, ginger, cotton, and livestock.[65]

Nevertheless, there was an inexorable push toward sugar monoculture from the 1690s. There may have been only twenty-six sugar estates in St. Andrew in 1754, but they took up the great majority of cultivable land in the parish.[66] Most large planters, moreover, owned far more land than they needed for sugar cultivation. The appropriation of land by large planters was well under way as early as the 1670s, but picked up pace in the early years of the eighteenth century, as planters both acquired fresh land for their growing slave forces working as ganged labor, and also bought large tracts of land for speculative purposes. Certainly, it was around this time that we hear the first murmurings of discontent lamenting how high land prices and excessive accumulation of land by planter elites were discouraging white settlement. William Wood in 1718 urged planters to "lay aside the false and narrow Notions and Schemes, entertain'd by to many of *them;* such as *that* the *Produce* of their *Plantations* will *sell* the *better,* the *fewer the Settlements,* which induces them to *Engross* great Tracts of *Land."*[67] By 1754 the number of landholders in Jamaica had doubled from 1670, but the numbers of small landholders had decreased from 384 to 263. In 1670 small landholders made up 53 percent of landowners. By 1754 small landholders made up only 16 percent of landowners. Meanwhile, the percentage of landowners who owned 500 acres or more (the amount of land necessary for a large integrated plantation) increased from 14 percent to 48 percent. By 1754, 78 percent of land was held in tracts of 1,000 or more acres.[68]

We need to qualify these statements by taking into account devastating disease epidemics after 1692. The number of white men able and willing to work on large sugar estates as overseers may have been small as a result of yellow fever and malaria. Nevertheless, those whites who survived epidemic fever and found work on large plantations may have been ideally qualified for implementing the radical novelties involved in maintaining plantation discipline. Many men who worked on plantations in the last decade of the seventeenth century and the first decades of the eighteenth were hardened to the rigors of plantation life by their previous experience in England's armies and in the Atlantic slave trade. Men who had served in the Anglo-French wars of 1688–97 and 1702–13 or who had sailed on Atlantic slave ships learned how to treat Africans harshly and to withstand the fear and terror of slave revolt. As Robin Blackburn has perceptively remarked, these were the only institutions in early modern life whose labor organization and harsh discipline mirrored those evident in the integrated large plantation.[69]

An Age of Warfare

The late seventeenth century was a period of almost constant warfare in the Americas between the English and the French. It was also a period when the numbers of men involved in the Atlantic slave trade dramatically increased. The rise of the large integrated plantation and the "military revolution" of the late sixteenth and seventeenth centuries seem to be linked.[70] Plantation societies were highly militarized, garrison governments in which military men, whether governors or planters, had great influence. The social hierarchy was largely organized around military assumptions, the leading men of which were militia officers. Every man of any distinction went by a military title: councilors were colonels and colonels were councilors. Such titles were more than just honorifics. The militia, despite the constant murmurings of governors that it lacked the discipline of the regular army, was generally effective. It mustered regularly and was often deployed both internally, against slave rebels, and externally, against the French. Some indication of how useful a military body it was can be seen in 1694, when 2,000 Jamaican militiamen repelled a large French expeditionary force that invaded and laid waste to Jamaica's southeastern parishes.[71]

It was not just officers and governors who were militarily minded. Ordinary white men were required to serve in the militia, were instructed to exercise regularly, and had to keep at least a gun, if not a horse, for their military service. The military abilities of these ordinary men were surprisingly good. They were good shots and good at drill. One likely reason the Jamaican militia was effective is that many militiamen had previous military experience. The late seventeenth century saw one of the greatest army mobilizations in English history. It also saw the creation of the English standing army. The size of that army was around 80,000 in the wars against the French between 1688 and 1713, meaning that around one man in seven was called to service. It was these men, of course, who were disproportionately represented among late seventeenth-century European immigrants to Jamaica.[72]

The new armies of the late seventeenth century were larger than and different in kind from previous European armies. Standing armies looked back to imperial Rome, with an emphasis on uniform training, discipline, and permanence. Two features of the standing army make it comparable to the plantation system. Like slaves, soldiers were subjected to relentless, monotonous work patterns. What soldiers did most of the time that they were not fighting was drill. Soldiers marched up and down relentlessly. William McNeill has noted the similarities of drilling to dance. He argues, from the perspective of having been a soldier himself, that repetitious drill "readily welded a miscellaneous collection of men, recruited from the dregs, into a coherent community, obedient to orders, even in extreme jeopardy." Ordinary soldiers conformed to whatever rules laid down because they "feared harsh punishment for infractions of discipline," and because "the rank and file found real psychological satisfaction in blind, unthinking obedience, and in the rituals of military routine."[73]

The standing army also had features similar to gang labor. As John Childs notes, what was essential for maintaining order in late seventeenth-century European armies was eliminating individual initiative: "each soldier had to be drilled and browbeaten to the point where he was little more than a machine." In addition, soldiers, like slaves, were subject to fierce discipline. Military punishments were tough and unyielding. Flogging was introduced in William III's reign as the principal mode of correction, making army discipline similar to that customary in slavery. But perhaps because soldiers were expendable in ways that slaves, as commodities, were not, floggings were considerably more severe in the army than on the plantation. A common soldier constantly saw men flogged, often to death or at least to permanent disablement.[74] Like planters, officers were able to impose their own punishments on the rank and file, and although in theory these punishments did not amount to loss of life or limb, except in cases of mutiny, sedition, or desertion, in practice officers could punish men as ferociously as they liked. Another feature of the late seventeenth-century standing army that bears comparison with plantations is that soldiers were generally recruited by officers who took responsibility for their wages and who in turn thought of their soldiers as their "property." Although soldiers tended to be paid wages, there was something about their status that was akin to enslavement. In short, men who had served in the standing armies of William III and Anne would not have found plantation discipline unusual or especially harsh.[75]

Men traveling to Barbados earlier in the century would also not have found the violence of the plantations alien. A large proportion of white immigrants to Barbados arrived during Britain's greatest internal conflict, the multiple civil wars in England, Wales, Ireland, and Scotland between 1642 and 1651. Immigrants to Barbados in the 1640s and 1650s had already experienced a military revolution before arriving to an island supposedly in the middle of a sugar revolution. The innovative military changes in organization, method, and, especially, the professionalism of the officer corps and the discipline of ordinary soldiers cast into large standing armies that had been pioneered by Maurice of Nassau, prince of Orange, and Gustavus Adolphus, king of Sweden, in the Thirty Years' War were introduced into the British Isles by the 70,000 or so men who had served in continental armies in the 1630s. These were professional soldiers rather than "swordsmen," commanded by officers who had been promoted less because of who they were than because of what they did. They served in armies that were rational, organized, and businesslike. Their armies employed aggressive infantry tactics as improved close-order drill made soldiers able to make better use of new military technology.[76]

That experience was extended to the population at large in the 1640s. The numbers of Britons involved in war mushroomed during the Wars of the Three Kingdoms. More men and women were exposed to the horrors of war between 1642 and 1651 than at any time since the Wars of the Roses in the fifteenth century. The mobilization of soldiers in the 1640s probably exceeded similar British mobilizations in either of the two twentieth-century world wars. Figures on mobilization are hard to come by, but Michael Braddick extrapolates how many men served in arms from data obtainable from one very well documented village, Myddle in Shropshire. He shows that probably around 40 percent of men of military age in the village went to war.[77] Many of these men were involved in horrific pitched battles with very high casualty rates. Perhaps 62,000 Englishmen died in battle between 1642 and 1646. In the English civil wars military losses were between 100,000 and 125,000. The losses of men in battle in this conflict were equivalent in numbers to the total population of England's four largest towns, excluding London.[78] England suffered less than Scotland and Ireland. In England the total loss of population attributable to conflict was probably around 3.7 percent, while in Scotland the losses were around 6 percent of the population. Ireland suffered a demographic catastrophe that was among the worst of any disasters arising from warfare in the early modern world: it is estimated that perhaps as much as 41 percent of Ireland's population (616,000 of 1,466,000 people alive in 1641) perished in the pogroms unleashed by Charles I and Oliver Cromwell. An additional 80,000 men were taken prisoners of war. This latter group formed a pool of labor for Barbadian planters keen to augment their labor forces.[79]

What do these figures mean for Barbados? They imply that a very high percentage of convicts and indentured servants (especially those coming involuntarily after having been prisoners of war) had had either direct or indirect military experience. That was especially true for the potentially 40 percent of the population who were Irish. The percentage of immigrants to Barbados who had been in the armies of the Wars of the Three Kingdoms was probably greater than the 40 percent of the population of Myddle who had gone to war, given the youthful age structure of Barbadian society. That military experience acclimatized them to a harsh world. Thomas Raymond, himself a former common soldier, commented that "the life of a private or common soldier is the most miserable in the world; and that is not so much because his life is always in danger—that is little or nothing—but from the terrible miseries he endures in hunger and nakedness in hard marches and bad quarters."[80]

But while many white Barbadians had military experience just at the time that the large integrated plantation was being implemented in the island, military experience among potential migrants to the Americas dropped dramatically in the next generation of American immigrants. Britons born in the 1620s were blooded by war; their children were not. After the Restoration in 1660 Charles II tried to maintain a professional army—doing so mostly by subterfuge, as English opposition to a standing army was intense, and concealing the army in Scotland, Ireland, and especially Tangier.[81] The English political elite favored using a militia for security. Initially it worked well, and the militia was well provisioned with arms and reasonably well trained. But during the 1670s the quality of county militia forces declined rapidly. In 1677 in the large county of Buckinghamshire, for example, the militia was comprised of just one regiment of foot and three troops of horse (less than the militia force of Barbados in 1679). It mustered and drilled once or twice a year. The number of men trained in firearms declined appreciably before the Monmouth Rebellion of 1685. The Wiltshire militia in that conflict performed very poorly, convincing James II that the militia possessed no military value and could not be relied upon. In reality, the idea of England's defense being conducted by citizen-soldiers was never properly countenanced by a landowning class more interested in disarming the populace in order to stop unlawful hunting than in promoting the use of firearms in a reformed militia.[82]

Henry Drax's overseer, to whom he addressed his instructions, was a living example of the differences between the military experiences of generations of Englishmen. Richard Harwood was the son of John Harwood, a Royalist soldier captured in 1643 and sentenced to servitude in Barbados. His son, by contrast, was no soldier. He became a planter in 1680 and prospered so well that the governor tried to appoint him to the council, over the objections of great planters, who saw him as a "mere overseer" and "suspected papist."[83] The late seventeenth century was hardly a pacifist paradise in the Americas. But American warfare was not like the warfare that had become customary as a result of the military revolutions of the sixteenth and seventeenth centuries in Europe. The primary kinds of battle that characterized plantation America in the third quarter of the seventeenth century were privateering and warfare against indigenous Native Americans.[84] Men with no formal military experience and who fought informally, sporadically, and mostly in guerrilla-type operations were unfamiliar with the kind of regimented discipline necessary to make enslaved Africans work in gangs. They were not temperamentally inclined to supervise such work.

But if the children born in the 1640s and the 1650s were a fortunate generation, their children were different, with lives more similar to those of their grandfathers than of their fathers. These people formed the cannon fodder of the massive armies that tramped across the low countries of Western Europe and that sailed across the Atlantic to the Caribbean from the 1690s to 1713. Men were impressed into service;

some became soldiers after being convicted of crimes, and others became soldiers rather than being burned in the cheek or hand. Once enlisted, they learned drill under the control of an increasingly professional officer class. Guerrilla warfare and the kind of ill-disciplined conduct that English soldiers were used to in the English militia and that characterized all kinds of soldiering in the colonies was discountenanced. Those soldiers who thought independently and challenged their officers—or who deserted or committed crimes—were court-martialed, flogged, or shot. When armies were disbanded at the end of the Nine Years' War in 1697, many men did not readily settle down, some becoming highwaymen and some moving to the plantations. The professionalism developed in the Nine Years' War was retained, out of which the modern British Army was born. Serving in a rational, ordered, and well-disciplined army was excellent preparation for plantation life.[85]

Slave-Ship Sailors

Sailors who had sailed in the Atlantic slave trade were even less likely to be alarmed by slaves' rough treatment. The slave ship was a prison in which there was open warfare between brutal sailors and brutalized captives. Manning of slave ships was very high because the ever-present risk of slave rebellion. It was not a gentle business. Sailors were free to discipline captives as they pleased, and even though ship captains had a vested interest in seeing as many of their slaves survive the voyage as possible, they had little hesitation in punishing captives quite harshly, even to the point of death. One need not belabor the point. What is important to note is that the slave ship did not just acculturate captives to their new status as commodities. It also acculturated English sailors into working out strategies to deal with slaves.[86]

The slave ship was a strange sort of vessel. It was part war vessel, loaded with guns, able to use its warmaking capacity against other vessels; part floating prison, presided over by prison guards who were also sailors; and part factory, converting people into commodities. Ordinary seamen occupied a curious and liminal position in this "vast machine." They began as sailors; they were transformed by their experiences on the coast of Africa and as jailers of captive Africans in the Middle Passage into white men who exercised violence over Africans, now seen as black people. Indeed, slave-trading enterprises were as much military as commercial activities. The slave ship was physically converted, if it had been used for other purposes, into a vessel in which security concerns were paramount. Builders added barriers and hatches peculiar to slavers through which captives, especially African men, could be closely controlled. The Middle Passage, moreover, was a cold war that erupted frequently into hot war: perhaps one of every ten voyages had a captive rebellion. Revolts occurred most often on voyages starting where Africans had particularly pronounced military traditions, such as Senegambia, Sierra Leone, and the Windward Coast. Slavers, moreover, were guided by security concerns when choosing their markets and gradually moved their attention to markets to regions like the Bight of Biafra, where captives could be more easily bought than elsewhere. Biafran slaves might fetch less money in plantation America and might be thought less desirable workers, but it was easier to transport these slaves across the ocean than to take slave men from regions where there was an extensive military tradition.[87]

Slave captains and their crews were constantly worried about security threats from African men. They kept them separated from women and confined them in parts of the ships that were farthest removed from ships' arsenals. They were chained two by two, manacled hand to foot, and loaded naked.[88] When brought up on deck, they were brought up individually. They were overseen by heavily armed sailors with blunderbusses and muskets, and the ship's cannons were loaded with small shot aimed toward the main deck where the slave men would be gathered. Captains were concerned about security above all other matters. William Snelgrave, for example, wrote extensively about how to control "ye strong rugged men Slaves" in "Instructions for a first mate when in the road att Whydah," written in 1727. These "rugged" men had to be kept under close control at all times and kept chained, with the chains being checked regularly. The first mate was to assign several sailors constantly to military duties, including sentries who fired muskets at every evening meal, so as to prevent "insurrection."[89]

What the slave trade created was a body of men—a "great brood of seamen," as Malachy Postlethwayt argued in his 1745 defense of the slave trade—who became "a formidable nursery of Naval Power." The whole system depended upon violence. It was exercised against sailors, described by slave-trader captain and reformed sinner John Newton as the "refuse and dregs of the Nation," and especially against captive Africans. Violence extended downward throughout the system. As a Liverpool writer argued: "the captain bullies the men, the men torture the slaves, the slaves' hearts are breaking with despair." It was a regime of terror, especially in the notorious Middle Passage, where cargoes of several hundred Africans, controlled by crews that generally numbered one sailor to every ten Africans, crossed the Atlantic in great misery. As the ex-sailor James Stanfield wrote in the late 1780s about slave-trade voyages to Jamaica before the start of the American Revolution: "this horrid portion of the voyage was but one continual scene of barbarity, unremitting labor, mortality and disease," with "flogging . . . a principal amusement." We have little such direct testimony about the nature of the late seventeenth-century slave trade, but, as Marcus Rediker points out, the principal characteristics of the trade changed little between 1700 and 1807. What changed least, moreover, was the disciplinary aspects of sailors' and captives' experience on the slave ship.[90]

The government of the slave ship depended upon exemplary punishment. Sailors were flogged for the slightest delinquency. Much worse violence was meted out to captives. John Newton recalled in testimony compiled in the late 1780s how an especially brutal slave-ship captain, Richard Jackson, in 1748 or 1749 had captives who started a rebellion aboard ship "jointed." According to Newton, "jointing" involved dismembering each man limb by limb with an axe until finally their heads were cut off. Jackson threw the bodies into the ocean for sharks to feed on. Then, in front of the "trembling slaves," gathered on the foredecks, he placed a rope round the heads of some captives and squeezed hard with a lever inserted in the point of the rope until "he forced their eyes to stand out of their heads." Even by the standards of life on a Jamaican sugar estate, the slave trade was exceptionally cruel and slave-trade sailors particularly callous. Newton argued that "a savageness of spirit . . . infuses itself . . . into those who exercise power. . . . It is the spirit of the trade, which, like a pestilential air, is so generally infectious that but few escape it." The terror was systemic, the violence relentless, and fear pervasive.

Most English seamen wanted no part of it. The crew of a slaver was the "very dregs of the community," because serving on a slaver was such a despised occupation that only the debauched, the desperate, the indebted, or the imprudent could be prevailed upon to do it. The high mortality rate for seamen and the deadliness of Africa's climate was one reason for its unpopularity among seamen, as were low wages and harsh treatment aboard ship. Sailors disliked being jailers and hated even more looking after slaves and cleaning up their excrement amidst the "nasty filthiness" of the trade. Their dislike was translated into extreme contempt for the captives they guarded. They beat them incessantly, cared little about their welfare, considered that the noxious smell of the captive's rooms showed that Africans were little better than beasts, and were principal agents in Africans' dehumanization.[91]

Seamen may have hated what they did on slave ships, thinking it demeaning and dangerous. But they learned skills that they transferred to the large integrated plantation. One person who recognized the close connection between the slave ship as "a large manufactory" and the barbarous plantation system driven by "Christian crimes and Europe's cruel sons" was Henry Smeathman, an extraordinary observer of Africa and the West Indies who was able to connect, through the ingenious use of termites and the termitary as allegories for colonization and plantations, the world of the plantation with the world of the military and the world of industrial factories. Deirdre Coleman notes how Smeathman, in one of the rare European descriptions of the slave ship as a scene of horrific inhumanity and furious industry, argued that a slave ship carried all the tradesmen necessary for starting a settlement.[92]

We don't have evidence of many men moving from slave ships to work on plantations, but there surely must have been some who did so. Record linkages exist between lists of sailors noted in the Royal African Company records and people present in the St. Andrews militia list for Jamaica in 1694. The results are inconclusive: 35 men in the militia list had the names of slave-trade sailors, but most of these names are common ones such as Williams, Brown, Johnson, and Carter. Only a few names in the militia list—Anthony Cornelius, Robert Ramne, Thomas Cornwall—are almost certain to be the same people as noted in slave-trade transcripts. Of course, there is no reason that these men were necessarily overseers rather than residents of Port Royal or Kingston, where most discharged seamen congregated. But records showing ex-sailors living in an inland parish indicates that they were working within the plantation economy.[93]

Certainly seamen involved in the Atlantic slave trade to Jamaica who were left behind in the island formed a pool of labor for the large integrated plantation. In 1745 4,119 seamen arrived in Kingston, of whom 1,074 came from North America and 966 from other parts of the West Indies. There were 18 slave voyages in a relatively light year for slave-ship arrivals. These ships took up 4,482 captives in Africa, of whom 3,831 arrived in Jamaica. If the ratio of slaves to crew was 10 to 1, then the number of seamen involved in the slave trade to Jamaica was on the order of 448, meaning that there were 1,631 sailors from Britain who were involved in other kinds of shipping. If we take a longer perspective and examine an average of slave shipments over a decade, from

1744 to 1753, then in an average year there were 28 voyages carrying 7,989 African captives, of whom 6,731 would have arrived in Jamaica, suggesting that 799 seamen were involved annually in the slave trade. In the 1690s and 1700s, when the slave trade was reduced in volume, the average number of seamen engaged in the slave trade to Jamaica was around 450 per annum. If the same ratios pertained for seamen in the slave trade and seamen in other areas of shipping, the number of seamen arriving in Jamaica each year was around 2,500 per annum.[94] Many of these people died: 18 percent of seamen on slave ships died in the last quarter of the eighteenth century.[95] Others would have caught a berth back to Britain, or to the West Indies or North America. But some ex-seamen may have become plantation workers, if only because they had no other choice of employment, such as a sailor discharged later in the century in Kingston "turned adrift, in a strange country, weak, lame, and possessing but little money!" Taking a job disciplining slaves may have been better than being consigned to the workhouse.[96]

The men who controlled Africans were violent because their charges were not pacifists. Africa was no less addicted to war and violence than early modern Europe. The slave trade accentuated the tendency of African states to engage in warfare. Just as in Europe, the larger nations of Africa were fiscal-military states in which the resources of the state were directed toward warfare, weapons, and the mobilization of resources. Some countries, such as Senegambia and Dahomey, aggressively waged war in order to secure captives for sale into the Atlantic slave trade. Eighteenth-century Dahomey, in particular, was a militaristic aggressor bent on conquest and expansion. It did not have its own way: the places it invaded were well-armed and full of warriors who contested Dahomean aggression. Thus, many of the Africans who moved to the Americas were experienced warriors, such as from the Akan region of present-day Ghana. Moreover, a large proportion of captives sent to the Americas, like the Irish who came to Barbados in the 1640s and 1650s, were captured soldiers. Their military experience gave them the boldness and confidence to make armed resistance possible.[97]

Revisiting *American Slavery—American Freedom*

If my argument about Jamaica is correct, what conclusions follow? Edmund Morgan was right that in order to understand the rise of the Chesapeake planter elite from the 1690s and the concomitant rise of the large integrated plantation system, we need to follow closely what happened to ordinary white men. Moreover, Virginia replicated what occurred in Barbados in the 1660s and mirrored what was happening simultaneously in Jamaica and the Leeward Islands in the 1690s. Morgan argued that the rise of Virginia's planter elite only occurred after a bitter class conflict in which planters won and heads of what Peter Thompson calls "little commonwealths" lost. Small planters may have lost the class battle of Bacon's Rebellion, but they were essential to the smooth functioning of Virginia society. Planters had to accommodate ordinary white men. These men found it impossible to achieve Nairne and Norris's dream of an autonomous independence as small landowners, but they had to be compensated for agreeing to working as overseers, subduing resentful African slaves.[98]

That compensation took two forms. First, they received high wages. By the middle of the eighteenth century, a successful slave overseer could command his own price. The costs of employing white plantation workers were substantial in mid-eighteenth-century Jamaica. Overseers got £100 to £200 per annum, subordinate workers between £25 and £50. White plantation workers earned substantially more than their counterparts in nonplantation agriculture in the American North and in Britain.[99] Second, the shift to a full-scale, mature plantation regime was accompanied by a heightened awareness of race. Whites were not only separated out from blacks economically, with blacks being slaves and workers and whites being masters or managers. There was also a gradual shift toward making race rather than freedom the principal marker of status. How plantation societies developed ideologies of "whiteness" and "blackness" is a theme for another book, but they helped shape the particular character of life in the American tropics.[100]

Second, while devastating for the million and more Africans caught up in the plantation "machine," the system was a breathtaking success for those fortunate enough to be the beneficiaries of the process. In the grand sweep of American history, only the advent of industrialization in the American North in the first third of the nineteenth century and the second industrialization of the last third of that same century was as transformative a process in American history. The principal benefits that the slow move to a mature plantation system brought were prosperity and stability. Prosperity is easily shown, as we shall see. Stability is a more problematic concept, drawn from J. H. Plumb's definition of "the acceptance by society of its political institutions, and of the classes of men or officials who controlled them."[101]

Acceptance of elite rule by ordinary white men was never uncomplicated or uncontested. Nevertheless, the incessant strife in British America in the seventeenth century had ended by the beginning of the eighteenth century. In almost every colony genuine ruling elites, separated by wealth, power, style of living, and ideology from the rest of the population, emerged. The rise of colonial elites and their increasing acquisition of power did not necessarily depend upon the establishment of a plantation system: the merchants of New England and the Middle Colonies did so without plantation slaves. But the most cohesive elite groups were in plantation societies such as Virginia, South Carolina, and Barbados. It was in these societies that "the politics of harmony" were most apparent, where oligarchical rule was most firmly established, where deference from the poor toward the rich was most observable, and where ruling-class solidarity was most pronounced.[102]

A final conclusion concerns African slaves. When we talk about how Africans coped under the relentless machine that planters built to exploit them, we note in passing the vicious treatment that they suffered. But what white men did to black men and women in order to make these people obey them was not an incidental by-product of the rise of the plantation regime. It was central to how it came about. To understand why black life was so degraded under that regime, we have to understand the mentality of the white men who beat them, raped them, and cowed them into submission. These men were formidable opponents. They did not scare easily, they were merciless and ruthless, and they used their contempt for Africans as a powerful weapon of oppression. Their attitude toward their African charges was similar to how European soldiers in eighteenth-century standing armies viewed their enemies: they demonized them. Brutalized themselves by their experiences in war, in the African slave trade, and on the plantations of British America, they acted as tyrants toward other brutalized people. The foot-soldiers of empire, they were the glue that held the plantation system together.[103]

White Attitudes toward Blacks

Why whites held the attitudes they did to blacks is a vast subject,[104] but a few points can be made The English had a palpable sense of difference from Africans from the start of English settlement in the Americas. That sense of difference made them insensitive to the treatment of Africans, allowing them to dehumanize and even demonize captives. First, they differentiated themselves from Africans on political grounds. Europeans did not consider Africans, by dint of their complexion, their seeming barbarism, and their paganism, to be political actors. David Eltis argues that Europeans, especially the Dutch and the English, both leaders in the shift to the large integrated plantation, had highly developed senses of insiders and outsiders in their societies. Europeans were insiders (even those Europeans who had committed crimes deserving of capital punishment) and Africans were not. The lines marking what one could do to insiders, and what one could do to outsiders, were clear. Notions that insiders could not be enslaved while outsiders could be led to moral restrictions on enslaving one's weaker or poorer neighbor, but not on purchasing a freely sold non-European who was already a slave in Africa.[105]

Secondly, English attitudes toward blacks were disfigured by racism. Africans were thought to be fundamentally different from, and inferior to, Europeans because of their supposed resemblance to beasts. Whether Europeans thought Africans to be humans like themselves, which, as Christians believing in monogenesis, they were bound to do, or thought of Africans as bestial creatures, over whom European dominion was acceptable, is complicated.[106] But slippage certainly occurred, especially in the area of gender. Europeans made the link between Africans and animality sufficiently often to suggest that the equation came often into their minds. They thought African women's apparent easy delivery of children was a sign that they were close to being animals. They also imagined that African women could suckle children over their shoulder as animals did, and they compared African women's breasts to those of goats. Africans, in short, were not fully human.[107]

Finally, the first English slaveholders differentiated starkly between the treatment of African slaves and the treatment of English servants. They treated Africans harshly because no one stopped them. As the English saw it, Africans were acquired in legitimate commerce and clearly defined in law as property. Historians have debated furiously over how Barbadians and planters in other plantation societies learned how to treat Africans differently from servants.[108] In the crucial switch from indentured servitude to slavery as the principal form of labor organization in the American colonies, great similarities existed between the condition of the least privileged servants, such as prisoners of war and Irish servants sent to America by coercion, and enslaved Africans. But there was always a difference between the two categories, occasioned in part because security concerns about poorer white Europeans were greater than about Africans.

Seymour Drescher points out, in a stimulating essay debating David Eltis's contention that it might have been possible to staff the plantations with servile labor drawn from England's prisons, orphanages, and

workhouses, that security concerns were very important in the development of English American plantations. The slave trade and slavery in
the plantations "depended upon the combined inability of Europeans
to project their domination into Africa and their ability to preserve the
severance of African ties with their original communities." In short, the
English could not control Africans in Africa (if local leaders in slave-
trading areas had not wanted to sell slaves to English traders, there is
little likelihood before the nineteenth century that the English would
have been able to acquire them), but they could control Africans in the
Americas, devising laws to keep them subjugated and employing people
with quasi-military skills to force Africans to do what they were told.
There is little evidence that many Englishmen, except during periods
of idle contemplation, ever contemplated using the English poor and
English criminals as slaves to work American plantations. Europe always
loomed larger than America in statesmen's calculations. If England's
jails were to be emptied, the inhabitants would be used in war across
the Channel, not in plantation agriculture across the Atlantic.[109] Even
if the English state had wanted to support private investors in making
Englishmen and Englishwomen slaves, they did not have the powers of
coercion to enact those policies, especially during periods of warfare,
when people fought partly in order to contest what they perceived to
be a tyrannical state. When Cromwell tried to implement the impress-
ment of men into the English navy (a less draconian policy than making white men slaves), he faced massive resistance. Drescher argues that
the "forced migration of large numbers of enslaved Europeans would
have been prohibitively expensive except in a permanently authoritarian state."[110] The English had a long tradition of opposition to slavery,
an opposition intensified by a civil war infused by a constant rhetoric
counterposing slavery to liberty. It would have taken a brave and foolish
statesman to try and counteract the common assumption in the seventeenth century that no resident of England could be made a slave. And
if he tried to do this, he would have met great resistance in a society
in which acquiescence to state desire was in the end mostly voluntary.
That resistance could only have been countered by imposing massive
force on local communities in a period when the English state had far
greater security concerns to deal with.[111]

Moreover, the costs of security in a plantation America full of white
slaves were prohibitive. Drescher argues that it is likely that putative
English slaves crossing the Atlantic would have resisted more effectively
than Africans, as they would have shared a common language, would
have been less terrified of ship crossings, and would have confronted

captors as men skilled in firearms. That may or may not be true: it is hard to prove a counterfactual. What is certain is that keeping white slaves on isolated islands in a period of continual European warfare would have increased defense costs. Drescher points to the invasion of St. Christopher by the French in 1666, when 400 African slaves were appropriated and 5,000 English settlers deported. If these settlers had been slaves rather than settlers or servants, and if the French had been prepared to keep the English as plantation slaves, they would have just taken over the plantations as they were. A West Indian island with European slaves would have been less a plantation zone than a slave bar-racoon, a place where European liberty was always at risk. A European venturing to invest capital in the islands would have been wary of going there in person if he thought he was virtual capital, able to be seized at any moment.[112]

The Rise of the Planter Elite in Jamaica

If Africans were undoubtedly the losers in the shift to the plantation sys-tem, it is pretty clear who the winners were: the great planters. Planters became one of the most distinctive social types in the Atlantic world, with wealth and influence unmatched by any elite group in the Americas before the American Civil War. Their origins, however, and the ways in which their ascent was aided by the institutionalization of slavery, the most problematic institution in Atlantic history, have often caused dis-quiet. As Allan Gallay concludes about the South Carolina planters who established hegemonic control over their colony in the early eighteenth century, "They shared no common purpose but to accumulate riches." He continues: "From first settlement, South Carolina elites ruthlessly pursued the exploitation of fellow human beings in ways that differed from the other mainland colonies, and they created a narcissistic culture that reacted passionately and violently to attempts to limit their indi-vidual sovereignty over their perceived inferiors."[113]

The origins of the great planter elite that came to dominate planta-tion society in the Chesapeake, the Lower South, and the West Indies is an oft-told story, but it is so important for the story of plantation America that it bears recounting again. Let's examine its rise in Jamaica as a way of complementing similar accounts for other plantation re-gions. The process by which great planters became rulers of their colony was broadly similar in Jamaica to elsewhere. One major difference was that large merchants and government placemen were also part of its

Table 2.1 Wealth and Slaveholdings of Assemblymen and Councilors, Jamaica, 1708

Name	Death	Wealth (£)	No. of Slaves
Philip Becket	1725	3,902	149
Peter Beckford	1735	145,749	1,669
John Blair	1728	6,323	419
Sir James Campbell	1737	21,983	921
Charles Chaplin	1736	22,361	704
John Clark	1721	4,641	180
John Cossley	1717	2,941	116
George Collier	1715	105	3
Roger Elletson	1730	2,399	70
John Flavell	1721	11,290	123
Thomas Flowers	1715	5,087	141
William Forrord	1713	3,938	103
Thomas Freeman	1718	3,542	140
Jonathan Gale	1727	28,753	606
John Halsted	1722	12,894	332
William Ivy	1724	4,684	92
John Lewis	1712	6,254	190
Odoardo Lewis	1713	2,601	92
Nicholas Lott	1724	3,202	56
John Moore	1733	2,218	69
John Peeke	1716	4,957	173
Edward Pennant	1736	29,627	610
Thomas Simson	1714	3,823	110
John Small	1712	1,659	139
Robert Thurgar	1714	1,200	4
Samuel Vassall	1714	1,387	53

Source: Inventories, 1712–37, IB/11/3/7–35, JA.

ruling elite. It was also richer and more powerful than any other British American eighteenth-century planter elite, dominating Jamaican society until the advent of abolitionism clipped their wings in the 1780s and even until well after the end of apprenticeship in 1838.[114]

Its origins extend back into the earliest days of settlement, but it only became established, as in the Chesapeake, in the first two decades of the eighteenth century.[115] Although slavery was established early in Jamaica, large plantations with hundreds of slaves did not become common until after 1700. We can see how the process of elite formation worked by analyzing the wealth and inherited position of the 47 men who formed the Jamaican Council and Assembly of 1708. This group was the beneficiaries of the assorted changes noted above. Table 2.1 details the wealth and slave ownership levels of the 26 men in this group who left inventories. Most were very wealthy, much wealthier than men in the previous generation. Before 1700 only very wealthy men left personal property of more than £4,000. The average wealth of the

1708 officeholders, however, was £12,975. If we exclude the extraordinarily rich Peter Beckford II (d. 1735), who died worth £145,749 with
1,669 slaves, the average wealth was still £7,664. There were 18 men
who owned over 100 slaves at their death, and 7 men who owned 300
or more. Others besides Beckford were very large slaveholders: Sir James
Campbell owned 910 slaves, Charles Chaplin had 704, Jonathan Gale
owned 606, and Edward Pennant possessed 610.

The 1708 Assemblymen and Councilors were a transitional class.
Over one-third were the children of the first generation of Jamaican
officeholders. Nearly two-thirds were able to transmit their wealth to
their children. Just one man, John Towgood, had a surviving son who
was not a major slave owner. Towgood's son died with just 10 slaves,
although he had a healthy personal estate of £3,294. More typical were
men such as George Bennett, whose son, George (d. 1748), died as
owner of 496 slaves and a personal estate of £19,559. A few men established political and economic dynasties. The two Beckford brothers,
Peter (d. 1735) and Thomas (1682–1731), had numerous rich descendants. John Lewis (d. 1712) was the owner of 190 slaves at his death.
The Lewis family remained major slave owners in Westmoreland Parish
for over a century: their most famous member was Mathew "Monk"
Gregory Lewis, the gothic author and diarist who chronicled his time in
Jamaica in 1815 and was the owner of 590 slaves. The Ellis family was
equally distinguished in northern St. Mary Parish. John Ellis (d. 1710),
the son of an early settler and legislator, was the father of a wealthy slave
owner, George (d. 1745), the owner of 158 slaves. He in turn had three
grandsons, who died with 285, 536, and 1,310 slaves respectively. Their
descendants continue to be significant London landlords.[116]

The children of the great planters of the 1700s and 1710s lived in a
world that was more dominated by large slaveholdings than ever before. Between the mid-1720s and the mid-1780s slave ownership was
widespread (over 80 percent of inventoried estates contained slaves), but
nearly two-thirds of slave owners were small slave owners, with fewer
than 16 slaves. These small slave owners accounted for less than 10 percent of total slaves. The majority of slaves, if Kingston owners are excluded from the equation, lived in large units of over 150 or more slaves.
The number of large slaveholdings increased to around 50 between the
1730s and 1750s, and to 69 in the 1770s. In addition, the average size
of slave forces increased from 25 to 35, with the average size jumping
to over 40 per slave owner in the 1730s and the 1770s. I will expand on
such data in chapter 4.

As in other plantation colonies, such as Virginia, the planter elite was made up of a cousinhood of interrelated families. The sons of the Ellis family, for example, married daughters from other wealthy planter families, including the Needham, Beckford, Long, and Palmer families.[117] Nevertheless, entry into the ranks of the upper slaveholding families was never closed. First, continuing white demographic disaster meant that estates came up for sale on a regular basis and also that existing large slave owners did not need to divide property in order to leave it to younger sons.[118] Second, high-status immigrants gained high wages soon after arrival in the booming plantation sector as attorneys, as lawyers profiting from Jamaicans' extreme litigiousness, or as government officials. Third, the slave trade and the lucrative trade with Spanish America, largely conducted out of Kingston, gave well-connected newcomers excellent opportunities to gain wealth.

There are several notable examples of immigrants who attained high office and very great wealth in eighteenth-century Jamaica. Edward Manning (1710–1756), for example, was a London immigrant who used his connections with the South Sea Company to become the most prominent merchant in Kingston in the 1730s and 1740s. He became an assemblyman and the leading representative of the merchant interest in a bitter fight against Spanish Town planters led by Sir Charles Price and Rose Fuller in the mid-1750s. He died a very wealthy man, with sugar plantations in Clarendon, St. Andrew, and St. Mary parishes, on which he worked 609 slaves. His successor as Kingston's leading merchant was Zachary Bayly, an immigrant from Wiltshire to Kingston sometime in the 1730s. By the time of his death in 1769 Bayly, who had removed from Kingston to nearby St. Andrew and invested his mercantile profits in major sugar estates in St. Mary Parish in northern Jamaica, had become one of the wealthiest men in the country. As his nephew and inheritor, the historian Bryan Edwards, noted, he had established a "princely" fortune, amounting to £114,743, including 2,012 slaves—the largest slave force recorded in inventories made before 1785.

Alexander Grant, whose career as a London Associate David Hancock has chronicled, was another immigrant to Jamaica who created a large landed estate through wealth gained as a merchant. Grant was born in Scotland in 1705, a member of an impecunious gentry family in a financially destitute country. He arrived in Jamaica as a physician and became connected with Peter Beckford, the eldest son of Peter Beckford II. His Beckford connections allowed him entrée into planter society in western Jamaica, where he became a landowner and married the heiress

Elizabeth Cooke. He left in 1739 for Britain. It was only after this that he became a serious planter. By his death in 1772 he owned 11,000 acres in Jamaica valued at £96,700 and producing gross sugar and rum receipts of £35,000 per annum. His Jamaican estate was valued at £72,895, with 672 slaves.[119]

The rise of Jamaica's planter elite, as in Barbados earlier, Virginia simultaneously, and South Carolina slightly later, was monumentally important for the history of the Americas. It produced the first genuinely American elite, prominent in leading the thirteen colonies into imperial rebellion, shaping irrevocably the society and economy of the West Indies, and which in the American South destroyed itself by declaring war against the industrial North in the conflagration of the American Civil War. The planter was the chief architect of the plantation complex and its major beneficiary. He (and it was usually he) was not unconstrained in his power, as the plantation was a colonial artifact, which meant that ultimate power in plantation societies resided in Britain. But he was powerful enough to feel like a god in his little kingdom. William Byrd II of Virginia wrote in the 1730s of the plantation as an idyll and the planter as God's representative on earth. By the third quarter of the eighteenth century the planter was a recognizable type, praised by defenders as a paragon of English gentility, a man of "noble and disinterested munificence."[120]

Starting in the early 1720s and extending through to the American Revolution, the great planters of plantation America controlled politics, society, and culture. Their dominance was based on their control of the most important assets of their societies: land, labor, and access to credit. It wasn't a pretty process. Men like Robert "King" Carter in Virginia and Peter Beckford in Jamaica were ambitious, assertive, and aggressive capitalists, with a strong philistine streak and a determination to gain advantages for themselves at the expense of everyone else. The men who made up the planter elite in this period shared several characteristics: a single-minded devotion to the acquisition of wealth and a corresponding lack of attention to the attainment of social graces, considerable involvement in transatlantic commerce, and success in the competition for access to the political and economic favors of colonial governors. They were ambitious, thrusting, hardheaded men who gave no quarter to political opponents or to dependents of any sort, let alone to enslaved people, whom they treated with excessive violence and cruelty.[121]

It was only well after planter elites had fully established themselves that planters tried to soften their behavior by developing and implementing an austere patriarchal code of conduct in which they exercised responsibility in return for having their authority recognized by others. They wanted to see themselves as both ancient Roman senators and contemporary British aristocrats. They also wanted to suggest that things other than crass materialism motivated their actions. At bottom, however, their status relied on money. That money was derived from their control of the large integrated plantation complex, a system they invented, perfected, and relied upon for their wealth, status, and control of politics. Great planters were capitalists, operating within the context of a capitalist colonial economy, always on the lookout for ways to increase their private profit, which was used to transform the landscapes they lived in so that they approximated as much as was feasible the polite and improved landscape of Georgian Britain. Yet behind the polished facades of the newly erected great houses and at the side of the proud men in fine clothes on horseback were the black workers who made the plantation complex possible, as well as the ordinary white people who acquiesced in great planter dominance because they shared in the benefits that the plantation system brought.[122]

Violence sustained the plantation system. The men who owned the large integrated plantations that transformed the slave societies of British America in the late seventeenth and early eighteenth centuries benefited most from the development of the plantation system, but they depended, as they well knew, on the willingness and ability of ordinary white men to inflict violence upon African slaves and to serve in colonial militias. Planters adopted with gusto the British system of associating rank with military office: they loved calling themselves "Major" or "Colonel." But behind the social display inherent in the adoption of such titles lay a firm reality. Plantations worked because white men were prepared to use military methods of coercion and control against slaves, all developed during one of the most highly militarized periods in British and British imperial history: first during the War of the Three Kingdoms, and then in the aftermath of the Glorious Revolution and the Treaty of Utrecht in 1713. That imposition of will was designed not to wage war, but to make money. The amount of money made was substantial, and it was transformative for Britain and its plantation colonies.

THREE

The Wealth of the Plantations

Introduction: The Transformation of British America

Planters, merchants, ordinary white people, and the occasional free colored person amassed considerable wealth in the plantation system as black chattel slavery was embedded into British American colonial life in the eighteenth century. Plantation societies were established throughout a long stretch of land, starting in the north somewhere near Baltimore in Maryland and by the early nineteenth century reaching into the northeastern tip of South America. These societies became the richest and most important parts of the British empire in the Americas in the second and third quarters of the eighteenth century. They became the focus of imperial attention and interest to a much greater extent than their more impecunious neighbors in the nonplantation colonies north of Maryland and southern Delaware.

The success of the plantation system based on black servile labor transformed the Americas. The colonization of America by the late seventeenth century seemed to be a gigantic failure everywhere except Barbados, the earliest adopter of the large integrated plantation system. By the mid-eighteenth century, however, the colonization of the Americas by the British had become wildly successful. The plantation system worked as intended, both in giving a few fortunate Americans and West Indians great wealth and also in creating political and social stability among previously fractious groups of American colonists. If British America became valuable to the British, as it did especially from the Seven Years' War onward, it was in no small measure due to the successful establishment of the large integrated plantation in Britain's tropical and subtropical colonies. The planters and merchants who controlled these societies cracked the code about how to make colonies worthwhile investments of empire. What worked was using slavery to produce tropical crops, such as tobacco, rice, indigo, and, above all, sugar. As Barbara Solow notes, "It was slavery that made the empty lands of the western hemisphere valuable producers of commodities and valuable markets for Europe and North America. What moved in the Atlantic in these centuries was predominantly slaves, the output of slaves, the inputs of slave societies, and the goods and services purchased with the earnings on slave products."[1]

Franklin and Smith on Slavery

Nevertheless, not everyone, even contemporaries, thought that the plantation system was an unalloyed benefit to the British empire. Benjamin Franklin, for example, in a pioneering essay on political economy published during the middle of the Seven Years' War, made a fervent argument that it was the northern, rather than the southern and island, colonies that most benefited the British empire. Franklin derided the West Indian colonies as not just morally retrograde, but in the long term economically less beneficial to Britain than societies not based upon slavery. It was a mistake, he argued, to base an economy upon slavery because, "every slave being *by Nature a Thief*," the institution corrupted British American character. When whites owned slaves, he argued, "the white children become proud, disgusted with labor and being educated in Idleness, are rendered unfit to get a living by Industry." His sense of a virtuous America rested upon a sense of northern virtue and southern and West Indian degeneracy. He depicted the plantation as economically backward and planters as atavistic throwbacks to a more primitive period.[2]

Franklin's condemnation of plantation slavery as terrible on moral grounds and undesirable in economic terms proved influential even in the eighteenth century, when the plantation system was at the height of its economic and political importance. At the very time that the

British empire was experiencing unprecedented expansion, from the mid-eighteenth century onward, political economists, notably Adam Smith, started to argue that colonial possessions were not as valuable as they seemed, and that slavery was an inefficient way of organizing labor. Smith's singular contribution to the political economy of slavery was to show that the "experience of all ages and nations demonstrates that the work done by slaves, though it appears to cost their maintenance, is, in the end, the dearest of all."[3] He thought that slave owners were doing things inconsistent with their best interests. Slaves were costly to work and maintain and had little interest in bettering themselves through working hard in order to attain consumer goods. Free labor was thus economically more efficient than, as well as morally superior to, slavery.

Yet Smith did not condemn slavery and the plantation system as fervently as his later admirers sometimes pretended. He was not, for example, as unequivocal in his condemnation of the plantation system as his abolitionist French disciple, Jean-Baptiste Say. Say spoke in favor of racial egalitarianism and thought slavery a moral wrong, although, even more than Smith, he assumed that New World planters were rational capitalists.[4] Say noted that profits of up to 18 percent per annum meant that French West Indian planters could recoup the price paid for a West Indian plantation within as short a time as six years, while a French farmer, making 3 to 4 percent profit per annum, would require a much longer time period to recoup his purchase price. For Say, therefore, the question about whether the slave trade should be abolished thus transcended cost-benefit analysis: very high profits were not enough to justify continuing an infamous commerce that went against justice and humanity.[5]

Where Smith was most critical of the plantation economies was how they took capital from metropolitan Britain that could have been better expended in other more economically beneficial and efficient activities. Britain funded the plantation system. Smith declared that "the stock which has improved and cultivated the sugar colonies of England has, a great part of it, been sent out from England, and has been by no means been altogether the produce of the soil and industry of the colonists." Without money from Britain, he argued, the "the progress of our North American and West Indian colonies would have been much less rapid, had no capital but what belonged to themselves been employed in exporting their surplus produce." Smith was careful to limit his musings to the British Caribbean. He did not think that English capital had played much of a role in developing Virginia plantations and thought that the capital "which has improved the sugar colonies of France . . . has been raised almost entirely from the gradual improvement and cultivation of those colonies."[6]

Smith's argument was predicated upon a larger attack upon mercantilism, a system he believed was bad for Britain because it diverted useful capital to dubious schemes of imperial advancement overseas and forced the colonies to be overly dependent on one single creditor. It is important to note, however, that Smith's argument that investment in the plantations was a misallocation of capital investment from Britain, a very influential one in shaping metropolitan opposition to plantation colonies in the beginning of the antislavery campaign and a primary one against imperialism in the eighteenth and later centuries, has been shown to be empirically flawed. Careful studies by Richard Pares in the 1950s on the colonies generally, and more recently by Russell R. Menard on the Carolina Lowcountry, show that the money used to finance the plantations did not come from Britain. Rather, much of it came from planters themselves, and from merchants in towns like Kingston, Bridgetown, and Charleston. Pares thought that "the profits of the plantations were the source which fed the indebtedness charged upon the plantations." Menard sees the development of Lowcountry plantations as arising less from strategic investments from London merchants than from farm building, local credit markets, and careful reinvestment by yeoman farmers, of which the most skilled and lucky became great planters. Nevertheless, just as Smith's stronger statements need to be qualified by reference to the availability of credit in the colonies themselves, so too do Pares's and Menard's contradiction of Adam Smith need to be qualified by an appreciation that British moneylenders, some from plantation societies themselves, cannot be as easily distinguished from colonial merchants as Smith imagined.[7]

In significant ways Smith was wrong about the plantation colonies of Britain, or at least his writings were misleading insofar as he moved the terms of the debate about the plantation system and its utility to Britain in unproductive ways. His criticisms were misplaced because he argued that the plantation system and British colonization was a net cost to the British nation. Colonies, it is true, cost a considerable amount in defense costs, and they may have been worse places to invest in than Britain's burgeoning industrial sphere. But the plantation system was highly efficient and highly profitable, except briefly during the American Revolution. Such a statement is true for all colonies south of Delaware but especially for the wealthiest part of the eighteenth-century empire, as a case study in patterns of wealth in Jamaica in chapter 4 will show. Moreover, as Kenneth Pomeranz has argued, the plantation system allowed Britain the luxury of being able to put less effort into obtaining tropical products than might have been the case if the colonies did not exist. They provided the "ghost acres" that allowed for significant substitution of resources. To compensate for the caloric inputs from sugar brought from the New World around 1700, about an extra 150,000 acres of wheat (out of 10 million acres of arable land) would have had to be put into production. In addition, sugar had many other multiplier effects that were useful for British economic growth, such as prolonging the durability of meats, fruits, and vegetables and allowing hot drinks to be substituted for beer, thus reducing the need for cereal.[8]

The Decline Thesis

Modern historians have offered other criticisms or comments about the plantation system that cast doubt upon its utility, efficiency, and overall value to the British empire. In the 1920s Lowell Ragatz argued that the West Indian plantation system was in terminal decline from as early as 1763, and in 1944 Eric Williams contended that the system was inherently fragile. Williams admitted that there was seemingly a great deal of wealth that came out of the West Indies in the eighteenth century before the American Revolution, but he insisted that this wealth was shallowly based and depended upon a system of labor and an elaborate series of capital arrangements that made the wealth of the plantations less secure than contemporaries thought. The whole system, he argued, was structured upon a chimera of debt and an excessive reliance upon the Atlantic slave trade. Planters were addicted to the short term and equally to luxurious consumption, meaning that they were living well beyond their means. When the American Revolution was fought, the weaknesses of the plantation system encouraged perfidious Albion to abandon the West Indies and compromise its prosperity by halting the slave trade. As Williams famously argued, Britain built up the plantation system and benefited greatly from it but was very ready to attack it as immoral and perhaps uneconomic as soon as other forms of economic organization, notably industrialization, rendered the plantation system less vital to British prosperity.[9]

Williams is but one of many modern critics who see the plantation system as not only inherently flawed as an economic system but also as based upon a monstrous social institution that was bound to fail once

Europeans realized its immorality. Franklin Knight, for example, argues that the Caribbean slave system bore within itself the seeds of its own destruction.[10] In reality, however, the plantation system provided great profits to those who instituted it and to the British empire in which it functioned. In this chapter I argue that it was as least as profitable, and probably a good deal more efficient, than any other form of money making that operated in the early modern world in Europe and its dependencies. And it was not inevitably bound to fail—not unless political decisions to weaken it were made.

Planters, of course, did not live up to the highest standards of efficient maximization of resources put forward by the best agricultural modernizers in Europe, especially in late eighteenth-century Britain.[11] In the Caribbean, for example, planters continued to use the hoe instead of the plow as a method of tillage until well into the nineteenth century, a practice derided by British agricultural innovators.[12] In the Chesapeake, planters were thought by some commentators to be especially slovenly husbandmen, a characterization that formed part of the historical debate around southern farming into well into the twentieth century.[13] Planters were also castigated for their extravagance, their overcommitment to archaic social ideals such as the code of honor, and a variety of social and cultural practices that got in the way of some aspects of profit maximization. They were condemned also for their lax financial habits and for being poor custodians of their properties, more interested in gaming, consumption, and politics than in the mundane and time-consuming business of managing their estates.[14] Certainly their accounting methods left a lot to be desired by modern standards. Very few planters before the late eighteenth century distinguished between current expenses and capital investments, making it very difficult to recreate their accounts. Relatively few kept systematic accounts of production and laborers' performance. By modern standards, planters were running blind about many aspects of their economic activities. They fail modern management standards pretty comprehensively.[15]

But meeting modern management standards is an unrealistic expectation for eighteenth-century businessmen. By most standards, modern and contemporary, the overall performance of the plantation system from the Chesapeake to the West Indies was extraordinary. Most planters were careful, committed, relatively cautious, and skilled managers of slaves and land who took great pride in how well they ran their estates.[16] Individual delinquencies by planters and merchants do not change the reality that the plantation system worked exceedingly well in bringing wealth to those who owned plantations, and prosperity to the merchants who lived in plantation societies. These "factories in the field" compared very well in their productivity and profitability to what was accomplished in other agricultural enterprises in the period of the ancien régime. Indeed, many planters were at the forefront of modernity, fully participating in the scientific discourse around agricultural improvement that was a feature of Enlightenment thinking in the eighteenth century. They applied scientific methods with great enthusiasm to improve their management practice. The planters and merchants who embraced such ideals, and who were attuned to dreams of transforming plantation landscapes into recognizably European places, wanted their improvements in plantation agriculture to become part of the larger intellectual discourse of the Enlightenment.[17]

The plantation system answered the question of how to make American lands enormously productive. As Lorena Walsh concludes in her extensive study of plantation management techniques in the Chesapeake before 1763, planters succeeded because they figured out how to use land effectively through their maximization of one of the two scarcest resources in the colonies, labor, and through the accumulation of the other scarce resource, capital. They were ever alert to new opportunities, be they better technology, more effective accounting, or new markets for old and then alternative and new crops. Their perseverance and ability to engage in crop diversification allowed them to take advantages of new opportunities quickly and expeditiously. It was a sign of their eagerness to work for profit, even if that eagerness to labor was really a willingness to exploit the forced labor of others for their own benefit.[18]

The large integrated plantation and the plantation system it generated were economically viable and profitable for as long as the system lasted in British America and the United States. No one now thinks that the plantation system was on its last legs in the American South in the 1850s and 1860s and would have just faded away without the intervention of a civil war. It was Union victory in the Civil War, not the inherent fragilities of the system, that destroyed the plantation system. Similarly, few historians now take seriously Williams's argument that the plantation system was contracting and failing at the time abolition emerged. Without the abolition of the slave trade (and even, in the case of British Guiana and Trinidad, despite abolition), the British plantation system in the West Indies would have expanded and continued to be profitable during the nineteenth century, just as it did in Cuba before the mid-1860s.[19] Robert Fogel's summary of the economic performance of the antebellum American plantation system also stands in for the British West Indian plantation system on the eve of abolition: "Although American slavery was deeply immoral and politically backward, it might, nevertheless, have been a highly efficient form of economic organization that was able to sustain high rates of economic growth and yield substantial profits to its ruling class."[20]

What is noticeable in Fogel's statement, however, is his apologetic tone. Concluding that the plantation system was economically rational and an economic positive good excuses the monstrous crime of black chattel slavery. Certainly some of the objections to Fogel's earlier and controversial work done with Stanley L. Engerman on the economics of slavery in the antebellum American South were based on suppositions that even to consider whether slavery as an immoral system was profitable was an intellectual activity so callous as to be itself immoral. To some observers it seemed morally irresponsible to even ask whether slavery was profitable.[21] One problem with the response to econometric analyses of the profitability of slavery was that it was couched within a discussion of whether free labor was better or worse than slave labor, a discussion that replicated in sometimes uncomfortable ways the political arguments against antislavery put forward by southern defenders of slavery in the prelude to the Civil War.[22] For students of plantation agriculture in the eighteenth century, such contexts are less necessary: there was no obvious counterpart to plantation slavery such as industrialization with profitable free labor. In this respect Franklin's encomium to free labor over slavery was so visionary as not to be part of contemporary debate.

The Rationality of Violence

Scholars of the plantation economy have largely reconciled themselves to concerns that what they are doing is a misallocation of their time and resources. Understanding the dynamics of the plantation system means understanding how it worked as an economic organization. That the institution lasted as long as it did makes sense only if it was an institution that made economic sense within the context of an evolving merchant and then industrial capitalism.[23] Nevertheless, even though planters thought of profit as a good thing, it is clear that such a summary is not enough, because how they accumulated their wealth was fundamentally problematic. For modern historians, as much as for Benjamin Franklin, the moral is ineluctably tied with the economic when assessing the performance of plantation economies. Our objection to the plantation system is as much theological as tautological: if slavery is the original sin of

British colonization of the Americas, then it must eventually be replaced by goodness, usually seen as initiated by the efforts of enslaved people in what is depicted as continual resistance to planter power.[24]

The immorality that is of most concern here is, of course, the immorality of slavery. Planters made the plantation system more efficient and more profitable mainly by perfecting means of extracting labor from enslaved persons. That extraction of labor involved a number of processes, all of which became more refined over time as planters ratcheted up work requirements and implemented new measures of psychological coercion.[25] It also involved considerable violence, as the previous chapter detailed. Violence was more openly practiced and more vicious in the West Indies than in the Chesapeake. There, mid-eighteenth-century planters increasingly turned to paternalism as the ideological structure underlying a defense of slavery.[26] Everywhere, however, violence sustained the plantation system. Planters sometimes pretended that the difficulty of managing slaves was a large psychic cost to white people, but the results of brutal treatment were mainly borne by enslaved people.[27]

The sad truth about the extent of violence on the eighteenth-century plantation was that violence against blacks worked, at least to keep enslaved Africans quiescent. Certainly, there was resistance, often considerable at the individual level, which enslaved people threw at the slave system. Nevertheless, organized resistance against white authority was limited once the plantation system was fully established. No slave revolt occurred during the eighteenth century in important plantation colonies such as Barbados, Virginia, Maryland, and Georgia. There were embryonic revolts in Antigua in 1732 and in South Carolina in 1739, both of which caused little damage to white authority but were put down with maximum force. The only slave revolt that shook white authority during the African period of slavery was in Jamaica in 1760, where Tacky, Apongo, and Kingston, three slaves possibly of Akan heritage, developed in great secrecy an island-wide revolt in which large numbers of whites were killed, extensive property was destroyed, and the colony came close to the precipice of white rule being overturned.

Yet this revolt too failed. The white response to Tacky was so ferocious that metropolitan Britons wondered about the motives of white Jamaicans in putting down the revolt and about what sort of people could exercise such brutality. The lesson for black people was clear: rebellion was likely to lead to failure, and failure resulted in slow death by torture for those directly involved in rebellion and massive retaliation against friends and families of rebels. Before the Haitian Revolution of 1791–1804 changed the rules of the game forever, planters were supremely confident in their ability to quash any potential slave rebellion. As Jeremy Popkin comments, whites in plantation societies thought of slave uprisings as akin to the earthquakes and hurricanes that afflicted the island—one-off disasters. The idea that uncivilized blacks could overthrow white rule and establish their own society was one most white planters found simply unthinkable.[28] What more concerned contemporaries in the first two-thirds of the eighteenth century when looking at the economic performance of plantations was not the damage it wrought upon black people but the increasing inequality that the rise of the great planter entailed for white people. Resentment against rich whites was relatively limited, however, although it began to become significant in previously deferential societies such as Virginia and Maryland during and after the American Revolution, when economic strains started to emerge within the Chesapeake plantation system.[29]

Politics, Inequality, and the Rise of the Plantation System

Sometimes the rise of the great planters and the increasing integration of a dynamic Atlantic economic system are seen as an almost organic consequence of natural evolution. It happened, it seems, as colonial societies developed sufficiently robust networks of exchange to allow entrepreneurial risk takers to take advantage of the opportunities thrust their way.[30] Yet the conditions by which one class took advantage of a favorable political climate following the resolution of English and English American political conflicts after the Glorious Revolution, so that they controlled everything of importance in plantation societies until the American Revolution in the thirteen colonies and the abolition of the slave trade in the British West Indies, followed from deliberate political decisions. The plantation system did not just evolve; it was created. The men who managed to control land and labor and create large plantations, with all that went them, were the winners in the great transition of the late seventeenth and early eighteenth centuries. Smaller planters (and, of course, all black people) were the losers in this transition. Their loss can be seen in the increased inequality that marked plantation societies in the eighteenth century. As early as 1680 inequality in Barbados had become marked. The 175 largest planters owned on average over 60 slaves and more than 265 acres of land, while ordinary white men owned only a few slaves each, if any.[31]

Other regions followed the Barbadian example, where the rise of the plantation led to increased wealth inequality. In the Tidewater regions of the Chesapeake, for example, the richest ten percent of the inventoried population in the Chesapeake increased their share of inventoried wealth from 40 to 70 percent after the plantation system was implemented in the late seventeenth century. The march of inequality was halted between 1710 and 1730 but then started again, especially after 1750. By the 1780s no place in the Chesapeake, and especially no place in the Tidewater, could be described as a "good poor man's country." Even when inequality was halted in the early eighteenth century, moreover, opportunity at the bottom of the social scale virtually stopped. [32] In South Carolina, growing wealth was initially not accompanied by significant wealth inequality. The share of wealth held by the top 10 percent of inventoried wealth holders increased from a moderately low 41 percent in the late seventeenth century, before the export boom of 1700–1740, to 44 percent for wealth holders dying between 1743 and 1745. After 1750, however, wealth inequality increased rapidly: the share of wealth held by the top ten percent of inventoried people in 1764 was 60 percent. It was at the top end, among the greatest planters and merchants, that wealth inequality was most pronounced. The great merchants and planters owned substantial amounts of improved land and large slaveholdings that benefited from sharply rising prices after the end of the Seven Years' War.[33]

The seeming reduction of opportunity for poorer white men and the increased economic distance between rich and poor in plantation societies should have concerned great planters. Rich white men needed to cultivate poorer white men, because the latter could cause the former an inordinate amount of trouble if they chose to oppose them. Throughout the eighteenth century ordinary white men proved a disruptive influence on numerous occasions, including engaging in piracy or smuggling in Jamaica in the early eighteenth century, adopting evangelical religious practices at odds with elite Anglicanism in mid-eighteenth-century Virginia, refusing to serve in militias in Virginia in the American Revolution except on their own terms, opposing Tidewater elites and making the War for Independence a civil war in the Carolinas, and insisting on doctrines of white supremacy against elite instructions in early nineteenth-century Barbados.[34]

How much trouble poorer white men could be within plantation societies is best illustrated not in British America but in Saint-Domingue at the start of the Haitian Revolution, between 1791 and 1793. In that colony the outbreak of the French Revolution not only pitted free coloreds against whites and eventually, after the slave insurrection in the northern province of 1791, black slaves against free coloreds and whites. It also aggravated class tensions between *petits blancs* and *grands blancs*, tensions that substantially destabilized society and allowed the slave insurrection to become a real threat to white rule in the colony rather than becoming transformed, as in Jamaica a century earlier, into a dangerous but controllable marronage (a term used to describe runaway slaves who created their own communities).[35] That antagonism soon broke into violence. In November 1791 a breakdown in trust between royalist whites and their free colored white and radical *pompons rouges*—poor whites who supported the French revolutionary movement—led to Port-au-Prince being burned down. *Petits blancs* were less politically active in Saint-Domingue's other main city, Cap Français in the north. There the white people who opposed rich whites were white sailors on ships in the harbor. On 20 June 1793 sailors' support of General François-Thomas Galbaud, who had been stripped of his office by revolutionary commissars and who had stirred up unrest about the activities of free coloreds in the town, and of the interests of revolutionary France led to a cataclysm of violence in Cap Français. It propelled the destruction of the town and formed the spark that destabilized the colony. As Jeremy Popkin argues, "This armed assault on the representatives of a national government by whites claiming to be republicans who distrusted the government's commitment to defend slavery . . . brought about a far more sudden and radical abolition of slavery than national leaders had foreseen."[36]

Nevertheless, normally whites in both French and British America were remarkably unified in support of the plantation system, no matter how much it contributed to economic inequality. Ordinary white men acquiesced to elite rule because they enjoyed a secure place in an all-white political culture. They participated in militia musters with enthusiasm, did their duty in county court sessions, and mixed with their "superiors" in gaming, horse racing, and athletic competitions, and they insisted on competitive elections in which gentry candidates were forced to appeal to their white inferiors for their votes.[37] Ordinary white men supported the plantation system for three reasons. First, the plantation system worked so well economically that enough benefits flowed down to ordinary white men in the form of increased wealth to make them satisfied. Secondly, ordinary white men profited from the plantation system insofar as many of them were plantation operatives and even more were slave owners. Thirdly, the plantation system was sufficiently diverse in such colonies as Barbados, Jamaica, and South Carolina, where there were thriving towns, that ordinary white men did not have to become part of the plantation sector in order to benefit from it.[38]

The Plantations at Midcentury

The plantation system, once implemented, led to economic success for everyone in it—except, of course, the African slaves crucial to its success. The plantation system brought great benefits to the British empire. British American exports increased substantially over the course of the late seventeenth century. In 1686 recorded imports from the plantations into London was valued at £884,176, an increase, despite a huge downturn in the tobacco trade, of 62 percent from the mid-1660s, which saw imports of £545,088. Of imports in 1686, the Chesapeake's share was 18 percent, the Lower South's was 1.4 percent, and the West Indies' was 77 percent. At the turn of the eighteenth century, the average annual value of commodity exports into London from British America was £838,814, of which most (a value of £621,793) were located in the British West Indies, mostly in Barbados, the Leeward Islands, and Jamaica.[39] The result of such production was to make whites in Barbados as wealthy in 1700 as whites in the Chesapeake in 1774, with white per capita wealth of £82. White wealth in Barbados had virtually doubled since 1665, with per capita wealth for the whole population increasing by 1 percent per annum or by one-third over thirty-five years.[40]

Seventy years later the average annual value of commodity exports in British America had increased nearly sevenfold to £6,475,078. The British West Indies were still the major contributor to these figures, with annual commodity exports of £3,910,600, but other regions also did very well. The plantation colonies of the American South and the British West Indies had annual exports worth £5,503,432, or 85 percent of all British American exports. Growth in the main plantation areas (the Lower South and the British West Indies) was especially strong. The average annual value of commodity exports per free person in these regions was £22.91 in the Lower South and £86.90 in the West Indies, compared to £0.90 per free person in New England and the Middle Colonies and £2.63 per free person in the Upper South. In some respects this division of wealth by region suggests that the increase in wealth was general, not just connected to the plantation system, as the share of colonial wealth taken up by New England and the Middle Colonies increased over the eighteenth century from 5.3 percent in the late seventeenth century to 14.9 percent between 1768 and 1772. Such a conclusion would be misleading, however, because it is clear that the great increase in wealth in New England and the Middle Colonies can be attributed almost entirely to the small but prosperous mercantile community oriented toward trade with the Caribbean. By the 1740s New England, Pennsylvania, and New York had developed an extensive shipping industry focused on taking provisions and various commodities to the West Indies.[41]

We can see the importance of the plantation sector in British America in the 1740s through a remarkable series of documents produced for private examination by British imperial officials in the 1740s by Robert Dinwiddie (1692–1770), surveyor general of the southern colonies from 1738 to 1749 and lieutenant governor of Virginia between 1751 and 1758. These records have been usefully looked at by Kenneth Morgan, who argues that these reports on military strength, shipping, trade, commodity output, and black population "offer a snapshot of the economic strength of Britain's American and West Indian colonies during the 1740s," a time of growing concern about imperial rivalry with France and Spain and a period during which concerns about the underlying economic health of the British West Indian and Chesapeake colonies were beginning to be allayed after years of economic decline in Jamaica and Barbados.[42] What is especially useful about Dinwiddie's analysis is that he demonstrates the priorities that shaped imperial thinking. The military strength of colonial militias was, for example, as significant as the wealth that the colonies produced. New England's major value to the British empire was its large population of men able to serve in military expeditions, such as that undertaken by Admiral Edward Vernon in Cartagena, in which many New Englanders served and died. New England's white population thus served as cannon fodder for the defense of the plantations.[43]

The second strength of Dinwiddie's analysis was that he saw the colonies in a wide perspective. By the 1740s, Dinwiddie asserted, British America was an integrated whole in which shipping from the northern provinces, especially New England, supported the production of tropical crops in the West Indies. Dinwiddie highlighted both the value of the plantation colonies to Britain and also the extent of trade (legal and illegal) conducted between colonies, especially Jamaica, and the French and the Spanish empires. His most significant contribution to the political economy of this period was showing that while plantation production was extremely important, so too was output in the nonplantation colonies. Both areas were closely connected, contrary to what Franklin was to argue ten years later. Dinwiddie, interestingly for a man connected to the southern and island colonies more than to the northern provinces, stressed the value of New England and Newfoundland, showing in particular that New England's export commodities had catapulted in value from £800,000 in 1743 to £1.8 million in 1748. Indeed, New England held the premier output position in North America, with only Jamaica in British America outstripping it in economic (though not military) importance to the empire in the 1740s.[44]

The plantations were important for Dinwiddie in three ways (excluding his interest in the slave trade and slavery): the production of tropical and subtropical commodities; the contribution of shipping to Britain's maritime strength; and trade, mostly clandestine, to French, Spanish, and Dutch America. Plantation production was extremely important. The plantation colonies were the most productive parts of British America, accounting for £2,120,000 or 57 percent of total produce of £3,745,000 and 22 percent of the accumulated value of American trade of £9,478,000. Production was increasing appreciably, with the total value of produce in the plantation colonies amounting to £2,810,000 in 1743 and £3,270,000 in 1748. The second area where the plantations were valuable was in shipping. In 1740 the American trade engaged 3,085 ships, of which 2,035 were from the colonies (1,110 from New England, Connecticut, and Rhode Island), employing 29,860 sailors who were "a very fine nursery" that was "of Infinite Service to Great Britain." By 1748 the trade was greatly enhanced, with the number of vessels increased to 3,770 and the number of seamen employed reaching 37,700. The value of this trade had increased from £2,758,000 (of which £388,000 was coastal trading and fishing, so thus should be discounted) in 1740 to £4,747,500 in 1748.[45] Finally, there was the trade engaged in with other European empires. In 1740 New Englanders were active participants, shipping logwood to the value of £100,000, mostly from the Bay of Honduras to the mainland colonies. By 1748 that trade had declined by half, but Jamaican trade with French and Spanish America had greatly increased and accounted for the great majority of the sizable increase in foreign trade from £425,000 in 1740 to £1,115,000 in 1743 and again in 1748.[46]

Dinwiddie argued from the evidence that he put before the Board of Trade in 1740; the secretary of state, the duke of Newcastle, in 1743; and his patron, Henry Pelham, the prime minister, in 1748 that the trade of America was "of inestimable value to the Nation of Great Britain." In 1743, however, he warned that France was becoming so strong on their sugar islands that if due attention was not paid to shoring up colonial defenses against France, soon "if we Should have War with France, [I] am

FIGURE 4. Painting by George Robertson, *View of Roaring River Estate, Westmoreland, 1778*, engraved by Thomas Vivares from a painting by George Robertson. © Courtesy of the National Library of Jamaica.

afraid they will be able to Invade & take all our Leeward Islands." By 1748 Dinwiddie's fear of French invasion had diminished. He gloried instead in "the immense Value, high Importance and prodigious national Benefit of this grand Source of Britain's Opulence." He attributed the "vast progress these Collonies have made" "to the Blessing of Heaven on the unwearied Industry of the Planters, to the singular Felicity they have of framing their own laws, and to the generous Credit constantly indulged to them by the Merchants here." It is notable that he foregrounded planters rather than colonists in general. Their "Opulence" was shown in the value of the slave populations of the sugar islands, which Dinwiddie considered only as property. In 1740 the sugar islands of the West Indies, by his computation, contained 231,000 slaves worth £20 per head. If the value of slaves was combined with the value of other property necessary to run a sugar plantation, then the "Value of the Sugar Plantations, abstract of the Soil" was £6,160,000. By 1748 that sum had increased to £7,428,125, mainly because Dinwiddie had arbitrarily increased the number of slaves in St. Kitts by 8,000 and had revalued slaves as being worth £25 per head.[47]

Dinwiddie's analysis pointed to plantations as being at the forefront of American prosperity. The majority of the profits they generated went to a relatively small group of men who built a highly productive system that was dependent on the poverty of the many. Their incomes derived from, as Barry Higman sums up, "the manipulation of a complex, agro-industrial technology, an integrated trade network and a brutal system of labor exploitation." The plantation was a great success because it was a precursor—contrary to traditional views that it was economically backward—to the modern industrial factory in its management of labor, its harvesting of resources, and its scale of capital investment and output.[48]

Plantations and Imperial Development

British imperial officials who wanted to maximize value in the empire saw that wealth was concentrated not where white people lived in large numbers, but where they were scarce. The wisest policy that Britain could have carried out in the British empire in the Americas would have been to deter European immigration to the Americas and place all their efforts on improving the slave trade and on fostering demographic growth in American slave populations. America, in short, could have been treated like nineteenth-century India. Doing so would have increased white levels of population in Britain, possibly would have reduced the imperial costs of maintaining empire, and might have allowed policy makers and investors to concentrate on improving plantation management on islands like Grenada and St. Kitts, where monoculture brought massive profits to a tiny planter elite, some of whom lived in Britain rather than in the tropics. In mainland America they should have concentrated on fostering development in economically high-performing regions such as coastal South Carolina and Georgia and let Virginia, Maryland, and North Carolina continue without much imperial assistance.

In some respects this policy was actually what operated in the eighteenth-century British empire. The extensive migration of Englishmen and a few Englishwomen to the Americas that had occurred in the seventeenth century dried up over the course of the eighteenth century, with migration from the metropolitan core of southern England substantially falling, especially to British North America, except for a burst of fresh immigration to Maryland and Pennsylvania in the years immediately before the American Revolution.[49] In the seventeenth century migrants to British America came from London, the southeast, East Anglia, and the west country. The total number of migrants from England

and Wales was 300,000, with a further 40,000 coming from Ireland or Scotland. In the eighteenth century the majority of migrants not from London (still the major region from which migrants left, but itself a center of migration from throughout Britain) came from northern England, the western districts of the Scottish borders and its Lowcountry (as well as from the Highlands and Hebrides), and southern Ireland.

The number of English and Welsh migrants to British America fell considerably after 1700. One estimate has it as low as 44,100 to British North America, but that is probably an underestimation. James Horn and Philip Morgan consider that 80,000 English and Welsh, 115,000 Irish, and 75,000 Scots moved to British America between 1700 and 1780, along with tens of thousands of German and Swiss migrants, with 70 percent of British migrants going to British North America being Scottish and Irish. Although Horn and Morgan probably also underestimate total migration by making migration to the West Indies lower than it was, their main point stands: English migration to the Americas declined over time. It seems clear, moreover, that English and Welsh migration was as high in the Caribbean as it was in British North America, and higher in the plantation southern colonies than in a northern colony like Massachusetts. New England received virtually no immigration over the course of the eighteenth century, especially not from England or Wales. Estimates for Jamaica suggest that European migration to that island was at least 30,000 and possibly as high as 50,000 between 1700 and 1750, and as much as between 100,000 and 125,000 in the whole colonial period in Jamaica before the outbreak of the American Revolution.[50] A careful study of total migration patterns from all of Britain, not just England, suggests that nearly 55 percent of migrants from Britain went to colonies where a plantation system was already established. Britons, especially Englishmen and -women from the metropolitan heart of the British empire, migrated to where there were abundant numbers of slaves and plantations.[51]

Astute British policy makers should also have realized that American dissent in the revolutionary period in the 1760s and 1770s was less prominent in areas with few English-born people and limited slavery. The center of revolutionary dissatisfaction in the 1760s and 1770s was Massachusetts; New England was the single core area of British America in which slavery was marginal. It received few immigrants after its one burst of migration in the 1630s and by the time of the Revolution had a population made up almost entirely of people born in the region. Average wealth in New England was also low. The number of white people in a plantation region and the wealth of that region were closely correlated.

The region of mainland America where white population growth was stagnant was wealthy Lowcountry South Carolina, especially its coastal tidal swamps, where the production of rice and indigo flourished but which were centers of deadly disease.[52]

These findings are magnified if we turn to consider wealth in the West Indies. The richest islands were those where white population was lowest and where the ratio between the black and white populations highest, such as the expanding sugar frontier of western and southeastern Jamaica and the sugar-producing islands of Antigua, St. Kitts, and Grenada. The wealth of St. Kitts and Antigua was especially arresting, as these islands had been settled early in the seventeenth century and might have been thought to have experienced, by the mid-eighteenth century, the same sort of environmental degradation that eighteenth-century Barbados suffered. Barbados had the lowest white per capita wealth of any West Indian island. It had the largest number of whites in the British West Indies, yet its total wealth in 1774 was unimpressive, making it as wealthy overall as much smaller islands like Antigua and St. Kitts. Its wealth made it more similar to Lowcountry South Carolina and Georgia than to Jamaica or Antigua. Significantly, its enslaved population was less productive than any other slave population in plantation America. It was the only colony in which the wealth of the colony divided per black person slipped below £100. Black per capita wealth (an artificial figure, as slaves saw little of this money, but one suggestive of black productivity rates) was £79 or 65 percent of black per capita wealth in Jamaica, 49 percent of black per capita wealth in the Lowcountry, and 35 percent of black per capita wealth in St. Kitts. Even enslaved people on the Tobacco Coast were more productive than slaves in Barbados, with black per capita wealth at £130.5, or 61 percent more than what it was in Barbados.[53]

From a hardheaded imperial viewpoint, extensive migration into the colonies and a rapid natural population increase in the Upper South and the interior regions of the Lower South was not a good thing, especially if few of the migrants going to these regions came from metropolitan England and its hinterland. What the backcountry regions of plantation colonies of British North America looked like from the perspective of London was places full of ethnic outsiders, mostly poor and increasingly discontented, who produced relatively little economic value for the empire and who got in the way of the productive members of the community (people who resembled the gentry, yeomen farmers, merchants, and independent householders who made up the political nation of England).[54] Populating the colonies with ethnic outsiders was not desirable, as was proven when the plantation colonies of British North America all supported their Massachusetts compatriots' call for revolution in 1775–76. It was not coincidental that it was the West Indian colonies, with a substantial number of people born in England or Scotland, that stayed loyal.[55]

Of course, the North American plantation colonies were useful as a dumping ground for convicts and as a convenient location on which to get rid of surplus populations from the poorer parts of Britain, such as Scotland and Ireland. But the composition of European population in these places—Ulster Scots, Irish, Germans, and deracinated native-born people of English descent—was disturbing from the perspective of English elites. This sentiment was shared by some of the elite in British North America as well. Benjamin Franklin famously admitted in his tract celebrating the growth of European population in the northern colonies that the racial mix in America reduced the resemblance of the northern colonies to Britain. Why, he asked, "should the *Palatine Boors* be suffered to swarm into our Settlements, and by herding together establish their Language and Manners to the Exclusion of Ours?" Similar, perhaps stronger, opinions were held by elite men in more southern colonies. For example, Anthony Stokes, chief justice of Georgia in the 1770s, reflected bitterly back in 1783 that the "swarm of men" flooding into the Georgia upcountry were scum, the descendants of criminals, and probably criminals themselves, who "will in time overrun the rice part of the country, as the Tartars in Asia have done . . . in the southern part of that country."[56]

British officials shared this disdain. The earl of Hillsborough, for example, a crucial figure in the breaking down of relationships between Britain and the thirteen colonies, was withering in his scorn for American arrivistes and for American society. Both Benjamin Franklin and George Washington detested him for his "malignant disposition towards Americans." The former condemned him as a man whose character was a compound of "conceit, wrong-headedness, obstinacy and passion." Franklin, who knew a bit about such things, experienced Hillsborough's disdain at first hand, when as secretary of state for the American department of Hillsborough rejected Franklin's credentials as the agent for Massachusetts "with something between a smile and a sneer," proving him, Franklin thought, to be "as double and deceitful as any man I ever met with."[57] The lowly social origins of American leaders and the heterogeneity and lack of civilization of "barbaric" ethnic outsiders were "facts" about American society that made politicians like Hillsborough very reluctant to give any attention to American criticism in the lead-up to the Revolution.

Settlement and Plantations

The above statements, suggesting that the most valuable American colonies were those where white population was smallest and where it struggled most to increase, are surprising because we privilege the development of American society and the growth of the white population of America over considerations of its contemporary economic importance. We follow Franklin in seeing the peopling of America by Europeans as vital to understanding its future greatness. This bias blinds us to the preferences of eighteenth-century imperial officials, who tended to be more impressed by the contemporary value of colonies than their potential future returns and who were influenced by colonial propertyholders living in England. These people are usually distinguished in the literature with the pejorative term of "absentees," implying that they were somehow delinquent in their responsibilities toward the colonies in which they were born and in which they had most of their wealth. It is better to think of such people as transatlantic brokers, negotiating a middle way between the colonies in which they derived their fortunes and the England in which they lived. It is a mistake to continue to treat these transatlantic brokers as if they were a drain on the societies from which they came and not accepted in the England to which they swore allegiance. From a British mercantilist point of view, it made perfect sense to encourage people who had made good in the colonies to return home and spend the money they had made in the metropolitan center. British leaders did not think that Massachusetts, which— although a useful source in the Seven Years' War for military recruits—was poor, rambunctious, and full of people no one had ever heard of, let alone met, was necessarily more valuable than St. Kitts, the wealthiest colony in the British empire, with its richest citizens able to be productive members of the English political nation.[58]

The colonization of British America led to two types of colonies: colonies of settlement and colonies of exploitation.[59] The first set of colonies had populations full of white settlers who claimed the benefits of English descent, especially political autonomy. The second set of colonies had small and transient groups of European residents, mostly men of some social background aspiring to wealth, hailing from metropolitan

England and its hinterland, presiding over massive populations of non-Britons. The model for the latter in the third quarter of the eighteenth century, of course, was the East India Company and its rule of Bengal.[60] Before the nineteenth century, it was the East India Company model of colonization, rather than the settlement model of British North America, that was favored by British statesmen on the relatively rare occasions on which they contemplated imperial matters. In the mercantilist model, what mattered was what economic gain colonies brought to Britain. Imperialists assessed matters using hardheaded analyses of national interest. Commerce was conducive to national hegemony, rather than to international harmony. Economic superiority was thus a positional good, and, as the Jamaican political economist Isaac de Pinto wrote in 1774, "Jealousy of commerce, and competition for power, create enmity between nations as well as between individuals." Of course, people disagreed about the right course to pursue in imperial matters. But it was unusual for British leaders to think of colonies in the way that Franklin urged in *Observations*: as homes to rapidly growing populations of British descent whose sheer numbers were worth celebrating. Their concerns were more mundane and immediate: how did colonies increase the wealth, power, and national prestige of the mother country?[61] Colonists, of course, had different concerns. They were exercised by whether their colonies were growing in population as well as in wealth, because by the middle of the eighteenth century the size and growth of a colony's population seemed as indicative of its future prosperity as its wealth and its contributions to national coffers.

British North America had many settlers in plantation areas who claimed full membership in British society by dint of their ancestors having removed from Britain to America in the seventeenth century. This means of populating plantation areas would have been a surprise to the men who conceived of Britain's first settlements overseas, although from the start occupying, cultivating, and inhabiting land was a defining strength of Britain's presence in the Americas, compared with colonization efforts in the Americas undertaken by Spain.[62] But the creation of surging populations of colonists was not the original intention of English colonization. The term "plantation" originally meant those farms on the outskirts of London that gave London its fruits and flowers. The service nature of the plantation to metropolitan needs was implicit from the start.

During the seventeenth century the idea of "plantation" evolved into two distinct concepts: the occupation of colonial space and entrepreneurial agriculture. By the eighteenth century these two definitions had merged. After 1700 the common definition of a plantation was a privately owned estate in tropical or subtropical British America that produced agricultural staples for the transatlantic marketplace. It was a novel meaning, in which the primary purpose of a plantation as a place that brought benefit to the metropolis was combined with a sense of the plantation as an exogenous location in which planters transformed wilderness into a settled, British place.[63] In America the second notion came to predominate colonial thinking. In Britain, however, the first notion had considerable purchase. Franklin's argument that the purpose of colonization was to produce populations of neo-Britons who would eventually come to outnumber metropolitan Britons was for most imperial thinkers a novel, bizarre, and ultimately unwelcome concept.[64] It played little part, for example, in Adam Smith's conception of empire as a means of promoting the economic wealth of the home country.[65]

When the English thought about plantations, and especially when they decided to invest in the empire, they focused on places where whites were small in number, blacks numerous, and plantation agriculture highly profitable. When English people of means decided to immigrate to the Americas in the eighteenth century, they favored Jamaica, Grenada, eastern Florida, and Georgia rather than the Chesapeake—and certainly not the American North.[66] Men without means, including those who were transported for crime, were less enamored of the most prosperous plantation places; rather, they stuck to colonies, such as New York, Pennsylvania, and above all Maryland.[67] Investors who flooded into imperial colonization schemes in the second and third quarters of the eighteenth century, by contrast, put their money overwhelmingly into the newly developing plantation lands of the Lowcountry and the West Indies. The big players in eighteenth-century colonial commerce disproportionately focused their attentions on new lands opened up to settlement, be they in Jamaica in the first decade of the eighteenth century or in the Ceded Islands, especially Grenada, in the decade following the Peace of Paris in 1763, rather than upon lands full of established settlers.[68]

Super Merchants

Simon Smith has examined the financial portfolios of "transatlantic super merchants" in the eighteenth-century British Atlantic and makes some useful points about their geographical orientation. He notes their concentration of interest in the highly profitable new plantation areas of the West Indies, where rates of return on loans were 7 percent between 1732 and 1753, compared to annual rates of return between 3 and 4 percent in English loans or annuities. Only East India stock provided comparable rates of return on investment, and in that area of investment there was a considerable amount of trading that was "indicative of what today we would call insider trading."[69] Smith analyzed the wealth strategies of Henry Lascelles (1690–1753), a Bridgetown merchant who returned to Britain in 1732, having established himself as a major landholder. Through extensive trade with and moneylending to the plantations and skillful deployment of capital in Britain, he died one of the richest men in England, worth £500,000. His wealth in the colonies was derived heavily from mercantile and slave trading with the eastern Caribbean. Upon his death in 1753 he had £226,772 invested in seventy-eight loans to West Indian planters, all but six in Barbados. One of the people he lent to was Gedney Clarke, Sr. The loan was unfortunate because his heir, Gedney Clarke, Jr., went bankrupt after the great credit crisis of 1772–73, a financial setback in Britain in which colonial credit was abruptly scaled back, especially in regions where the Clarkes had considerable involvement, notably the Dutch colonies in South America and in the Ceded Islands. Clarke Sr. was originally from a prominent and well-connected family of Salem, Massachusetts. He used those connections to develop a real estate and planting empire in Virginia, Nova Scotia, Barbados, Tobago, Grenada, and the Dutch colony of Demerara-Essequibo. His long-term trading relationship with the Lascelles was cemented when his eldest son married Henry Lascelles's niece.[70]

What is significant about the Clarkes' holdings is that they did little business in the elder Clarke's native Salem, but concentrated instead on investing in West Indian plantations. Clarke Sr.'s major real estate holdings were in plantation America, with land worth £1,344 in 1755 in Virginia; a further two estates and land in Bridgetown, in Barbados, worth £16,007; and land in Demerara-Essequibo worth £80,000. Altogether the gross asset value of his plantation land was £105,000. Between 1755 and 1772 he and his son diversified those holdings by reducing the Demerara-Essequibo holdings and buying property in Grenada and Tobago worth over £100,000, while increasing his Barbadian holdings to £38,815 in value.[71]

The Clarkes' involvement in Demerara-Essequibo is the most interesting of these investments. These colonies were raw frontier settlements with great opportunities. Barbadian merchants thought them highly desirable places to invest, even if some merchants were deterred by the undeveloped nature of the place, the enormous number of black slaves compared to white men, and the proximity and example of Berbice, where a slave revolt had occurred in 1763 that threatened to destroy the plantation system in that colony.[72] Investment in Essequibo in the mid-1740s, when Clarke Sr. was making his first forays into the region, was all the rage in Barbados. The governor of Barbados, Henry Grenville, noticed Clarke's investment in Dutch America soon after the 1746 opening of the colonies up for foreign settlement, concluding that "Esequibe Estates are much in Fashion here." These were significant investments. Clarke thought in 1762 that "a Sugar Plantation must be reckoned at not less than £10,000 here and a Coffee Plantation about £8,000." Clarke Sr. was strongly committed to Demerara-Essequibo, restocking three plantations with eighty female slaves in 1764, the year of his death. His son, however, was less sanguine about the colony's prospects. He thought the government corrupt and riven by factional division, was concerned about the possibility of slave revolt, and lamented a terrible drought in 1769 and drops in commodity prices in 1770. Clarke Jr. sold out and used the profits to buy estates in Grenada and Tobago, both new areas of plantation development. Sadly, he bought these plantations at inflated prices during a prolonged economic boom, using borrowed money, the debt for which he could not afford to service. The credit crisis of 1772–73 pushed him into bankruptcy. Buying into new plantation areas was not always wise, as a downturn in both the Ceded Islands and also the Dutch South American colonies proved in 1772 and 1773. But it was these places that attracted investor interest.[73] After 1763 money poured into the new plantation areas, leading to a classic bubble in slaves and land values.[74]

If successful colonization was inversely related to the size of white population (the more whites, the less valuable a colony was; the smaller the population, the more wealth for the home country it produced), why has this seemingly counterintuitive fact about eighteenth-century colonization been so little commented upon? One reason is that what we might call the "population principle" was deeply ingrained in the mid-eighteenth-century imagination. It was close to impossible for eighteenth-century Britons, living at a time when the percentage of the world's population that was British was increasing at an unprecedented pace, to think that a growing population was anything other than an entirely good thing.[75] The congruence of British industrial wealth, a growing imperial presence throughout the world, and a population notable for its fecundity did not seem coincidental to late eighteenth-century Britons. Indeed, the very model of an Englishman was a gentleman coming out of church with a blooming wife and a brood of healthy children.[76]

Conversely, populations that were not increasing seemed both immoral and also economically inefficient. As the liberal abolitionist Thomas Babington Macaulay exclaimed in 1832, "Why is all America teeming with life and why are the West Indies becoming desolate? Even 'the worst governed state of Europe—in the worst managed condition of society—the people still increase,' whether in Ireland, Russia and the slaves of North America."[77]

Population, Development, and Guiana

We tend to share eighteenth-century European assumptions about how the vitality of a population says something about the prosperity of a society. White West Indians seemed very unimpressive people in an industrializing country like Britain that could increase its wealth at the same time as it sustained large population increases. By contrast, white colonial populations in tropical settings that were unable to increase their population naturally, and whose syphilitic, invalid population flocked to Britain's spas, were thought deficient. At a time when the ideal English gentleman was like the fecund George III, with his fifteen children, the fast-living, sallow-faced planter who eschewed the bonds of holy matrimony and brought few children into the world was a symbol of corruption due to an excess of luxury and excess nervous simulation. As Mark Harrison comments, people in this period of rapid English population increase were strongly inclined to believe that "whether produced in colonies, the ballroom or the factory, the manliness of a proud and martial nation were [sic] being undone by illness." Manliness went with reproduction; effeminacy could be implied by childlessness. White populations in Britain and America were expanding rapidly throughout the eighteenth century, especially after 1750. But West Indian populations—hybrid, debilitated, effeminized—were declining in numbers. This decline was a sure symbol of corruption, race mixing, and cultural philistinism. The fear of West Indian disease and population decline was intensely worrying to some imperial reformers because it raised the specter of irreversible degeneration.[78]

We also think that small free populations in slave societies were vulnerable to slave revolt. Colonial British Americans could count just as we can, and what they noted when they did the numbers was that the ratio of blacks to whites in the most successful plantation societies in the West Indies and in the Lowcountry was disproportionately in favor of blacks, sometimes in ratios of 15:1. When the ratios were so much in favor of the black population, contemporaries and modern historians have assumed, slaves were likely to revolt. That is not, however, how eighteenth-century slave owners saw matters. Slave revolts in the eighteenth century were actually few in number and were relatively easily put down. A small white population was not as vulnerable as it seemed, especially when it was protected by imperial forces and when it used overwhelming violence against slave populations routinely and with imperial support.

The ideal British American colony from the perspective of London money men was one in which British settlement was limited, slavery was the dominant form of economic organization, the management of property was delegated to salaried employees resident in the colonies for only a few years before either returning or becoming plantation owners themselves, and there was abundant fresh land available for plantation expansion. In short, when they thought of imperial investment they looked for American counterparts to India rather than to settler colonies such as Australia or Canada.[79] This perspective about what constituted the ideal colony and the perfect colonial relationship with imperial power helps to explain why so many Britons in 1763 supported what now seems to be an indefensible position, which was to take Guadeloupe in the peace negotiations with the French rather than the vast expanses of Canada. To modern audiences, the choice seems obvious. A small sugar-producing island with very few white inhabitants was no match for a vast, continent-sized possession full of natural resources and with a healthy climate that would lead eventually to a large and flourishing population of white settlers. But that was not how many imperialists saw it at the time. The decision to take Canada, made mostly on grounds of defense, was roundly criticized in Britain as being a blatant instance of self-interested lobbying by a West India lobby determined to keep sugar prices artificially high by restricting supply. Foreigners were also puzzled. Britain's decision, for example, to keep Canada perplexed the authors of the *Histoire des Deux Indes*, a best-selling interpretation of Europe's impact on the New World and the New World's impact on Europe, first published in 1770. British actions meant that "from this time England lost the opportunity . . . of seizing all the avenues, and making itself master of the sources of all the wealth of the New World." Britain, they thought, could have easily taken Mexico and from there the rest of the South American continent.[80]

Islands like Grenada and St. Kitts fulfilled most of the conditions for plantation expansion but were too small for it. Jamaica was more appropriate, though by the late eighteenth century it too was beginning to run out of fresh arable land to cultivate. The British found their ideal plantations in 1803 in the three Dutch colonies that later became British Guiana. These were colonies where most of the property was owned by nonresidents, the slave population was large and disproportionately greater than the small white population, and the amount of cultivable land was seemingly limitless. At 83,000 square miles, British Guiana dwarfed any other British West Indian plantation colony in size. Ironically, however, at least from the perspective of fans of plantation expansion, four years after taking over these colonies Britain gave itself a self-inflicted blow in respect to creating wealth in British Guiana by abolishing the slave trade, the lifeline to colonies that did not enjoy natural demographic growth in their enslaved population. The mid-nineteenth-century imperial theorist Herman Merivale, who was no great fan of slavery, thought it probable that the abolition of the slave trade injured West Indian trade to such an extent that Britain "surrendered the means of preserving and extending our colonial opulence." He had British Guiana especially in mind when making this statement, believing it "one of the most productive countries on the face of the globe," and one that, "had the slave trade continued[,] . . . would have exceeded Cuba in prosperity."[81]

Certainly the prospects for future growth when Britain first started to get seriously involved with Dutch Guiana seemed limitless. The colonies were caught up in the American and French revolutionary wars, changing hands between the Netherlands, France, and Britain six times between 1780 and 1803. The British were the most dominant players in these takeovers, and by 1802 seven out of eight plantations were in British hands. The years immediately before Britain took over were ones of remarkable prosperity and growth. Profits were very high. In 1799 a coffee planter estimated that he could make a profit of £6,000 on one crop alone. Planters poured into the island from other British colonies, notably Barbados. As a result, between 1780 and 1802 sugar exports rose 433 percent, coffee exports increased by 233 percent, and cotton exports expanded by 862 percent. The British takeover encouraged even more investment, especially in slaves. The slave population doubled in the decade before 1802, and another 20,000 African captives were brought to the colonies between 1803 and 1805, increasing the slave population by one-third. The large integrated plantation was central to such growth. Gradually Berbice, and especially Demerara and Essequibo, became devoted to sugar monoculture, produced on merged plantations with larger slave forces than anywhere else in the British West Indies or the United States. The percentage of slaves working in sugar in

Demerara-Essequibo increased from 33 percent in 1813 to 79 percent in 1834, making the colony one of the most extreme sugar monocultures in the Caribbean. It was also one of the most productive places in the West Indies, as Merivale recognized. The amount of sugar production per head increased from 0.20 per slave between 1815 and 1819 to 0.65 between 1830 and 1834. In the latter time period, productivity was 0.21 in Barbados, 0.22 in Jamaica, and 0.40 in Grenada. British Guiana and neighboring Trinidad increased its share of West Indian sugar production from just less than 20 percent between 1811 and 1823 to one-third in the last decade of slavery in the British West Indies. The result was great wealth accruing to Guiana sugar planters—and a plantation system that was notoriously harsh and so destructive of slave health that it never achieved anything close to natural reproduction.[82]

Great new fortunes might not have been possible in Jamaica or Barbados in the first decades of the nineteenth century, but they were certainly made in Berbice and Demerara-Essequibo. The most famous fortune belonged to the Liverpool merchant John Gladstone, father of the British prime minister William Gladstone. John Gladstone invested heavily in Demerara, buying the *Success* plantation in two tranches in 1812 and 1816 and stocking it with hundreds of slaves. It was a very profitable purchase. Gladstone made good money from his £80,000 investment, returning £10,000 per annum. He achieved double-digit returns (between 10 and 15 percent per annum) on *Success* and his other Guiana plantations and recouped his initial investment within just seven to eight years. His investments in British Guiana allowed him to increase his net worth from £333,000 in 1810 to £502,550 in the 1820s.

Other men who invested in British Guiana were nearly as wealthy as Gladstone. In the compensation lists given out in 1834 as recompense for slave property held by planters on the eve of emancipation, British Guiana planters were prominent beneficiaries. The person who received the single biggest compensation in 1834 was the Irish-born M.P. James Blair, whose 1,598 slaves on Blairmont fetched him £83,530. After abolition the colony's slave owners received double compensation per slave, as did slave owners in the older islands, reflecting the greater potential of the colony for future growth and the high price of slaves there. There were 2,674 awards for 84,075 British Guiana slaves in 1834 worth £4,281,032, amounting to 26 percent of all British West Indian compensation. Only Jamaican slave owners, who were much more numerous, received more money, getting £6,121,446. The largest awards, however, were disproportionately given to British Guiana planters. Of 382 awards over £10,000, 358 went to people who had estates in British Guiana.

British Guiana planters feature prominently in William Rubinstein's list of the wealthiest Britons dying in the first half of the nineteenth century. Thomas Porter, for example, died with British Guiana and British wealth over £100,000 in 1815, while James McInroy was worth £172,913 on his death in 1813. Of sixty-five signatories to a petition from a group of London "Proprietors and Mortgagees of Estates in the Colonies of Demerara and Berbice" in 1826, ten were worth more than £100,000 at death. Significantly, this high concentration of wealth was all new money: these fortunes had all been made since 1796. British Guiana, in short, was for Britain the nineteenth-century sugar frontier, just like Louisiana during the same period in the United States. New people were making new money on new land. As Nicholas Draper comments, British Guiana wealth in slave property after abolition "formed a new asset class that attracted recognizably modern, mobile capital" from very modern capitalists.[83]

The wealth of British Guiana was limited by the campaign of abolitionists first to end the slave trade and then to end slavery altogether, as Merivale acknowledged. Sugar imposed a huge demographic cost on slaves. Very few plantation regions devoted to sugar monoculture, and none that were in the earliest stages of development, were able to maintain slave populations without a substantial input of new laborers. The abolition of the British slave trade was a severe challenge to early nineteenth-century sugar planters in the Caribbean, with the exception of Barbados, where the population was increasing naturally.[84]

The Nineteenth-Century American South

No such problem existed in the American South. The establishment of the United States of America, with a government committed constitutionally to the protection and expansion of slavery, made possible, once Native American resistance to white settlement had been overcome, new plantations and large populations of enslaved people in Georgia, Alabama, Mississippi, and the newly acquired lands of Louisiana. A flourishing internal slave trade, with slaves from the slave-exporting states of Virginia and Maryland sent to the Deep South and Louisiana, was crucially important in securing the success of these new plantations: Virginia was nineteenth-century Louisiana's Angola.[85] Without an excess slave population in Virginia that could be sent south to Louisiana, the economy of the Deep South could not have grown so rapidly in the antebellum period. Moreover, without the boost that slave sales provided for cash-strapped Virginia planters, relative economic decline in the Tidewater would have been precipitous rather than gradual.[86]

In the 1780s these deep southern areas were poor, thinly settled places, inhabited by a congeries of people from several European empires and with a diverse red, white, and black population. As Adam Rothman notes, "Compared with other places in the Americas, the region scarcely registered at all in the roll of slave societies." Plantation agriculture was limited to a small strip of settlement in the Lower Mississippi Valley. By the 1820s, however, it was "the leading edge of a dynamic, expansive slave regime incorporated into the United States and firmly tied to the transatlantic system of commodity exchange."[87] This remarkable transition was due to two plantation crops, cotton and sugar, and to the increasing integration of the region into the Atlantic world. This integration left planters susceptible to economic fluctuations in Europe but also allowed them to benefit from the great expansion of British cotton manufacturing.[88] Slaves multiplied in number: in the Mississippi Territory, for example, the number of slaves increased from 3,499 in 1801 to 16,703 in 1810. As in Georgia and South Carolina previously, Louisiana planters looked to Caribbean examples for their modus operandi. They adapted Caribbean plantation techniques to their local ecologies and used advanced forms of technology pioneered in the British and especially the French West Indies, such as irrigation schemes and Otaheite sugarcane. As Rothman concludes, "They continued to improve their methods of production for the next half-century, belying the idea that slavery and technological progress are incompatible."[89]

Not all plantation schemes worked, however. The graveyard for plantation schemes was in eastern Florida, where massive interest in an area in which the promotional literature was wildly hyperbolic led to a variety of quixotic, grandiose, and expensive failures.[90] Some of these failures came about because promoters of settlement schemes failed to learn lessons from previous failures, such as the Scottish settlement at Darien in Central America in the late seventeenth century, and the French settlement at Kouroo in northern South America in the aftermath of the Seven Years' War, in which plans to establish plantation agriculture using the labor of virtuous free white husbandmen and their families fell apart owing to the exigencies of disease, climate, and motivation.[91] The most notorious such failure in eastern Florida after the Seven Years' War was New Smyrna, a utopian settlement promoted by Sir Andrew Turnbull. He thought that "Greeks would be a very proper people for settling in His Majesty's southern provinces of North America" due to their hatred of Roman Catholics, their "remarkably handsome" women, whose charm would make British settlers want to marry them, their experience with subtropical crops, and their desire to be out of the Levant and away from Turkish despotism. It was a disaster of monumental, almost comical proportions. Two years after it was founded, half the settlers were dead, and the rest were close to revolt. They suffered from severe discipline and from the rigors of a harsh, mosquito-ridden environment. As Bernard Bailyn concludes, "While in the salons of French intellectuals New Smyrna was being praised for its enlightened and benevolent intentions, in the wilderness clearings of Florida and elsewhere in the Deep South it was condemned for its terrible waste and brutality."[92]

Other large investors were no more fortunate. Wealthy investors like Denys Rolle, a rich Devon landholder, tried to populate his 80,140 acres in Florida with a ragtag collection of England's poor, who came to Florida in an old-fashioned way, as indentured servants. His scheme failed disastrously. Rolle was inexperienced in plantation business, and his utopian and impractical scheme might have been predicted to fail. The earl of Egmont's desire to recreate feudalism in the Florida wastelands was probably also doomed from the start. But even experienced and successful businessmen with plantation experience failed in Florida. Sir Archibald Grant of Monymusk, for instance, was a relative of Sir Alexander Grant, a London merchant, an M.P., and a substantial Jamaican landowner. He got assistance from Sir Alexander in setting up his scheme. The Grants lost money too. All of them sought to import white settlers and use indentured servants to clear land suitable for plantations. Each scheme failed.[93]

Even seemingly sensible and well-executed schemes that relied on slave labor rather than indentured servitude to transform swampland into plantations were unsuccessful. The London merchant and serial entrepreneurial investor Richard Oswald correctly decided to use slaves, not white servants, to work Florida fields. Having chosen, after much research, to invest in Florida rather than the Ceded Islands, as he did not want to "risk his life and fortune to purchase in a sickly island when there is a great choice of valuable land at North America to be had for a small consideration," he bought 20,000 acres forty-five miles south of St. Augustine. He stocked it, and adjoining planters' estates, with slaves from three slave ships that derived from his slave factory in Sierra Leone. The scheme was very well-planned and excellently resourced. It should have worked, but it failed, mainly because his land was a bog, useless for anything except growing indigo. His failure proved the truth of what the South Carolina merchant planter Henry Laurens claimed: East Florida was "a Paradise from whose Bourn no Money e'er returns." Oswald failed, despite his keen business sense and intelligent preparations, because the soil and climate were not propitious, because the region lacked suitable infrastructure, and, most important, because he could not get or keep decent white managers. It also failed because Oswald was ambivalent about his goals. In Florida, Oswald ceased his life-long insistence that profit was the main thing in order to treat what he was doing as an experiment, "with neither a clear model to copy nor a clear road to follow." His insistence on growing sugar and his determination, late in a life in which philanthropy had hitherto played little part, to relieve London's poor by giving them a new home in Florida were his two biggest mistakes. It showed that improvement schemes dreamed up in London did not always work in the demanding environment of plantation America.[94]

Less wealthy planters who lived in the region where Oswald failed were either more fortunate or, probably, more realistic and more skilled. They transferred seasoned hands from South Carolina and Georgia to break in their estates. Through their labor they turned vast amounts of inhospitable swamps and hammocks (well-drained and higher lands in the swamps) into profitable fields. They augmented that labor with substantial importations of slaves from Africa, including slaves brought in by Oswald. Soon Florida planters were growing rice, cotton, indigo, oranges, and a small amount of sugar, as well as harvesting lumber and preparing naval stores for export. These planters made good profits before the American Revolution intervened, forcing planters after 1784 to move to South Carolina, Georgia, or the Caribbean.[95]

Temporality

What a discussion of the travails involved in creating plantations in Florida reveals is that temporal concerns were very important in determining the evolution of plantation societies. Paying attention to time is unusual. We usually concentrate upon regional differences in understanding the course of economic growth in the plantation sector.[96] We tend to concentrate on subregional differences between plantation regions rather than differences over time, noting, for example, considerable variations between subregions in the Chesapeake tobacco-growing areas and different planting regimes in various Caribbean islands, depending on geography and crop mix.[97] But temporality is important too. Thus, while the shift to the large integrated plantation occurred pretty much simultaneously in Virginia, Jamaica, South Carolina, and Antigua between 1690 and 1720, the ways in which that shift happened differed appreciably depending on whether the economy was booming, as it was in the Lowcountry, or in severe stagnation, as in Virginia.

In some ways, of course, the West Indies and the Tobacco Coast marched together in the seventeenth century. The long slump in tobacco prices in the Chesapeake between 1680 and 1729 was accompanied in the 1680s by a similar slump in sugar prices in Barbados. Even though sugar prices improved in the 1690s, war ravaged the West Indian colonies in the War of the League of Augsburg between 1689 and 1697 and the War of Spanish Succession between 1702 and 1713. Production costs soared, shipping losses were heavy, and freight rates were close to unsustainable. War transformed the tobacco trade in this period also, turning it from a relatively open trade to one heavily controlled, with high barriers to entry and politically driven by strategically placed great planter-merchants. The West Indies, especially Barbados, survived these problems better than the Chesapeake, but West Indian planters' move to the large integrated plantation system was influenced by the imperial situation they found themselves in, as well as by plantation building.[98]

In the second quarter of the eighteenth century, the Lowcountry and the West Indies shared similar trading conditions. The long slump in the tobacco industry ended by the 1730s, and the Tobacco Coast entered into a long period of prosperity, hampered only by some downturn during the wars of the early 1740s, the late 1750s, and the early 1760s. By contrast, the West Indies experienced a marked slowdown in the 1730s, when low sugar prices ushered in a decade of recession. A threatened slave revolt in Antigua and a prolonged and unsuccessful war against Maroons in Jamaica aggravated the downturn. South Carolina followed the West Indies into a sharp and prolonged recession from about 1740, which was also accompanied by the first serious slave revolt in its history.[99]

The plantation societies of the British Atlantic world were at their height in the third quarter of the eighteenth century. Rates of profit in the West Indies were extraordinary. J. R. Ward estimates the average annual rate of return was 10.1 percent before the Seven Years' War, a healthy 13.5 percent in that war, and an appreciable 9.3 percent return between the Peace of Paris and the outbreak of the American Revolution. Such a rate of return compares very favorably with economic activity in Britain. Profits on government bonds yielded 3 to 3.5 percent annual return, while moneylenders could rely on between 6 and 8 percent on colonial loans. Returns to money laid out in agricultural improvements in England were between 6 to 12 percent. The slave trade gave somewhat higher returns, but generally below 10 percent, especially once losses from failed ships are counted in. In the Lowcountry a well-managed estate could make 10 percent return per annum in the boom years in the late 1760s and early 1770s. Virginian rates of return were somewhat below this rate but were still healthy.[100]

The results for individual income were similarly impressive. At the top end, the largest planters could clear sums per annum equivalent to the incomes of Britain's wealthiest aristocrats. Richard Pennant, the heir to two generations of rich sugar planters in central Jamaica, cleared upward of £6,400 per annum from his several plantations and over 600 slaves in the 1740s. By the early 1770s he was averaging £13,331 per annum net profit from the labors of his 1,016 slaves. The wealthiest South Carolina planters had net incomes of between £5,000 and £6,000 in the early 1770s, while Daniel Parke Custis, one of the richest planters in Tidewater Virginia, netted planting profits of £1,323 per annum from his 283 slaves between 1757 and 1759. In Maryland Richard Tilghman, the owner of 60 slaves and several thousand acres on the Upper Eastern Shore, cleared £241 annual net profit between 1740 and 1757 from his plantations. These figures show the differences in scale between wealthy men in Maryland, at the margins of the plantation system, where wealthy planters in the mid-eighteenth century probably made between £100 and £500 per annum from all sources, and Jamaica, where incomes of several thousand pounds a year were the norm for large sugar planters and rich merchants. These figures also demonstrate the much greater productivity of sugar over tobacco and grain production. Pennant's slaves produced net revenues per capita from planting of £10.5 in the 1740s and £13.1 in the 1770s. Custis expected only £4.7 net revenue per slave in the late 1750s, while Richard Tilghman produced £4 per enslaved person in the 1740s and 1750s.[101]

Risk and Failure

Of course, the possibilities of great profit were accompanied by considerable risk. Fortunes were made in the plantation sector, and plantation regimes provided wealth to most whites. But many planters failed, some catastrophically. Thomas Thistlewood's harsh portrait of his employer, John Cope, showed how even someone who was fortunate enough to inherit two large sugar estates from his father-in-law in 1754, containing 2787 acres and 442 slaves in one of the most prosperous plantation areas in British America at the time of its greatest prosperity, could fail.

Planting was an inherently risky business, and, contrary to contemporary descriptions of planters that pictured them as poor economists indifferent to anything except the mindless pursuit of pleasure, a good planter needed the full range of early modern business skills, as well as agricultural expertise. Samuel Martin of Antigua asserted in his highly regarded guide to plantership that the planter must be "adept in figures, and all the arts of economy, something of an architect, and well-skilled in mechanics," as well as an expert sugar boiler and distiller, an astute manager of both white servants and black slaves, and a "very skilled husbandman." Cope possessed few of these skills, as Thistlewood lamented privately in his diaries and once in a letter of complaint to his employer. In 1763, having served under Cope for nearly twelve years and increasingly disparaging about his many deficiencies, Thistlewood exploded in a letter to his employer following a relatively trivial dispute: "Sir, I have often thought you Certainly make it your Study how to lay this Estate under the greatest Inconveniencies . . . I have never expected better Treatment from you Whilst in your Service." He left Cope's employ on bad terms, angry that Cope was insisting on early payment of the wages he owed Cope's wife for keeping Molly Cope's slave, Phibbah, as his wife. This petty action, "while he is greatly in my debt," was proof positive of Cope's "strange meanness—but Mr. Cope is capable of any meanness whatever."[102]

Cope was not so much mean as incapable of managing his emotions, and of systematically ordering the affairs of his estate. He was a prime example of someone unable to follow Martin's sage advice. He overspent and underinvested and was a poor employer and a harsh master. He was fond, in Thistlewood's opinion, of sleeping with young slave girls and was a devoted carouser. His personal weaknesses did not bother Thistlewood unduly, but his deficiencies as a plantation manager certainly did. Thistlewood prospered; Cope, despite all his advantages in life, did not. He was able to survive as a planter in the halcyon economic boom of the 1760s and early 1770s even though even in these years he only escaped from being thrown into prison for debt by marshaling a set of favors from powerfully placed patrons. He was also unlucky. The hurricane of 1780 hit him hard, devastating his estate and what was left of his wealth. He was forced to sell Egypt, the small sugar estate Thistlewood worked on from 1751 to 1764, for £8,300 in 1784. When he died on 1 March 1792, his estate was valued at a mere £3,151, a tenth of the amount that was left by his father-in-law, William Dorrill, when he died in 1754, and £220 less than his less privileged but more talented erstwhile employee. It was looking at Cope that persuaded Thistlewood not to become a sugar planter. In 1779 he made an aside that many ordinary whites might have made: "To be the owner of a sugar works is to have external dignity for inward or external grief."[103]

Naturally, in any system individuals prosper and fail, although the plantation system favored risk takers so systematically that the number of individuals who failed in plantation societies was comparatively large by early modern standards. The greatest example of failure was that suffered by William Beckford II (1759–1844), the English-based Jamaican planter who in 1770 inherited the greatest plantation estate in the West Indies. Beckford was an accomplished and creative romantic novelist, specializing in gothic tales. But he was a dreadful businessman, neglecting the Jamaican properties that formed the basis of his wealth and through neglect allowing his attorney to gradually alienate his property to the attorney's own benefit. He was an obsessive collector and a builder of magnificent follies, expensive hobbies that eventually destroyed his estate. William Byrd III of Virginia (1728–1777) also had a particularly spectacular fall from prosperity to poverty. He inherited one of the greatest of all Virginia estates, including 179,000 acres, more than 1,000 slaves, ships, and commercial properties. By the early 1770s it was almost all gone, some due to unwise speculation in western lands, most from reckless extravagance. He epitomized elite excess. The outbreak of the American Revolution, in which both the royal governor of Virginia—John Murray, Lord Dunmore—and his fellow Virginian George Washington rejected his offers of help, led him into a deep depression, aggravated by his extreme indebtedness. On 2 January 1777 he committed suicide.[104]

What is more interesting than a few individuals rising and falling is entire planter groups in decline. One special case was the great planters of Tidewater Virginia and southern Maryland. Few Chesapeake planters fell so far as Byrd, though Benjamin Harrison V (1726–1791) came close, but the great Chesapeake planters as a whole found themselves in financial straits in the years immediately before the American Revolution. The traditional interpretation attributes their decline to excessive spending and heavy indebtedness to British mercantile firms. Planters, exemplified by William Byrd III, experienced generational decline. The children and grandchildren of the aggressive merchant-planter entrepreneurs of the early eighteenth century concentrated (unlike their ancestors) on social success and politics rather than on improving their estates. They were competent managers, but their neglect of trade limited their economic horizons and bound them into activities that rendered them vulnerable to changing economic circumstances, such as those that cropped up after the American Revolution. Moreover, when they did take financial risks, such as western land speculation, that risk taking diverted resources from more profitable activities. The transformation of an occupationally diverse planter class into a more narrowly focused group of agricultural specialists was logical and economically rational, given the changing nature of the Atlantic economy. But it meant that planters could not take advantage after the Revolution of developments outside the plantation economy, such as manufacturing and commerce in the booming town of Baltimore.[105]

The Growth of Wealth over Time

Other planter classes also made choices based on short-term economic exigencies that would come to haunt them when conditions in the Atlantic economy changed. Thinking in the short term rather than planning for the long term was a particular planter weakness, especially in the British West Indies, where high mortality rates and engagement in an inherently risky business such as sugar planting encouraged people to think of the here and now rather than the immediate, let alone the distant, future. Some contemporary observers noted planters' lack of persistence and lamented it. Edward Long's *History of Jamaica*, for example, is one long complaint by a thoughtful observer of the malign effects of Jamaicans' lack of a persevering nature.[106]

The extensive correspondence of the wealthiest early nineteenth-century Jamaican planter, Simon Taylor, a man who turned a substantial inheritance into a massive fortune as a highly effective attorney on large sugar estates, managing properties for British owners, outlines the constant tension between high annual returns and investing for the future. Taylor had continual run-ins with the overseer on Golden Grove Plantation, John Kelly, in the prosperous 1760s and 1770s over Kelly's management techniques. Kelly worked his enslaved labor force as hard as he could in order to produce extremely high annual returns. What is important to note here is that both Taylor and Kelly were extremely skilled planters; their dispute was over principles more than over the quality of their management practices. Taylor thought that the most important duty of a planter was to preserve his laboring stock. He was motivated less by humanitarianism than by cost concerns. There is precious little sign of any concern for enslaved people in his correspondence, and he had no sympathy whatsoever for abolitionists, especially William Wilberforce, whom he damned as a diabolical enemy of the empire. Slaves were expensive, and if the sugar regime was so harsh that the customary waste of lives was greater than it should be, then the cost of replacing labor was exorbitant.[107]

Taylor used a telling analogy to make his point. He told his employer, Chaloner Arcedeckne, owner of Golden Grove Estate in the sugar-rich parish of St. Thomas in the East, that "Negroes" could wear out just like machines: "They are not steel or iron and we can see neither gudgeons nor capooses last in this country." Gudgeons and capooses were small but vital parts of the vertical sugar mill that bore considerable stress. If they were too stressed, they broke, and everything ground to a halt. Slaves were like gudgeons and capooses. If they were worked, as Taylor believed they were worked at Golden Grove, "above their ability," they would collapse and die. He believed in a constant flow of enslaved people: he recommended that Arcedeckne buy £10,000 "worth of Negroes." That would have been about 150 to 200 new workers, which would bring the estate back to the 540 slaves it had when Chaloner's father, Andrew, owned the estate, instead of its current 380.[108]

Kelly thought differently. In a way he was a poor man's version of Taylor. Starting from nothing, he became a man of some wealth, using the large sums he earned as a skilled overseer to buy slaves. He owned 140 slaves by 1774, 120 of whom he sold to Arcedeckne for the large sum of £8,714, payable by installments until 1778. Before that time he earned nearly two times as much income per annum from hiring out his slaves as he did in wages. He focused very much on the short term, aiming to produce larger and larger sugar crops. He was good at what he did, however, and doubled sugar production on his estates between 1765 and 1775. Golden Grove was ideal territory for sugar planting, but turning theory into practice required a skilled manager. Kelly was that manager. Working slaves very hard, with "the poor wretches" never getting, according to Taylor, more than five or six hours' respite from work each day while harvesting and digging cane holes, Kelly produced 740 hogsheads of sugar in 1775, over double the 350 of 1769. It was "the most extraordinary crop that was ever made on any one estate in Jamaica," worth £14,000.[109]

Kelly's success kept Taylor quiet. What really bothered Taylor, however, was how Kelly continued such a punishing regime in the tough times of the American Revolution after 1778, when supplies from America dried up and slaves faced significant privation. He thought Kelly worked slaves so hard that "their hearts have been broke." Kelly gave them so few rations and favored his own slaves so methodically over his employer's when allocating out provisions, that the Golden Grove

FIGURE 5. William Clark, *Exterior of a Distillery, on Weatherell Estate.* British Library © British Library Board.

slaves "were Starving" and a "very feeble Set indeed." Golden Grove, Taylor argued, would not support "a Gang of Negroes while he [Kelly] had anything to do with it," and soon the property, with slaves "killed by overwork & harassed to Death," would be a Land without Negroes." Kelly refused to accede to Taylor's wishes and was eventually fired in 1782.[110] Here, long-term perspectives won out over short-term desires. That was not what always happened.

As is clear from comparing estimates of plantation wealth and the annual estimates of produce exported to Britain and to French and Spanish America in the 1740s made by Robert Dinwiddie, it was not just the overall wealth and income of the plantation colonies that was impressive, but also the rate of growth over time. All areas of the plantation world became more profitable over time, but the concentration of slaves in the British West Indies meant that total product and the amount of capital stock increased more rapidly there than anywhere else.[111] Rises in total wealth were translated into increases in personal wealth. Between 1685–89 and 1765–69 average inventoried personal wealth in Jamaica grew nearly fivefold, from £628 to £3,058. Growth was constant, except for a plateau of wealth increase in the 1730s and the 1740s. Between the 1680s and the 1700s average wealth (excluding realty) per wealth holder increased by 22 percent. The increases in each twenty-year period between the 1720s and the 1760s were 26 percent, with the biggest spike, 52 percent, from £809 to £1667, between the 1700s and the 1720s, when the transition to the large integrated plantation was completed.

In South Carolina a similar process occurred, although average wealth was much lower and the rates of increase generally higher. At the start of settlement, average wealth was a respectable £204, just under one-third the average wealth in Jamaica. Forty years later average wealth had increased 43 percent to £357, although since wealth in Jamaica had catapulted forward in that period the average South Carolina decedent was now only 21 percent as rich as his Jamaican counterpart. By the mid-1740s the average wealth of a South Carolina wealth holder was £539, a one-third increase over twenty years. By 1764 average wealth had increased to £1,145, indicating a massive 53 percent increase in twenty years as rice bust turned to rice boom. This huge upward spike in wealth in the 1750s and 1760s allowed the gap in wealth to be closed a little between South Carolina and Jamaica, with the average South Carolinian being 37 percent as wealthy as the average Jamaican. That gap lessened, however, in the 1770s as Jamaican wealth really took off, with average wealth increasing by percentages not seen since the 1710s to £4,033 between 1770 and 1774, a 37 percent increase over a decade.[112]

Increases in individual wealth in the tobacco-growing areas of the Chesapeake were more modest and not so constant over time. But there were increases. In Maryland average inventoried wealth increased 55 percent from £151 in the late seventeenth century to £333 in the decade before the American Revolution. Unlike in Jamaica and South Carolina, in the Chesapeake individual wealth did not increase alongside the implementation of the large integrated plantation, mainly because that transition happened when terms of the tobacco trade were at a low ebb and when the natural population increase meant there were a lot more people provide for than in the seventeenth century. Indeed, between 1680 and the 1700s average wealth probably plateaued or even declined. In the first half of the eighteenth century, average individual wealth growth was minimal. In St. Mary's County on the lower western shore, an intensively studied parish with very good records, average wealth hit a low point in the early 1730s, when it dipped below £100. Wealth climbed from the late 1730s before halting for nearly twenty years and then rapidly increasing in the quarter century before the American Revolution. These figures suggest that the transition to the large integrated plantation brought relatively few benefits to the region; but what is more persuasive is that the move to a new form of economic organization disproportionately benefited those who adopted it in two periods of unprecedently bad times, between 1689 and 1713 and between 1720 and 1732. The transition to the large integrated plantation prevented hard times becoming catastrophic economic disaster.[113]

The plantation system was especially prosperous after the end of the Seven Years' War. Planters in these years mastered the technologies of large-scale production of staple crops, advanced rapidly in means of managing and improving their slave labor forces, and had enviable access to sources of capital for investment and reinvestment, both locally and in the Atlantic world. Unsurprisingly, the success of sugar and rice planting led ambitious, entrepreneurially minded young men with capital and connections to develop fresh plantation systems in new areas such Grenada and Georgia. In this they emulated their late seventeenth-century ancestors, who transferred the Barbadian system to the Leewards, Jamaica, and South Carolina. The difference was that new planters had the experience of over a century of planting in the Americas to guide them. Unlike during the seventeenth century, when the transition to the large integrated plantation system was slow and contested, after the Seven Years' War the expansion of the plantation system was rapid, uncontested, and focused from the start on plantations rather than building slowly from small farms.

Georgia and the Ceded Islands as Plantation Societies

One advantage of a chronological framework when looking at plantations in British America is that one can detect plantation development phases. The first phase was its creation in Barbados in the mid-seventeenth century, and its gradual transmission into the Chesapeake, the Leewards, Jamaica, and South Carolina in the early eighteenth century. The next phase was the growth of planter elites in the second quarter of the eighteenth century and their ability to devise increasingly sophisticated models of plantation management in order to attain sizable wealth. Everywhere in plantation America those aims were achieved by the early 1750s. By this time all areas of the plantation world were integrated into an increasingly interdependent Atlantic economy in which both the production and the marketing of staple goods was being perfected.[114] By the end of the Seven Years' War in 1763, it was clear that the plantation system was the most effective means of utilizing American land. Eric Williams was wrong that the plantation system was on the verge of precipitous decline after the American Revolution. The

American Revolution threw a wrench into the works and led to economic and political problems for planters in the Caribbean and economic meltdown in the Lowcountry. But by the time the French Revolution led to the cataclysmic destruction of the richest plantation society, Saint-Domingue, the British and American plantation systems had recovered from revolutionary difficulties and were steaming ahead.[115]

By this time ordinary white people had come to terms with the plantation system. Even though ordinary white people played only minor roles in the expansion of the system from the 1750s on, their lack of opposition to a move from subsistence farming to profitable plantation agriculture meant that new plantation societies in the West Indies (Grenada, Guiana, and Trinidad) and in North America (Georgia and the Deep South) did not have to suffer the same struggles to get established as they had in seventeenth-century Virginia and Jamaica. In a replay of what had happened in Barbados in the 1640s, the evolution of plantation culture in these societies proceeded so rapidly that the various stages of development seemed to betoken a revolution rather than gradual change.[116] Ordinary white people did not always participate directly in the plantation economy: there were opportunities outside the plantation system, notably in the large plantation towns of Baltimore, Charleston, Bridgetown, and Kingston, where people could acquire decent competencies. Unlike in the seventeenth century, these alternative opportunities were pursued within economies in which the large integrated plantation was dominant.

We can see how the process worked by examining Georgia's rapid transition from a struggling colony producing little of importance into a flourishing plantation society in the fifteen years between 1750 and 1765. On the surface, Georgia seems to have gone through the same evolution from subsistence farming to plantation agriculture that happened elsewhere. It did so rapidly and without significant contestation from below, emulating in its speed of transition what had happened in Barbados a century before, but without that island's social tensions. In the third quarter of the eighteenth century, Georgia's Lowcountry was transformed from a handful of hardscrabble farms into nearly three hundred plantations producing rice for export to Britain. That it became a society dedicated to nearly monocultural staple crop production on large integrated plantations was deeply ironic given its founding ethos. Georgia had been founded in direct opposition to the evils of the plantation system in nearby South Carolina, born from a worthy but unrealistic philanthropic vision in which it was to become a model society of yeoman farmers in which slavery was banned and in which residents would find moral redemption in subsistence farming. It was founded, in short, as a rejection of the Barbadian plantation model. It did not work. The first years of settlement in Georgia saw it struggle to survive: it had no economic base to sustain a slowly growing white population and nothing to encourage moneyed men to invest.[117]

Figures show how quickly Georgia was transformed into a flourishing plantation society. Rice production jumped tenfold in fifteen years, and the population increased from 1,700 whites and 300 blacks in 1749 to 12,000 blacks and 5,000 whites in 1772. In the developed plantation parishes of St. Philip and St. John, the ratio of blacks to whites was as high as seven to one. Charleston and Savannah merchants played crucial roles as investors, introducing up-to-date irrigation technology, buying up large shipments of Africans, and often becoming Georgia planters themselves. In 1774 Georgians bought 1,500 Africans direct from Africa and a further 1,300 of 4,200 put up for sale in Charleston. The result was an increase in the black population of Georgia by 18 percent in a single year.[118] As much as 25 percent of the rice crop in the 1770s was produced by twelve or thirteen planters, most of them with good connections in Georgia politics. The largest planter was James Wright. He owned 523 slaves on eleven plantations who produced around 3,000 barrels of rice, which accounted for 17.2 percent of total rice production in the colony.[119]

These large planters had access to considerable capital from Savannah and Charleston, as well as from Britain. They could also draw on their own resources, being reasonably prosperous men on first entry into Georgia. Many, like Jonathan Bryan, who established the first rice plantation in the region and eventually owned 32,000 acres and 250 slaves, came from the Carolinas.[120] Others were Scots from St. Kitts. All migrants brought with them the culture of their home colonies and a fierce desire to acquire African slaves. That desire also extended to planters who came from Britain. William Knox, a British absentee planter, wrote to his agent James Habersham, in 1768: "What is the matter that you have bought no Negroes for me this season? No, pray don't let any of your confounded Punctillio get the better of your good sense and friendship for me in this business. Negroes I must have or I shall never forgive you."[121]

Their efforts led to dramatic profits: the annual rate of return was as high as 15 to 20 percent immediately before the American Revolution.[122] Planters also brought with them the repressive slave code of South Carolina and added a few twists of their own, such as mandating capital punishment for poisoning.[123] In short, these entrepreneurial capitalists drew on a century of experience in the British Atlantic World, one that started in mid-seventeenth-century Barbados, to develop a highly profitable and extremely exploitative plantation system in the southernmost British North American colonies. What they developed, moreover, was almost a pure monoculture. Georgians showed little interest in growing anything other than rice, of which a greater proportion than that from South Carolina was traded directly to Britain. Their share of Lowcountry rice production soared from 5 percent to 13 percent of exports in less than a decade.[124]

Even larger profits were possible in the rapidly developing plantation areas of the Ceded Islands. Money poured into the Ceded Islands, especially Grenada and the Grenadines, after the Seven Years' War. To an extent, such investment was unsustainable, as was to be proved in the credit crisis of 1772–73 when not just Gedney Clarke but a number of overeager and overextended investors from Barbados and Britain found themselves in financial trouble. The land commissioners in the Ceded Islands were inundated with requests from purchasers wanting land ideally suited for growing tropical crops, French settlers in the islands were equally eager to sell, and merchants in Britain were keen to advance substantial credit on easy terms. The scale of investment in Grenada, in particular, increased in a decade "to an incredible amount," as a group of Grenada planters explained to the Board of Trade to help them understand how "in a few Years near the whole property of the Island became British, either by purchase, Mortgage, or other Securitys."[125]

The result was great debt and massively increased production. Sugar production increased more than fourfold in Grenada between 1762 and 1772. Average wealth per white capita increased to £2,751 and the amount of wealth per capita divided by the black population to £175. The region became close to a monoculture. This happened first in Grenada, where by 1819 83 percent of slaves worked in sugar, mostly in its windward parishes, and then in St. Vincent, which became the leading sugar producer in the Windward Islands in the last decades of slavery. Both St. Vincent and Grenada had very high rates of productivity, with slaves in the islands producing more tons of sugar per slave (0.5 ton per slave between 1815 and 1819 in St. Vincent and between 1820 and 1824 in Grenada) than in any other British American colony before Demerara got into high gear in the late 1820s. Productivity rates in these islands were twice as high as in early nineteenth-century Jamaica. Planters in the Ceded Islands also produced other tropical goods, notably coffee, cotton, and cocoa in Dominica and cotton in the miniature plantation economy of Carriacou in the Grenadines.[126]

David Ryden has outlined how, after the Seven Years' War, plantation development in this area could proceed very rapidly in an examination of a census of plantations in late eighteenth-century Carriacou. He shows how for a brief moment some investors in the plantation sector built large plantations very quickly in an industry—cotton before the invention of the cotton gin in 1792—often assumed to have been dominated by small planters. From producing virtually no cotton before the 1770s, planters in Carriacou produced 1 million pounds of cotton per annum by the 1780s, amounting to half of all of Grenada's cotton production and 9–14 percent of cotton production in the British West Indies. Between 1776 and 1790 Carriacou planters increased cotton production by 30 percent, abandoning other crops to become a cotton monoculture and doing so on estates that rivaled sugar estates in size and profitability. The largest plantation, Dumfries, owned by the London merchant William Todd had 544 acres and 275 enslaved workers. It produced 96,000 pounds of cotton in 1790, worth £5,000 on the London market. These cotton estates exhibited strong economies of scale, producing 280 pounds of cotton per annum per enslaved worker. Todd's slaves produced 349 pounds of cotton per slave annually. The heyday of cotton in Carriacou was short-lived, ending after the invention of the cotton gin opened up cotton production in the United States' vast Southwest. But in its heyday, as one observer put it in the 1780s, "the Carriacou Estates have prospered more uniformly and generally than any other of our West Indian islands."[127]

Two Plantation Models

A study of the development of plantations in the Ceded Islands and in Georgia in the second half of the eighteenth century shows that everywhere plantations were established they brought wealth not only to planters and many ordinary white men and their families, but also to imperial Britain. But though the majority of plantation societies were prosperous, they were not all the same. Indeed, by the late eighteenth century two models of plantation systems had developed in British America. The first system, centered on the Chesapeake but moving through the early nineteenth century to the cotton frontier of the American South and Southwest, had large populations of whites, many of whom were not connected directly to the plantation sector; and a naturally growing slave population, meaning that planters were not reliant on either the Atlantic or the domestic slave trade. The second system was the sugar-growing economies of the West Indies, with very small white populations and large slave populations that were sustained, at least before 1807, only by an efficient and dynamic Atlantic slave trade. The end of the slave trade in 1807 proved a severe challenge to the continued viability of this system.[128]

The development of two kinds of plantation societies reflected two different demographic regimes. Much united the plantation societies of British North America and the British West Indies, but demography separated them. The American South had a naturally growing and diverse white population and, after the 1720s in the Chesapeake and by the 1770s in South Carolina, a naturally growing enslaved population. By contrast, neither the white nor the enslaved population grew naturally in the British West Indies. The nature of population growth in each plantation system shaped the kinds of slave societies that developed. It also helped influence responses to British policies toward America in the revolutionary period. It was inconceivable, given their dependence on the Atlantic slave trade and on extensive trade in provisions and food from other places in the British empire, that West Indians would contemplate a commercial boycott of British goods such as that so enthusiastically enacted in the Chesapeake by wealthy planters in 1769.

Some leading Virginia gentlemen would have liked to extend this boycott of commercial goods to the slave trade. Virginia legislators tried in 1767 and 1769 to impose double duty on imported Africans and in 1772 tried to abolish the slave trade to Virginia altogether. One of the leaders of this campaign was Thomas Jefferson, who had been scarred by a brief and unsuccessful experience as a slave trader. Jefferson became convinced by his experience that participation in the slave trade was a means whereby Britain ensnared people like himself in debt and led to his passionate denunciation of the slave trade in his draft of the Declaration of Independence. Not all Virginians were convinced. The attempt to abolish the slave trade to Virginia united imperial officials, British slave merchants, and ordinary white men, especially in the developing Virginia Piedmont, seeking to buy their first slaves against wealthy planters. Poorer planters wanted to increase the availability of slaves and reduce slave prices through an enhanced supply of Africans.[129]

Jefferson's campaign was thus notably two-faced. Virginia's planters later proclaimed that they supported an attempt to suspend the slave trade in 1772 because of concern about the immorality of the trade. Some also suggested that they voted as they did because they feared Virginia had too many slaves and thus was becoming vulnerable to slave rebellion. Arthur Lee drew on parallels with Rome, "brought to the very brink of ruin by the insurrections of their Slaves," and warned Virginians that their greater number of slaves than in Rome and annual importations of several thousand captive Africans per annum would be a "fearful odds, should they ever be excited to rebellion." In fact, opposition to the Atlantic slave trade from established Tidewater planters had little to do with either morality or apprehension of slave agency. Tidewater planters had no difficulty selling slaves in a flourishing internal market. They no longer, however, needed to buy slaves, especially expensive Africans, because their slave populations were growing naturally. Keeping the duty on slave imports very high and discouraging slave ships from coming to the Chesapeake kept the prices of their own slaves, who were sold to smaller planters or to burgeoning markets farther south, very high. Twelve years before the attempted ending of the Atlantic slave trade by the Virginia House of Burgesses, Governor Francis Fauquier accused "old Settlers who have bred great Quantity of Slaves, and would make a Monopoly of them by a Duty which they hope would amount to a prohibition" of waging a class conflict against "the rising Generation who want Slaves" at reasonable prices. Jefferson had much individually to gain from the policies he urged Virginia to adopt. It was the demographic structure of Virginian slavery, not a concern over the nature of the Atlantic slave trade, that drove Jefferson and wealthy slave-owning legislators to take the action they did.[130]

As noted above, the most important development in the history of slavery in the Chesapeake was a very early transition to a naturally growing enslaved population. The transition occurred in the 1720s in Virginia; in the 1770s in South Carolina; in the 1810s in Barbados; and not until after emancipation, in the 1840s, in Jamaica. In Virginia the rate of natural increase was so high that by 1790 it had 293,000 slaves, with a further 103,000 in other areas of the Chesapeake, meaning that the enslaved population of the region was much greater than in Jamaica, despite an almost negligible Atlantic slave since the 1760s and significant enslaved outmigration. From a high point of 15,700 Africans shipped to Virginia in the 1730s, the decades of the 1750s and 1760s saw fewer than 10,000 Africans arrive at America, and in the first half of the 1770s fewer than 4,000 Africans came to Virginia. By this time the percentage of Africans in the enslaved population was vanishingly small: less than 16,000 in 1770, decreasing to 4,740 in 1790, by which time African-born slaves were just 2 percent of the enslaved Virginian population. In the most highly populated slave regions of Virginia, between the York and the Lower James Rivers, African migration had dried up to a trickle, with only 519 Africans going there between 1761 and 1774.

By the Revolution, Tidewater Virginia had an overwhelmingly creole enslaved population.[131]

The decline in the number of Africans in the enslaved population helped the transition to a native-born population go even faster. By the 1740s, the decade when it became clear that Tidewater Virginia did not need an Atlantic slave trade to keep increasing population levels, over 30,000 of a population increase of 40,000 came from natural increase. By the 1780s virtually all of the nearly 70,000 increase in slave numbers came from births to creole women. Slave women were producing more than enough children to replace the adults of previous generations, and they were having their children sufficiently young to allow for large families and rapid intergenerational growth. Creole slave women were healthier than African-born women and thus had both larger families and also families in which most children survived to adulthood. The result was rapid population growth among a people who, noted one clergyman as early as 1724, "are very prolific among themselves."[132]

Virginia planters noted that slave women were good and frequent breeders. A clergyman argued in 1756 that slave women were "far more prolific . . . than white women," due, he believed, to their simple diet and their "being used to hard labor."[133] Whites noticed such things but did little directly to encourage a vibrant native-born demographic regime. It is possible that some planters were persuaded to adopt ameliorative policies after the Seven Years' War in order to preserve and improve slave health.[134] But the majority of the evidence suggests that attempts to improve slaves' demographic performance were limited and took a back seat to planters' determination to improve agricultural productivity. As everywhere in plantation America, Virginia planters were conscious agricultural improvers. That improvement did not mean lessening work demands on enslaved people. Pregnant women were given little respite from work, and children and old people alike were worked extensively in backbreaking labor. Improved health conditions owed relatively little to planter initiatives. They flinched at the potential loss of labor through pregnancy or sickness but were not much concerned with slaves' welfare or worried about them dying. Agricultural improvement tended toward making work more efficient and productive rather than on making sure that human capital was healthy.[135] And even when planters appeared to be acting in ways that would increase slave fertility through good treatment, their objectives behind such indulgences were suspect. Planters after the turn of the nineteenth century occasionally gave pregnant women and new mothers payments and better food, but, Thomas Jefferson explained, such actions were in planters' self-interest, since he thought "a woman who brings a child every two years more valuable than the best man on the farm."[136] What best explains the better demographic performance of Virginian over West Indian slaves was not the attitudes of masters, but a less malign disease environment and the less arduous demands of working on tobacco or grain farms rather than in rice, indigo, and especially sugar. Better nutrition resulting from slaves' not having to grow their own food on provision grounds may also have contributed to population growth.[137]

Slave demographic performance was quite different in the West Indies, especially in the heartlands of sugar production such as eighteenth-century Jamaica and nineteenth-century British Guiana. Both fertility and mortality were problematic: relatively few women were mothers and most of their children died at birth or in infancy; and slave life expectancy, especially for new arrivals from Africa, was extremely poor. The West Indies suffered a crisis of reproduction, with negative rates of natural increase—often highly negative—everywhere before the American Revolution, and everywhere, except perhaps Barbados, in the period between the Revolution and the abolition of the slave trade. In Jamaica, for example, 575,000 importations from Africa in the eighteenth century resulted in a slave population that increased by only a little more than 250,000. Without the slave trade, demographic decline would have been catastrophic. The adoption of ameliorative measures toward slave women after 1800 helped arrest demographic decline, but the numbers of enslaved persons still fell 12 percent in Jamaica between 1807 and the abolition of slavery in 1834.[138]

The results of the differing demographic regimes in Virginia and Jamaica have been explored to remarkable effect by Richard Dunn. He has made a painstaking and revealing reconstruction of the individual and collective lives of over 2,000 slaves on Mesopotamia Estate in Westmoreland, Jamaica and Mount Airy in Richmond County, Virginia. He shows that the contrasting histories of these two slave populations illustrate the most basic difference in slave life in the two plantation regions. Mount Airy was a very large plantation, with 381 slaves in 1809 and 378 in 1828. It enjoyed a healthy population increase, with 252 births and 142 deaths over twenty years. It was a plantation in flux, though in different ways than in Jamaica. Hardly any slaves were purchased (just 4 between 1809 and 1828), and relatively few (36) were brought in from other estates belonging to the Tayloe family that owned Mount Airy. Many more slaves were moved off the estate, with 109 being transferred off Mount Airy and the majority of the slaves on the property eventually moving to new plantations in Alabama from the 1830s. Another

44 slaves were sold from Mount Airy in the early nineteenth century. Neither plantation regime was beneficial to enslaved people, but the circumstances of the two regimes were very different. From the mid-eighteenth century to emancipation in 1834, life on Mesopotamia was shaped and stunted by deadly work regimens, rampant disease, and dependence on the Atlantic slave trade for new laborers. The only way that Mesopotamia's owners kept slave numbers constant was through heavy importation of slaves, either from neighboring estates or through the Atlantic slave trade. Between 1762 and 1807 the owners of Mesopotamia purchased 112 Africans, and between 1762 and 1833 they bought 307 slaves from local sources. They needed to do this because the number of births between 1762 and 1833 was just 416 and deaths were 751. At Mount Airy, where births consistently outnumbered deaths until emancipation in 1865, "surplus" slaves were sold or moved to distant work sites, and families were routinely broken up. Flux was a feature of life on both plantations, both where family life was very difficult to achieve and also where families flourished, at least demographically.[139]

Dunn chose to track the lives of two women, one from each estate, to show the vicissitudes of slave existence in mature plantation systems defined by quite different demographic structures. Sarah Affir was a field hand on Mesopotamia who suffered constant poor health and the death of her children while they were still young, and who seems to have lived a miserable life, alleviated only by producing a son out of an alliance with a white man who was able to move out of field work and whose quadroon child was almost able to escape the worst of slavery. Like most slave families in Jamaica, Sarah's was haunted by death.[140] This story, well-documented, is perhaps more familiar as a historiographical example than the nuanced biography of Esther Grimshaw and her daughter, Winney, that Dunn also relates. Esther was born around 1799, the second of three surviving children of native-born domestic servants. She worked as a spinner for thirty-four years. A spinner was a less arduous job than working in the field and one where a slave was less likely to be sexually compromised than as a domestic. By the mid-1840s she was sick and worn out. The work was not easy, even though it was a better occupation than enjoyed by many female slaves. She used cotton and flax grown on the farm and wool sheared from plantation sheep to make slave clothing, work she performed in addition to being a mother. She married Bill Grimshaw, a skilled carpenter, in the early 1820s and proceeded to have seven children, six of whom survived into adulthood, between 1824 and 1837. But things went badly wrong for her in 1845. In that year her husband was flogged and escaped from the estate. He became the only permanent absconder from Mount Airy, eventually ending up in New Brunswick by 1851 (after which date we know nothing more about him). The owner of Mount Airy, William Henry Tayloe, took his revenge by breaking up Bill and Esther's family, sending most of her children to his new cotton estate in Alabama, moving Esther to distant slave quarters away from her remaining children, and, in July 1846, selling her and her nine-year-old son away from Mount Airy for $300, most of which was paid in respect of the child. Tayloe's callous attitude toward a slave who had worked for him for over thirty years and who had provided him with six slaves collectively worth thousands of dollars is summed up in his contemptuous entry next to Esther's name in a list of slaves: "sold, or rather given away."[141]

Tayloe's comments show that we cannot think of the Virginia slave regime as being less harsh than that of Jamaica, or of Virginian masters as less calculating and as better paternalists than West Indians. The demographic experience of slaves varied between the two places, but the slave-management practices put in place were similar insofar as they were founded on the idea that manipulating human capital in the form of enslaved people was the essential means of making money. The Tayloes were sellers, not buyers, while the Barhams of Mesopotamia were buyers rather than sellers. On the surface, the lives of slaves working on a sugar estate in eighteenth-century Jamaica were immeasurably worse than in nineteenth-century Virginia. Dunn made this comparison in an earlier article on the two plantations, declaring that "if one had to be a slave, Mount Airy was a better place than Mesopotamia."[142] Thirty-seven years later, he is more circumspect, arguing that whether in Jamaica or in Virginia the institution of racial enslavement was pernicious to the core.

The reason Sarah Affir prospered less than Esther Grimshaw was because she worked in sugar. Sugar was a uniquely destructive plantation crop. In no place where sugar was cultivated did slave populations increase; indeed, mortality on sugar plantations was extremely high, family formation was stunted, and slave health was excessively poor.[143] But planters' attitudes toward enslaved people were much the same, whether the slave owners were absentee Caribbean grandees or Chesapeake livestock and grain producers. Slaves were there to work and to make money for their owners. Slave owners adopted ameliorative measures only in an effort to improve productivity, not standards of living, let alone to address the moral issues tied up in slavery. A devotion to agricultural improvement united planters throughout plantation America, especially after the mid-eighteenth century. Plantation-management strategies were transformed by ideals of Enlightenment science, improvements in accounting systems around human capital, the rise of numeracy and political arithmetic, renewed attention to the efficient use of time, and methods of slave management that forced slaves to give up time spent in leisure for time devoted to work. The aim of planters involved in the Enlightenment project of agricultural improvement was to manipulate and organize work time so that slaves began to exhibit work values aligned with what historians call the "industrious revolution."[144] Order, science, and new ways of disciplining and compelling labor were features of agricultural improvement everywhere in the late eighteenth- and early nineteenth-century plantation world. If this meant some more attention paid to slave health and morbidity, the advent of scientific management also made work harder and more efficient.[145]

Free Populations

It was not just slave populations that were different in the mid-eighteenth-century American South and the British West Indies. The free populations were different also. There were overlaps: the white population of the South Carolina Lowcountry suffered, though not to the same extent as did whites in Jamaica or Guiana, from excessive mortality, mainly as a result of yellow fever.[146] But whites in the American South prospered in ways that never occurred in the West Indies, even in Barbados, where white population was largest and most diverse, with a balanced sex ratio and starting by midcentury to grow naturally. The story is familiar—part of the peopling of America narrative—but still worth retelling, as the nature of the white and free people of color populations significantly affected plantation development in British America.

White population growth made a major difference in British North America because so much of it occurred outside of the plantation sector, in the expansive lands of the American southern interior. The percentage of whites and blacks stayed roughly constant in British America between 1750 and 1780 at around 40 percent. But because the population of the American South expanded more rapidly than that of the West Indies, the lower percentage of whites to blacks in the American South meant a gradual decline in the percentage of total population in the slave colonies of British America that was black, falling from 59.4 percent in 1750 to 54.7 percent in 1780. Migration to British America was dominated by African migrants: during the long eighteenth century, from 1676 till 1820, 69.5 percent of 3,665,800 migrants were African. But rapid white population growth in places where slavery was either relatively marginal, such as North Carolina or Maryland, or virtually absent, as in the southern interior of South Carolina and Georgia, meant that in the American South the numbers of whites kept pace before the American Revolution with a fertile black population. A huge surge of migration of 200,000 people from Europe, half from Ireland and many from the Scottish Highlands, to the developing plantation areas from Kentucky through to Mississippi after the American Revolution, as well as considerable internal white migration, kept the percentage of white population above that of blacks. English migration to Virginia was limited (645 emigrants in 1774 and 1775), and that to the Carolinas, Georgia, and Florida was inconsequential (134). The only plantation area where English migrants went in considerable numbers was Maryland, where 2,146 went in 1774 and 1775. Many of these migrants were convicts, adding to the nearly 4 percent of the white adult population who were convicts. The majority went to Baltimore and that part of northern Maryland which bordered on Pennsylvania. Most European migrants were German, in the northern interior, and Ulster or Catholic Irish, as well as Scottish Highlanders in the upcountry areas of the interior South.[147]

These migrants built societies that were associated with plantation worlds but were not part of those worlds in the same way as in the West Indian islands. Some of these areas, like the middle country and part of the upcountry of South Carolina, transformed into plantation districts in the early nineteenth century. A commitment to slavery was nearly universal, even among people who never managed to acquire slaves and who lived in areas where slaves were few. But the size of the nonplantation sector and the very large number of people who were only tangentially involved in plantation life meant that planters had to gain white support through ideological commitment to a common cause as much as through shared economic benefits. Some of those ideological commitments concerned issues far removed from plantations, such as the fierce desire of many people in the interior to acquire Native American land and remove Native Americans from power and property. Native American population levels in the South decreased during the eighteenth century but were still substantial. On the eve of the Revolution, for example, the number of Africans, Europeans, and Native Americans in Georgia was roughly equal.[148]

The size of the white population in the American South not connected to plantations gave white planters strength in numbers but complicated white relationships in ways that were less pronounced in the West Indies, except perhaps in Barbados, where, as noted above, a relatively large group of ordinary white freeholders made themselves politically and socially important and challenged planter control on several occasions, notably in a fiercely fought election in 1819. The relations between planters, yeomen, and poor whites has been a staple of scholarship on the antebellum South, with earlier generations of scholars arguing that white people were united through a shared commitment to white supremacy. Recent scholarship has tested such assumptions, suggesting that class divisions between southern whites diminished whiteness as a uniting value for people far down the social scale and suggesting that even among aspirational whites the social relations of the household, rather than shared racial identity, was what connected white men.[149] Exploring the relations between differing sections of white people in the American South before 1820 is a task for a separate book, but a few brief points might be made.

First, while ordinary property-holding white men and propertyless white men with yeoman aspirations generally accepted the rule of white planters, they did so, as has been noted several times in this book, conditionally and with reservations. Commitment to white supremacy and potential access to purchasing slaves, while desirable, was not enough. Planters needed to be responsive to the concerns of ordinary white men, even in the home of deferential politics in America, the Chesapeake. Riots over tobacco regulation led by small planters in Maryland in the 1730s and, even more tellingly, dissension over the terms of yeoman involvement in armed resistance to Britain in the Revolution point to the limits of planter authority.[150] Secondly, some white people stood outside respectable white society and thus outside the boundaries of white solidarity. David Brown calls these people "vagabonds" and believes that by the late antebellum period men permanently moored in the bottom social stratum, with little chance of improving their social station, may have amounted to as much of 7 percent of the free working population, or approximately one-third of the 22 percent of the free workforce who were designated as propertyless laborers. Their numbers increased during the antebellum period, but there were a sizable number of vagabonds at all times in southern history. These men were not slaves, but neither were they full members of white society. Unlike aspirational whites, many of whom participated in the plantation economy as overseers, managers, and eventually freeholders, vagabonds had little economic clout, were sometimes passed over as laborers in favor of enslaved people, and were "wedded to a culture of crime, backwoods fighting, and interracial fraternization."[151]

Wealthy planters often viewed the vagabonds with contempt. The classic description, establishing a discourse that has lasted for centuries, was written by the Virginia grandee William Byrd II in 1728. Traveling to the border of Virginia and North Carolina, he encountered a people whom he thought especially lazy and shiftless. These men were so averse to labor and such poor specimens of manhood that they even reminded him of Native Americans, who also "impose all the work upon poor women." After contemptuously describing their "slothfulness," Byrd concluded that it was a "thorough aversion to labor that makes people file off to North Carolina, where plenty and a warm sun confirm them in their disposition to laziness for their whole lives."[152] The laziness, debauchery, and illiteracy of this group led more highly placed whites to put forward theories of biologically inherited depravity as a means of explaining their seemingly non-British behavior. Similar kinds of denigrations were hurled at the poorest whites of Barbados, derogatorily termed "redlegs" from their slavelike exposure to the sun as toiling workers. George Pinckard traveled to Barbados in 1795 and found poor white people obtaining "a scanty livelihood by cultivating a small patch of earth and breeding up poultry." He had not found such a "numerous class of inhabitants, between the great planters and the people of colour," in any of the "more recently settled colonies." He was disturbed by what he saw, as he thought these people "reduced to a state not much superior to the condition of free negroes." This status violated racial understandings of the industry of white people. It encouraged more extreme commentators to declare that "the poor whites are the lowest, and most degraded, residing in mean hovels." They were dirty, dependent on "negro charity," and seemed loathsome and vulgar: "I have never seen a more sallow, dirty, ill looking, and unhappy race, the men lazy, the women disgusting, and the children neglected: all without any notion of principle, morality, or religion."[153]

Thirdly, free people of color complicated easy equations of white and free, black and slave. The number of free people was very small until the last third of the eighteenth century and was always much smaller than in Iberian America, where free coloreds often outnumbered slaves, or in French America, where free coloreds made up nearly half of the free population of Saint-Domingue by 1788, and where they were both wealthy and politically assertive.[154] No substantial community of free people of color existed in British America in the eighteenth century. By the last years of slavery in the West Indies, the free colored populations had grown but in many places were still small. Barbados had only 838 free coloreds in 1786 and 5,146 in 1829—1.1 percent and 4.4 percent of the black population respectively. Free colored populations were also small in South Carolina and Georgia. The Lowcountry had 2,199 free coloreds in 1790, 6,355 in 1810, and 8,589 in 1820, amounting to 2 percent of the black population. Only in Jamaica, where there were 28,800 free coloreds by 1825 and 42,000 by 1834, and in Maryland and Virginia, which together had 76,629 free coloreds in 1820, were populations of free people of color sizable.

Some of the smaller West Indian islands had significant populations of free coloreds: in Grenada there were 2,742 free people of color in 1820, amounting to three-quarters of the free population and 9 percent of the black population. It was only in Maryland, however, that the free colored population was over 25 percent of the black population, but even there the free people were a small minority of the total population, given the large numerical predominance of whites. Free people of color were comparatively more important in the West Indies than in the American South, mainly because they, alone of any racial group, experienced considerable natural increase, and because white populations remained stagnant. By 1830 there were 98,435 free coloreds in the West Indies, with the biggest populations in Jamaica and in Trinidad, compared to just 52,871 whites, of whom nearly 15,000 lived in Barbados, which was the only major West Indian island where the white population considerably outnumbered free coloreds. By contrast, the American South had 121,265 free coloreds in 1820, of whom just 20,153 were in the Lowcountry and the Deep South. They were massively outnumbered not just by the 1.5 million slaves in America, but by 2.75 million southern whites.[155]

During the eighteenth century free people of color were seldom political or social actors, though they were sometimes acted upon by whites determined to keep them in their place. They became more prominent in the nineteenth century, especially in Jamaica, where they began to demand their rights and enjoyed some success in altering white political dominance.[156] Such assertiveness was not possible in the American South. A large and growing white population, increasingly committed to ideas of white supremacy, kept in check the aspirations of free people of color. The result was that free people of color found themselves in a precarious place. Their position in plantation society required them to ally with planters and to adopt their dress, language, and political ideas, especially a tentative support for slavery. But they were never part of plantation society. Rather, they were trapped between planters who despised them and slaves with whom they did not identify.[157]

Conclusion: Wealth and Poverty

The wealth of the plantation system was spread unevenly and was noticeable for the inequality it engendered, but the wealth it produced was
sufficient for most white people to feel they benefited from the system. As
the rich got richer, ordinary whites also prospered, albeit more slowly. In
plantation societies the most endemic poverty was found where plantation agriculture was weakest, notably in the interior and on the Tobacco
Coast. Yet even among the seemingly poorest white men and women in
plantation America, poverty was not especially pronounced in the eighteenth century.[158] Even in the Chesapeake, where the number of landless white men increased rapidly in the last forty years of the eighteenth
century, a considerable proportion of laborers were not destitute or even
especially struggling. Typically, laboring without land was a stage in the
life process. Laborers were young men who were either waiting to inherit
land from their fathers or else learning a craft. Christine Daniels argues
that they "often achieved at least a meager competency" even if sometimes they "lived close to disaster." Most acquired land if they worked
hard and were both thrifty and fortunate.[159] Among white people in
plantation areas, perhaps only convicts, comprising one-quarter to one-
third of all British migrants to British America in the eighteenth century,
with most going to Maryland, were really poor. Moreover, convicts were
the only white people disciplined like slaves. They faced increasingly
difficult times over the course of the eighteenth century, and very few
escaped poverty.[160] In general, however, relatively few white people in
plantation America were poor, or at least abjectly poor as in continental
Europe. As Philip Morgan concludes, "For white folk, colonial America
was a middling person's country, where the majority enjoyed a modest
competency, far more so than their European counterparts."[161]

That modest competency may have been the reason there was so
little class tension in the eighteenth century over differential access
by rich and poor whites to the plantation system . Another reason for
this limited class tension was that the real poor were the enslaved, not
ordinary whites. When blacks are included in poverty estimates, then
plantation societies were not just extraordinarily unequal by historical
standards, but that inequality was distributed so that few white people
were near the bottom of wealth distribution reckonings.[162] Black people
were not just poor but often on the verge of starvation owing to over-
work and rational slave-management methods. Moreover, the extent of

black poverty and the closeness of blacks to starvation were reversely correlated to increasing white wealth: the richer whites were, the poorer were blacks.

Slaves were not just dependent; they were also disposable. Their work made the plantations systems flourish. Contrary to commonsense arguments, however, that suggest that only a foolish planter jeopardized the health and working capacity of enslaved people through overwork and malnourishment, the most modern and rational planters, and those most attuned to contemporary management methods, were quite prepared to destroy their slave population through relentless work as long as a thriving African slave trade brought in a constant supply of new slaves. In a period when Britain and America were embarking upon rapid and unprecedented kinds of economic change as industrialization started in earnest, the plantation system looked deceptively unchanging. It was not. What changed most were the increasingly sophisticated management methods used to raise slaves' productivity levels. It meant that from the time of the Seven Years' War and well into the nineteenth century a whole range of white people realized that the plantation system was a great way to make substantial wealth, especially while a highly exploitative use of labor could be maintained through the Atlantic slave trade. Plantations were far from being on their last legs when abolitionists started to campaign for the abolition of the slave trade.

FOUR

"A Prodigious Mine": Jamaica

The Wealth of Jamaica

The jewel in the British imperial crown in eighteenth-century plantation colonies was undoubtedly Jamaica. It may have been a failed settler society, with white population persistently low after the disasters of the 1690s, especially the advent of regular bouts of deadly epidemic disease. The proportion of black to white was too high for contemporary comfort, and the colony was full of transients with relatively little commitment to developing a coherent community ethos and collective identity in the ways that happened in established colonies of British North America. But Jamaica was a stunning success in imperial terms. It was not only the plantation colony par excellence, the colony in which the large integrated plantation was most dominant, and in which the values and structures of the plantation was most pronounced. Strategically, it was also immensely important to Britain as a strongly defended island set among the established American colonies of Spain and the growing colonies of France in the Antilles. Most important, it was the wealthiest part of the British empire. Overall colonial wealth might have been slightly higher in the longer settled and much more populous colony of Virginia, and individual planters in St. Kitts and Grenada may have been able to acquire more wealth from their enslaved population than Jamaicans; but no eighteenth-century British American colony matched Jamaica as the quintessential plantation colony, with the richest and most influential planter ruling elite.

By the eve of the Seven Years' War in 1756, the natural historian Dr. Patrick Browne declared Jamaica "not only the richest, but the most considerable colony at this time under the government of *Great Britain.*" It was an island that surpassed "all the other *English* sugar-colonies, both in quantity of land and the conveniencies of life." It was "so advantageously situated, in regard to the *main continent,* that it has been for many years looked upon, as a magazine for all the neighboring settlements in *America*" and "the quantity or value of its productions, the number of men and ships employed in its trade [and] the quantity of valuable commodities imported there from various parts of *Europe.*" Browne wanted to show in part how far Jamaica "may yet be improved."[1]

The British prime minister Lord North used to say of Jamaican planters that they were the only master he ever had. That was a considerable overstatement, but their wealth and political clout, exemplified in the mid-eighteenth century by the wealthy London magnate and absentee planter William Beckford (1709–1770), was sufficient for Jamaicans to get their way about most political matters affecting their island.[2] The power that the small white population of Jamaica had was based on the extraordinary ability of its planters to grow sugar and the equally extraordinary abilities of its indigenous merchant class to extract bullion from Spanish America. Britons were mightily impressed. Despite its well-deserved reputation as a white person's graveyard, Europeans flocked to the island to acquire great fortunes. Most died; some did indeed make fortunes. William Beckford's family was one family that became immensely rich in Jamaica. His father, Peter Beckford, died in 1737 with land and personal property that probably exceeded £500,000. Sir Simon Clarke, son of a baronet and highwayman transported to Jamaica in the early 1720s, was just as wealthy. He died in 1777 in western Jamaica with a personal estate worth £192,565 and total wealth similar to that accumulated by Beckford forty years earlier. Zachary Bayly, a Kingston merchant who diversified into large-scale sugar planting, died in 1769 with a princely fortune of £114,743, including 2,010 slaves. Thomas Hibbert, an English migrant from Manchester, left no accounting of his wealth but was probably richer than Bayly. One sign of his wealth was that when he died in 1780, his heir sold 2,000 acres in Kingston that Thomas had owned, which must have been worth a colossal sum.[3]

Some of the greatest fortunes were made virtually from scratch. Thomas Thistlewood gossiped in 1765 that "old Philip Haughton died worth 400 thousand pounds currency had 70 thousd: Sterling in the bank at home yet about 20 years worth about 10 thousand currency." The richest of all Jamaicans were John Tharp and Simon Taylor, who profited immensely from booming sugar prices in the 1790s as Saint-Domingue dissolved into civil wars. Tharp died in 1805 with £362,000 in personal property, including 2,990 slaves.[4] Simon Taylor (1740–1813) was richer, even with a slightly smaller slave force, with 2,228 slaves valued at £124,578. Most of his money was in British investments, and his total estate was valued at £739,207, or twice that of Tharp and over three times as much as Peter Beckford's in 1737. His wealth was legendary: the wife of the governor declared after meeting him in 1805 that he "was by far the richest proprietor in the island, and in the habit of accumulating money so as to make his nephew and heir one of the most wealthy subjects of his Majesty." Richard Sheridan estimates his annual income in the early nineteenth century at a princely £47,000 per annum, or between five and eight times as much as the average British peer and the same as the legendary income that Robert Clive of India was reputed to have earned in 1760. His real and personal property added together was very likely to have been over £1 million.[5]

These were the extreme ends of wealth in a wealthy white population. In 1774 average wealth for white male wealth holders can be estimated at £4,036; for white adults, at £2,691; and for all whites, at £2,018. Contemporaries would not have included black people as beneficiaries of the wealth that the plantation generated—they were in this instance property rather than people—but some measure of the extraordinary wealth that Jamaica created lies in the fact that average wealth for all of Jamaica's 209,617 residents was £134, over three times the wealth of the average person in England and Wales or in the northern colonies of British North America.[6] That wealth made Jamaica very valuable, the colony whose loss the British could have least afforded, as can be seen in how it prioritized its defense over supporting British troops at Yorktown in the last act of the American Revolution in British North America in 1781. It was, as Charles Leslie wrote in 1740, "a Constant Mine, whence Britain draws prodigious riches."[7]

There are several reasons to study wealth in eighteenth-century Jamaica. It is a useful colonial case study of how the rise of the large integrated plantation transformed British American life in the eighteenth century. It is also a good example of how economic and social diversity was possible even within a society where commitment to plantation agriculture was total. A colonial plantation society made money from plantations, but also from other economic activities, such as urban merchandising, as in eighteenth-century Kingston.[8] Kingston was the

Table 4.1 Largest Slaveholders in Jamaica, 1674–1784

Name	Death	No. of Slaves	Estate (£stg.)	Parish
Zachary Bayly	1770	2,010	114,743	St. Andrew
Peter Beckford	1739	1,669	145,789	Clarendon
Richard Haughton	1742	1,432	33,092	Hanover
William Beckford	1774	1,356	81,620	Britain
Thomas Blagrove	1767	1,338	54,720	St. Ann
Henry Dawkins	1745	1,315	78,341	Clarendon
John Ellis	1784	1,310	60,493	St. Mary
John Vassall	1748	1,167	53,088	Westmoreland
Thomas Blagrove	1756	1,053	67,399	St. Ann
John Blagrove	1755	929	56,324	St. Ann
Sir James Campbell	1737	921	21,983	Westmoreland
Richard Beckford	1756	910	59,490	Clarendon
Alexander Macfarlane	1756	791	53,239	Kingston
Robert Needham	1739	779	28,086	Vere
John Foster	1731	766	34,630	St Elizabeth
Thomas Hall	1773	752	41,867	Hanover
Robert Stirling	1764	750	54,531	Kingston
John Bryan	1775	741	69,905	. . .
Isaac Gale	1750	735	63,018	St. Elizabeth

Source: Inventories, 1674–1784, IB/11/3/1–64, JA

Table 4.2 Wealthiest Jamaicans, 1674–1784

Name	Death	Wealth (£stg.)	Debts (£stg.)	Slaves (value in £stg.)	No. of Slaves
Sir Simon Clarke	1778	192,565	174,757	9,196	171
Edward Foord	1777	147,293	142,679	2,817	69
Peter Beckford	1739	145,749	96,459	33,510	1,669
Samuel Delpratt	1784	141,930	139,160	2,770	67
Zachary Bayly	1769	114,743	42,857	62,860	2,012
John Morse	1782	98,982	71,977	19,629	490
George Paplay	1770	96,814	70,065	21,417	616
Aaron Baruh Lousada	1768	83,196	75,352	5,851	145
William Beckford	1774	81,621	0	70,713	1,356
Henry Dawkins	1745	78,342	28,407	26,294	1,315
Alexander Grant	1773	72,895	27,194	43,818	672
John Bryan	1775	69,905	27,946	31,574	741
Charles Mitchell	1762	68,676	49,244	11,193	306
Alexander Harvie	1767	68,566	38,561	20,332	445
Thomas Blagrove	1756	67,399	23,803	34,614	1,053
Scudamore Winde	1776	67,338	58,738	3,355	70
Malcolm Laing	1782	63,285	58,180	1,850	93
Isaac Gale	1750	63,019	31,555	16,401	735
John Ellis	1784	60,943	0	55,053	1,310

Source: Inventories, 1674–1784, IB/11/3/1–64, JA

Table 4.3 Population in Jamaica, 1662–1834

Year	Total Population	Slaves	Whites	Free Colored
1662	4,207	554	3,653	NA
1673	15,536	7,768	7,768	NA
1693	48,000	40,635	7,365	NA
1730	83,765	74,525	8,230	1,010
1752	120,000	106,592	10,000	3,408
1774	209,617	192,787	12,737	4,093
1788	254,184	228,232	18,347	7,605
1834	369,670	311,070	16,600	42,000

Source: Trevor Burnard, *Mastery, Tyranny, and Desire: Thomas Thistlewood and His Slaves in the Anglo-Jamaican World* (Chapel Hill: University of North Carolina Press, 2004), 16; B. W. Higman, *Slave Populations of the British Caribbean, 1807–1834* (Baltimore: Johns Hopkins University Press, 1984).

landing point of the great majority of African slaves who came to the island between 1692 and 1807. It also provided plantations with capital needs and consumer goods. But it was more than just an adjunct to the plantation system. It had a vibrant local economy, with a flourishing property market, it was a significant market for a large surrounding community, and it was the place where trade with Spanish America was conducted. One sign of its importance and its relative independence from the gyrations of boom and bust in the plantation economy was that it did not suffer the catastrophic fall in land prices that affected rural Jamaica in the aftermath of the end of the slave trade in 1807 but instead enjoyed a constant rise in land values during the whole abolition of the slave-trade period.[9]

We know relatively little about society and economy in the island from the 1690s through to 1780, and our knowledge is especially poor for the period between 1690 and 1730. The early eighteenth century remains, in Philip Morgan's words, "*the* Darkest of the many Dark Ages of Caribbean history."[10] This chapter thus provides useful empirical information about a period and a place we know little about. It is surprising that so little is known about Jamaica in this period. By comparison with other plantation societies in the Americas, sources are relatively abundant. It has, for example, an excellent collection of vital records on population (parish registers, notably from the parishes of Kingston, St. Andrew, and St. Catherine), inheritance (a series of extant wills starting from the early 1670s), landownership (patents and deeds), and in particular wealth (inventories of personal property) that allow us to track individual and collective trends over time. This chapter relies heavily on evidence from one of these sources. I have examined 10,222 Jamaican

FIGURE 6. Large engraved map of Jamaica with hand-colored outline. In *A New General Atlas . . .* (Edinburgh: George Ramsay, 1817). Private possession.

inventories taken between 1774 and 1784. The strengths and deficiencies of this source are described in the appendix to this book. There is also a series of excellent records on various aspects of Jamaica's social and economic life from the early 1750s that allow us to examine the whole of the island at a particular period of time, including a survey of landownership, a detailed breakdown of economic activity in St. Andrew Parish and data on people and property in Jamaica's major towns of Kingston and St. Jago de la Vega.[11]

Edward Long's *History of Jamaica*

Jamaica was fortunate in having had its social and economic patterns described in several contemporary histories. In addition to a considerable corpus of works commenting on various aspects of Jamaican life, polemical accounts of its politics, and some impressive natural histories, Charles Leslie wrote an impressionistic survey in 1740 (Thomas Thistlewood thought it terribly inaccurate), and James Knight wrote a more considered account around the same time that is as yet unpublished.[12]

In the 1790s the Jamaican planter Bryan Edwards wrote a popular and influential three-volume history of the West Indies in which Jamaica was treated extensively.[13]

The most impressive history of the island, however, is Edward Long's three-volume account, written in 1774. Long (1734–1813) has become a notorious figure in eighteenth-century intellectual life and is usually written about as a leading proponent of scientific-racist thought.[14] But he was much more than just a passionate defender of whiteness and a promoter of black inferiority. His history of Jamaica is a compendium of important social and economic information about the island and a carefully worked out argument seeking greater British support of the island and calling for a change in how white Jamaicans behaved. Long, a wealthy planter who died in the same year, 1813, as Simon Taylor did, though not as rich, was an absentee planter when he wrote his great work, but he had significant Jamaican experience in the twelve years he spent there between 1757 and 1769, in which time he served as a judge in the vice admiralty court. He was immensely well connected. His great-great-grandfather, Samuel Long, had been a legendary Speaker of the Assembly in the 1670s and 1680s and a determined opponent of excessive gubernatorial authoritarianism. His brother-in-law was Jamaica's governor at the time of Tacky's Revolt.[15]

Not surprisingly, given his pedigree, Long was a strong Whig, fully supportive of Jamaican legislative assertiveness. But while he was a proudly patriotic defender of the virtues and values of the Jamaican planter, he was not an unthinking enthusiast for everything that white Jamaicans did. Indeed, he was often highly critical of how Jamaicans were not living up to their great promise.[16] He thought that France ran its plantations in Saint-Domingue better than the British ran theirs in Jamaica. France fostered, he thought, long-term planning for economic advancement—unlike Jamaica, where both government and planters were addicted to short-term opportunism. France, he argued, was "like a skillful gardener" who was "careful in the choice of plants, and treated her colonies as a favorite nursery, in which none should be fixed that were not vigorous, healthy, with all the promising appearances of thriving luxuriantly, and producing good fruit." By contrast, Britain, he lamented, "treats her plantations as a distant spot, upon which she may most conveniently discharge all her nuisance, weeds, and filth, leaving it entirely to chance, whether any valuable production shall ever spring from it."[17]

Nevertheless, even if planters in Saint-Domingue were advancing over those in Jamaica, Jamaica was doing well because, Long argued, it was a productive place and because the general character of the inhabitants was admirable. In general, Jamaica was "rather getting forward rather than declining in its most valuable settlements." Its history over the hundred years since it was first established, he concluded at the end of volume 2 of his history, made it an ideal place to restart one's life and gain a fortune, being "the asylum of the distressed and unfortunate, where all may enjoy sustenance." Recent developments had shown how much it had "improved" as a place of residence, meaning that recent arrivals had the "advantage, unknown to our ancestors, of coming to an established society, which, from the number of towns and settlements, has every accommodation and convenience that can be desired."[18]

One aim was to chronicle that improvement. In general Long was a very careful observer. He mostly reported on the statistics of Jamaica in an honest, transparent, and checkable way. There was only one area (outside his thoughts on race and on Africans) where he was appreciably influenced by an unproven bias. He systematically overstated the numbers of white people in the island and overestimated how many Jamaicans were living in Britain. Thus, he argued that there were 17,949 whites in the island in 1768, when a census in 1774 suggested that the number of whites was only 12,737. He got to this figure by assuming a rate of increase in the number of white servants from estimates made in the 1730s that his later arguments, about how planters did not care to stock their plantations with white underlings, showed to be logically contradictory. He also thought that the percentage of white propertyholders living in Britain was about one-third of the resident white population, when it was in reality closer to 10 percent. His blind spot was related to his underlying concern with climatic theories of development. He thought Jamaica much healthier than it was, especially if people lived moderately. He had little idea of how destructive epidemic disease was in the island.[19]

But Long's estimates of wealth were otherwise carefully founded and backed up by empirical evidence. His data showed conclusively that Jamaica had developed considerably since English settlement started in 1655, and that it was advancing particularly rapidly in the years following the end of the Seven Years' War. The island, he estimated, had 70 sugar plantations in 1670 producing 1,333 hogsheads of sugar. By 1739 the number of plantations had increased to 429, producing 33,000 hogsheads of sugar and 13,200 puncheons of rum. By 1768 the number of sugar estates was up to 651, and sugar production was 68,160 hogsheads, with a further 27,200 puncheons of rum. Jamaica supported 166,904 slaves and 135,753 livestock and provided £27,292 in revenue to the government. Long thought that a medium-sized sugar estate with 100 slaves cost £14,029 to establish, produced 100 hogsheads of sugar and 50 puncheons of rum, and returned net profits of £1,400 per annum after contingencies of £580. Larger estates benefited, he argued, from economies of scale. An estate with 300 enslaved workers produced three times the amount of sugar and run but made more than three times the profits: £4,000 per annum, with contingencies of £2,000. By any standard, it was a prosperous place.[20]

Long also carefully worked out Jamaica's exports and imports. Jamaica's trade balance was heavily in its favor, especially with Britain, where it exported £1,310,919 of tropical goods in 1768, up from £539,500 in 1751.[21] Imports from Britain, North America, and Africa were £1,054,290, making the trade balance in Jamaica's favor £256,628. Long thought that much of this favorable trade balance was eaten up by the money spent by absentees in Britain and interest payments, but against this was money that Jamaica received from Spanish America. In addition, he thought Jamaica provided Britain with intangible benefits, such as "being a nursery for seamen and support of trades for ship-building." It increased possible trade with Africa as well as providing income to "transient traders" who, "having reaped by merchandize, or other possession, competent fortunes, return full laden to their native hive." Jamaica was indeed a prodigious mine: "What a field is here opened to display the comforts and blessings of life, which this commerce distributes among so many thousands of industrious subjects in the mother country! If we should carry our ideas still further, and imagine double the number of acres to be occupied in the island, and equally cultivated, it would then yield a profit of full two millions and a half yearly to our mother country; a grand project this of future maturity, which offers a large sphere for the exercise of patriotism!"[22]

What is especially valuable about Long's analysis is that he gave a detailed description of the economic activity of the parishes of the island, accounting for the geography of each place and delineating each parish, and both rural and urban places, by virtue of what it produced. The Jamaica of the Seven Years' War period, when Long first arrived in the island, took over a century to develop. It was considerably smaller than Cuba or Saint-Domingue, but it was much larger than all of Britain's island colonies in the Lesser Antilles. It contained relatively high mountains, large stretches of swampy morasses, and arid interiors, as well as fertile savannahs. Its diversity extended to temperatures, rainfall, geological formations, flora and fauna, soil types, and access to roads and harbors. But Jamaica always had sufficient arable land to accommodate agricultural development. Indeed, at the start of the Seven Years' War much good land was still uncultivated.[23]

Wealth Estimates

Jamaica was a settled place with a shifting frontier. The northwest and southeast edges developed spectacularly from the 1740s onward, after Jamaica had established peace in 1739 with the Maroons who controlled Jamaica's mountainous interior. In 1730, 23 percent of enslaved people lived in the northern, western and far eastern parishes of Jamaica. Slaves in the prime sugar-producing northwestern parish of St. James increased by 90 percent between 1740 and 1745, trebled between 1745 and 1761, and increased by 250 percent between 1761 and 1788. That year the percentage of slaves in the formerly peripheral parishes of St. James, Hanover, Trelawney, St. Mary, and St. Thomas-in-the-East was 44 percent, up from 13 percent in 1734. In St. James alone the numbers of slaves had increased from 2,297 in 1734 to 37,864 in 1788 (by which time the parish had been divided into two, with a new parish of Trelawney established in 1770), or from 13 slaves per acre in the former year to 129 slaves per acre in the latter year. One-half of the sugar estates in 1788 were in parishes that had been undeveloped in 1734.[24] The financial importance of these developing frontier regions is seen in the increasing tax payments they made to the government. In 1740 residents of St. James and Hanover Parishes paid £466 in taxation. By 1768 this sum had increased to £4,730, and in 1788, with the addition of Trelawney, the northwest parishes contributed £11,424 to Jamaican coffers.[25] Property prices were high in these newly developing areas, with many large integrated plantations. If we take the very rural and long-established Clarendon Parish in central Jamaica as a reference point for property prices in the second half of the eighteenth century, then land prices in far western Hanover Parish were nearly double those in Clarendon. Land prices in Trelawney and St. James were nearly 50 percent higher, as was also true in the north-central parish of St. Mary. Land in St. Thomas-in-the-East was 27 percent higher than in Clarendon.[26]

Jamaica's economy was more diverse than that of any West Indian colony settled by the English in the seventeenth century. This diversity resulted from the island's varied physiography and the slow pace of settlement, a pace hindered by Maroon resistance in the first third of the eighteenth century. Its diversity meant that it was never a sugar monoculture. Planters combined other export staples such as coffee, cotton,

FIGURE 7. Painting by anonymous, engraved by John Boydell, entitled *To Edward Morant, Esq. A Prospect of RIO BONA Harbour, in the Parish of ST ANN'S and the Tavern, Wharf and Stores, in the Parish of ST JAMES, the North side, JAMAICA* (1770). Private collection.

allspice, and indigo with sugar production. Plantations specializing in different crops could be found in different parts of the island, creating the potential for internal trade between plantation units. Particularly vital to the Jamaican economy were livestock pens and well-developed provision grounds where slaves were expected to grow their own food on their own time. Their institution showed just how hardheaded and devoted to profit Jamaican planters were. They were unprepared to devote good plantation ground to food production and wanted to minimize how many provisions they bought from North America (with only marginal success), so they forced slaves to cultivate their own food crops.[27]

Long was correct to see Jamaica as having developed remarkably in the 120 years of English settlement prior to his departure from Jamaica. Using methods to determine wealth in 1774, Jamaican wealth increased from £314,434 in 1673, to £4,633,734 in 1722 to £10,338,236 in 1754 and to £27,680,517 in 1778.[28] Just as the 1774 estimate was close to that estimated by Long in that year, so my estimate for wealth in 1754 is within the margin of error of a careful estimate made in 1751. An anonymous author estimated total wealth as £10,587,400, of which £5,334,000 was made up of slaves and livestock, £2,642,400 was held as real estate, £1,968,000 was in the form of urban housing, and £643,000 was in the euphemistically named form of "commerce."[29] Annual income came from two principal sources: trade with Spanish America, which Robert Dinwiddie, as noted above, estimated at £1,115,000 in 1748; and plantation produce, which was £832,897 in 1744 and £1,191,556 in 1762.[30]

The People of Jamaica

The people who participated in this great expansion of trade and wealth were as diverse as any group of colonial peoples in the British America. Jamaica's population comprised three principal groups. The first was free settlers, mostly initially from England but over the course of the eighteenth century added to by considerable numbers of migrants from Scotland.[31] Irish settlement was relatively small compared with that of islands in the eastern Caribbean. What Jamaica had, however, that distinguished it from other British West Indian possessions, with the possible exception of Barbados, was a comparatively large, influential, and wealthy Jewish community. Most of these were Sephardic Jews who had settled in Port Royal (later moving to Kingston in the early eighteenth century) after having been expelled from Surinam and from Portuguese Brazil.[32] Jews occupied an indeterminate social position in Jamaica. They faced considerable prejudice (Long, for example, was nearly as ferociously anti-Semitic as he was virulently racist) and were excluded, as they were everywhere in the British empire, from civic participation. But Jews fell on the free and the white side of the two great social axes in Jamaica, and eventually were given full civil rights, several years before Jews gained civil rights in Britain.[33]

In the seventeenth century Jamaica was an English colony, with most European migrants coming from metropolitan England. Using records on indentured servants, convicts, and free settlers in the seventeenth century, 84 percent of free settlers for whom we can establish a place of original residence and 89 percent of servants and convicts came from England. The percentage of English emigrants declined over time, such that only 62 percent of free settlers with an original place of residence identified who died and left wills between 1720 and 1770 were English. Scots started to come to Jamaica in larger numbers beginning in the mid-eighteenth century. Between 1720 and 1770 they accounted for 18 percent of free settlers leaving wills with a place of origin noted. They were reported by Long to be one-third of the white population by the American Revolution. Most English migrants came from metropolitan England: 57 percent of migrants came from London, Middlesex, and the home counties, and 78 percent of English migrants left from London to come to Jamaica. Only 5 percent came from the north of England. These English migrants tended to be of relatively high status, especially those who became large planters, several of whom were from gentry backgrounds.

English settlers who moved freely to Jamaica came from backgrounds similar to those of free migrants who went to the Chesapeake. They came from the middle to upper ranks of London's mercantile community, from the lower tiers of the provincial gentry, or from the ranks of skilled tradesmen. The social origins of English migrants who moved under indenture to Britain, especially in the eighteenth century, were also comparatively high: only 30 percent of servants arriving from London between 1719 and 1759 were agricultural laborers, and 36 percent were unskilled. Evidence suggests that English indentured servants to Jamaica were more highly skilled than their counterparts in the American South. The typical European migrant to Jamaica was single, male, in his late teens or twenties, from metropolitan England, and from an urban mercantile or trade background. These migrants fostered a society that was highly materialistic, secular, competitive, exploitative, violent, and capitalist.[34]

The second group of migrants to Jamaica was easily the largest: West African slaves, arriving in increasingly large numbers, from most of the major regions from which the British shipped captive Africans, save for southeast Africa. No one region of transshipment dominated the trade. The areas from which most Africans came to Jamaica varied over time. Over the whole period of the slave trade, the largest number of slaves came from the Bight of Biafra, accounting for 35 percent of African arrivals, but in the early eighteenth century, when the transition to the large integrated plantation occurred, Benin and Angola were the principal places of transshipment, accounting for two-thirds of Africans arriving in the island between 1701 and 1725. Slaves were present in Jamaica from the start, the Spanish having owned small numbers of enslaved Africans prior to English conquest of the island in 1655. Their numbers exploded in the late seventeenth century. From parity in numbers with whites in 1673, slaves were 85 percent of the population in 1693 and nearly 90 percent by the mid-eighteenth century. Their numbers steadily increased after the end of the American Revolution, reaching a peak of 356,990 in 1811, then falling to 311,070 on the eve of emancipation in 1834.[35]

The dreadful demography of slavery meant that the enslaved population, just like the white population, was heavily dominated by recent migrants in their twenties and thirties. There were few children. In 1789 the Jamaica Assembly estimated, in a self-serving analysis designed to hide the destructiveness of the sugar economy, that the proportion of Africans in the population was about 25 percent. While the percentage of Africans in the Jamaican slave population was probably lower in the 1780s than it had been before, as a result of the decline in the Atlantic slave trade during the American Revolution, it is hard to imagine that the percentage of Africans in the slave population had slipped to just one-quarter of all slaves.

In 1817, ten years after the slave trade closed, the percentage of Africans in the Jamaican slave population was 37 percent. Michael Craton has made educated extrapolations from work on slave populations for the eighteenth century and estimates that the percentage of Africans in Jamaica was about 90 percent in the late seventeenth century, 80 percent in the second quarter of the eighteenth century, and 75 percent at the time of the American Revolution. These figures are probably a bit high. On Sir Charles Price's Worthy Park Estate, 43 percent of his slaves were African between 1787 and 1791, rising to 61 percent between 1793 and 1796 after heavy involvement in the Atlantic slave trade. A listing of slaves on York Estate, in western Jamaica, in 1778 indicated that the percentage of Africans on that large sugar estate was 48 percent. Both York and Worthy Park were long-established plantations and could be expected to have substantial creole (or native-born) enslaved populations. My guess is that the percentage of Africans on more newly established or smaller estates was higher than that on York or Worthy Park, suggesting a percentage of Africans before the American Revolution of between 50 and 60 percent of the enslaved population.[36]

African Ethnicity

Four regions—the Bight of Biafra, the Gold Coast, west central Africa, and the Bight of Benin—accounted for over 90 percent of captive Africans, with the Bight of Biafra and the Gold Coast together contributing nearly two-thirds of Jamaican slaves.[37] The Bight of Biafra, as shown in table 4.4, was the most important catchment area before 1676, but it

Table 4.4 Ethnic Origins of African Migrants to Jamaica by Percentage over Time

Region	Total	1655–75	1676–1700	1701–25	1726–50	1751–75	1776–1800	1801–8
Bight of Biafra	35.1	62.1	15.5	1.6	33.9	31.7	43.8	51.2
Gold Coast	26.8	8.5	11.3	44.8	26.7	31.1	24.3	20.4
Angola Region	15.9	11.0	28.8	10.5	23.9	9.2	17.6	18.9
Bight of Benin	12.2	18.5	36.7	34.7	9.3	11.2	6.5	4.8
Windward Coast	4.6	0	0	1.2	1.4	10.7	2.9	2.2
Sierra Leone	3.3	0	1.3	0.6	1.2	4.3	4.0	2.1
Senegambia	2.0	0	6.0	5.4	3.1	1.9	0.9	0.4
Southeast Africa	0.1	0	0.4	0.7	0	0	0	0

Source: David Eltis, "The Volume and Structure of the Transatlantic Slave Trade: A Reassessment," *WMQ*, 3d ser., 60 (2001): 17–46; *TSTDB*. Note: Includes only slave voyages for which port of embarkation is known.

declined in importance in the early eighteenth century before becoming once again important in the late eighteenth century. In the last fifteen years of the Atlantic slave trade, over half of all Africans shipped to Jamaica came from the Bight of Biafra. In the second quarter of the eighteenth century, however, slaves from the Gold Coast were prominent, along with slaves from Benin. West central Africa was an appreciable provenance zone throughout the whole period.

A conspicuous feature of African migration to Jamaica was the heterogeneity of African ethnic origins.[38] The structure of the slave trade to Jamaica meant not only that the variety of African ethnicities represented on the Kingston seafront, where most slaves were sold, was remarkable, but also that buyers of slaves purchased slaves from many African provenance zones. There were only five five-year periods when more than half of all slave arrivals came from just one region of Africa. In twelve five-year periods, no single region provided as much as 40 percent of all slave arrivals.

In practice, buyers took whatever slaves they could get, purchasing slaves from different regions. The wealthiest planter in seventeenth-century Jamaica, Peter Beckford I, bought 189 slaves in fourteen separate shipments. Of these slaves, 75 were from the Gold Coast, 66 were from the Bight of Benin, 25 were from west central Africa, and 22 were from the Bight of Biafra. If we link slaves sold by the Royal African Company before 1708 with their slave purchasers, we find heterogeneous buying patterns. Of twenty-one large slaveholders who were men who listed slaves in their inventories similar in number to those that they bought from the Royal African Company, seventeen bought slaves from at least three regions of Africa. Most slaves came from Benin, Biafra, and the

Gold Coast, which is not surprising given purchasing patterns in the 1670s and 1680s. There was no clear pattern, however, in the proportion of slaves bought from each region.[39]

The best guide to early ethnic diversity is a census of St. John Parish in central Jamaica taken in 1680, in which it is possible to link data from the Royal African Company with census material to identify the slave purchases of eleven male residents. These men bought 299 slaves from five African regions. The greatest number (128) came from the Gold Coast, with a further 54 from Benin, 81 from the Bight of Biafra, 17 from West Central Africa, and 19 from Senegambia. None of the five largest slave buyers bought their captives from just one region. Nearly two-thirds of Lieutenant Colonel Whitgift Aylmer's 49 slaves came from the Gold Coast, but neither Colonel John Cope nor Captain William Bragg bought from that region. Cope's slaves came mostly from Biafra and the Gold Coast. By contrast, Major Thomas Ayscough, who had a particularly diverse slave population, bought 24 slaves from the Gold Coast, 12 from Benin, 13 Senegambians, and 6 Biafrans. The ethnic foundations of slave populations on the properties of the first sugar planters were thus distinctly heterogeneous. That heterogeneity increased as slaves from different areas of Africa mixed, mated, and produced progeny with varying African heritages and diverse Jamaican experiences.[40]

Patterns of slave purchasing accentuated ethnic heterogeneity. In the seventeenth century slave sales saw many purchasers, each of whom bought only a few Africans. The few men who bought large numbers of slaves tended to be Port Royal and Kingston merchants, none of whom were fussy about which region of Africa they bought their slaves from. Over time the importance of Kingston merchants in the Atlantic slave trade greatly increased. By the mid-eighteenth century most slave buyers were Kingston merchants buying slaves for resale to planters. The result was a considerable mixing of ethnicities in the pens and yards of Kingston before slaves were sent out in generally small numbers to work plantations. Just as in Africa, where Africans lived on barracoons before being funneled onto ships for transshipment to the Americas, Kingston was where African captives were "seasoned" into becoming slaves.[41]

The only naturally increasing group in the Jamaican population, apart from Jews (who seem, from impressionistic evidence derived from vital records, to have had healthy rates of natural increase),[42] was free people of color. The first free people of color were freed in the late seventeenth century, but their numbers were negligible until the second quarter of the eighteenth century. They increased in numbers mainly after the turn of the nineteenth century. In 1730, 1,010 free people of color lived in Jamaica, rising to 3,408 in 1762, 4,093 in 1774, and 7,605 in 1788. In 1788 free people of color were 3 percent of Jamaica's population and nearly 30 percent of the free population. Numbers increased by 234 people per year in the 1770s and 1780s. The rapid rise in the rate of freed population increase after midcentury can be seen in the parish registers for St. Andrew, St. Catherine, and Kingston. Figures on free people derived from parish registers need to be interpreted with care, as not all ministers included free people in church ceremonies. Nevertheless, baptisms of free people of color in all three parishes doubled, and funerals for them increased four- or fivefold between 1740 and 1780, suggesting an explosion in the numbers of free people of color in the island.

The geographical distribution of free people of color was uneven. Like whites, free people of color clustered in Kingston and St. Jago de la Vega. Kingston was home to over a quarter of the free people of color in 1730 and 43 percent of the free people of color by 1788. In addition, free people of color tended to be female rather than male, children rather than adults, and as likely to be colored as black. The census of 1730 provides the only breakdown of the freed population by sex and age. It shows that whereas adult men were less than 16 percent of the free people of color population, adult women made up 37 percent and children a further 47 percent of free people of color. This bias toward women and children was maintained over time. Women and children accounted for 75 percent of deaths of free people of color in Kingston between 1753 and 1774. Free women of color outnumbered free men of color in St. James Parish in 1774 by more than three to one.[43]

Migration to Jamaica thus led to a cultural heterogeneity that eroded regional cultures inherited from Britain or West Africa. For whites, migration to a "hybrid and heterogeneous" Atlantic world meant that "even the most humble English inhabitant in the most remote colony found himself living in a world far more culturally complex than anything he would have experienced in England." Jamaica was one of the most cosmopolitan and polyglot places in British America, full, as Richard Burton evocatively proclaims, of "the deracinated, the deranged, the debauched and the desperate" from all areas of Britain, with a smattering of buccaneers in the seventeenth century from many European nations, as well as Portuguese-speaking Sephardic Jews from the Netherlands, Brazil, and Surinam. The African population was even more mixed, as the doctor and fellow of the Royal Society Hans Sloane found when he visited a sugar plantation in the interior of the island and watched a dozen Africans make music that was variously from the Angola, Papaw, and Coromantee regions of Africa.[44]

Settlement and Growth: Three Estates and a Parish

The settlement history of Jamaica can be divided into two periods—the period of relatively small plantations before 1700, and the period of the dominance of the large integrated plantation from the second quarter of the eighteenth century. Jamaica took some time to become a plantation society dominated by large sugar estates. After 1700 larger slaveholdings became more common, and the average number of slaves per slaveholder increased. The proportion of slaveholdings that were fewer than 5 slaves halved in the first twenty-five years of the eighteenth century compared with the late seventeenth century, while the percentage of slaves owned in large estates with 150 or more slaves increased by over 250 percent over the same period. The number of estates with more than 150 slaves increased from six in the 1700s to sixteen in the 1710s and twenty-seven in the 1720s. It was this latter decade that saw the emergence of truly gargantuan slaveholdings. After 1725 the pattern of Jamaican slaveholding was set. On the eve of emancipation, slave ownership was general within the white population, with 12,453 slave owners in a population of 16,750. It was also concentrated, with the 7.5 percent of slaveholdings with 100 or more slaves containing 62 percent of all slaves. The largest slaveholding was an estate with 750 slaves in St. Dorothy Parish in the east of the island, while 119 Jamaicans had estates with 300 or more slaves.[45] The patterns a century earlier were much the same as in 1832. Slave ownership was widespread—three-quarters of inventoried estates contained slaves—but most slaves were owned by only a small number of slave owners. The 5.3 percent of slave owners inventoried between 1725 and 1784 who owned over 150 slaves accounted for 49 percent of all slaves and 51 percent of slaves living in rural parishes. The percentage of slave owners who owned more than 150 slaves within the slaveholding class nearly doubled from 1710 to 1730, as did the proportion of slaves held in slaveholdings of this size.[46]

We can see how this process worked in looking at the history of one of the wealthiest families in Jamaica. The first Pennant in Jamaica was Giffard Pennant, a Welshman who established plantations in central Jamaica in the seventeenth century. At his death in 1676 he owned over 10,000 mostly undeveloped acres in Clarendon and St. Elizabeth Parishes, 59 slaves, and an estate worth £2,048. He was one of the wealthier planters in the late seventeenth century. The Pennant fortune, however, grew to be substantial during the lifetime of Giffard's son Edward (1672–1736). At Edward's death he owned 8,365 mostly

Table 4.5. Jamaican Slave Forces by Percentage of Slaves in Various-Sized Slave Forces

	1674–99		1700–1724		1725–84		
Number	Percentage of Slaves in Slave Forces of Various Sizes	Percentage of Slave Forces Containing Various Nos. of Slaves	Percentage of Slaves in Slave Forces of Various Sizes	Percentage of Slave Forces Containing Various Nos. of Slaves	Percentage of Slaves in Slave Forces of Various Sizes	Percentage of Slaves in Slave Forces of Various Sizes, Kingston Excluded	Percentage of Slave Forces Containing Various Nos. of Slaves
1–5	7.6	47.1	3.3	34.6	2.5	1.9	36.4
6–15	17.0	28.2	10.5	28.9	7.0	5.6	26.5
16–35	21.0	14.1	14.0	16.3	10.4	9.3	16.1
36–75	20.7	6.1	18.9	10.2	13.9	14.2	9.7
76–150	21.8	3.6	24.7	6.6	17.5	17.9	5.8
151+	11.9	0.9	28.6	3.2	48.7	51.1	5.3
No. Obs.	8,694	554	30,296	1,114	22,0657	190,829	6,078

Source: Inventories, 1674–1784, IB/11/3/1–64, JA

developed acres and 610 slaves among personal property worth £29,627. That wealth eventually descended to his grandson Richard, who used his Jamaican wealth and marriage to a Welsh heiress to establish large slate works in north Wales. His Jamaican plantations underwrote that industrial expansion in about the only example where the Williams thesis of plantation money underwriting British industrialization is correct. Net profits from sugar and rum on the Penrhyn properties in Jamaica increased from £6,400 per annum in 1765 to over £10,000 per annum in the 1770s and nearly £20,000 per annum in the 1780s and 1790s. The hurricanes of the 1780s and the political turmoil of the American Revolution had a small effect on overall profits, but by the early 1790s their adverse effects had been overcome. The Penrhyn properties entered into a sustained period of profitability, with net profits in 1792 reaching £23,382 and the profit per laborer (Pennant owned 1,228 slaves) being £19.04 per annum. That rate of profit meant that an African paid for himself or herself (the average price for newly arrived Africans in 1785–89 being £60.23) in a little over three years.[47] Unlike some Jamaican planters, who suffered after the abolition of the slave trade in 1807, the Pennants maintained high profitability until the 1820s. The large estates of George Hay Dawkins Pennant, for example, were very profitable even after the abolition of the slave trade. He made gross profits of £33,977 in 1811 and £32,576 in 1812, which, even after allowing for inflation and some increased expenses, suggests he was coming close to the estate's 1792 peak net profit of £23,382.[48]

It was not just the owners of large properties who prospered during the eighteenth century. The Spring Estate, a sugar-producing property in St. Andrew, has left good correspondence and an excellent set of accounts that allows us to trace profits from the 1720s through to the early nineteenth century, although there is a twenty-year gap between 1727 and 1747. It was a medium-sized estate with 123 enslaved workers and three white employees in 1754 on 600 acres, of which 120 acres were planted in sugarcane. It produced 80–90 hogsheads of sugar in a good year and 55–60 in an ordinary year. Established in the late seventeenth century by Aldworth Elbridge, from Bristol, after the death of Aldworth's brother Robert eleven-sixteenths of the plantation passed to Robert's widow, Mary, in Kingston, and then to Robert's brother John, who lived in Bristol. The remaining five-sixteenths of the one-half of the plantation were owned at midcentury by the Kingston merchant Thomas French, who kept them until his death in the mid-1780s.

Mary Elbridge found looking after the plantation hard work. She lamented to her English relative Henry Woolnough in 1739 that as he had but "recently come into the family" he could not "be Sensible what I have done to Serve not only the Plantation which I have laboured and entangled myself for this past twelve years" and made "more money of it and Saved more than ever was under any person Management." She felt undervalued: "I shall say no more than that I have been used with a Great deal of ungratitude." She thought it "very hard to be made so uneasy in my old days and in the latter part of my life" by English relatives who were refusing to sell their share of the plantation, despite her having improved it, as she thought, so that by 1739, after several hard years, it was worth £8,000, up from the £3,600 at which "Col: Dawkins previously valued it." She begged her relatives to sell soon as she wanted to "have a little quiet and ease from the troble and vexation of negros."

Mary died in 1744, and her Bristol relatives kept the estate. They did so even though the profits, which had been around £1,000 per annum in the 1720s, slipped to £414 per annum in the mid-1740s. They invested money in putting more land into cane and expanded slave numbers so that by 1754 it was producing 89 hogsheads of sugar and 27 puncheons of rum. In the 1750s profits jumped to £1,518 per annum, a profit level that continued relatively constant until the early 1780s, after which it increased a little to £1,755 per annum. The baronets Sir James and Sir John Hugh Smyth, the Bristol owners who had inherited the plantation in the 1750s and who had bought out Thomas French at his death in the mid-1780s, were convinced by their Jamaican agents, Hibbert and Co., that the estate could be made much more profitable. In 1788 they wrote that net profits were low owing mainly to "Mr French's want of economy." They pointedly noted that the estate had suffered "no droughts and sugar has sold well," and that it had "not suffered from fire insurrections foreign enemies etc." They recommended increasing the slave labor force by twenty from its current eighty-two slaves and predicted that they would clear £2,625 per annum from 70 hogsheads of sugar and 35 puncheons of rum. As it turned out, the estate vastly exceeded their predictions. The destruction of Saint-Domingue proved a bonanza for Jamaican sugar planters. The Spring Estate returned over £4,000 per annum in the early 1790s, peaking at a magnificent £5,819 in 1792. The profits were used to purchase new African slaves from the Gold Coast. The great returns of 1792 were never surpassed, but the estate still cleared £3,049 in 1800.[49]

One advantage of using the Spring Estate as an example of plantation production in Jamaica is that it was located in St. Andrew Parish, a long-settled parish neighboring Kingston that was partly a prime sugar producer, partly a locus for the development of coffee in its many hills, and partly a garden retreat known for its relative salubrity, to which many Kingston merchants were attracted. The two most important were Edward Manning (d. 1756), who kept some of his 610 slaves in the parish, and Zachary Bayly (1720–1769), the uncle of the historian Bryan Edwards, and as the owner of 2,010 enslaved people the largest slave owner listed in Jamaican inventories before 1784. What is especially helpful is that in 1754 its custos, or chief magistrate, Edmund Hyde, compiled a very detailed census of land use that allows us to evaluate agricultural production in depth at one point in time. St. Andrew was not a normal Jamaican parish, but then, no parish in the island was normal. And in its particular kind of diversity, how land was used in St. Andrew shows the importance both of sugar and of the large integrated plantation in the island's economy, and also how sugar and large estates based on slave labor could sustain considerable diversity.[50]

St. Andrew contained 68,877 acres, of which 24,703 were undeveloped and probably undevelopable. Of the remaining acreage, nearly 19,000 was in woodland and 13,000 in pasturage, leaving 3,443 acres devoted to sugar, 804 to coffee, 398 to ginger, and 76 to cotton. A further 7,332 acres were devoted to provisions. There were 155 proprietors, of whom 147 were men, a figure somewhat less than the 219 properties noted in a list of landholdings made in 1754 and the 221 proprietors noted on a map by Thomas Craskell and James Simpson compiled in the late 1750s. The most important properties were the twenty-four sugar estates on which nearly 45 percent of the parish's 7,947 slaves were held, the average estate having 174 slaves and five estates having over 200. The largest estate was that of Philip Pinnock, a high-ranking politician, who had 280 slaves and 16 white employees on 2,872 acres, of which 242 were in sugar. The most productive estate was the 2,434 acres, of which 310 acres were in cane, owned by James Gibbon, with 229 slaves. Gibbon produced 230 hogsheads of sugar and 34 puncheons of rum worth £6,647. He also had 229 cattle. Sugar was easily the most profitable commodity, accounting for £51,159 of the £67,135 plantation revenue. Sugar and rum accounted for 87 percent of plantation revenues, with coffee worth £6,419 or 10 percent of total revenues.[51]

Only one sugar property produced just sugar. That property was one of two sugar properties owned by Edward Garthwaite. There were fourteen sugar plantations on which provisions were grown and livestock were cultivated. Less wealthy men produced coffee or ginger: there were thirty-eight coffee estates and thirty-five properties producing ginger. They also hired out their slaves to sugar estates during harvest times and probably provided themselves as salaried employees to sugar planters

Table 4.6 Average Wealth of Inventoried Jamaicans, 1674–1784

Year	No.	Average Wealth (£stg.)	Average No. of Slaves	Average Value of Slaves (£stg.)	Average Value of Debts (£stg.)
1674–99	780	466	11	179	109
1700–1724	1,469	911	21	356	160
1725–49	2,752	1,688	28	614	619
1750–84	5,221	2,444	28	981	981

Source: Inventories, 1674–1784, Jamaica Inventories, IB/11/3/1–64, JA

Table 4.7 Average Wealth of Inventoried Jamaicans by Occupation over Time, 1674–1784

Occupation	No.	1674–99 (£stg.)	1700–1724 (£stg.)	1725–49 (£stg.)	1750–84 (£stg.)
Esquire	1,044	1,392	3,465	7,171	10,266
Merchant	990	1,207	1,985	2,932	4,188
Planter	2,328	395	860	1,028	1,269
Gentleman	719	440	604	1,074	726
Doctor	400	109	646	768	1,361
Tradesman	1,114	237	339	564	777
Mariner	426	177	211	477	689
Jew	439	2,122	1,982	1,643	3,796
Woman	1,192	414	561	645	1,034

Source: Inventories, 1674–1784, IB/11/3/1–64, JA

in order to supplement their earnings. That is what happened on the Spring Estate, where Humphrey Seaward, a small planter from an established St. Andrew family, acted as overseer from 1762. Livestock was a major activity, with twenty-two men specializing in livestock, and 88 percent of properties having some livestock. One hundred and eight propertyholders, or 70 percent, owned cattle totaling 4,161 head.[52]

This summary of land use in St. Andrew in 1754 demonstrates that many white people enjoyed considerable prosperity, whether they were wealthy sugar planters, moderately well-off coffee planters, or owners of livestock pens. Table 4.6 outlines the general tendencies in wealth distribution in Jamaica over time, and table 4.7 examines these wealth patterns by occupation. They show that while most of the gains in wealth over the eighteenth century accrued to the wealthiest portion of the white population, gains in wealth were sufficiently widespread that most white people felt they shared in the benefits brought by the advent of the large integrated plantation.

Components of Wealth: Land

The principal components of individual wealth were land, slaves, and debts. Let's deal with each in turn. Landownership is little studied for Jamaica, as it is for most plantation societies in British America, despite its obvious importance.[53] Researchers have veered away from studying land patterns for several reasons. First, land records, while voluminous in quantity, at least in Jamaica, are difficult to access and hard to interpret. The land conveyance deeds held at the Island Record Office follow a formulaic format that includes the date of the sale, the buyer's and seller's names and their place of residence, the selling price, the size of the property, and generally the economic specialization of the property. The context of the deeds is often missing, meaning that occasionally sale prices seem absurdly low, probably indicating that a transfer of property had taken place before it was formally recorded. In other instances a deed was not recorded for a couple of years after the transaction was done, with no explanation for the delay. Secondly, land was especially variable in quality and thus in price. A small plot of land on Kingston's waterfront or 200 acres of fully planted in sugarcane in a developing parish was immensely valuable; an undeveloped 1,000-acre tract of land in the interior mountains was virtually worthless. Consequently, while the figures presented below indicate general trends, they cannot substitute for a close study of the land market.[54]

This summary of land patterns relies on quantitative studies. I have examined all the deeds for land sales conducted in St. Andrew Parish between 1694 and 1780, following on an earlier analysis of land sales in the parish before 1690 done by W. A. Claypole.[55] The results are summarized in table 4.8. In addition, Ahmed Reid and David Ryden have done an analysis of land patterns in the island as a whole in selected years before 1810 that provides information about changes in land prices over time. Furthermore, the governor of Jamaica in 1753 ordered a listing of all landholders in the island, which was done in 1754, that allows for a comprehensive snapshot of land patterns at one point in time.

St. Andrew Parish was settled early. Until the mid-1670s smallholdings predominated, but large plantations started to take over from the 1680s. The character of St. Andrews changed after 1700. From being at the center of plantation developments in the seventeenth century, it became more peripheral in the eighteenth. By 1739 it produced just 4.4 percent of the colony's sugar and paid only 6.6 percent of the colony's poll tax. By 1768 sugar production had slipped to 3.8 percent of

Table 4.8 Land Sales in St. Andrew Parish, 1695–1780

Years	No. of Sales	Acres	Price (£stg.)	Ave. Price
1695–1704	159	17,193	9,491	0.55
1705–14	270	32,570	30,942	0.95
1715–24	230	24,169	23,295	0.96
1725–34	173	18,291	52,447	2.87
1735–44	204	28,006	44,666	1.59
1745–54	241	23,018	53,403	2.32
1755–64	329	33,308	162,514	4.88
1765–80	328	42,245	246,503	5.84

Source: Land Deeds, IRO.

the island's total sugar production, and St. Andrew's share of the poll tax was 5.3 percent.[56] Until the 1670s the price of land was minimal. It increased appreciably in the 1680s, so that good land reached over £1 per acre, but there was still a lot of other land available for lower prices. The big jump in prices came in the second decade of the eighteenth century. Prices were £0.55 per acre between 1695 and 1704 but jumped to over £0.90 per acre after 1712.

By this date a well-developed sugar property was expensive. Lewis Archbould sold his sugar estate of 160 acres for £2,000 in 1710 to Richard Rigby, a prominent political placeman. Increasingly, as the large integrated plantation became the norm in the parish, by the 1720s such prices became normal. It was hard to get land for less than £1 an acre after 1713, and by 1725 the average price of land had jumped to £2.77 an acre. Economic slowdown in 1730s led to a drop in the average price of land to under £2 per acre. But good property was still sold for excellent prices. In 1742, for example, Edward Yeamans sold 190 acres to Charity Collins for £3,000. It was after the start of the Seven Years' War that land prices increased rapidly. The average price of land increased to £4.88 per acre between 1756 and 1764, and to £5.84 in the 1770s, while the average number of sales jumped from 241 to 329 per decade. Good estates went for large sums. In 1751 a 500-acre estate was sold for £4,325, and in 1758 the same size estate fetched £6,400, while a 386-acre sugar estate was sold to Mathew Gregory, a member of Council, for £10,000. By the mid-1760s Lewis Archbould's grandson, Henry, sold 1,400 acres to Daniel Moore, a Kingston merchant, for £23,000.

The vibrant land market in St. Andrew after 1750 was replicated in Jamaica as a whole. Reid and Ryden's analysis of the Jamaican land market in selected years shows that between 1750 and 1810, there was an average of 328 sales per annum or 19,000 land sales over sixty years, with around 3,720,000 acres changing hands, or roughly 1.5 times the total size of cultivable land in the island. Reid and Ryden estimate that around 2.6 percent of land turned over every year, which was greater than in eighteenth-century South Carolina and in Essex in England. Their estimates of annual turnover are probably low, especially for the mid-eighteenth century, as they chose 1760 as one of their reference years. That was the year of Tacky's Revolt, a major slave uprising that brought the land market virtually to a halt. There were only 89 land sales in that year, compared to 396 a decade earlier, 164 a decade later, and 341 in 1780. The land market became more active over time. By 1790 there were 426 transactions a year and a very high 668 transactions in 1800, a year in which the annual turnover of land was around 4.6 percent. The volume of land sales mirrored economic cycles. There were few in 1760, when the future of the island seemed in doubt, and very high numbers of sales in the booming years of the 1790s, when profits from sugar were considerable. Land was always expensive, especially good land suitable for sugar or town lots in Kingston and to a lesser extent in St. Jago de la Vega. In the late 1790s, however, land prices moved beyond what was sustainable. Buoyed by the boom in sugar prices, purchasers of land in the decade before the abolition of the slave trade participated in an over-stimulated market and paid outrageous sums for productive plantation land, which bore little relationship to real returns. It was the people who bought land in this decade who were particularly badly affected when the bubble in Jamaican agricultural land prices burst after 1807.[57]

The Jamaican land market in the second half of the eighteenth century was affected by two things in particular. Kingston was especially important, accounting for nearly one-quarter of all transactions. It experienced a much greater rate of turnover—9.5 percent—than any other parish; only its also mainly urban neighbor, Port Royal, with 7.9 percent annual turnover, approached Kingston's frenetic activity. There were in addition a larger number of female buyers and sellers (women tended to sell to each other) in Kingston than in rural areas. Outside Kingston women seldom entered the land market, being only 7.7 percent of sellers and 4.1 percent of buyers in Reid and Ryden's survey, and selling landholdings on average only one-third as large as those sold by men. What was distinctive about Kingston's flourishing land market was that from the turn of the nineteenth century it was decoupled from what was happening in the countryside. Land prices continued to soar in Kingston after 1805 even while they were collapsing elsewhere.

Kingston real estate was always expensive and became increasingly more so. Between 1750 and 1810 prices soared by 425 percent, and be-

Drawn by James Silvester   Engraved by D.T. Egerton

Monument of the late Thos. Hibbert Esqr.

at Aqualta Vale, St Marys

Published Apr 1 1824 by Hurst Robinson & Co 90 Cheapside & E Lloyd Harley St London

FIGURE 8. Thomas Hibbert (1708–1780) was "one of the principal and most opulent merchants in Kingston." He bought a 3,000-acre estate in Aqualta Vale, on the north side of Jamaica. In 1815 his descendants still owned this property, on which there were 896 slaves and 633 head of cattle. *Monument of the Late Thos. Hibbert, Esq. at Aqualta Vale Penn, St Mary's*, plate 9 in James Hakewill, *A Picturesque Tour of the Island of Jamaica* (London, 1825; reprint, Kingston: Mill Press, 1990). Private collection.

tween 1750 and 1770 they increased by 67 percent. Land prices increased by a further 30 percent between 1770 and 1790 and then nearly doubled between 1790 and 1810. The extraordinary increase around the turn of the nineteenth century reflected the intensification of trade between Spanish America and the British empire that occurred during Britain's long war with Napoleonic Europe. Kingston was at the epicenter of this intensified trade. By 1808 Thomas Coke described Kingston as "the emporium of foreign commerce of the whole island," with great merchants building large houses on the edge of town. It also was the place where a large percentage of refugees from Saint-Domingue settled, pushing up prices in a town where new building was limited by geography. In effect, Kingston turned after 1807 to trade with Latin America, replicating what merchants had done in the 1730s and 1740s—effectively separating the town from the plantation economy.[58]

FIGURE 9. *View of Harbour Street, Kingston,* plate 3 in James Hakewill, *A Picturesque Tour of the Island of Jamaica* (London, 1825; reprint, Kingston: Mill Press, 1990). Private collection.

Elsewhere in Jamaica sugar was the major influence on land prices. A sugar plantation was over two and a half times as valuable as average land, even though most sugar estates generally included a mix of land types. Edward Long estimated in 1774 that the best cane land, producing four hogsheads per acre, was worth £57 per acre, with ordinary cane land valued at £20 per acre. Provision grounds, by contrast, he valued at £7 per acre, and woodland and other barely productive land was worth £2 per acre. The value of cane land on a sugar estate was slightly more than 70 percent of total real estate costs.[59] Land suitable for sugar, because it was so valuable, squeezed out land that might be used for other activities. The market operated so that sugar plantations were on the most productive land; other types of agriculture were on less productive plots.[60] Using the long-established rural parish of Clarendon as a reference point, Reid and Ryden show that land on the Jamaican frontier, where the large integrated plantation was especially dominant, was considerably more expensive than land elsewhere. The most expensive land in rural Jamaica was in far western Hanover, where an average acre was nearly twice as expensive as in Clarendon. Land in Trelawney, St. James, and St. Mary in northern Jamaica was worth nearly 50 percent more than land in Clarendon. St. Thomas-in-the-East also had expensive land, the average price of an acre being 27 percent higher than in Clarendon. Conversely, the scrubby land of southwestern St. Elizabeth and the rainy parishes of Portland and St. George were valued between 25 and 50 percent lower than land in Clarendon.[61]

Land prices mirrored how well the Jamaica economy was doing, and for most of the second half of the eighteenth century, Jamaica was prosperous. Between 1750 and 1790 prices rose steadily. Good years in the 1760s saw relatively little overall increase in land prices, mainly because there was probably still some land available from the excess holdings of planters, as Thomas Thistlewood found in 1765 when he bought 600 acres in Westmoreland Parish.[62] Between 1770 and 1780 prices increased more rapidly, by 37 percent, but fell again by 18.5 percent in the 1780s. The booming 1790s, however, saw a rapid increase in prices, such that by 1800 the price of agricultural land was 60 percent higher than in 1750, with a 40 percent increase in one decade alone. The abolition of the slave trade in 1807, however, saw a catastrophic decline: by 1810 land prices were 5 percent less than what they had been in 1750. Thus, the abolition of the slave trade proved disastrous for planters who had poured capital into overvalued Jamaican sugar plantations in the 1790s, even though slave prices and sugar production did not follow land prices into irreversible decline until nearly fifteen years later.[63]

Rising prices encouraged Jamaican planters to accumulate land. Well-placed Jamaican planters encouraged land engrossment so that land was taken out of circulation and not made available for development. They did so, it was argued by imperial officials who opposed their actions, in order to artificially boost land prices through the manipulation of supply-and-demand cycles. Metropolitan officials and imperial governors linked the slow growth of white population, Jamaica's disorganized militia, its confrontational politics, and its large areas of undeveloped land to a single issue: the accumulation of thousands of acres of uncultivated land by planters who controlled the political process and who used their power to acquire land through dodgy titles. Moreover, the most prominent of these planters, notably William Beckford, the largest landowner in the island, were resident in Britain, adding fuel to accusations that absentees were not acting in the best interests of the island. Imperial leaders introduced scheme after scheme to force Jamaica's largest landholders to either relinquish title to undeveloped land or else develop that land. Each scheme, however, failed. Sir Charles Price, the influential speaker of the House of Assembly in most years from midcentury to his death in 1772, was especially prominent in efforts to ensure that no real action was taken to stop land engrossment. Price, the owner of between 10,000 and 15,000 acres in the 1750s and over 20,000 acres by his death, was a dedicated land speculator who at his death was discovered to have gotten most of his land acquisitions through fraud.[64]

Charles Knowles, Jamaica's governor between 1752 and 1756 and the loser in a mighty contest between an assertive planter-controlled Assembly and an increasingly domineering imperial center, fulminated to the duke of Newcastle in 1754 that "powerful princes" held "vast Tracts of Land" under uncertain title. Their engrossing policies, he argued, meant that planters were able to keep the price of sugar high by keeping out potential new recruits and by preventing having their uncultivated lands "being improved into Sugar Plantations." He wanted to reduce "these Mighty-Men" by making sure that some of the excess land that they owned "were resumed by Law and Vested again in the Crown." In order to prove his claims of considerable land engrossment, he commissioned the clerks in the receiver general's office in St. Jago de la Vega to compile a list of landholders in the islands, derived from the quit-rents books. The subsequent list provides a guide to who owned what land in Jamaica on the eve of the Seven Years' War. This careful accounting of landholdings amply confirmed Knowles's point that land engrossment was rife. Landownership was widely spread but very concentrated, with greater amounts of land held in large parcels than in 1670, where mean acreage was relatively small, the spread of landholding size between large and small relatively limited, and most land was cheap and acquired through inexpensive government patent.[65]

Landowners

The list of landholders of 1754 carefully enumerates the landholdings of 1,595 landholders who between them owned 1,684,198 acres. Nine in ten landowners were male, and men owned over 95 percent of all land. Landowners living outside of Jamaica owned some land, but most (over 95 percent) were resident in the island. The largest 477 landowners, those people who owned 1,000 acres or more, possessed 73.7 percent of all land; the top 159 possessed 844,567 acres, or 50.2 percent of total acreage. William Beckford, one of the relatively rare absentee landowners, owned over 20,000 acres; a further ten men owned between 10,000 and 20,000 acres; and a further 212 individuals owned over 2,000 acres each. Many of these large landholders owned parcels of land throughout the island, with over 30 percent of owners having title to land in more than one parish and ten men, including Price and Beckford, who had land in more than five parishes. A large percentage of these large landholdings were "ruinate" or uncultivated. Long estimated that a very large sugar estate with 300 slaves producing 300 hogsheads a year would require 900 acres of land, of which 88 might be in woodland, while an average sugar estate producing 100 hogsheads could be run on 300 acres. The detailed listing of land in St. Andrew suggests that 53 percent of all land and one-quarter of land held by sugar planters in that parish was woodland or uncultivated. What landowners were doing was exactly what Knowles accused them of: keeping excess land in a land bank. They did so, however, for more prosaic reasons than to keep the price of sugar artificially high (a strategy no individual planter had the power to implement and one that was also beyond the collective efforts of assemblymen), or to limit white settlement (it was hardly in planters' interest to do this, given how much they needed to pay in deficiency tax due to a low white population). Rather, they did so in order to profit from future increases in the price of real estate. It was a sensible strategy. A 1,000-acre plot of land patented for virtually nothing in St. Andrew Parish prior to 1670 was worth £680 in the 1690s, £950 in the 1710s, £2,060 in the 1740s, £4,880 during the Seven Years' War, and £5,884 by the eve of the American Revolution. Some of that increase in land value came from improvements to the land, but most came from price appreciation. The landholders of 1754 were sitting on a gold mine, and they knew it. They struck financial gold in the boom years of the 1790s, when the prices paid for sugar estates surpassed all reasonable expectations of return.[66]

By 1754 three broad patterns of landownership in Jamaica existed. The first was on the frontier, in the newly developing sugar monocultural areas of the northwest and far east. In these regions, almost all landowners were men, and there were high mean and median levels of landownership. In the older settled parishes around the urban centers of St. Jago de la Vega and Kingston, both mean and median landholding levels were lower than average, and the number of landholders, including appreciably more women than on the frontier, was comparatively large. The third kind of landownership was in the towns, notably Kingston. In the early 1750s the value of Kingston private real estate was worth, conservatively, about £500,000, with further money tied up in churches, barracks, wharfs, and other public buildings. It was a town of renters as much as owners: in 1745, 292 landlords rented out 786 of the 844 occupied properties and got £114 rent on average from their properties per annum. The richest landlords made substantial sums from renting. In 1769 the Pereira family made £2,046 per annum from 39 urban rentals, while the Gutterez family realized £1,285 per annum from their 30 properties and Samuel Adams made £810 from his rentals. Investing in urban property was favored by people who worked outside the plantation economy. Not many merchants were landlords: only one merchant dying between 1745 and 1760 with personal property worth more than £2,500 had more than one rental property in Kingston in 1745. Of the forty-nine landlords who made more than £160 in rental income per annum, there were three carpenters, an ironmonger, a mariner, two gentlemen, three doctors, eleven Jews, four women, and a free person of color. That year the total value of rents was £40,379, or £38.86 per householder, with rents ranging from a nominal sum to £325. Before 1770 investing in Kingston real estate was financially viable but not as lucrative as investing in the plantation economy. The number of rented properties that returned money increased from 786 in 1745 to 961 in 1769, and the total value of rents in the town increased by 4 percent per annum from 1745 to 1753, and then from 2 percent per annum from 1753 to 1769. In 1769 total rents had increased by 55 percent from 1745, to £62,690. People made money less in increased rents than in more intensive development of undeveloped properties, from the 175 properties that were not returning rent in 1745 but were doing so in 1769.[67]

Components of Wealth: Slaves

Land in the countryside increased in value because it was worked by slaves, a category of wealth that also became increasingly more valuable over time. In an important article, David Eltis, Frank D. Lewis, and David Richardson provide empirical evidence and theoretical models explaining the strong economic performance of British West Indian slave economies in the eighteenth century. They used a database of slave prices for new African slaves in the Atlantic slave trade combined with sugar-price data to show that plantation agriculture in the region was highly productive by preindustrial standards. Between 1700 and 1807 slave productivity rates increased by 56 percent, or an average annual rate of 0.4 percent, varying between 0.23 to 0.49 percent per annum at different times. They see four periods of accelerated productivity: the 1640s to the 1670s, mainly in Barbados; the early 1710s to the early 1730s, when the large integrated plantation developed in Jamaica; the early 1760s to the mid-1770s; and the mid-1790s through to the mid-1800s. They also note a sharp decline in productivity in the 1730s and early 1740s, when sugar prices collapsed and slave prices in the Atlantic slave trade accelerated. Their data, which extend to the end of the slave trade, suggest that West Indian planters entered a bubble economy in the early 1800s, when slave prices rose to levels beyond slaveholders' capacity to sustain through increasing slave productivity. Planters stock-piled slaves in these years in the expectation that the slave trade would end soon.[68]

Eltis, Lewis, and Richardson posit four possible reasons that productivity gains were so rapid in eighteenth-century Jamaica. Slave populations may have experienced lower mortality rates during the eighteenth century. Data on slave mortality prior to the late eighteenth century is scarce and inconclusive, but Eltis, Lewis, and Richardson plausibly suggest, working from population benchmarks, that annual attrition rates in the western Caribbean (including Saint-Domingue) between 1670 and 1700 were 4.85 percent. These rates declined to 3.45 percent between 1700 and 1750 and to 2.77 percent between 1750 and 1790,[69] figures that accord with estimates made by Michael Craton about slave mortality trends and with slave price data from the early eighteenth century.[70] In this period, the average price of a slave noted in an inventory was around three-quarters of the price of a new African slave, suggesting that there were many unhealthy slaves on Jamaican plantations, that there were relatively high percentages of children in slave forces,[71] and that buyers of slaves who purchased from estates rather than from ships added in a substantial discount in order to account for the risk of excess mortality. Eltis, Lewis, and Richardson also suggest that improved planting methods and new and more productive varieties of sugarcane, such as the Otaheite strain introduced from the Pacific in the late eighteenth century, made plantation agriculture more effective. Studies of late eighteenth-century plantation agriculture in the British West Indies provide ample evidence of planters' innovative agricultural tendencies. In addition, improved infrastructure, especially in shipping, and more effective financial intermediation, especially better credit facilities, led to greater slave productivity.[72]

The last factor that Eltis, Lewis, and Richardson note as leading to productivity gains was human capital improvements. This is probably the most significant and most dynamic part of the increase in productivity gains and can be traced, if imperfectly, through data obtained from inventories. Slaves accounted for over 40 percent of all slaveholders' inventoried wealth in the mid-seventeenth century, rose to 53 percent

Table 4.9 Slave Prices in Jamaica, 1674–1784

Year	No. of Observations of Slaveholders[1]	Average Price of Slave in Inventories[2] (£Stg.)	Average Price of New African Slave in the Caribbean[2] (£Stg.)	(2)/(3) (%)	Average Price of Sugar, London, Shillings/ Hundredweight.[2] (£Stg.)	(2)/(5) (%)	(3)/(5) (%)	Average Value of Slave Property[3]	Average Percentage of Personal Property Made Up of Slaves[4]	Average No. of Slaves Owned By Jamaican Slave Owners[5]
	(1)	(2)	(3)	(4)	(5)	(6)	(7)	(8)	(9)	(10)
1674	11	13.41	19.86	67.5	23.50	57.1	84.5	103.06	30	7
1675–79	128	14.81	19.35	76.5	21.78	68.0	88.8	202.89	46	14
1680–84	64	13.63	16.72	81.5	20.38	70.9	82.0	254.97	46	19
1685–89	176	13.62	18.44	73.9	21.52	63.3	85.7	213.62	41	16
1690–94	171	14.99	20.19	74.2	35.26	42.5	57.3	217.69	48	15
1695–99	6	16.61	23.33	71.1	39.38	42.2	59.2	227.07	45	16
1700–1704	165	17.97	23.51	76.4	43.28	41.5	54.3	392.96	48	25
1705–9	39	16.62	25.06	66.3	33.40	49.8	75.0	431.78	51	26
1710–14	270	15.74	23.00	68.4	55.15	28.5	41.7	355.85	59	24
1715–19	291	17.69	18.39	96.2	32.33	54.7	56.9	485.95	52	27
1720–24	343	18.67	24.99	74.7	25.50	73.2	98.0	582.34	52	31

1725–29	327	19.41	30.55	63.5	26.00	74.7	117.5	597.50	50	30
1730–34	343	19.60	22.82	85.9	19.75	99.2	115.5	830.32	45	41
1735–39	319	18.95	28.25	67.1	22.10	85.7	127.8	995.12	53	50
1740–44	513	21.94	28.46	77.1	29.88	73.4	95.2	694.02	49	33
1745–49	617	27.82	26.19	106.2	35.00	79.5	74.8	868.10	49	33
1750–54	413	25.60	30.90	82.8	33.14	77.2	93.2	951.74	48	38
1755–59	588	29.22	30.93	94.5	39.08	74.8	79.1	1,046.36	52	36
1760–64	591	33.83	32.23	105.0	36.00	94.0	89.5	1,099.35	55	33
1765–69	668	34.89	39.22	89.0	36.84	94.7	106.5	1,205.74	52	36
1770–74	491	38.90	43.01	90.4	36.18	107.5	118.9	1,813.69	58	46
1775–79	629	43.10	43.07	100.0	45.36	95.0	95.0	1,484.10	57	35
1780–84	577	45.10	44.44	101.5	49.10	91.9	90.5	1,502.21	55	33

Source: Inventories, 1674–1784, IB/11/3/1–64, JA; David Eltis, Frank D. Lewis, and David Richardson, "Slave Prices, the African Slave Trade, and Productivity in the Caribbean, 1674–1807," *Economic History Review* 4 (2005): 679. I have not adjusted, as did Eltis, Lewis, and Richardson, observations of prices by English price indexes, since the link between Jamaican prices and English prices has not been tested.

[1]In Jamaican inventories for time span.

[2]By current price.

[3]Slave owners only, Jamaican inventories.

[4]For Jamaican slave owners in Jamaican inventories.

[5]In Jamaican inventories.

of inventoried wealth by the late 1700s, and increased to a peak of 59 percent of average inventoried slaveholders' wealth between 1710 and 1714. Slaves declined in significance as a percentage of inventoried wealth after the late 1710s, reaching a low of 45 percent in the early 1730s before gradually increasing again to 57 percent in the 1770s. David Ryden estimates the average annual gross returns on slave investment between 1752 and 1807 at 17.8 percent. It therefore made sense for slave owners to do their best to improve the human capital that produced those returns.[73]

One sign of the value planters placed upon their slave investment was that slaves were described and tabulated in inventories in increasingly sophisticated ways. Over time, slave owners moved from noting slaves as an undifferentiated mass to adding more and more characteristics about individual enslaved people. After the 1730s appraisers of inventoried estates increased information about individual slaves and became increasingly able to differentiate among slaves based on such things as their occupation, health, age, ethnicity, and, sometimes, color. Increasing information enabled slave owners to price slaves accurately. By the late 1760s the price of slaves was within 8 percent of the value of sugar, which Jamaicans considered the best guide to how slaves ought to be priced. As one observer put it in 1803, when sugar prices fell "the price of Negroes must Fall, at least if they bear a proportion to the fall in Produce."[74]

Slaves were expensive enough for slave buyers to take a great interest in their purchase. Thomas Thistlewood, for example, wrote at length in his diary about how "in regard to buying off Negroes" he preferred to buy adolescents under eighteen "as full grown Men or Women Seldom turn out well." He pointed out the several ways by which slave merchants prepared slaves so that they looked "Fatt and Sleek" on a ship, though they could not maintain their condition once on a plantation.[75] Over time the selling of slaves became more market oriented, especially as the trade came to be dominated by leading Kingston merchants, who bought slaves wholesale in order to sell them at retail. Buyers may have had strong opinions about what sort of slaves they wanted, but they were not the principal players in a complex system that relied ultimately upon decisions made by African merchants about the Africans they provided for sale, and upon slave captains determining at which slave port they would sell their human goods. The supply of African slaves improved after private traders supplemented and then supplanted the Royal African Company in the early eighteenth century. Nevertheless, the demand for slaves was always so strong that Jamaican slave purchasers took what was available rather than what they wanted.[76]

Slave Ownership and Slave Prices

Slave ownership, like landownership, was widespread and highly concentrated. Three-quarters of inventoried wealth holders owned slaves. The very wealthiest Jamaicans poured as much money into buying slaves, which were still relatively cheap, as they could. Some changes in the structure of slaveholding can be traced in the number and prices of slaves as detailed in inventories as compared to the price of newly arrived Africans and in the price of sugar in London as a proxy for the state of the Jamaican economy.

It was a period of rapidly rising sugar prices, with the price of sugar increasing from 35 shillings per hundredweight in the early 1690s to 55 shillings per hundredweight between 1710 and 1714. The average price of new African slaves also increased, but more slowly, from an average of £20 in the 1690s to £23 between 1710 and 1714. One reason the price of slaves did not increase as much as that of sugar was that the volume of slave arrivals doubled per annum between the early 1690s and the late 1720s. The slave trade also became more efficient in this period, achieving the same profit margins on larger volumes, thus allowing merchants to keep price increases down. The result was that the ratio between the price of slaves and the price of sugar reached all-time lows, with the price of a new African being just 42 percent of the price of sugar between 1710 and 1714. This large price differential encouraged planters to stock their plantations with as many slaves as they could at a time when slaves were less expensive relative to sugar than at any time in Jamaican history, and when soaring land prices were keeping smaller operators from starting new sugar plantations. Between 1705 and 1709 the price of new slaves declined by 9 percent, while the price of sugar increased by 51 percent. The effect of these interrelated developments meant that the average investment in slaves increased from £220 in the 1690s to £585 in the 1720s, an increase of 166 percent, even though the average price of enslaved people barely increased. The average inventoried slave was valued at £17.17 between 1700 and 1704 and at £18.95 between 1735 and 1739.

The second major shift in slave prices came in the late 1740s. After a long period of stagnation, London sugar prices rose appreciably in the early 1750s. Prices during the Seven Years' War were 39 percent higher than a decade earlier. Slave values had started to increase a few years before sugar prices began to rise. By the late 1760s the average price of a new African slave in the Caribbean was 46 percent higher than it had been twenty years previously, while the average price of a slave in Jamaican inventories was 65 percent higher in the late 1760s than in the early 1740s. By the early 1780s the average price of an inventoried slave was £45.10, or just over double what a slave had been worth in the early 1740s and three times as much as a slave had been valued at in the early 1690s.

After the Seven Years' War the previously considerable differential between the prices of slaves from Africa and the prices of slaves on the plantation virtually disappeared. Table 4.10 shows that from the 1740s an inventoried slave was worth over 90 percent of the price of a new slave. Given that the general Jamaican slave population contained more old people, more children, and more sick slaves than were found on newly arriving slave ships, this lessening of the price differential points to how planters improved their human capital. Increasing life expectancy rates, as seen in falling attrition rates, played a part in rising slave prices. Changes in credit arrangements, which led to a drop in interest rates from 10 percent before 1738 to 8 percent between 1738 and 1751 and 6 percent after 1751, also had an effect on rising slave prices.[77]

The decline in the price differential for inventoried slaves and the price of new Africans was probably a combination of better information about the individual characteristics of slaves, lower slave mortality, and highly positive confidence in the future of plantation agriculture in the island. Certainly individual slaves became more accurately priced over time. Between the 1760s and the 1780s the price of slaves was within 8 percent of the value of sugar. Eltis, Lewis, and Richardson suggest that productivity must have, at a conservative estimate, doubled between 1700 and 1790. Work by David Ryden and J. R. Ward supports this interpretation. Ward divided aggregate output by the number of slaves working in sugar to show appreciable gains in output per hand from the 1730s onward. Ryden argues that whereas aggregate worker productivity was 512 pounds of sugar per sugar-estate slave in the 1750s, it had nearly doubled to 974 pounds of sugar per slave by the 1790s.[78]

The Jamaican slave force also improved over time in several key characteristics. Slave forces became close to being gender balanced, despite a small bias toward men in deliveries of Africans to Jamaica in the Atlantic slave trade. This gender balance probably reflected the better survival rates of women over men. The male percentage declined slightly over

Table 4.10 Slave Prices in Jamaica, 1674–1784: Comparison of
New Africans and Inventoried Africans

Decade	Average Price of Inventoried Slave (%)	Average Price of Inventoried Slave in Slave Forces of 150+ (%)
1670s	75.0	63.4
1680s	75.8	65.9
1690s	74.1	67.8
1700s	75.1	69.3
1710s	82.5	75.4
1720s	69.1	74.4
1730s	77.1	78.9
1740s	92.0	89.7
1750s	89.1	88.3
1760s	98.6	97.2
1770s	89.4	98.7
1780s	101.6	100.7

Source: See table 4.9.
Note: Prices are shown as a percentage of prices of a newly arrived African slave.

time, from 55 percent between 1725 and 1734 to 53 percent between 1775 and 1784. What was more consequential was a sizable increase in the percentage of the inventoried slave population that was adult. It increased over time from a low of 72 percent in the decade between 1715 and 1724 to 78 percent in the decade between 1775 and 1784. Productivity rates were high in part because the productive element of the slave population was so high. Data from one well-chronicled inventory with a large slave force from 1775 and two estate records from 1778 and 1779 where ages were included along with other information about slaves show that 1,134 of 1,900 slaves working in sugar (60 percent) in the late 1770s were aged between fifteen and forty-four, prime working years.[79]

Planters adopted slave-management strategies that were the polar opposite of those adopted in the Chesapeake, where from the 1740s there was a naturally increasing slave population. In the Chesapeake planters encouraged slave breeding and fostered positive pregnancy regimes in order to increase the number of children born on their estates who, upon reaching adolescence, could be sold in the burgeoning slave trade between Virginia and Louisiana.[80] In Jamaica, however, planters did virtually nothing to encourage women to have children, at least while the Atlantic slave trade provided them with a ready stream of new slaves and before abolitionists forced them onto the defensive in regard to their treatment of pregnant women. Their low regard for children can be seen in how they valued them in inventories, where slaves noted as children were valued between 1775 and 1784 at £8.70, a third of the price given to slaves designated as boys or girls and nearly six times less than that of adult males. Most of the value attached to children, moreover, went to slaves past infancy. Infants were seldom valued at all, being listed with their mothers without a price being attached to them. Infant and child mortality rates were so high that planters saw little point in trying to support pregnant mothers or to help women with infant children. Indeed, they resented women who became pregnant or had children, as this reduced their pool of prime working hands.[81]

Planters concentrated on improving the skills of their male slaves while leaving women to do the majority of fieldwork. The quickest and most effective way of increasing individual slave values was in training the most likely male slaves to be tradesmen. Before the 1730s planters faced opposition from white tradesmen who believed that if slaves became tradesmen, these whites would be squeezed out of the marketplace. For a variety of reasons, the most important being that white tradesmen themselves were busy training slaves in trades, white Jamaicans stopped listening to white tradesmen's complaints about competition from slave tradesmen. Beginning in the 1730s larger planters began to train up slaves as tradesmen. It made financial sense to do so: slave tradesmen brought a strong premium in the market. In the 1770s slave tradesmen were valued at £84, while healthy men slaves of working age who were not tradesmen were priced at £62. The average price for men in general (including the sick and the elderly) between 1775 and 1784 was £51 and for women it was £38. The differential between tradesmen and prime male hands was thus 27 percent, while the gap between a slave tradesman and the average male slave (including unhealthy and superannuated slaves) was 65 percent. Bearing in mind that only the most promising male slaves were trained as tradesmen, if a slave owner converted a field hand into a tradesman, he increased revenue and was able to move less good slaves into the field while moving more productive slaves into trades.[82] More sustained attention to other aspects of the plantation process meant that these human-resource decisions had few negative consequences, since plantation productivity increased despite the likely lower quality of field hands.[83]

The value of investment in slave property could also be increased by making slaves work in sugar. Urban slaves, who tended to have a wide range of skills, were valued less than unskilled rural slaves. The average price of slaves owned by residents of Kingston who left inventories between 1770 and 1784 was £37.86, compared to £44.82 for slaves owned by residents of north-central parishes and £48.93 for slaves owned by people resident in the far western parishes. Slaves owned by planters were on average £5 more expensive than those owned by merchants. Moreover, slaves working on large integrated plantations became increasingly valuable compared to other slaves. In the seventeenth century, as table 4.10 shows, slaves owned by slave owners who possessed 150 or more slaves were worth less than two-thirds of the average price of a newly purchased African in the Atlantic slave trade. Over time, however, that price differential narrowed. Between the 1680s and the 1780s slaves owned by slave owners with 150 or more slaves moved from being worth 63 percent of the value of a new African slave to being worth exactly the same as a newly purchased African. This narrowing of a significant price differential between newly arrived Africans and all slaves is all the more significant given how arduous conditions were on sugar plantations (where most such slaves worked), leading to terrible morbidity and mortality rates. The lowering of the price differential reflected productivity gains in sugar and the high expectations Jamaicans had for future profits in sugar production.

Slaves made white Jamaicans wealthy in two ways. First, Jamaican slave owners used slaves to produce income. In the second half of the eighteenth century, the income made from slaves may have reached close to its natural preindustrial limits. Barry Higman estimates that in 1800 per capita productivity in Jamaica was £29.20, an extraordinary degree of productivity for preindustrial times.[84] Second, slaves formed an essential and increasingly important part of individual wealth portfolios. The rapid increase in slave prices in the second half of the eighteenth century made slaves appreciating assets. It is no surprise that ordinary Jamaicans bought slaves as soon as they could afford to, often before they had become property owners. Being a slave owner and thus a master meant something in a society in which lordship over dependents brought great social prestige. But the main reason that Jamaicans bought slaves was that they were likely to increase in value. A slave force of 100 slaves was worth £3,489 in 1765 and £4,310 ten years later, an increase of £82.10 per annum over and above what slaves produced in income. Of course, making that sort of money required luck, especially low slave mortality, but in some years in the 1760s and 1770s slaves were appreciating by as much as £1 each per annum, making investment in slaves very worthwhile. The increasing number of slaves in Jamaica and their increasing value made investment in slavery an ever more important component of Jamaican wealth. The value of slaves in Jamaica in 1722 can be estimated at £1,757,460; in 1761 it had increased to £5,819,857, and in 1778 the value of slave property was £10,567,783. Jamaican slaveholders by the time of the American Revolution thus had large amounts of money invested in slavery. In 1775, 148 inventoried slaveholders listed 7,049 slaves, or an average of 48 slaves each. The total value of these slaves was £306,474 and the average value of slaves in the inventoried estates of 1775 was £2,071. The largest slaveholders were among the greatest slaveholders in plantation America. There were eight men dying in 1775 who had slave forces that were worth over £10,000. John Bryan had 741 slaves worth £31,574, John McLeod had 417 slaves worth £20,400, and John Nixon had 350 slaves worth £17,295.

Components of Wealth: Moneylending

The final major component of Jamaican wealth was money lent out to others. Estimating debt levels in Jamaica is difficult owing to an absence of quantifiable data about how much people were in debt. It was commonly assumed that planter debts were enormous, amounting to millions of pounds in the years immediately before the American Revolution. But while indebtedness was undoubtedly greater in the West Indies than elsewhere in plantation America, and while Jamaica was an extremely litigious society in which actions over debt were the major reasons for litigation (between 1772 and 1791, 80,021 executions for £22,563,786 were lodged in the provost marshal's office in St. Jago de la Vega on judgments in the Jamaican supreme court), debt was not unmanageable. Merchants were not fools. They lent money because they expected to make good returns: they expected to collect the majority of their debts. When sugar prices were high, slave imports were certain, productivity rates were improving, and credit was available, planters could be reasonably sure that taking on prudent amounts of debt would not compromise their estates.[85]

We can make some general observations about levels of debt in Jamaica from what is noted about credit in inventories. First, the amount of money lent by Jamaicans to other Jamaicans was considerable. The average indebted estate listed £1,946 in debts. Many Jamaicans lent out vastly more than that sum. Of the 137 people who died with estates valued at more than £20,000, the average amount of debt per estate was £20,827, and total debts were £2,853,232. The biggest moneylenders lent extremely large sums. There were nine men (seven of whom were Kingston or St. Jago de la Vega merchants) who lent out more than £50,000, with Sir Simon Clarke, Edward Foord, Samuel Delpratt,

Peter Beckford, Aaron Baruh Lousada, John Morse, and George Paplay each outlaying more than £70,000 in loans to other Jamaicans. To keep this in perspective, only one man in colonial Maryland—Charles Carroll of Annapolis—lent money on the Jamaican scale, with £57,400 out on loan in 1776. Virtually no one else in Maryland at the start of the American Revolution had more than £15,000 out in loans. Secondly, the amount of money lent out increased considerably over time. During the eighteenth century it became ever more common for white Jamaicans to lend money. The percentage of inventories containing debts increased from 43 percent for people dying before 1700 to 61 percent for people dying after 1749. Consequently, the average amount that debt made up of the average estate increased over time: from under 20 percent for people dying before 1720 to over 30 percent for people dying after 1764. By the early 1780s, 34 percent of the average Jamaican estate was held as debts, with that percentage increasing to 52 percent for the two-thirds of indebted estates.

The data in table 4.11 show that in the late seventeenth century the average total of credits per annum listed in Jamaican inventories was £3,283. This figure nearly tripled in the first quarter of the eighteenth century, increased to £68,143 per annum in the second quarter of the eighteenth century, and exploded to £146,312 for the years between 1750 and 1784. By the 1760s a tabulation of debts in inventories suggests that every year 160 decedents lent out over £161,141 to fellow Jamaicans. As the white adult male population in the 1760s was around 5,000, of whom at least half were wealth holders, the amount lent out in any given year in the 1760s should probably be increased around fifteenfold, to nearly £2.4 million. By the American Revolution the annual amount lent out by the 140 decedents who died between 1776 and 1784 was £184,964, suggesting, if the same ratios are used as above, that the amount given out in loans within Jamaica probably approached £3.5 million per annum in this period.

Although no debts were recorded in 45 percent of inventories (undoubtedly underestimating the numbers of people who lent money to others), and although nearly 60 percent of all testators had estates in which money lent out made up less than 20 percent of their personal estate, there were 1,843 people (18 percent of all testators) for whom debt made up between 60 and 99 percent of their personal wealth. A considerable percentage of these moneylenders lived in Kingston and surrounding areas. Jamaican whites tended to congregate in towns: 45 percent of the monies lent in Jamaica belonged to residents of Kingston, Port Royal, or St. Andrew, with residents of Kingston alone accounting

Table 4.11 Sum of Loans Recorded in Jamaican Inventories, 1674–1784

Years	No. of Inventories	Total Debt per Annum (£stg.)	Average Debt (£stg.)
1675–1700	780	3,283	109.44
1700–1724	1,469	9,383	159.69
1725–49	2,752	68,143	619.04
1750–84	5,221	146,312	980.83

Source: Inventories, 1674–1784

for 39 percent of monies lent out. People living in Britain accounted for a further 7 percent of monies lent, with residents of St. Catherine Parish, which contained the colonial capital and the small town St. Jago de la Vega, holding 12 percent of debts. Kingston moneylenders thus dominated the debt market. The average percentage of total estate value of Kingstonians leaving over £15,000 made up by debts was 67 percent. Some moneylenders made most of their money from this means: Solomon Nunes Flamingo died with an estate of £15,254, including six slaves, and with debts of £14,564 or 95 percent of his estate, while Joseph Hutchinson had debts owed to him that amounted to £17,946 of his estate of £19,390.

Jamaican moneylenders lent both small and large sums to debtors, whereas British lenders concentrated on big players. Between 1723 and 1753, for example, the Barbadian merchant turned Yorkshire landowner Henry Lascelles lent out £226,772 to 78 people in the Lesser Antilles, for an average loan of £2,907. The debt portfolios of two of the largest moneylenders in Jamaica during the American Revolution below show somewhat different lending patterns. Samuel Delpratt, a Kingston merchant who died in 1784 with an estate of £141,930, either by himself or with his partners—Edward Foord, who died in 1777 with an estate worth £147,294, and Richard Clark, who died in 1778 worth £48,342—made 351 separate loans to 328 people. Sir Simon Clarke, the son of a baronet transported to Jamaica in the 1720s for highway robbery, was the largest moneylender in western Jamaica, dying in 1777 with personal property of £192,565, of which debts payable accounted for £174,757. Clarke's inventory listed 132 loans to 126 people. Delpratt and partners made 149 loans of less than £100 in Jamaican currency and 82 loans between £100 and £249 in Jamaican currency. Clarke made 80 loans of less than £250 in Jamaican currency. Delpratt's average loan was £759, while Clarke's average loan was £1,250. Table 4.12 summarizes their loan portfolios.

Table 4.12 Size of Loans, Samuel Delpratt and Sir Simon Clarke, 1778 and 1784

Size (£)	Samuel Delpratt			Sir Simon Clarke		
	N	Sum (£stg.)	Percentage	N	Sum (£stg.)	Percentage
10,000+	10	230,302.81	61.7	5	136,691.44	59.2
2,500–10,000	10	52,035.58	13.9	9	53,612.26	23.2
1,000–2,500	19	33,854.97	9.1	10	17,051.21	7.4
500–1,000	32	22,416.23	6.0	11	7,789.46	3.4
250–500	49	17,745.33	4.8	17	7,405.22	3.2
100–250	82	11,216.29	3.0	17	5,860.25	2.5
Under 100	149	5,454.41	1.5		2,538.27	1.1
Total	351	373,025.62	100		230,948.11	100.0

Source: Inventories, 1778, 1784, IB/11/3/59, 63, JA

Nevertheless, despite the seemingly ecumenical characters of their debt portfolios compared to that of Lascelles, these Jamaican money-lenders mostly lent money to a few highly leveraged people. Delpratt made ten loans of over £10,000 in Jamaican currency and another ten loans of between £2,500 and £10,000 in Jamaican currency, accounting for £201,671, or 76 percent of all money lent out. Clarke made fourteen loans of over £2,500 in Jamaican currency, amounting to £135,931, or 82 percent of his loan portfolio. The biggest loans were made as mort-gages. Delpratt and his partners had twelve mortgages outstanding owed to them at Delpratt's death, valued at £146,920, or 55 percent of his loan portfolio. Bonds accounted for a further 30 percent of all debts while 108 debts made as notes accounted for 5 percent of money lent out. Clarke made nine mortgage loans worth £86,900 and sixty-six bond loans worth £63,383, accounting for 91 percent of all his debts. Some of these mortgages and bonds were gargantuan. Clarke lent £34,204 to Wheeler Fearon and £14,444 to Fearon's kinsman Thomas Fearon. He also lent £25,311 on mortgage to the estate of the late John Reid. Delpratt and his partners were major creditors for four sugar estates. They lent £29,231 to Clifton Hall and Marlborough Estates, £22,188 to Mount Sinai Estate, £21,581 to Burlington Estate, and £24,772 to the Bondbrogen Estate of Mrs. Sarah Gale.

Merchants such as Samuel Delpratt and Edward Foord parlayed the money they made through slave trading into moneylending. Unlike some merchants, such as Zachary Bayly, Alexander Harvie, and Thomas Hibbert, who diverted their profits into buying sugar estates stocked with hundreds of slaves, Delpratt and Foord remained Kingston mer-chants, with relatively small slaveholdings. The three partners owned

192 slaves between them, the largest number being held by Foord, who had 69 slaves. In the absence of other evidence, we don't know how these three merchants acquired slaves, but it is possible that a number of the slaves that the three men owned were gained as an outcome of defaulted debts rather than acquired for productive use. These men concentrated on moneylending rather than planting. But their wealth was dependent on the success of planting, given that 76 percent of their credits were large loans of over £10,000 in Jamaican currency intended to finance expenditure on large sugar estates.

The loan portfolios of merchants, farther down the food chain, who died in 1782 show how people other than large sugar planters borrowed money from Kingston moneylenders. Judith Gordon, for example, had £2,613 out on loan in the form of eight bonds and six notes. Most of the money (£2,448 or 94 percent) was lent to a single individual, John Hitchman, a Kingston merchant. George Campbell did not have a large loan portfolio: he had only six loans. Of these, 4 went to people borrowing between £250 and £500 in Jamaican currency, and one was a small loan of £11.97. Other moneylenders, however, specialized in small loans. David Austin made thirty-two loans, totaling £749, all under £100. Thomas Russell, a more substantial moneylender than Austin, was even more catholic in his lending practices. He tended to deal with ship captains and mariners and made 138 loans, worth £5,670, with the average loan being £41.09 and 120 loans being less than £75.

Trade and Merchandise

The analysis of debt patterns in Kingston inventories shows that while the plantation economy was extremely important in creating and sustaining wealth, Jamaica was not just a planting colony. As Richard Pares argued in regard to the diverse sources of Kingston trade in the 1730s and 1740s, when the planting economy was in the doldrums Jamaica was "as much a trading colony as a plantation." Kingston was heavily involved in a variety of export trades, notably the shipping of tropical commodities to Britain. It was the leading British West Indian exporter of sugar and rum to Britain and North America and the largest entry point for slaves in British America. Kingston traders were successful entrepreneurs: for example, Zachary Bayly, merchant prince and uncle and benefactor of the historian Bryan Edwards; and Thomas Hibbert, a migrant from Manchester who arrived in Kingston in 1734 and by the

1770s had become the largest consignment merchant in Kingston, with a reputation for financial probity that allowed his bills of exchange to be accepted without question in mercantile houses throughout London.[86]

Nevertheless, not everyone in Kingston was involved in long-distance maritime trade. Caribbean towns had diverse economies, with an internal dynamic that meant that they were more than just an adjunct to the wider rhythms of the plantation world. Towns were more than shipping points for the staple trade. Kingston was also where Jamaicans accessed the British Atlantic world of consumer goods and services. Although the countryside hosted some merchant stores and plantations themselves provided some essentials, most whites and many blacks needed the services available in an urban economy to get essential staples and luxury products. Hence, unlike in the Chesapeake, major towns in plantation regions like the West Indies and the Lower South grew in part because consumers flocked to them, rather than to a nearby country store.[87] Kingston had a thriving local market for meats, fruits, and vegetables, as Edward Long testified. He thought the market so good that "the most luxurious epicure cannot fail of meeting here with sufficient in quantity, variety and excellence, for the gratification of his appetite the whole year around."[88]

Kingston had three major trades that kept its inhabitants occupied and wealthy, alongside the significant business of keeping itself fed, housed, and entertained. First, it was the leading entrepôt for the Atlantic slave trade. The importation of African slaves into the Americas was the largest and most complex international business of the eighteenth century. Jamaica's insatiable desire for slaves was mainly satisfied by Kingston merchants. Between 1700 and 1758 Kingston was the sole port of entry for Africans shipped into Jamaica and the major port for such shipments between 1758 and 1807. During this time nearly 830,000 slaves were imported into Jamaica (another 150,000 were shipped there and then sent to Spanish America). Assuming an average price per slave of £30, the total value of this trade amounted to nearly £25 million, or close to the total wealth of Jamaica in 1774. Perhaps £200,000 per annum passed through the hands of Kingston merchants.[89] Henry Bright, a Bristol factor resident in Kingston, called the trade to Africa the "chief motive of people venturing their fortunes abroad."[90]

Secondly, Kingston was the epicenter of legal and illegal commerce with Spanish America. As early as the 1680s Spaniards began coming regularly to Jamaica for slaves, trading, dyestuffs, and indigo. They were welcome because they paid for their goods with much-needed gold and silver. English authorities constantly advised Jamaican officials not to interfere with foreign traders because the "flock of bullion" invigorated the Jamaican economy. Daniel Defoe thought that "the secret Trade to Spain is the real and only Occasion of the great Concourse of People . . . to the Island of Jamaica." The first eighteenth-century explosion of trade with Spanish America started in the wars of the late seventeenth century and was especially pronounced during the War of the Spanish Succession. The informal slave trade to Spanish America thrived, with 18,180 slaves exported from Jamaica between 1702 and 1714. The well-informed Robert Allen argued that until 1706 "Jamaica flourished & abounded more in Spanish gold & silver than it ever did before." In 1707 Jamaican merchants shipped an extraordinary £275,000 in goods to the Spanish colonies.[91]

These illegal connections continued, increased, and were explicitly encouraged by imperial officials throughout the eighteenth century. As late as 1758 one French observer claimed that "the greatest source of Jamaican wealth was Spanish trade to areas like Portobello, even in times of war."[92] The second heyday of such trade was in the 1730s and 1740s. The volume of illicit trade between Jamaica and Spanish America was so great that Jamaican planters, notoriously opposed to merchants' interests, were prepared to turn a blind eye to how their own lawful navigation was molested by the Spanish due to offenses by British and Jamaican interlopers. Instead, they turned their resentment against the Spaniards. Shipping between Jamaica and Spanish America was considerable and only increased when Spanish irritation at British depredations, and British insistence that smuggling should be protected and encouraged, led to war in 1739. Trade prospered during wartime, especially in the early 1740s. It was still strong in 1744 and 1745, when one in five ships entering Jamaica came from the Spanish colonies. By 1746 the trade had declined to under 8 percent of shipping. That Britain was prepared to provoke a war in order to increase trade with Spanish America is testimony to its importance in a period when planting was in the doldrums and Kingston merchants were in the ascendant. South Sea factors used their legal trade in slaves as a cover for making fortunes in contraband. Their secret books show that they traded £6,000,000 of goods and slaves clandestinely in the 1730s. In return, they and private traders imported perhaps £250,000 in Spanish goods and over £500,000 in Spanish bullion annually. Bullion allowed Kingston merchants, alone of British American merchant groups, to escape dependence on foreign capital. Until midcentury Jamaica was awash in currency, and although

Gresham's law operated and the "good" currency was siphoned off to Britain and North America, enough remained to ensure that Kingston merchants were cash rich.[93]

The third eighteenth-century boom in trade between Spanish America and Jamaica came after the end of the American Revolution. Kingston was the port of preference for Spanish Americans seeking slaves because, as one merchant argued, "we fit out our ships for this trade more expeditiously and cheaper than the French can; our people understand the manner of carrying on the trade better, and our manufactures are better adapted to it."[94] Officially, 3,400 slaves were sent to Spanish America from Jamaica in 1786, but the numbers may have been higher: one contemporary source suggests shipments of 5,182 slaves in 1787 and 11,042 slaves in 1788 from the whole of the British West Indies. The growth of trade in manufactures was even more dramatic, especially in the early 1790s. British exports to Jamaica virtually doubled between 1788 and 1796 to £1,695,353, most of which went to Spanish America. The destruction of Saint-Domingue enabled Kingston merchants to overwhelm French competition for Spanish trade, becoming the "general magazine of the Spaniards from the gulph of Mexico," as one French correspondent lamented. The leading merchant house in Kingston alone was reputed to make sales of between £100,000 and £300,000 annually, of which the "great part" was to Spaniards. By the early 1790s Jamaica was the dominant player in Spanish American trade, exporting nearly £1,000,000 in manufactures to the region in 1795 and importing £653,541 in bullion.[95] Contraband trade was even greater. Adrian Pearce suggests that Caribbean trade to Spanish America, large proportions of which emanated from Kingston, increased by 300 to 400 percent between 1763 and 1808.[96]

Finally, Kingston was a lively port where a range of goods arrived and were distributed throughout the island by merchants of all kinds. The poll tax list for 1745 indicates that there were ninety shops or stores in the town, of which fifty were on Port Royal Street, facing the harbor, with the majority of the rest on adjoining streets. Port Royal Street also had extensive slave yards: the 1745 list notes 1,167 slaves on that street, with a further 1,011 on Orange Street and 824 on Harbour Street. These must have been the most densely slave-populated streets in eighteenth-century British America. Among the residents of Port Royal Street were extremely wealthy merchants involved in the consignment trade with Britain, such as Samuel Dicker, who left £30,014 at his death in 1762; Robert Stirling, who died in 1764 with a personal estate valued at £54,531, including

750 slaves located on several sugar estates in St. James in the far west of Jamaica; Samuel Adams, who died in 1773 with £21,238 and 356 slaves; and Nicholas Bourke, a prominent merchant-politician who also became a planter and who, upon his death in St. Catherine Parish in 1772, had £27,879 in personal property and 486 slaves.

But alongside these transatlantic merchants were a variety of other Kingstonians, such as Phiba, a "free negro" who owned one slave on a property upon which no rent was assessed. In addition, there were twenty-one women on Port Royal Street, only eight of whom paid rent. Indeed, Port Royal Street, on which eighty-two properties were excused rent, had the highest proportion of properties in the town where no rent needed to be paid. It had a collection of shops and taverns where smaller merchants and shopkeepers lived, such as Philip Weston, a tavern keeper who died in 1747 worth £449; John Kendrick, a sailmaker who left £795 at his death in 1758; and Daniel Silva, a silversmith who died in 1745 with £260 in personal property. Further inland, such as on Harbour Street and Orange Street, the premises of wealthy merchants were less prominent, with the shops of more modest merchants, shopkeepers and tradesmen dominating the landscape. Some wealthy merchants, such as Aaron Baruh Lousada, worth £83,197 at his death in 1767, had offices on Harbour Street, but more typical residents were small merchants like Richard Bateman, worth £167 at his death in 1746; Peter Baker, a shipwright worth £167 when he died in 1758; and John Brown, a wigmaker worth £512.[97] Kingston was an extraordinarily active port. Between 1744 and 1746, 342 ships each year with 4,444 sailors, of which 23 were slave ships from Africa with 5,567 captive Africans, arrived in the town. One hundred and fifty-eight ships came from the northern port cities, 68 from Britain and Ireland, and 60 from Spanish America.[98]

The result of all these interrelated sources of commerce was that by the mid-eighteenth century Kingston was the richest town in British America. Wealth in Kingston was of a different level from that in the port towns of British North America, with the wealthiest merchants such as Thomas Hibbert, who died in 1780 worth probably around £500,000, far outstripping the wealthiest merchants in Charleston or Philadelphia. This was considerable wealth even by Jamaican standards, as tables 4.13 and 4.14 reveal. The average Kingstonian left nearly £1,000 in the early eighteenth century and nearly £2,500 in the third quarter of the eighteenth century—almost exactly the same amount left by those dying in the countryside. Some of this wealth was laid up in slaves and consumer goods, but the greatest source of wealth was in financial instruments.

Table 4.13 Wealth in Kingston over Time

Years	No. of Inventories	Wealth (£stg.)	Slaves (£stg.)	Debts (£stg.)	No. of Slaves
1700–1724	262	987	131	304	8
1725–49	852	1,444	223	796	10
1750–84	1,439	2,452	499	1,448	13

Source: Inventories, 1700–1784, IB/11/3/7–64, JA

Table 4.14 Wealth in Kingston by Occupation and Status

Occupation	N	Wealth (£stg.)	Slaves (£stg.)	Debts (£stg.)	No. of Slaves
Esquire	135	11,068	2,809	6,412	86
Merchant	616	3,604	360	2,385	13
Tradesman	365	816	218	347	7
Jew	238	3,167	399	2,119	15
Woman	371	671	223	244	9
Free black	48	268	171	16	6

Source: Inventories, 1700–1784, IB/11/3/7–64, JA

Between 1750 and 1784 Kingstonians left an average of £1,448 in debts receivable and £499 in slave property. The richest men, the great transatlantic merchants who controlled the town's politics and who built grand houses near the Parade at the center of town, had the largest share of this wealth: 135 men were noted as esquires and died with an average wealth of £11,086, and 616 merchants died worth on average £3,604. But wealth was spread well down the social hierarchy. Tradesmen were well-off: the average tradesman in Kingston dying after 1724 left £869.

Not everyone in the town was rich. Indeed, it was a place of great extremes, with higher than normal concentrations of poor people. White women—often single householders—and free people of color congregated in the town, and it was home to large numbers of poor and rootless sailors, who, when, as often happened, they succumbed to fever, were likely to be buried in a pauper's grave in Kingston's overflowing churchyard or in the grounds of its inadequate hospital. Surviving records hint at poverty in a town awash with riches: nearly 1,300 people, or 19 percent of all people dying between 1753 and 1774, did not have enough money for a funeral and were buried "by the parish." Poll tax lists note people excused because of poverty from paying town rates; nearly 20 percent of inventories were less than £100, with decedents possibly owning just a few sticks of furniture, some clothes, and possibly a horse, a gun, and a slave; and vestry minutes document the substantial sums that Kingston residents were expected to give to alleviate white poverty (church and poor taxes averaged £2,131 per annum between 1745 and 1751, or over £1 per white resident and £3 per white householder). Welfare provision for poor white people was substantial, especially for poor widows.

Conclusion

Jamaica was, along with Barbados and perhaps South Carolina, the British American plantation colony par excellence, but it was also just one of many plantation societies, each with its own distinctive features. In Jamaica the expectation of early death accompanied the promise of great wealth, giving a certain insouciance to social interactions: no other plantation colony in eighteenth-century British America experienced quite the dreadful demographic regime that Jamaica suffered, and none experienced it over such an extended period. And of course, even in a very rich colony, only a minority of white people became wealthy, and many stayed poor. Jamaica was also more diverse than the classic monocultural plantation economy, growing a variety of plantation products alongside sugar. In 1805 it exported almost 100,000 tons of sugar, the most of any place in the world, and in 1810 it had become the largest coffee producer in the Americas.[99] It also had a dynamic nonplantation sector, focused on Kingston, where trade was as important as planting. The variety of activities available within the plantation economy, only some of which were related directly to plantation agriculture, demonstrated the depth and diversity of plantation economies. Slavery was central to every economic, political, and social activity, but it was a facilitative institution, securing wealth for the great majority of the white population.

Jamaica was undoubtedly the most important plantation economy in British America, the economy that contributed the most over a long period to imperial coffers, and the colony whose loss Britain could least afford. It was the island that most shaped British and British American imaginings of what a plantation society was like, and it was the place that most contributed to abolitionist attacks on the planter character. Until the late 1780s, however, such denigration of Jamaican mores and any questioning of the value of Jamaica to the empire were limited. The more common response was seen in the feverish outpouring of enthusiasm by

Trinity Estate
St. Mary's

Published June 1, 1824 by Barret, Robinson & Co. 56 Cheapside & E. Lloyd, Harley St.

FIGURE 10. The eighteenth-century owner of this estate was Zachary Bayly, like Thomas Hibbert a Kingston merchant who purchased several large sugar estates, including Trinity Estate, one of the best sugar properties in the island. The estate had 1,110 slaves in 1815 and produced close to 1,000 hogsheads of sugar per annum. Tacky's Revolt began in 1760 on this estate. *Trinity Estate, St Mary's, The Property of C. N. Bayly, Esq.*, plate 12 in James Hakewill, *A Picturesque Tour of the Island of Jamaica* (London, 1825; reprint, Kingston: Mill Press, 1990). Private collection.

Britons when they heard the news that Admiral Rodney had defeated the French at the Battle of the Saintes, thus "saving" Jamaica from invasion. Jamaicans were even more beside themselves and competed for the honor of commemorating Rodney. The Spanish Town planter group won and constructed the most costly public monument until then built in the British empire. The statue, by John Bacon, still resplendent in the town square of a much reduced and dilapidated Spanishtown, features Rodney as a toga-clad Roman senator commandingly surveying, with extended arm, Jamaica's loyal subjects. It was housed in a splendid octagonal temple linked by curved colonnaded walkways to two office buildings that flanked the monument on either side. The Roman pretensions were appropriate for a colony where planters humored themselves by giving their slaves classical names and which emulated its classical predecessor in being an immensely wealthy society built on slavery.[100] It showed, moreover, that Jamaicans thought they had survived the tumults of the American Revolution and that they were headed for a bright future as a plantation society based on slavery.

FIVE

The American Revolution and Plantation America

The Great Divide

The American Revolution was a pivotal event in the history of plantation America. If we accept the argument put forward in this book—that the rise of the large integrated plantation brought great economic success to British America—then the ways in which the American Revolution disrupted the relationship between plantation America and Britain are surprising. That Britain would go out of its way to alienate its natural supporters in British America was an act of great folly.[1] It made little sense in an imperial system in which officials were mostly interested in defense, European great power strategy, and immediate commercial returns.[2] It makes even less sense when seen from the perspective of British American planters, considered from Maryland through to Jamaica. Despite occasional grumbles about how Britain was not allowing them to treat their slaves as they wanted and some complaints about how they could not make legislation as they thought they were entitled to do, wealthy planters and merchants in plantation British America had little reason to want to break away from Britain in the mid-1760s. The result of the American Revolution was mixed for planters, depending on whether they were resident in North America or in the West Indies. One major result, however, of the conflict was that the unity of the plantation world was broken, as plantation British America split in two on the formation of the United States of America.

For planters, the imperial crisis of the 1760s and the 1770s was fraught with danger. The plantations depended upon foreign trade with Europe, especially with Britain. Revolution was bound to lead to economic crisis. Moreover, planters' cultural aspirations were profoundly tied to British conceptions of order, gentility, consumption, and prosperity. Some younger planters in the Chesapeake and the Lowcountry may have welcomed the coming of the Revolution, seeing it as an opportunity to exercise autonomy over their own affairs. The American Revolution allowed some younger men the opportunity to leapfrog over older men as political leaders in the transformation of the politics of places like Virginia, as can be seen the ages of some its leading planter politicians, such as Thomas Jefferson and James Madison (aged thirty-five and twenty-five, respectively, in 1776).[3] The majority of planters, especially older men brought up within the ambit of a beloved imperial system in which Britain stood for freedom, military prowess, tolerance, and wealth, were deeply ambivalent about severing the umbilical cord linking them to the motherland. A Virginia planter, Landon Carter, born in 1710 and facing domestic opposition from ungrateful children and grandchildren as well as recalcitrant slaves, was typical. He supported the Revolution but despised the republican principles and leveling attitudes of firebrands like Patrick Henry. He yearned continually for "the whole British World . . . as they were in 1763."[4]

Planters had reason to feel ambivalent. The Revolution broke down traditional relationships and encouraged a democratizing of society and a heightened commitment to emotional release that planters of the old school found distinctly uncomfortable.[5] It was disruptive and challenging for plantation societies. Its most significant long-term effect was an artificial separation of the British empire even more pronounced than what happened to the French Atlantic empire in the aftermath of the Seven Years' War, when France was forced to cede its northern possessions to Britain. The aftermath of the American Revolution saw the northern and southern sections of the prerevolutionary British empire separated, with the new United States of America intruding itself between Canada and the West Indian islands. The more significant shift was in plantation America. The natural links between slave societies in British America were broken, reducing in the long term the ability of slave societies to unite against outside opposition.[6]

Britain

The American Revolution had important consequences for the various parties involved in plantation America. The place that suffered least was Britain. The loss of thirteen North American colonies was a personal disaster for a few people, notably Lord North, the prime minister, and probably also George III, who had committed himself fully to the war and who found the loss of the American colonies intensely hard to bear. But by 1782 a new administration was in office. Moreover, the memory of the loss of America was already replaced by jubilation at Admiral George Rodney's great naval victory at the Battle of the Saintes. The long-term effects of the American Revolution on Britain were thus limited, especially in a period of sustained economic prosperity and dominance in the mid-1780s. As J. G. A. Pocock observes, "The Revolution was less of a traumatic shock to the British than a display of their capacity for losing an empire without caring very deeply."[7]

We need to discuss the effect of the Revolution on Britain because Britain's political influence on plantation colonies was immense. The limited effect of the loss of the thirteen colonies heavily influenced Britain's attitude to the plantations that remained in the British empire after 1783. It was in Britain, for example, that the impetus for abolitionism occurred, and in Britain where visionary ideas of an empire without slavery and the slave trade were formed. Many Britons had thought, during the War for American Independence, that losing the thirteen colonies would be a devastating blow to British prestige and power. It turned out not to be so catastrophic. The memory of the bloody nose that the United States gave the most powerful military nation in Europe quickly faded. The general prosperity of the 1780s and Britain's growing self-confidence convinced British rulers that their long-standing imperial impulse to bring the colonies under tighter control was right.[8]

Britain recovered remarkably quickly from the travails of war, in part because the Revolutionary War was not fought on British territory. The 1780s saw a boom in government and personal finances. National income rose at a record rate in the decade after 1782, and national expenditures dropped dramatically. The cotton industry in particular soared in value in the 1780s as the fruits of the early Industrial Revolution began to pay off. The accession to the office of prime minister of the twenty-four-year-old William Pitt the Younger in 1783 provided Britain with stronger leadership than it had had since Pitt's father had been in charge of the nation. Pitt had a degree of financial wizardry about him that encouraged supporters to think him a sort of wunderkind. The 1780s was thus a decade of expansiveness, self-confidence, and moral certainty, seen not just in the increasing spatial reach of the empire from Africa to Asia, the Americas, and Australia and the Pacific, but also in Britons' insistence that the empire in India and the West Indies had to conform to Britain's increasingly self-righteous sense of itself as a moral paragon. Britain, its serenely self-possessed elite believed, could be both rich and morally superior.[9]

Britain was also much better placed in Europe in the late 1780s than it had been during the War of American Independence, when it had been diplomatically isolated. The changing position relied heavily on the decline of France, Britain's feared and formidable rival. France's decline was in part due to the huge debt that France had incurred fighting on the American side. It was sliding into disaster and disarray, a state of affairs confirmed by the start of the French Revolution in 1789. The Dutch were also foundering, and neither Spain nor Portugal was doing well. By contrast, Britain had a very healthy trade balance in its favor in the 1780s and was on the verge of controlling the lion's share of non-European resources and markets. Even the weather was good, with endless sunshine in 1787 leading to a bumper harvest. The public was content. After the Gordon Riots of 1780, in which thousands of people were injured in protests against supposed favoritism toward and the good treatment of Catholics, the 1780s were years of remarkable social order and acquiescence to authority.[10]

Britain's strong position economically, culturally, and diplomatically in the 1780s allowed it to care little about America. Britain thought it had little to learn from a United States that lurched from crisis to crisis before the ratification of the Constitution in 1788. After the Constitution, however, events in America reached a satisfactory solution, as the United States adopted the kinds of fiscal-military measures that kept Britain's finances in order during the eighteenth century. It also dropped the republican excesses of the immediate aftermath of the American Revolution, which were widely disparaged in the British press as naive and stupid. Moreover, Britain soon recovered its economic position in America without the headache of having to deal with colonials or provide defense to the thirteen colonies. By the 1790s Britain was once more America's main market, its chief supplier of imports, and a major provider of American immigrants.[11]

The success that Britain enjoyed in the 1780s immediately before the start of the French Revolution, and the particular nature of the British

FIGURE 11. By the late 1780s abolitionists had succeeded in depicting white West Indians as brutal tyrants. Note in this famous etching the way in which the artist gives the white West Indian vaguely simian features, suggesting a close link with the African slaves he was brutalizing. James Gillray, *Barbarities in the West Indies* (Hannah Humphrey, 1791). Hand-colored etching. © Courtesy of the Warden and Scholars of New College, Oxford.

empire that remained once the thirteen colonies had departed, made imperial officials reluctant to deviate from established practices. One lesson they did not learn was that settler elites needed to be treated carefully, and that their interests and their prejudices had to be respected. They certainly did not think that if Britain acted in ways that settler elites disagreed with, they needed to do it in such a way that settlers recovered from their setbacks with a modicum of dignity. The British empire from the 1780s onward became more, not less, authoritarian, and ever more dependent upon metropolitan direction exercised tightly among a close group of like-minded military men. Governors after the American Revolution were unwilling to put up with any opposition from settlers, especially those who upheld the principles of local autonomy that had led the residents of the thirteen colonies into revolt.

Such imperial obstinacy and self-confidence proved especially problematic for West Indian planters. Britain acted less consultatively, and less in the interests of West Indians, after the American Revolution than before. In 1784, for example, strongly against West Indian protests, they severed the West Indies from North America by insisting both on a stronger mercantilist policy and on recognizing the United States of America as a foreign nation whose ships should be banned from British ports. Increasingly, and a couple of years before the abolitionist crusade of 1787–88 altered metropolitan–West Indian interests, West Indian lobbyists in London found themselves unable for the first time in the eighteenth century to get their way over West Indian policy matters. This diminished political influence, moreover, coincided with a change in metropolitan opinion, such that West Indian planters were seen less as gauche nouveaux riches who brought benefits to empire than as crude, cruel, sexually lascivious deviants, given to "mongrelization" in their relations with black women, and as intellectually and morally bankrupt. This movement was led by abolitionists but was increasingly embraced after the late 1780s by polite metropolitan society.[12]

The Deviant West Indian

The image of West Indian planters declined rapidly in the 1780s. It was a bad omen for West Indians, because it coincided with one policy that continued after the war: the vision of an empire without slavery. A few thinkers had thought this impossible before the American Revolution, but more people tried to envisage such an empire in the 1780s. It led in 1788 to the settlement at Botany Bay in Australia and to the first major colonization effort by the British in which a British colony was established whose founders maintained a commitment to the principle that their new settlement would remain free of slavery.[13]

This alternative discourse to the commonplace belief that slavery was essential to British colonization in tropical regions was first developed in the works of Maurice Morgann, an advisor on colonial affairs to Lord Shelburne. Morgann wrote the first plan for the gradual emancipation of slaves in 1772, animated by Lord Mansfield's decision in *Somerset vs. Steuart*. He thought it wiser to incorporate Africans into civil society than to have them as slaves. If slavery did not exist in the West Indies, then the empire would stand on "sure foundations of equality and justice." Morgann was especially interested in how freed Africans in the colonies could be used as soldiers. He thought that they were as malleable to British interests as the Highlanders of 1745 had proven within the British Army. He even entertained notions that freed blacks would marry Europeans and, as in Spanish America, become a mixed-race people whose combined strength would "shake the power of Spain to its foundations."[14]

Such an equation of the British empire with Spanish imperial models was anathema to West Indians like Edward Long, who thought the Spaniards a mongrel race. But what concerned planters more than these theoretical racial heresies was Morgann's belief, drawn from his experience as an imperial official in a rapidly growing and racially more diverse empire after the Seven Years' War, that slaves were subjects, just like white colonists. Other imperial officials, such as the proslavery slave owner William Knox, shared Morgann's view that slaves were subjects. Most planters, however, especially in the West Indies, saw slaves as property: "when the English humanitarians attempted to take the view that he was a subject, they were advocating a theoretical and practical innovation which only slowly gained acceptance in the controversies over amelioration and emancipation." Edward Long saw the problem plainly when Lord Mansfield decided the famous *Somerset* case. "It is preposterous," Long proclaimed, "that Negroe slaves emigrating from our plantations into this kingdom are to be deemed *free subjects of the realm* . . . As our trade esteemed Negroe laborers merely a commodity . . . so the parliament of Great Britain has uniformly adhered to the same idea . . . and hence the planters . . . deemed their Negroes to be fit objects of purchase and sale transferable like any other goods or chattel."[15]

Antislavery was aided by the spread of free-soil principles, suggesting that Britain was a land without slavery or slaves. After *Somerset vs. Steuart* in 1772 had become enshrined in law, at least in popular misconceptions of what Lord Mansfield had actually decided, these principles helped transform American slavery from normative to legally peculiar. Slavery became a legal anomaly in British law, an institution that had to be positively authorized by local courts and legislatures and that governments were free to limit or abolish. Such changes in the legal position of slavery had little effect on slavery during the American Revolution but became very important in the 1780s as Britain began to assert broad new powers over other slaveholding empires, including the United States of America. The shift in emphasis was often more important in theory than in practice. To an extent the shift was welcomed by planter elites, who had been long pressing for slavery to be treated as a local rather than an imperial issue. But the shift in law also suggested that slavery was abnormal, not normal. It meant that abolitionists had the upper hand over slaveholders in discussions over whether slavery was normal or aberrant. By the time abolitionism became a major social movement in the mid-1780s, even slaveholders were willing to admit that slavery was not an ideal institution. Proslavery campaigns, the first of which began in the British West Indies in the late 1780s, were on the defensive from the start.[16]

Thus, some intellectuals and a small group of activist abolitionists had begun to see slavery as an imperial problem by the mid-1770s. The American Revolution did relatively little to advance dreams of an empire without slavery. The standard historiographical argument about what David Brion Davis has called "the problem of slavery in the age of Revolution" tends to suggest that the American Revolution greatly advanced the cause of abolitionism by popularizing the idea of universal liberty and stigmatizing the institution of slavery. The evidence is decidedly mixed on this count, mainly because the one nation that had the power to seriously harm the institution of slavery in plantation America—Britain—showed little inclination to do so during the War of Independence.[17] Britons were ambivalent about the problem of slavery in the Americas, to the extent that they considered slavery a problem at all. Lord Mansfield, after all, was the judge not only in *Somerset*, which slaveholders thought was a blow against their interests, but also in the *Zong* case of 1783, which came to be seen as an outrageous defense of inhumane slave traders.

In the American Revolution Britain tended to support slaveholders and slavery rather than undermine the institution. At times Britain used the plantation colonies' reliance on slavery to their own military advantage. Virginia and South Carolina planters were outraged by Lord Dunmore's prerevolutionary offer of freedom to any slave who joined British forces in 1775, galvanizing them into revolutionary activity more effectively than the Coercive Acts of 1774. General Henry Clinton's offer during the war itself, in 1778, to extend Dunmore's suggestion to all slaves owned by rebels outraged the planters further. Enslaved people saw these offers as opportunities to gain freedom and deserted their masters in large numbers in order to flee to British lines. The ferocity of fighting in the South after 1778 made slavery especially precarious in the region. Probably 35,000 enslaved people were lost to Patriot masters in Virginia, South Carolina, and Georgia in the three years of warfare in the South. Losses were especially traumatic for planters in Georgia and South Carolina, where between one in four and one in six slaves were lost through death, desertion, or military confiscation. Yet, unlike Abraham Lincoln in the Civil War of 1861–65, who used the problem of dealing with slaves in military possession as a step on the road to emancipation, British commanders showed no enthusiasm for liberating slaves.[18]

As members of a slave-owning and slave-trading empire, British generals were not friends of the enslaved. The British Army was the single largest slaveholder in the American South by 1781; it sold many thousands of slaves to the West Indies and was reluctant to use blacks as soldiers. Moreover, many Britons were horrified by what Dunmore and Clinton had done, seeing such desperate military actions as signs of incompetence and beneath the dignity of a civilized nation. They were also concerned about what such reckless extensions of freedom would mean to their strategy of winning over slave-owning Loyalists to their side. In short, Britain did little to use the exigencies of war to help destroy slavery in the South. It is pretty clear that they could have done serious damage to slavery as an institution if they had wanted to. The war in the South after 1778 devastated the plantation economy there, especially because significant slave losses could not be made up by new arrivals from the Atlantic slave trade. Many southern planters were as concerned with protecting their slave property as they were with fighting the British army, leading to persistent tension between planters and the nonslaveholding soldiers expected to fight for the revolutionary cause. If Britain had encouraged slaves to flee to them in the expectation that they would not be sold into slavery in the West Indies but instead would be freed, and if it had mounted a serious campaign to undermine slavery in the region, it is possible that planter patriotism might have withered. As Christopher Brown comments, "Slavery in the British Empire survived the American Revolution, in part because the British government wanted it to." Their commitment to slavery was clear in their determination to keep the British West Indian plantation colonies, even if that meant abandoning their claims to the thirteen colonies.[19]

Indeed, the American Revolution delayed rather than advanced the cause of abolitionism in British America. The strong presence of slaveholders in the Constitutional Convention suggests that slaveholders were considerably more powerful than the small group of North American abolitionists. It is possible, however, that the end of the American Revolution opened up a space for antislavery politics that had not existed before. The major American antislavery organizations in the American North were all founded in the 1780s. Some slaveholders, especially in the Upper South, came not only to believe that slaveholding was incompatible with revolutionary principles, but also acted upon such principles by manumitting enslaved people. The number of free blacks in the Chesapeake increased sixfold to 12,000 between 1782 and 1792. The Revolution also encouraged Britons to see American slaveholders as hypocrites, demanding liberty for themselves while imposing enslavement on others. Britons in the mid-1780s tended to focus less on abuses in the slave colonies than on moral outrages in India as a means of asserting themselves as morally superior and the empire as morally deficient. Nevertheless, both James Ramsay and Thomas Clarkson, very important early British abolitionists, succeeded in linking abolitionism to British national identity in ways that distinguished Britons from evil planters.[20]

Abolitionism, Proslavery, and the War in the American South

It is more likely that the new antislavery politics of the mid-1780s in Britain and America reflected a new beginning after the American Revolution, rather than the Revolution being itself a catalyst for change. The War for American Independence saw a diminishing of the small upsurge in voices speaking out against slavery that had started in the early 1770s. These voices almost disappeared during the worst years of the war for Britain. At the time the crew of the *Zong* was throwing African captives into the dark seas off the coast of southwestern Jamaica in November 1781, antislavery sentiment had stopped in Britain. It didn't really start again until Thomas Clarkson (who had never heard of Quaker opposition to slavery when he started writing his Cambridge essay against slavery in 1785) published his best-selling abolitionist essay in 1786, the same year that Edmund Burke started his agitation to have Warren Hastings impeached for misconduct in India.

The big spike in activity against antislavery started only in late 1787, expanding until it became a media sensation in 1788. Before that date interest in antislavery was small. The trial of the *Zong* crew in 1783, for example, attracted only limited attention before becoming a cause célèbre after being publicized by John Newton in 1788 and Olaudah Equiano in 1789. The years immediately after the end of the war saw British slave traders restarting their activities on a greater scale than ever before, large investment into British West Indian plantations, and renewed attention to the military defense of the West Indies. Extraordinarily, the abolitionist campaign became a leading social movement in just a few months, during a period of extreme optimism about Britain's future and in the middle of a flurry of activity in which Britons simultaneously tried to solve the ills of people at home (their propensity for vice and immorality, in particular) and to reform humanity on a global scale.[21]

The main result for slavery of the American Revolution is that it stopped Britain from implementing fully its long-term ambition, contra Mansfield, to transform British America into a set of colonies in which the imperial center, not the colonists, set the rules about slavery.[22] Of course, if the American Revolution had not been fought, implementing abolition from the center would have been more difficult. West Indian opposition to metropolitan interference with slavery would have been buttressed had West Indian planters' voices been joined to those of the formidable body of slave owners resident in the American South. Another result of the Revolution was to strengthen the hands of planters in a new United States of America committed to slavery. The commitment to slavery varied by region. It withered away in the North, became less prevalent in those parts of America close to the Middle Atlantic industrial economies, and was made much stronger in the plantation South. America was a slaveholding republic with a political system in thrall to slaveholders, an increasingly efficient and large-scale internal slave trade, and a booming capitalist economy commanded by wealthy planters, powered by steam engines, and dependent on the coerced labor of slaves. The new centers of slavery in the nineteenth-century American South were the sugar-growing region of Louisiana and the cotton kingdom of the Mississippi Delta. The American Revolution liberated slaveholders in the places where slaves were most important, the southwestern frontier, from a powerful centralized government that planters feared might attack slavery. When they looked across at the West Indies in the early nineteenth century, American slaveholders were convinced that they had made the right decision to fight in 1776 rather than stay loyal to an imperial power that insisted in interfering in colonial affairs.[23]

Such certainty would have been foolish in the early 1780s. The American South suffered dreadfully during the War. Virginia and Maryland suffered less than South Carolina and Georgia, but the war aggravated tensions between elite planters in the Chesapeake and lower and middling sorts. The region had relatively few Loyalists, but not all men who adhered to the Patriot position were as willing to enlist in the Continental army as wealthy planters wanted. Ordinary Virginians' main concern was over equity: rich men used poorer men to serve in their stead and insisted that the plantation system had to be preserved at all costs. Small planters especially resented having to recapture runaway slaves. Leaving their insecure properties in order to recover the property of wealthier men seemed to violate revolutionary principles.[24] Of more moment was the damage that war did to the tobacco trade. In 1775 planters had exported 100 million pounds of tobacco to Europe per annum, but they managed to sell only 2.2 million pounds per annum to France between 1778 and 1780. In 1777 and 1779 they sold an additional 28.5 million pounds to Amsterdam. Farmers turned to subsistence agriculture as the export trade disappeared. South Carolina and Georgia faced much worse problems, since Britain concentrated all its military attentions after 1778 on the South. The region descended into civil war. By October 1781 South

Carolina in particular was a scene of devastation, with Charleston occupied by British troops and the Lowcountry rice plantations suffering the depredations of marauding troops while slaves either escaped or starved to death. A monetary crisis added to their problems. The South's share of nonhuman national wealth dropped from over half to a little less than a third between 1774 and 1799. The rural South did not recover from the Revolution until after 1815.[25]

The West Indies

The Revolution was much less immediately traumatic in the West Indies than in the American South.[26] Indeed, before 1778 the West Indies experienced only minor economic discomfort, chiefly from disruption in trade and higher freight costs. Plantation profits declined, but not markedly. The situation changed after France and Spain entered the war in 1778. Their entry led to substantial economic problems in 1780 and 1781, compounded by the effects of a series of disastrous hurricanes, the worst of which devastated Barbados and Jamaica in September and October 1780.[27] Compared to British North America, the effects of war on the British West Indies were not transformative. Some islands in the Lesser Antilles changed hands, and Jamaica might have suffered an invasion from a large French expeditionary force in April or May 1782 if Admiral Rodney had not beaten the French Admiral De Grasse at the Battle of the Saintes.[28] Slaves suffered much worse than whites, with planters claiming that many died of hunger occasioned by lack of provisions from America and from the devastation caused by multiple hurricanes.

Nevertheless, the economic damage caused by the American Revolution did not last long. By the late 1780s plantation production was back to full steam, and the Atlantic slave trade was fully reestablished. The turmoil that in Saint-Domingue during the French Revolution as the island exploded into civil war between whites, free coloreds, and previously enslaved rebels proved extremely beneficial to the British West Indies. The 1790s saw the British West Indies reach a height of productivity that it had not enjoyed previously. Planters were so confident of future prosperity that the prices of slaves and land increased to unsustainable levels. It is thus difficult to see the American Revolution as more than a modest economic setback in a century-long story of material progress for the British West Indies.[29]

The main problem for West Indian planters was that they could not practice their normal exploitative methods of working their slaves. They found it hard to work their slaves past exhaustion and into ill health in ways they were accustomed to in peacetime. Doing so in wartime meant that their slave forces quickly declined. Before the war losses from over-work were compensated by a flourishing Atlantic slave trade. The slave trade declined precipitously after 1776, falling to a nadir in 1780, when only 3,763 Africans were shipped to Jamaica and 5,835 to the British Caribbean. By comparison, 60,480 slaves were shipped to Jamaica in the three years immediately before the American Revolution and 91,347 to the British West Indies. Planters argued that the American Revolution and hurricanes caused a crisis of slave subsistence. Figures show slave population growth in Jamaica slowed dramatically during the American Revolution. It increased by 38,612 between 1768 and 1775 but slowed to 12,710 between 1777 and 1782. The major reason, however, for the de-cline in slave population was a decline in slave imports, which dropped to 5,754 per annum during the war, under a third of the level reached in the five years before 1776.

Contrary to what planters self-servingly argued, increasing slave mortality was caused by planters continuing their destructive slave-management policies rather than by privations resulting from a decline in provisions shipped from North America and multiple hurricanes. Once the slave trade picked up again after the mid-1780s, the West In-dies economy prospered and slave populations grew. As Lord Grenville summarized the West Indians' importance to Britain in 1787, the "com-merce of our colonies was growing" and "promised a rapid increase in circumstance that could not bit prove extremely beneficial to the mer-chants and planters of our West India Islands."[30]

Problems with the supply of slaves to Jamaica in 1780 and 1781 led to the cause célèbre that was the trial of the *Zong*. This case was in retro-spect the most important event in the West Indies during the American Revolution. The story of the *Zong* was horrific but can be easily sum-marized. In an ill-judged decision by a slave captain hoping to take ad-vantage of war-related disruptions in the slave trade in Africa, a captured Dutch slave ship was sent to Jamaica under the command of an inex-perienced slave captain, Luke Collingwood. It was a disastrous journey. The crew of the *Zong* eventually found themselves miles off course, off the southwest of Jamaica, with leaking water cisterns and in fear of an imminent slave revolt. The crew decided to throw 132 slaves off the ship in three separate mass murders. The owners of the *Zong* then submit-ted an insurance claim for the murdered slaves. The insurance brokers refused to pay out, and the case ended up in front of Lord Mansfield, who found against the owners but accepted the assumption that humans could be thought of as cargo. Granville Sharp used the case to publicize the inhumanity inherent in the slave trade. He got little traction at first, but when the abolitionist campaign kicked off as a major social reform movement in 1787–88, the outrageousness of the *Zong* affair and Mansfield's comments equating humans with property made it central in raising public disgust about the realities of the slave trade.[31]

The *Zong* case showed that slave traders had so effectively equated humans with property that "the taking away of the life of a black man is [of] no more account than taking away the life of a beast." The black abolitionist Ottobah Cuguano spoke for abolitionists in general in 1787 when he described Captain Collingwood as an "inhuman monster" and his employers as "inhuman connivers of robbery, slavery, murder and fraud." For Cuguano the *Zong* case showed that "our lives are accounted of no value, we are hunted after as prey in the desert, and doomed to destruction as the beasts that perish."[32] The importance of the *Zong* lies beyond the simple facts of the case.[33] Opponents of the slave trade never failed to express disgust at what had happened off the seas of Jamaica in late 1781 and seldom missed a chance to fulminate against the inhumanity of a legal system that saw the murder of 132 Africans solely as an interesting example of marine insurance law.[34]

It was thus not economics but politics that was the real problem facing the West Indies after the American Revolution. Jamaican planters came under scrutiny, mostly unfavorable, as never before.[35] Britons accepted the new principles of an imperialism that was beginning to bestride the globe but felt distinctly queasy about particular aspects of its commerce and governance.[36] To an extent this concern over the meanings of empire arose out of the multiple disruptions that resulted from the aftermath of the American Revolution and led to migrations of Britons to Africa and Australia, free blacks to Sierra Leone, and American Loyalists to a range of places, including Jamaica.[37] White West Indians were the first in a long line of Loyalists abandoned by Britain. Beginning in 1783, British imperial officials showed repeated readiness to refuse to recognize as properly British significant sections of people who claimed cultural and political membership in the British empire, thus liberating itself from its own imperial loyalists.[38] Planters were not seen as they saw themselves: British gentlemen, of upright character and firm morals, capable of moderation, self-restraint, and refined gentility. Depictions of planters' wealth were undercut by undercurrents of decadence coded as luxury, effeminacy, gluttony, racial degeneracy, and sexual hybridity.[39]

A Global Event

The American Revolution distorts how we view plantation British America. In the first place it was an event that affected plantation British America indirectly rather than directly: the Revolution was not caused by the way in which plantations organized themselves. Second, we have to appreciate just how important a role the American Revolution plays as the foundational event in the historical imaginary of the most powerful nation in the world. It is hard to see the American Revolution as an event in Atlantic and indeed in British history, given its importance as an event with a peculiarly American resonance. It is instructive, however, to see the American Revolution as an Atlantic event with global repercussions, and one that was neither an end to colonial history nor the start of American history, but a midway point in a much larger process that was part of the Age of Revolutions.

This approach runs up against some very deep-seated historiographical assumptions. First, it is hard to escape the lure of teleology: the American Revolution is usually written about as bound to happen, more or less, in the way that it did in fact happen and as bound to be successful, more or less, in the ways that it eventually began to be seen as successful. Because the American Revolution had such important effects, it is difficult to appreciate how accidental, contingent, and preventable it actually was. It was a conflict that should never have happened, fought on premises that were, in the end, trivial. It was also fought around a set of principles that in wiser hands could have been easily resolved. British Americans were mostly happy in 1763 to be British, proud of their achievements in the half century before the Revolution, and they believed they contributed a great deal to the British empire. If Britain had not embarked upon a series of misguided actions that provoked massive resistance in America and had not persisted in trying to coerce people who believed they were free, it is highly unlikely that there would ever have been a push toward independence. British America would have probably been like other white settler colonies, moving slowly to local political autonomy within a shared acceptance of the virtues of imperial belonging and limited monarchical rule.

The American Revolution was thus a surprising event. It was the wrong war, fought for the wrong reasons, in order to implement a political system—republicanism—that most Britons and more than a few British Americans thought quixotic, morally suspect, retrograde, and likely to lead to the sort of disaster that had happened during England's brief experimentation with republicanism in the 1650s. British Americans, like Britons, were happy until the mid-1770s to live under a limited constitutional monarchy. Attachment to constitutional monarchy was especially strong in the plantation colonies. In December 1765 legislators from South Carolina complained that they were described as republicans when "no people in the world could be more averse to republicans than the British Americans." How a conservative people led by slave owners committed to hierarchy came to rethink their governing assumptions so that authority came from the people rather than from the king, and implicitly from God, and with some support given to democratic principles in which elite dominance was greatly weakened, is the most surprising aspect of a surprising event. It certainly was not foreordained.[40]

Moreover, many Britons and British American Loyalists predicted from the start that such rash experimentation, based on a philosophy that ascribed laws to nature and then derived natural rights from such laws, would fail: Jeremy Bentham called it "nonsense on sticks." The troubles that the United States of America faced in the 1780s and into the 1790s confirmed prejudices against republicanism.[41] Rather than being the great hope of mankind, America was on the verge of irretrievable disaster, led by men who did not know what they were doing, in a form of government that all theorists on republicanism said could not work. America was like the Netherlands, a once flourishing center of commerce and planting that had frittered away its natural advantages by adopting a poor system of government. Americans seemed to Britons and West Indians to have dissipated their future greatness by picking a quarrel with Britain over abstruse matters of political philosophy revolving around the extent of parliamentary authority in British America in which the differences between the parties at the outset of conflict were minimal (Americans, like Britons, accepted that in the end the British Parliament was sovereign) in order to institute a system of government that no one wanted and that was making their people poor and contentious.

Was the American Revolution Progressive?

The adoption of a national constitution in 1788 made things better, Britons thought, but only because it showed that Americans had seen the light, had abandoned utopian schemes of human improvement, and were returning to a system of government remarkably similar to Britain's constitutional monarchy. If British ministers had shown remarkable folly in allowing events in the thirteen colonies to get to the pass they did in 1776, Americans had been even more foolish in following the advice of radical extremists like Thomas Paine. Britons especially, but also West Indians, compared their contentment and prosperity at the start of an equally foolish experimentation with utopian politics across the Channel beginning in 1789 to what they saw as American decline, especially in the plantation colonies. They thought that the American Revolution was an unfortunate aberration in a century-long history of happy progress under benign imperialism, and that any lessons it held for the British empire about what to do in the future were entirely negative. That Britain continued and intensified its commitment to the kind of imperial policies that had got it into so much trouble in America from 1765 onward is one sign of the unimportance it attached to the ambitions professed by American revolutionaries.[42]

Some perceptive observers thought otherwise. Benjamin Franklin, for example, disagreed that the American Revolution was a failure. His long and well-chronicled journey from committed imperialist in the 1760s to the most internationally famous supporter of the new American government in the 1780s showed that he came to believe that republicanism was a good thing, just as he came to understand that slavery was morally and economically indefensible. But he agreed that the American Revolution was an unnecessary accident brought on by ministerial incompetence. Like most Americans of his age (he was born in 1706), Franklin was a reluctant revolutionary. He was happy under British rule until the Stamp Act. Before that he was a fervent imperialist and an American booster who imagined an imperial British America with a glorious future as the population and economy of the American colonies multiplied over time. He crowed in *Observations on the Increase of Mankind* that the rapid population increase in North America will mean there "will in another Century be more than the People of England, the greatest Number of *Englishmen* will be on this Side of the Water. What an Accession of Power to the *British* Empire by Sea as well as Land! What Increase of Trade and Navigation! What Numbers of Ships and Seamen!" These new Britons would be firm defenders of empire, as "there is not a single native of our country who is not firmly attached to our King by principle and affection." Britain had to do nothing to maintain that affection, he believed. There was no danger, he thought, of America's "uniting against their own nation, which protects and encourages them, with which they have so many connections and ties of blood, interest and affection and which 'tis well known they all love more than they love one another." Indeed, Franklin continued, "I will venture to say, an union amongst them for such a purpose is not merely improbable, it is impossible."[43]

Franklin's *Observations* is a useful text for understanding plantation America because it hints at what Franklin thought was the greatest threat to continued British American prosperity. Franklin alludes to two things in his pioneering tract. First, if Britain would just refrain from interfering in the activities of the northern colonies, they would prosper, because providing a growing population with domestic necessities was economically beneficial. Secondly, he suggested that British America was not unified. His text was an early and sustained attack upon West Indian pretensions, and in it he expounded on how slavery diverted resources from worthwhile and sustainable long-term goals. Slavery poured resources into activities that Franklin thought only marginally important and fundamentally immoral. He suggested there were fundamental differences between the two areas evident even before the start of the Seven Years' War and argued that at some stage Britons and Americans would have to make a choice: would the British empire be an empire devoted to liberty, with free labor prioritized over slave labor, or an empire of slavery, with the interests of slaveholders dominant?

Franklin, as was his wont, was right, though his correctness seems more evident in retrospect than it did at the time. It is difficult to replay the tape of history as if the American Revolution did not happen, but one possible scenario that might have happened if Britain and the thirteen colonies had resolved their differences is that another conflict, this time over slavery, would have emerged once abolitionism became a major social movement in the 1780s and 1790s. If the issue of difference between Britain and British America had been slavery rather than the relatively trivial issue of parliamentary sovereignty, then the southern and island colonies would have found common cause, and the dividing line between warring parts of British America would have been placed further north. Probably the northern colonies would have remained in a British empire without slavery while the plantation colonies might have formed an independent confederation, as South Carolina eventually, in 1860, decided it should have done in 1776.

Somerset

In this respect, the galvanizing event that served in the plantation colonies the same purpose as did the Boston Tea Party in convincing Americans that Britain was prepared to compromise colonial liberties was the *Somerset* case of 1772. William Murray, Lord Mansfield, gave a statement to a packed courtroom on 22 June 1772 that demonstrated the rare ability to be oracular and gnomic at the same time. He found that James Somerset, an enslaved man from Virginia via Boston living in London with his master, could not be forcibly removed to Jamaica. The most extreme reading of what Mansfield decided in 1772 was that he provided the legislative means whereby slavery was set on the road to extinction. He produced strong words about how slavery was not an institution that did credit to Britain, declaring that "the state of slavery is of such nature that is incapable of being introduced on any reasons, moral or political, but only positive law . . . It is so odious that nothing can be suffered to support it but positive law."[44]

For the most fervent abolitionists, Mansfield's dictum suggested that Britain was finally willing to condemn slavery both in Britain and also in the colonies. One observer even thought that plantation America might be willing, in a sort of unholy alliance, to trade fiscal autonomy for full protection of slavery. He told Benjamin Franklin that if America was willing to accept parliamentary sovereignty, then Britain would allow the extension of *Somerset* into the colonies. It was reasonable, David Hartley argued, to suggest to America "that they sh[oul]d treat an act of Parliament flowing from general principles of humanity and justice, with a different reception, to what has been given to acts of vengeance." The aim, he thought, was to force planters to "correct a vice, that was contrary to the laws of God and man."[45]

That was not a reading, however, that Mansfield encouraged. His finding suggested a fundamental break in the colonial understanding of how slavery should be treated, but it was a judgment given reluctantly. This may be why the reasoning underlying the case—that slavery was mostly a local issue—was never adopted as a policy by the British state. Throughout the case Mansfield, who was very aware of the value of the plantation colonies and the slave trade to Britain and who was enough of a political animal to worry about the consequences of a judgment that attacked the legal basis of holding Africans in chattel slavery, was disturbed at what would happen if he were forced to rule upon the matter under debate. Throughout the case he urged the two sides to settle so that he would not have to make a decision.[46] His judgment in the end was short (it lasted not much more than a minute when presented in court), and he refused to elaborate on what he meant. It may have been a momentous decision, but it did not have many practical legal consequences for enslaved people. Franklin was not too far from the truth when he derided the importance of *Somerset* as a judgment that merely meant that one slave only could not be made to board a ship bound for Jamaica.[47]

Nevertheless, even if Mansfield was reluctant, his judgment was freighted with consequences, as people knew at the time. Mansfield knew what he was doing when he declared that slavery could only be instituted by positive law. He was making a deliberate effort to demolish the legal justification for slavery on any other basis not just in England, but in the colonies. His ruling meant that slavery existed only within those jurisdictions that had passed laws specifically to protect it. Slavery was thus circumscribed. Commentators have spent much time debating what *Somerset* meant in terms of law. Daniel Hulsebosch, for example, downplays its impact, arguing that it was less a harbinger of emancipation than an attempt to interject flexibility into the imperial legal order by restructuring the geographic range of laws protecting the disciplinary power of slave masters. He thinks that scholars have made too much of Mansfield's positive-law remark, being, he suggests, a typical compromise by a politically aware judge who wanted to uphold the primacy of his area of law over competing jurisdictions without undermining British commerce. The positive-law remark, he contends, was put forward as a way of avoiding the inflammatory claim that slavery was forbidden under English common law. If Mansfield was dealing a fatal blow to the idea that slavery was legal in England, he was doing so without making slaveholders change many of their practices save being more careful bringing slaves into and out of the kingdom.[48]

But however hedged Mansfield's dictum on slavery was, it heralded a decisive shift in the struggle between masters and servants, especially in Britain, where the opinion was rightly seen by England's black population of 10,000 people as a substantial broadening of their rights under what the law termed was a condition of slavish servitude. Because slavery had to be positively sanctioned, it could be selectively altered or abolished, as indeed happened in Pennsylvania, Massachusetts, and New York during and after the American Revolution. It also raised substantial issues about compensation if Parliament ever chose to abolish slavery. Such a prospect lay well in the future. But *Somerset* meant that slaves could sue for freedom if they were to be removed from England; and, as Mansfield well knew, the ruling was likely to lead to increased slave runaways, as slaves came to realize that they could become free or protected from excessive force in both England and the colonies. The practical effect on slaveholders, therefore, was that they had to be careful about moving slaves from one jurisdiction—*Somerset* was mostly a case about a conflict of laws—to another jurisdiction, especially if they intended to dwell in Britain.[49]

Some slaves took advantage of *Somerset* to claim freedom. On 30 September 1773, for example, John Fannie, the owner of two runaway slaves in Botetourt County, Virginia, wrote in the *Virginia Gazette* that he had "some reason to believe they will endeavor to get out of the colony, particularly to *Britain*, where they imagine they will be free (a notion now too prevalent among the Negroes, greatly to the Vexation and Prejudices of their Masters.)" Slaves in plantation America who thought that *Somerset* freed them were quickly disillusioned, but the case had more purchase in Britain. The advertisements in papers for slave sales or for returning runaways disappeared virtually overnight, while in Scotland James Knight, a slave of the Jamaican slave owner John Wedderburn, successfully used the example of *Somerset* to gain his own freedom.[50]

West Indian planters were certainly exercised about *Somerset*. The colonies deployed three of their strongest intellectuals to argue against the law: Jamaican Edward Long, Barbadian Samuel Estwick, and Antiguan Samuel Martin.[51] Their arguments against *Somerset* were learned, if profoundly racist. Probably the most significant effect of their testimony was not on British public opinion (it had none), but its role as forming the bedrock of intellectual thought for the first expression of proslavery sentiment in British America.[52] Opposition to *Somerset* was more muted in the mainland colonies, even if planters in those colonies were generally prepared by the early 1770s to see ministerial conspiracies in every British action. Thomas Jefferson, for example, who became convinced that all forms of despotism and corruption were British in origin, leading him in 1776 to try to include an unconvincing rant against the British for responsibility for their "cruel war against human nature" in forcing the slave trade upon a reluctant American population, was not especially concerned about *Somerset*, but he was concerned about the Privy Council overturning laws by Maryland and Virginia to tax and regulate slave imports.

The difference between the Chesapeake and the West Indies in this instance was that Chesapeake planters had no need for the Atlantic slave trade, given their growing slave population. It had many reasons to support attempts to suppress the slave trade. It has often confused people why Jefferson, a slave owner, would make what seemed like perverse and bizarre statements about British culpability for the slave trade that denied American complicity in its development. Jefferson lambasted George III as a king who had "prostituted his negative for suppressing every legislative attempt to prohibit or restrain this execrable commerce." He did so because he was an American in a plantation area that no longer needed an external slave trade. Virginia planters were free to reject imports from Africa by British traders from 1774 as part of American nonimportation agreements. Jefferson was worried about how the Atlantic slave trade increased Chesapeake debts to British merchants. He knew that restricting the supply of slave labor would benefit planters like him who had surplus slave labor. He also thought it good politics to displace blame for the slave trade onto Britain and thus portray colonial Patriots as innocent victims of a mercantilist system that forced them to engage in an "execrable commerce" that enslaved "a distant people who had never offended" Britain, "captivating & carrying them into slavery in another hemisphere, or to incur miserable death in their transportation thither."[53]

Virginians who thought the slave trade should be stopped because it was, as Fairfax County planters proclaimed in 1774, "wicked cruel and unnatural" were unconcerned about the implications of *Somerset*. The practical consequences of *Somerset*—hindering slaveholders from taking slaves back and forth from the colonies to Britain and making their investment in slave property in Britain less secure than it had been—were not that important in the Chesapeake or even in South Carolina, given how few American slaveholders moved to Britain. West Indians were more affected, but in 1772 they were at the height of their post–Seven Years' War prosperity and political influence. They could afford to ignore theoretical attacks upon their investment in slaves.

Moreover, their antagonism toward British ministers and British judges were tempered both by the clear unwillingness of Mansfield to follow through on the implications of his judgment, and also by Mansfield's decision in 1774 in *Campbell vs. Hall*, a case brought by a Grenada planter protesting about the power of a local collector of duties to impose taxes after the Crown had divested itself of the right to tax when it had granted Grenada an assembly on 7 October 1763. Mansfield's decision in *Campbell vs. Hall* supported West Indian arguments that their constitutional rights were not subject to the whim of the royal prerogative, thus taking away one of West Indians' principal complaints. If the West Indian planter lobby could succeed so easily in an area of constitutional concern at a time when Britain was denying almost every constitutional issue that North American colonists thought important, then it felt confident it could protect its right to control slaves as it saw fit if that became a political issue. If *Somerset* had been decided in 1775 or 1783 it might not have been so confident, but in 1772 West Indian self-confidence was at an all-time high.[54]

In retrospect, what should have disturbed West Indians about *Somerset* was not just that it had the theoretical potential to draw a line whereby slaves had protection on one side of the Atlantic only, but also that West Indian planters were portrayed in a new and disturbing fashion which suggested that if Britain was enlightened, then British America was benighted. The arguments that the prosecutors made on behalf of James Somerset were encased within a discourse in which West Indian planters were compared to tyrannical Turks and to Russian serf owners. Sergeant Davy argued that Virginia law could not prevail in England because otherwise a Turk could bring his Circassian slave to England and rape her with impunity. More to the point, if Virginia law had any purchase in England, then Steuart would be allowed to beat Somerset to death with impunity, or to maim him for daring to run away. These acts, however, would be crimes in England, and so had to be disallowed. Behind Davy's argument was not only an implicit racism (what would happen if foreigners brought not just black but white slaves, possibly Englishmen enslaved in Barbary, to England?) but also an assumption that Americans and West Indians were somehow not proper Englishmen. When West Indian and American planters brought their slaves to Britain, they were not only bringing in alien Africans who themselves were a source of corruption for the lower orders, they were also bringing themselves: men compared to oriental Turks or vicious Russians or to the African barbarians from whom they purchased their slaves. The prosecutor, Francis Hargrave, made explicit English fears that colonial masters were corrupt and that they were foreigners who wanted to bring the laws of infant colonies and "a barbarous nation, Africa," to the home country.[55]

What bothered both the English prosecutors and also Granville Sharp, the person most involved in bringing this case to court, was planters' excessive use of force. That readiness to use force was as problematic as slavery itself. Hargrave's colleague, John Alleyne, conjured up a vision of West Indian masters whipping slaves in fields outside London. He hinted that if *Somerset* was decided the wrong way there would be a gradual acceptance of the "horrid cruelties" of America and an advancement of slavery as the English became familiar with it and accepted planters' "high despotism." Physical despotism, as he knew all listeners understood, was just a short step away from political despotism. Granville Sharp lamented that the arrival of West Indian absentees bringing to England their customs, their despotic ways, and their black slaves debased the whole country. Sharp became a humanitarian reformer in the late 1760s—not just because he sympathized with Africans, but also because he found slave owners objectionable tyrants. He became involved in abolitionism in 1765 after he saw an Antiguan slave owner, David Lisle, beat his slave, Jonathan Strong, nearly to death in a London street. Sharp nursed Strong back to health and was horrified when Lisle sought his property back and when Strong's new owner, James Kerr, threatened to sue Sharp for theft.

Sharp also made a direct link between what planters were prepared to do to their black slaves (far too many of whom were coming into England, he thought, degrading working-class life and contributing to an upsurge in crime), and what they would do to ordinary poor English people if they were allowed. He was certain that if England permitted planters to keep slaves in England, pretty soon they would increase the number of slaves in the country, taking away the livelihoods of white people. Once the English poor had become destitute, they would involve them "in the same horrid Slavery and oppression; for that *is always the case wherever Slavery is tolerated.*" West Indians inadvertently fueled this fire by suggesting the inevitability of miscegenation. Edward Long went so far as to claim that lower-class white women were attracted to black men for reasons too "brutal" to mention. That was more colonial contamination than most English people were prepared to contemplate. Mansfield's ingenious solution of a *cordon sanitaire* in which colonial slave owners were not free to bring their enslaved property to England was a good way of containing that contamination.[56]

A Civil War

In reality, of course, the American Revolution was a civil war, as well as a war by some Americans against the British state. It was the first of two civil wars in Anglo-America, the second of which was fought in 1812. It was also the first of two civil wars of Americans against Americans, the second one of which began in 1861.[57] One effect of the Revolution was to create a massive diaspora of people, including many planters and their slaves, that in total numbers was proportionately higher than the emigration of people from revolutionary France and its possessions.[58] That the American Revolution was a civil war is a truism. But its implications have been imperfectly worked out, mainly because we do not factor either the American interior or the British West Indies into our calculations of who supported or did not support the Americans who rebelled in 1776. Why Britain punished Boston for the Boston Tea Party has often puzzled historians. But Britain had a good reason to give Massachusetts a short, sharp shock, believing that the Coercive Acts of 1774 would be generally supported in British America. They did not expect West Indian planters—nor many people in the interior, including Native American allies— to support American rebels. To an extent they were right. Thomas Iredell, a wealthy and irascible Jamaica legislator and planter, advised his nephew, North Carolina's James Iredell, later a Supreme Court Justice, to "Keep yourself perfectly Neuter in those disputes both in words and Actions unless you choose to see yourself adrift with it, maybe a Family at your Heels." The veiled threat was real: once the war began, Thomas Iredell disinherited his revolutionary nephew for "having taken an oath of Allegiance to Congress in violation of your first to this Country."[59]

American historians have argued that British ministers severely underestimated American support for Boston rebels. The ministers may have been better accountants than we have thought, for we consistently underestimate the extent of Loyalism in British America. It is generally assumed that between one-fifth and one-third of Americans were Loyalist.[60] What is meant by such a calculation is that 20 to 33 percent of white British Americans living in the thirteen colonies supported the Revolution. British America was a bigger entity than white people in the thirteen colonies. Most Native Americans lived far away from the centers of revolutionary discontent and so should not be counted in any enumerating of Loyalists or Patriots, but most Native Americans living near the eastern seaboard supported the British. The number of Indian allies of the British was probably around 100,000 people.[61] In addition, the great majority of African Americans either supported Britain, in the vain hope that the British might free them from enslavement, or lived in the Caribbean, where they had no choice but to be loyal. Support for the rebellion was strong in Massachusetts, New Hampshire, the Tidewater Chesapeake, the port cities of the North, and much of the Lowcountry. But Loyalism was strong in New York, the interior of the South, and the Northwest, and was dominant in Atlantic Canada and the British West Indies. The percentage of Loyalists among the white population of British America may have been closer to 40 percent than to 20 percent and was well over half of the total population once Native Americans and African Americans were included. It was well over 50 percent in plantation America.

It is important to remember that only half of British American colonies joined Massachusetts in revolt against Britain in July 1776. Only thirteen contiguous colonies in British North America needed to explain why they had dissolved "the political bonds" connecting them to Britain and to justify why they claimed "the separate and equal status to which the Laws of Nature and of Nature's God entitle them." Colonies north of New Hampshire and colonies in the Atlantic Ocean and in the Caribbean stayed loyal. This loyalty was what British ministers expected. In particular, they assumed that all colonies in which slavery was the primary social and economic institution would be too afraid of slave rebellion to risk making grandiloquent assertions of liberty. Slavery would keep these "yelpers after liberty," as Samuel Johnson contemptuously described American planters, quiescent.[62] Ministers expected the break in the imperial "snake," as depicted in Benjamin Franklin's famous woodcut "Join or Die," to occur further along the chain of colonies than it in fact did.

Why did the break in the colonial chain of colonies occur so far south, and what did that break mean for the plantation societies of colonial British America? This question is hardly an unexplored topic. Nevertheless, it is one whose answer is usually invested with a degree of teleological determinism. We usually ask why the southern mainland colonies joined the rebellion, as if this result were foreordained rather than one that careful contemporary observers had every reason to think unlikely, especially in South Carolina and Georgia, where slave populations were large.[63] We also look at the plantation colonies of the British West Indies during the American Revolution and ask why these colonies stayed loyal, rather than explore whether they might have joined the Revolution.[64] But if fear of slave rebellion was so determinative of British West Indian attitudes during the American Revolution, making them loyal even when they were sympathetic to American republican ideology, why did such fear not also cause South Carolina to stay loyal? Conversely, if South Carolina was impelled into revolution precisely because it wanted to control its slave population and doubted British intentions in this respect, why did similar assumptions not encourage Jamaican planters to join the rebellion?

These are not minor questions. That Virginia would join the revolution is reasonably explicable. Republican sentiment was strong in Virginia, the planter elite wanted to assert their moral authority against the British government as a way of shorting up support for their political rule among poorer whites, and economic distress made Virginians anxious about the harm that British actions were doing to their economy. South Carolina's revolutionary orientation makes less obvious sense. South Carolina's decision, however, to join its northern brethren was important both in how the War of Independence ended up and also in the resulting commitment of the United States to black chattel slavery as a constitutionally approved institution. Although South Carolina planters and merchants may have had their doubts during the Revolution about the wisdom of their decision to join northern rebels, given the viciousness of warfare in the South, its decline into internecine civil war, and the massive disruption that war created within the plantation economy, the rightness of their decision to rebel was confirmed by events after the Revolution. By the early nineteenth century they had consolidated their power within the new state and in a nation committed to slavery. Jamaican planters, on the other hands, had reason to regret their choice to stay loyal: their loyalty was rewarded, as they saw it, by British betrayal once abolitionism became a major social movement from the mid-1780s.[65]

In determining why South Carolina rebelled and Jamaica remained loyal, we should recognize that planters were less incapacitated by fear of what slaves might do to them if they rebelled than is commonly supposed. That they had a wary worry about slave violence is clear. It is also clear that enslaved people took advantage of the fog of war to pursue their own agendas at the expense of planters.[66] In the end, however, planters were not paralyzed by fear of slave rebellion, especially before the events in Saint-Domingue in the first few years of the nineteenth century showed planters the capacity of black soldiers to inflict serious damage on planters' property and persons. In 1776 British American planters had every reason to think that a slave rebellion, of which there had been remarkably few in British American history, and only one (Tacky's Revolt in Jamaica in 1760) that had posed a significant threat to planter power, would be easily overcome.[67]

The Slave Trade, Slavery, and Slave Revolt

One factor determining whether planters in different colonies would or would not rebel against Britain was the extent to which the Atlantic slave trade sustained slavery. Planter responses to British ministerial actions were influenced by the demographic condition of the enslaved population. By the 1760s the slave societies of the American South were experiencing natural growth of the enslaved population; the West Indies, by contrast, relied on the Atlantic slave trade to maintain population numbers. Jamaica and other West Indian colonies that rebelled were indeed compelled by fears over slavery to stay within the empire whether or not they supported British actions, but the fear they had was not about whether slaves would revolt if they perceived that planters were divided in their political loyalties. It was, rather, that if war broke out the lifeline ensuring the profitability of the plantations that was the slave trade would be stopped. In the American South planters had the political luxury of being unconstrained by dependence upon British merchants for fresh supplies of Africans. As it turned out, the decision of planters in the American South to declare for war had disastrous, nearly fatal, consequences for maintaining plantation slave numbers. If slave populations had not experienced natural population growth before and after the Revolution, the losses during the war would have made the plantation system in the American South unsustainable.[68]

Britons thought they would get more support for their cause in the plantation colonies than they did, mainly because they assumed that colonists in places with a large slave population were too scared of internal dissension to contemplate armed revolt. They also assumed, based on their experience with the West Indies, that planters' insatiable desire to buy more slaves left them dependent on British commerce. On 26 October 1775, for example, William Henry Lyttleton, member of Parliament for Bewdley and a former governor of both South Carolina and Jamaica, and thus a man with expertise and experience with the psychology of planters and the nature of plantation society in British America, gave a notorious speech to the House of Commons predicated on weak revolutionary sentiment in plantation America. Foreshadowing what Lord Dunmore, the last royal governor of Virginia, was going to do just two and half weeks later, Lyttleton outlined a strategy whereby the southern and island colonies of British America could be isolated from the northern colonies.[69] Comparing the thirteen colonies to a chain, he noted that the northernmost colonies, with their abundance of white residents, were the part of the chain least likely to break under British pressure to reform. The weaker links, Lyttleton suggested, were those that corresponded to the southern colonies of South Carolina and Georgia, where the white population was nearly outnumbered by the black enslaved population.

Making an implicit criticism of the futility of the Coercive Acts as a means of bringing Massachusetts to heel,[70] Lyttleton argued that Britain should concentrate on separating the vulnerable southern colonies from their alliance with northern colonies. He was convinced that Britain could use the racial demography of the South to turn the southern colonies against rebellion. South Carolina and Georgia, he believed, were paralyzed by fear of what their enslaved population might do to them if given the chance. Lyttleton suggested that Britain should use British troops stationed in America to stand firm against outbreaks of settler patriotism. He argued that a few regiments should be sent to the southern colonies of British North America, which were weak "on account of the number of negroes in them," with the understanding that "the negroes would rise, and embrue their hands in the blood of their masters." Moreover, he advocated these troops be augmented by rebel slaves who had run away from their plantations, and by exploiting the military obligations of the few free people of color in the two colonies. He believed that southern planters were so afraid of slave rebellion that a show of force on the British side, especially if it included a touch of racial antagonism, would quickly bring the southern provinces to heel. This view was commonly shared. The most prominent Patriot in the colony and the leader of Charlestown's Sons of Liberty, Christopher Gadsden, expressed concern about South Carolina's ability to support its northern brethren, given the threat that the large enslaved population of South Carolina posed to the colony's security. Writing to the Boston radical Samuel Adams, he admitted that South Carolina was "a weak Colony from the Number of Negroes we have amongst us and therefore exposed to more formidable Ministerial Tricks."[71]

Lyttleton's idea was a prime example of such a ministerial trick.[72] The large slave population in the southern colonies could be used to create divisions within British North America. His idea was not taken up, however, by his fellow members of Parliament, who were wary of promoting slave rebellions even in the exigencies of wartime.[73] By the time news of the speech had reached Charlestown, however, the even more inflammatory proclamations made by Lord Dunmore in neighboring Virginia had caused great alarm. Dunmore had preempted the political process by declaring war against the Patriots on 7 November 1775. A week later he promised freedom to the slaves of rebels who might run away from their masters and join the royal cause. Hundreds of slaves defected to Dunmore, allowing him to form and arm a Royal Ethiopian Regiment.[74] South Carolinians were doubly worried because they had just foiled, or so they believed, a potential slave insurrection in June 1775 that they argued had been developed into a conspiracy by a wealthy free black ship pilot, Thomas Jeremiah. Jeremiah had been tried and convicted; he was executed (hanging followed by a public burning of the body) on 18 August 1775.[75]

Lyttleton's plan was ingenious but likely to backfire, which may have been why it was not taken seriously in London. Some historians argue that rumors of British attempts to stir up enslaved people and Native Americans so that they would take up arms against South Carolina and Virginia planters confirmed planter beliefs in ministerial wickedness. It firmed up their conviction that the best way to protect their investment in slavery was to join in rebellion against a government that threatened southern slavery. What Lyttleton suggested, and what Dunmore proposed, was ample confirmation that their fears about British ministerial intentions were correct.[76] For Ira Berlin, the revolutionary years in the Americas gave blacks "new leverage" in their perpetual struggle against their owners, the war offering them "new opportunities to challenge both the institution of chattel bondage and the allied structures of white supremacy."[77] The Haitian Revolution, in particular, proved that one could not keep enslaved people down forever.[78]

There is little evidence, however, that slave resistance was especially widespread either before, during, or after the Age of Revolutions or that planters were especially concerned about slave revolt. The extent of slave rebellion in eighteenth-century British America was not great. Some important colonies, such as Virginia, Maryland, and Barbados, experienced no slave rebellions in the eighteenth century. That slaves rebelled at all is remarkable, given the ferocity with which slave rebellions were put down by white planters able to exploit the full panoply of state-sanctioned violence on their behalf. But they did not rebel often enough to cause planters serious concern. By 1776 no planter in Virginia or Barbados and virtually no South Carolina planter except long-lived ones with excellent memories would have recalled slaves taking collective action. Even in Jamaica, where there was a series of small rebellions in the late seventeenth century and another small rebellion in 1765, as well as a foiled slave conspiracy in 1776 in addition to the major revolt of 1760, long periods—such as the first sixty years of the eighteenth century, for example—passed without a slave revolt. Moreover, rebellions did not increase in the Age of Revolutions. Indeed, the frequency of rebellions and conspiracies in the British Caribbean reached an all-time low between 1776 and 1815. During the American Revolution, the British Caribbean was particularly quiescent, despite suffering hardship and famine. Slaves took advantage of the war in the American South to run away in large numbers, and they made small gains in the nature of their working lives, gains that were quickly destroyed as violence on the plantations dramatically increased in the immediate postwar period, when planters sought successfully to restore traditional patterns of control and deference. But no slave rebellions occurred in the midst of planter disarray and slave hardship. The closest slaves got to rebellion were a few quickly discovered and harshly punished conspiracies in 1774 and 1775 that may have been no more than rumor.[79]

Those colonists who had not experienced a major slave revolt were sometimes inclined to downplay the horror of such an event. Barbadians, for example, had been "so long exempted from insurrections" that they "do not appear to harbour any considerable suspicions on that head" and felt "but little of that corporeal dread of blacks which seems to pervade some of the islands."[80] Jamaicans were not so complacent. They continued to worry about slave revolt during the 1760s and 1770s. Indeed, they used their fear of slave revolt as an ostensible reason not to join with North Americans in rebellion. In words that echoed what their bête noire, William Henry Lyttleton, was to express a year later, the Jamaica Assembly sent a formal petition to the British Crown protesting British actions in British North America, declaring that they could not express their discontent as violently as colonists were doing on the mainland because their fear of slave rebellion and their dependence on British defense had reduced them to such a "weak and feeble" state that they could not offer physical resistance.[81]

One should not overestimate, however, the extent to which Jamaicans were paralyzed by fear of slave rebellion. Jamaica was quite willing to resist British authority and to express its hostility to British actions in forthright language when it wanted to do so. When the Board of Trade remonstrated with Jamaica about legislation passed in the immediate aftermath of Tacky's Revolt, the Jamaican Assembly declared that "they are by no means disposed to submit their sentiments to the determination of their lordships nor ever will, at any time, suffer them in any respect to direct or influence their proceedings whatsoever." The language that it used in the extensive controversy between the Assembly and Lyttleton in the mid-1760s was similarly extreme and uncompromising. Nicholas Bourke's dazzling defense of settler rights against royal authority contrasted Jamaicans as "men zealous for the constitution and liberties of their country" with Lyttleton's supposed support for "the absurd and slavish Doctrines of DIVINE and HEREDITARY RIGHT and PASSIVE OBEDIENCE and NON-RESISTANCE."[82] White Jamaicans experienced a number of revolts after Tacky and before the Declaration of Independence, but they had put them down easily and bloodily yet with relatively little loss of white life. As far as Jamaicans were concerned, violent repression worked, at least insofar as it killed those slaves prepared to rebel and gave other slaves contemplating rebellion a stark warning of the torments that awaited them if they were captured. Slaves who contemplated rebellion did so, therefore, in the knowledge both that their enterprise was likely to fail and that the result of failure would be a grisly death by slow torture. Given the small likelihood that a slave revolt would succeed, slaves who rebelled were therefore opting for a form of self-destruction. Many more slaves chose not to seek self-destruction through rebellion but instead sought death through suicide.

Thistlewood recorded ten suicides in his diaries between 1768 and 1782, making suicide the second-leading cause of recorded slave deaths, after infectious disease.[83]

Militarily trained colonial governors were contemptuous of the martial spirit of white Jamaicans, while civilian governors found Jamaican methods of slave management highly deficient. But white Jamaicans were sufficiently martial and well disciplined to be able to cow their slaves into submission. One of the primary explanations for white success at keeping blacks down was their ready recourse to strategies of terror. Jamaican slavery was especially brutal, even by the elevated standards of New World cruelty. White Jamaicans were absolutist tyrants, with a torturer's charter that allowed them to do whatever they wanted. As the planter historian Bryan Edwards put it, the occasional planter kindness "affords but a feeble restraint against the corrupt passions and infirmities of our nature, the hardness of avarice, the pride of power, the sallies of anger, and the thirst for revenge."[84]

Why Jamaica Stayed Loyal

The conventional explanation for why Jamaica did not rebel in 1776 is that it couldn't. Its commitment to slavery and its geographical position as a British island in a sea surrounded by French and Spanish enemies meant that it relied on British troops to an extent unparalleled anywhere else in British America. This conventional explanation, however, is not very convincing.[85] The history of eighteenth-century conflict in Jamaica, and Jamaica's difficult terrain, suggest that subduing rebellious forces, even when there was an army already established in the island, was a hard task. The rebel slaves of 1760 were subdued only with difficulty. In the long first Maroon War, which lasted well over a decade in the 1720s and 1730s, the Maroons were never beaten. Jamaica was unable to force them to surrender and had to come to terms of peace with them in 1739.[86] Attacking Jamaica from the outside was even more difficult. The historical experience of European involvement in the Caribbean was that the malign disease environment was the central fact that shaped geopolitics in the region. John McNeill's study of the geopolitics of fever in the eighteenth-century Caribbean shows how intra-European armed struggles were fought out mainly in landscapes undergoing rapid environmental change in which the impact of debilitating fevers, especially yellow fever, was the principal determinant of the outcome. An invading army could succeed only if the island was small and had poor fortifications, and only if victory was won very quickly. If a European army was forced into a siege against determined defenders with good fortifications for any extended period, then yellow fever would do its work. The easiest way to destroy a European army in the eighteenth century was to send it to the Caribbean. Jamaica's terrible disease environment would have kept it safe, just as malaria in South Carolina preserved it from British takeover. Even though it was an island in the Greater Antilles, and even though it was surrounded by Spanish and French foes who aspired to capture the island, Jamaica never was successfully invaded while in British hands. Indeed, when the British took Jamaica in 1655, it was a poorly defended and sparsely populated outpost of the Spanish empire; it was to be the last time that a European took a large island from another European power and kept its territory safe.[87]

Jamaica did not rebel, furthermore, because it did not want to rebel. It was Loyalist in outlook, not revolutionary. One reason for its Loyalism was demographic. Jamaica was an immigrant society, a substantial minority of its white population having been born in Britain. It was hardly surprising that native-born Britons identified instinctively with Britain rather than with North America. In mid-1776 the Jamaican overseer Thomas Thistlewood recorded, with approval, the toast of a fellow immigrant overseer in favor of British success against the American rebels: "John Hartnole's wish to the No: Americans. Cobweb Breeches, hedgehog Saddles, jolting Horses, Strong Roads & tedious Marches, to the Enemies of Old England."[88] Loyalist sentiment went beyond a reflexive commitment to Britain, expressed in loyal addresses to the Crown and patriotic toasts. It was also seen in dislike of North American pretensions, especially, by 1776, in outright antagonism toward the residents of New England. As Isaac De Pinto, a Jamaican Jew writing in France, commented, one "only had to read the history of New England . . . to take notice of the temper and character of its inhabitants." New Englanders were "fanatics and barbarians," devoted to violence and naturally imperialist. All the lands to the south of America, including French and Spanish America, as well as Jamaica, should fear if America became independent under the control of New Englanders because, "by reason of their great population and natural hardiness" and being "in want of metals in general, and of bullion in particular," they would seek to "invade and subjugate Mexico and Peru."[89]

Moreover, unlike Virginia, which suffered economically following the credit crisis of 1772,[90] Jamaica prospered in the crucial years leading up to the Declaration of Independence. There were few economic reasons encouraging rebellion, and many compelling loyalty. For white Jamaicans, the years between the Seven Years' War and the American Revolution were, as George Metcalf concluded, "a brief golden age for the plantocracy."[91] Although the island does not have an especially impressive resource base (being small, mountainous, and not well connected to European shipping routes), by the early years of the eighteenth century it had become the leading sugar exporter in the British empire.[92]

White Jamaican planters were powerful in part because they had influential allies in Britain. There were perhaps as many as seventy West Indians, with Jamaicans prominent among their number, in the House of Commons. They were closely connected to the higher reaches of British society, creating a West Indian fraternity not replicated among North American colonists. The West India interest in Britain enjoyed singular success from the 1730s to the 1770s over legislation involving the West Indies. The main reason for their success was that their concerns fitted well with government policy. The islands retained their preferential tariff on sugar and rum despite its costs to consumers because it conformed to prevailing mercantilist theories and because the government was convinced that the West Indian islands were essential to imperial power. That the West Indies willingly submitted to imperial policies when the North American colonies so fiercely resisted them also aided the island's case, encouraging British ministers to reward such "dutifull" colonies with discriminatory legislation.[93]

Why South Carolina Rebelled

South Carolina did not have had the political clout of the West Indies, but it had a similar social structure, especially in the Lowcountry, which was famously described as being "more like a negroe country" than a European one.[94] It was also prospering economically as the Revolution approached.[95] The center of resistance to Britain was concentrated in the plantation areas of the Lowcountry, areas that very closely resembled the British West Indies in socioeconomic character.[96] Why, then, did South Carolina rebel when its richest and most influential residents had so much to lose? The subsequent events in the South after the British invasion in 1780 were sufficient cause to make those wealthy planters who in 1776 contemplated such things as likely to occur to think loyalism the best option. South Carolina's plantation society was placed under severe strain as the colony descended into violent civil war, and as Britain concentrated its most concerted military efforts on besieging Charleston and disrupting South Carolina's lucrative export trade in rice. It was only the debilitating effects of malaria on General Cornwallis's troops that preserved Patriots' precarious security.[97]

Constitutional issues best explain South Carolinian intransigency in the early 1770s. Before 1770 South Carolina tracked Jamaica in its constitutional pretensions. In the Gadsden election controversy of 1762, South Carolinians successfully got rid of a governor they did not like, just as Jamaicans did four years later. Unlike Jamaica, however, South Carolina was involved in another bitter dispute with Britain over constitutional issues in the Wilkes Fund controversy between 1769 and 1775.[98] As Jack P. Greene argues, the controversy was "instrumental in bringing South Carolinian politicians to a full realization of the nature of the political challenge involved in Britain's new colonial policy."[99] It was the bridge to revolution. But no such bridge developed in Jamaica. The difference between the two colonies was that in South Carolina the Wilkes Fund controversy encouraged local politicians to think hard about the imperial situation. In Jamaica, by contrast, the constitutional concern was with local parochial politics. Andrew O'Shaughnessy distinguishes between the two parts of the British American empire in the 1770s: North Americans were concerned with the power of parliament, while West Indians thought mostly about prerogative struggles with the Crown. Thus, when *Campbell vs. Hall* was decided in 1774, most West Indian complaints against Britain faded away.[100]

South Carolinians were not instinctive revolutionaries. Their political culture was based on a lobbying tradition that emphasized the importance of "interest" over "deference" as a basis for establishing political harmony. By contrast, Virginia had a political culture in which "deference" worked more intensively. The political culture of "interest" worked very well in South Carolina. The province's whole experience in the mid-eighteenth century had been that of a favorite child within the empire. It made South Carolina's elite leadership reluctant revolutionaries, the most conservative of all Patriots. They did not share the revolutionary ideology so powerful in Virginia and Massachusetts. By 1774, however, they came to believe that the Crown was acting against South Carolina's interests.[101]

South Carolina's willingness to join in the American Revolution caused problems for its southern neighbor. Georgians, oriented more to the West Indies than to Virginia but tied to South Carolina, were the most reluctant revolutionaries in North America. Georgia was in the middle of a prolonged boom in rice production and was enthusiastically buying slaves from Africa. Its stage of development and its growing wealth made it eager for British consumer goods. The colony, to the ire of northern Patriots, showed no interest in adopting strategies of nonimportation, and before 1775 its commitment to opposition to Britain was limited. Indeed, most large rice planters were Loyalists and suffered greatly in the War for Independence. John Graham, for example, heavily in debt to London merchants, was ruined by the war when his vessel, which was loaded up with rice and deerskins, was destroyed by Patriots in March 1776. It cost him £40,000 because, he thought, he would not rebel "against my King and Country." James Wright, the governor and the largest planter in the region, was forced to flee, even though before the Revolution his astute management of Native American affairs had won him the acclaim of his countrypeople. He was very dismissive of backcountry opportunists who he believed had taken control of the colony for their own self-interest, calling Georgia revolutionaries "a parcel of the meanest people." Whatever the politics of the Revolution, the civil war that ensued in the region after 1780 left Georgia devastated. The coastal region, where rice production flourished and where the large integrated plantation was dominant, was especially affected. It became the handmaiden of the Upcountry after the American Revolution, with new planters adopting models of commercial agriculture that bore little resemblance to the gang system on large plantations that existed in the Lowcountry.[102]

Jamaica never shared the belief of significant segments of the population in Georgia and South Carolina that Britain was tyrannically destroying their liberties. Moreover, unlike South Carolinians, Jamaicans were never invited to join in North American continental congresses. In was in these intercolonial environments that South Carolinians both encountered other colonials who had grievances against the Crown and also learned that their particular kind of lobbying tradition—a tradition that encouraged South Carolinians and some Georgians to embrace radical behavior in which they were very willing to threaten to withdraw from negotiations if some benchmark demands were not met— worked very effectively in forcing northern delegates to acquiesce to South Carolina positions. That position worked extremely well in 1774, when South Carolina insisted that if rice was not excluded from the list of goods subject to nonimportation agreements, they would walk away from the Continental Congress. This continued to be South Carolina's political strategy in dealing with opposition from other colonies and states until secession in 1861.[103]

In contrast to Jamaica, where the threat of slave revolt was used as an excuse to stay out of the conflict, planters in South Carolina supported independence as a way of protecting slavery from perceived British attacks.[104] Indeed, as Bob Olwell and J. William Harris argue, slavery itself provided a vital impetus in the decision for revolution. As events would later prove, it was South Carolinians rather than Jamaicans whose assumptions were correct. By declaring for revolution, white South Carolinians, despite some hair-raising moments during the Revolutionary War when slaves were a potential destabilizing threat to political survival, ensured the survival and solidification of their principal social institution. It took a civil war for South Carolina to be forced to give up slavery.[105]

Ordinary Whites and the Coming of Revolution

A central theme of this book has been that ordinary white men were not just spectators in the great developments that transformed plantation societies in British America, but vital actors in making those developments reality. What role was played by ordinary white men, by which we mean free white men who often owned enough property to qualify as voters, but who usually did not aspire to play a role in active politics, in the movement toward American independence? Nowhere did ordinary white men take the lead in deciding whether to support rebels in Massachusetts. That role was taken by planters, who defined the "common cause" of America, and who produced the ideas spread through pamphlets to more middling people. Ideas tended to trickle downward. One would expect this in societies deeply committed to hierarchy and the preservation of inequality. As Barbara Clark Smith notes, a common assumption in the eighteenth century was that "a cobbler should stick to his last." The right of the well-born to rule, and the foolishness of "leveling" tendencies in which the poor were raised to equal status with the rich, were beliefs held throughout society. Power and authority were located at the top, in monarchs and in God, and were replicated further down the social scale in the authority of men over women, parents over children, masters over servants and slaves, and humans over animals.[106]

Yet, as Clark also notes, another cliché of eighteenth-century British American politics was that "A Cobbler in his Stall can easily tell whether the Nation is well or ill governed." Moreover, the cobbler and other ordinary white men felt that they had a right to protest when they felt that their rulers were treating them poorly. They accepted that they were the ruled, rather than rulers, and did not aspire to office, but that did not mean they were politically quiescent. Ordinary men had many ways to protest the actions of their social betters. Cobblers might not make laws, but they had numerous means, enshrined in law and in practice as part of the birthright of British subjects, whereby they could instruct their rulers to desist from unjust actions. Rulers found it difficult to rule without the people's consent, and there was "a surprising range of occasions on which ordinary men's status was sufficient and ordinary men's knowledge was enough to establish significant political agency."[107]

Ordinary white men in plantation societies were zealous defenders of their rights. Commentators felt that such prickly concern about the recognition of their position was a distinctive feature of white society. For Bryan Edwards, writing about late eighteenth-century Jamaica, "a marked and predominate [sic] character to all the white residents was an independent spirit and a display of conscious equality throughout all ranks and conditions," quite different from the situation in Europe, where "men in the lower orders of life" never felt themselves "on a level with the richest." By contrast, even the poorest white man in the West Indies "approaches his employer with an extended hand." Thomas Thistlewood demonstrated on several occasions the value he placed on rich men's treating him in the manner he thought his position in society deserved. On election day in 1766, for example, he refused to accept a handshake proffered by the wealthy assemblyman William Lewis because previously Lewis had ignored him "altho' I have resided 15 or 16 years in this parish." He confided with satisfaction in his diary that Lewis was "affronted for which I did not care," declaring that "he had never had such a Sett-down before" and that he "threatened to be even with me Which I did not Note at all." For conservatives, such assertions by ordinary white men violated the natural order. William Beckford of Hertford Pen, a neighbor of Thistlewood, bemoaned "the levelling principle that obtains among the white people of Jamaica," which "annihilate[s] the bonds of power and the good effects of subordination." Janet Schaw, a Scottish gentlewoman visiting the West Indies and the southern colonies, similarly dismissed ordinary white people's pretensions. Encountering ordinary people in Wilmington, North Carolina, she expostulated that "there is a most disgusting equality among American clown[s]" and that "I am sorry to say that I cannot look at them without connecting the idea of the tar and feather." But it was the ruling elite, not ordinary white people, who were forced to accommodate themselves to American egalitarianism. A South Carolina minister, John Bullman, found this out the hard way in 1774 when he railed in a sermon against the "illiterate

Mechanic," a man, he asserted, "who cannot govern his own household" or pay his debts and who "presumes he is qualified to dictate how the State should be governed." His words violated a political compact between ruled and ruler, whereby the ruler did not insult ordinary white men and (by implication) their "uncontrollable" wives: Bullman was dismissed from his post by his vestrymen.[108]

Bullman's fate illustrates the limits of deference in British American plantation areas. Colonial America was a place of often rambunctious egalitarianism. The coming of the Revolution did not necessarily release a pent-up demand among ordinary white people for a more democratic society and an end to deferential behavior. By comparison to Europe, ordinary white men in plantation societies had considerable freedom and could insist that no laws be passed that violated their interests. White male assertiveness was present at all social levels, as was distaste for elite pretensions and overly exclusionary social practices. When the American Revolution came, ordinary white men, even if they supported the authority of wealthy planters against British rule, insisted that they should be consulted. In Virginia, for example, often considered the homeland of deferential politics and a colony with a large and committed group of Patriots right from the start of the Revolution, ordinary white men refused to serve in militia forces in which they were unable to select the officers who commanded them and rejected plans by which officers received military pay far higher than that given to ordinary soldiers. If planters did not "please the people," then the people would not fight. One of the ironies of the Revolution is that many of these freedoms, derived from long-standing conceptions of the limits of ruling-class power and the necessity for lawmakers and rulers to get consent for their actions from the population at large, were reduced and eliminated after the revolutionary settlement of 1783.[109]

For most ordinary whites, the coming of the American Revolution brought little benefit. There were a few enthusiastic supporters of the revolution among ordinary people, as in Charleston, South Carolina, where the relatively plebian Sons of Liberty were a powerful force from the Stamp Act in 1765 in augmenting wealthy planters' ambition to break free of Britain.[110] But many more ordinary whites either stayed neutral as long as they could or else actively opposed the coming of the Revolution. Neutrals may have accounted for 40 to 60 percent of the population in the plantation South. Whether ordinary whites supported the Revolution often depended on their experiences with ruling elites before the war started. They joined the Revolution enthusiastically when wealthy planters had treated them well before the war; they stayed loyal to Britain when landowners they respected took that position; and, as in large areas of the Carolinas, they engaged in bitter civil war when the prerevolutionary experience had been one of conflict and class division. Even if they did join the Patriot cause, as in Loudoun County in Virginia, they were careful to correct preexisting grievances. In that county, tenants resisted service until better tenancy agreements were negotiated. And servants and convicts in places such as Maryland made sure that if they were called up to fight, they would have their conditions of indenture or convict service reduced or expunged. The Regulator bloodshed in 1771 in North Carolina, where settlers from the politically underrepresented western areas of the colony engaged in bloody conflict with planters from the wealthier eastern plantation areas, was one region where "religious dissent and class resentment made a combustible mixture." In July 1775 ordinary white men from areas where conflict in the Regulators' period was intense sent a pointed message to "the Coast" that if a commercial embargo planned by Patriots went ahead, they "would come down and burn all the Houses on the Coast, and put the people to the Sword."[111]

Ordinary whites hesitated to follow planter Patriots in the Chesapeake, the Carolinas, and Georgia because going to war was devastating. Most of the burdens of war fell upon ordinary white men, especially men who could not be saved from service because they were needed as overseers to keep enslaved populations under control. The War of Independence in the South, especially in South Carolina, which bore the brunt of the devastating Southern Campaign of 1780–81, was close to an economic cataclysm, triggering the greatest decline in southern economic growth rates until the Great Depression of the 1930s. Between 1775 and 1782 the South faced a perfect storm of reduced trade, monetary depreciation, wartime destruction, and burdensome military requisitions. Most of the burdens fell on poorer whites, especially on whites unable, like wealthy planters, to defer military service by paying a substitute to serve in their place. Allan Kulikoff estimates that the number of white laborers in the South shrank by nearly 25 percent between 1776 and 1780, mostly from death by disease either in military service or as a result of wartime privations.[112]

With these losses, the question is why some ordinary white men in plantation British North America were still willing to fight for the patriot cause. Many men, of course, were not. Ordinary white men in the West Indies showed no desire to join the patriot cause. There was no pressure on them to do so from wealthy planters. In that age of considerable prosperity, ordinary white men were content with the oligarchic rule of great planters, especially after the advantages of being white were accentuated by a series of laws passed in Jamaica and Barbados in the aftermath of Tacky's Revolt in 1760. As in French Saint-Domingue, by 1776 racial codes were systematically reformed so that color, rather than wealth or status, became the defining qualification for social and political inclusion. Buttressed by a developing ideology of whiteness, largely excused from military service by the presence of British soldiers and the recruitment of free people of color into the militia, enjoying abundant opportunities for employment, and as largely British-born people who were instinctively pro-British in outlook, ordinary white men in the West Indies had little reason to want to test matters by supporting rebellion. The same tendency toward Loyalism was true for East and West Florida. These were Loyalist bastions, with virtually no support for rebellion among any section of the populace. The Floridas were full of settlers who had been British soldiers and had a higher than normal number of people connected to and dependent upon British government largesse. Indeed, East Florida relied heavily upon a parliamentary subsidy to finance its government and its extensive defense needs. During the war the Floridas proved a handy refuge for Loyalists fleeing Patriot aggression further north. It was also a logical place for planters in the West Indies to turn to for food and other goods that they had previously purchased from British North America.[113]

Loyalism was also pronounced among ordinary white people in large sections of the interior districts of the Carolinas and Georgia, where by 1776 up to two-thirds of the white population of the Lower South lived. A strongly pro-American historiography previously denigrated Loyalists in this region as "venal, bloodthirsty and traitorous" and suggested that one reason for British failure in the Lower South was that they "grossly underestimated the extent of Loyalism" in the region. More recent scholarship disputes this interpretation. While it may be that in much of the South Carolina Upcountry "whigs more consistently represented the broad class interests of many backcountry settlers," there was a sizable minority of ordinary white men whose loyalism arose from a commitment to political principles that abhorred rebelling against a lawful monarch. In Georgia Patriots had little support among either wealthy planters or ordinary whites until news of fighting in New England started to swing the balance in favor of Patriots. Many white men, confirmed Indian haters who lusted after Native American land, also moved to the Loyalist camp in protest against what they considered British indulgence of Creek allies. But many men in Georgia and the Carolinas stayed loyal to the British throughout the Revolutionary War.

Jim Piecuch concludes that, far from the stereotype handed down in a nationalist historiography, Loyalists in the Lower South, even outside the Floridas, were "numerous, courageous, and steadfast in the face of brutal persecution." He noted that long before the British southern campaign of 1780–81, Loyalists in both South Carolina and Georgia, with ordinary white men prominent in their ranks, had taken up arms to fight American rebels, turning the contest as early as 1776 into a "genuine civil war." Loyalists fought rebels without either British prompting or without British support.[114]

Indeed, when Loyalists fought Patriots they were in many cases handicapped by British ineptitude. The failure of Loyalism in the American South arose not because the British underestimated ordinary white support for the Crown, but because they mismanaged what support they had. That the British did not know how to assuage the feelings of ordinary white men was apparent, even when they turned their attention seriously to defeating Patriots in the South, as the resourceful and skilled Georgia governor James Wright lamented after Yorktown. He argued that lots of Loyalists had flocked to Georgia by 1780, "Expecting His Majesty's Protection and Safety, from the Tyranny & Oppression of the Rebellion." But, he continued, "When the Loyal Subjects in that Province were beginning to Raise their Drooping Spirits & to Collect and Improve the Remains of their Scattered & almost Ruined & lost Property," the leader of the British army in the south, General Cornwallis, departed abruptly from Georgia. The result was disaster: "before the Minds of the People were Settled, & wholly Reconciled to a return of their Allegiance . . . [rebels] assassinated & Otherwise Cruelly Murdered, as Many Loyalists as they Could come at, & upwar[d]s of an Hundred Good Men, in the Space of one Month, fell Victims to their Loyalty, & the Cruelty of the Rebels."[115]

Well before this abandonment, however, the British had failed to pay sufficient attention to the sensitivities of ordinary white men. The most conspicuous failure was Lord Dunmore's threats to grant enslaved people freedom if they abandoned their plantations and fought for the British, threats repeated by General Clinton in 1778. It was not just wealthy planters who were alarmed by Dunmore's intemperance. It appears that many ordinary white men resented British attacks upon the slave order, even if some of our evidence for this discontent was penned by elite Patriots in celebratory mode. Richard Henry Lee commented that "Lord Dunmore's unparalleled conduct in Virginia has, a few Scotch excepted, united every man in that large colony," while Archibald Cary exulted that the proclamation "has had a most extensive good consequence" as

"Men of all ranks resent the pointing of a dagger to their throats, thru the hands of their slaves." His argument was that Dunmore was the rebel, not white Virginians, because he "has armed our slaves against us, and . . . excited them to a general insurrection." Dunmore thought along the same lines, boasting that his declaration "has stirred up fears in them which cannot easily subside." People in other provinces took notice: the *South Carolina Gazette and Country Journal* claimed that Dunmore "has worked up the passions of the people there almost to a frenzy." Thomas Jefferson used those passions to include the horror of the declarations made by Dunmore as the culminating grievance listed against George III in the Declaration of Independence.[116]

The problem with Dunmore's Proclamation of November 1775 was not that it did not work; in fact, it did work in the short term, especially in creating hopes among blacks that they could gain some degree of freedom. It worked even better in sowing dissension within white ranks. The poorest white men, notably convicts, who numbered in the thousands in Virginia, welcomed the Proclamation because it gave them the chance to improve their situation through military service. Servants and especially convicts fled in large numbers to the British flag, severely disrupting plantation management. The Proclamation also had an effect on many ordinary white men, deterring them from joining the Patriot cause from apprehension that opposition would lead to slave revolt, social disorder, and the strengthening of British authority, and thus ultimately to the destruction of their property and loss of their lives. In parts of Virginia where Loyalism was strong, such as the Norfolk area, many people were encouraged by Dunmore to declare their loyalty to the British Crown. Within a few days of the Proclamation, perhaps 3,000 men in the counties around the town of Norfolk had taken an oath of allegiance to the governor. As Michael McDonnell argues, the short-term effect of Dunmore's Proclamation was to undermine the Patriot cause. He notes that "Dunmore's offensive exposed real cracks in the face of patriot claims of unanimity, much to the surprise and embarrassment of gentry leaders." The long-term effect, however, of Dunmore's precipitous actions was that they set in motion a complex chain of events that ultimately led to Virginia's independence. The problem for Dunmore, however, was that he was not fully in control of events in Virginia. His Proclamation was a bold throw of the dice. It initially worked, but it then served to undermine him and emboldened the Patriot gentry into making the final step into revolution, encouraging ardent Patriots to accelerate plans to raise a regular army. They made more determined efforts to force wavering whites to either join with them or face retribution. And, most important, they conspired to let the town of Norfolk burn to the ground while blaming the destruction on Dunmore. The burning of Norfolk was Virginia's Rubicon. Dunmore's Proclamation forced waverers to take sides and allowed Patriot leaders to call the governor's bluff.[117]

Many wiser British leaders than Dunmore believed his Proclamation to be a huge mistake. As events in Virginia showed, it was very difficult to control the unintended consequences arising from attempting to transform the racial and social order of a plantation colony. In the end, Dunmore's Proclamation drove Virginia from dissension into outright revolt. It is noticeable that the only governors to make such rash pronouncements about arming and then freeing slave soldiers were William Henry Lyttleton and Lord Dunmore, both conspicuously unsuccessful and contentious politicians. The governors of Georgia, Jamaica, South Carolina, Maryland, and Barbados kept their own counsel about arming slaves in 1775 and 1776, proceeding cautiously and slowly.[118] Most officials in the southern colonies, moreover, rejected proposals to establish slave regiments in case these proposals stimulated a profound revolution in racial order that might undermine slavery. Many British leaders felt that Dunmore's proclamations achieved little in military terms and only served to unite against them the large numbers of white men invested in slavery. The more general practice during the Revolutionary War was to discourage men of color to take up arms. One fear was that if free people of color fought, then they would be entitled to citizenship rights, something to which ordinary white men strongly objected. The more normal response by both the British government and rebel leaders was to try and expand the number of men committed to slavery. In 1781, for example, the state government of South Carolina introduced Sumter's Law, which promised slave labor and land out of property seized from Loyalists to men who signed up to serve in the military. Georgia started to award slaves to recruits in 1782. In short, there were strong incentives given to ordinary white men to fight not so much for independence, but for the continuation and expansion of slavery and for the chance to become slave owners themselves. The vaunted American war for liberty was, in the South, a war to perpetuate slavery, which in part accounts for the very low level of manumissions in the Lower South and the almost total absence of antislavery sentiment in any part of the population. Many ordinary Americans fought in favor of the Revolution not just to support slavery in general, but specifically to acquire slaves. In Georgia and Upcountry South Carolina, that ambition was often achieved.[119]

A commitment to the maintenance and expansion of slavery was common throughout plantation America. What most differentiated the Loyalist West Indies and the politically divided plantation areas of British North America was not commitment to slavery or differing fears about the possibility of slave revolt, but was the presence or otherwise of Native Americans. Indians had not entirely disappeared from the Caribbean by the mid-1770s—the fate of the Black Caribs in Dominica was a heated imperial issue. But Native Americans were small in number in the places where they still had a presence, and their political significance was limited. That was most certainly not the case in the Lower South, home to numerous and powerful Native American nations, many of which, for a variety of reasons, sided with the British during the 1760s and 1770s. France and Spain also both had substantial holdings along the Gulf Coast and in the Lower Mississippi Valley.[120]

Southern whites were much more hemmed in by outsiders than were West Indian whites. After the Revolution, many Americans found the promise of land and slaves in Spanish Louisiana and now Spanish West Florida appealing, and thousands transferred their affections from the United States to the Spanish monarchy. Before the Revolution, however, the Spaniards living in coastal towns on the Gulf Coast were more threatening than encouraging. Spanish presence stopped American expansion. One reason for ordinary white men to cast their lot with rebellious Americans was that their pugnacious attitude toward the Spanish empire promised them more possibilities of land in Spanish territory than did relying on the British crown. The quick surrender by the British of Loyalist West and East Florida in the Peace of Paris was confirmation that the British placed global diplomatic concerns over settler ambitions. They were even more impressed by Patriots' hostility to Native American land rights and by their refusal to accept Native American constitutional arguments. The willingness of the new United States to ride roughshod over long-standing assumptions that the South was a land of multiple sovereignties, all of which had to be respected, satisfied the ambitions of land-hungry and slave-hungry Americans more than did the less aggressive and more diplomatically sensitive policies of European empires.[121]

Republican Ideology and Slavery

One question remains. If fear of slave rebellion played a major role in shaping southern and island attitudes in the decision for revolution, as is often posited in the literature, surely the ideologies of republican liberty expressed in the Declaration of Independence, the clear evidence shown by slaves in their actions during the War for Independence that they thought that sentiments about liberty also referred to their condition, and the example of northern colonies in adopting schemes of gradual emancipation should have forced those southerners who fought for liberty between 1776 and 1783 to reconsider their position on slavery. How was liberty for republican Americans compatible with the entrenchment of slavery in the American South? For a few slave owners, most notably Virginians, the contradictions between fighting for liberty and holding slaves in bondage were sufficient to lead them to manumit slaves. The most prominent example of a Virginian who recognized the contradictions of republican slaveholding was George Washington, the only president to manumit significant numbers of enslaved people, albeit only at his death.[122]

The main effect of the American Revolution on slavery, however, was to allow its expansion into the Mississippi Valley and the Deep South. The Constitution was a resolutely proslavery document: the number of slaves manumitted outside the Chesapeake was pitifully small, and racially exclusionary policies toward blacks were ever more rigid and more easily enforced. If the themes that the founders proclaimed were the themes of the Revolution were actually true (the extension of universal and unalienable rights of life, liberty, and the pursuit of happiness throughout the world), the inability of the founders to cut out the cancer of slavery from the new nation suggested that the American Revolution was a counterrevolutionary disappointment. Gary Nash makes a particularly strong argument along these lines. He notes that the American Revolution was a limited inspiration internationally. Its only importance was as a colonial revolt by settler elites, not as an example of a campaign for liberty, as Americans imagined. The unwillingness of most southern founders to confront Carolina slave owners over slavery, Nash argues, was a betrayal of revolutionary principles. Jefferson was the most prominent and disappointing example of cowardice, reduced to arguing that the fate of slaves had to be left to "the workings of an overruling Providence." That this sort of equivocation over slavery was a rejection of the principles of 1776 was clear to the one true revolutionary, Thomas Paine, who lamented the retreat of Americans from "a *new system* of government in which the rights of *all* men should be preserved."[123]

Nevertheless, this is not how southern whites saw matters. Their version of liberty was negative liberty, in the definition made famous by Isaiah Berlin, meaning freedom from interference by other people.

They counterpoised that idea of liberty to an idea of slavery, which was based upon the idea of constraint. Key to both liberty and slavery was the idea of human agency: it was people themselves who determined whether they were to be free or to be slaves. This notion that humans rather than providence or luck helped determine status helps explain why slave owners used the discourse of slavery so often in explaining why they needed to resist British attempts to take away their liberty and thus make them "slaves." It was a short step from believing that human agency kept people free to believing that those people who were enslaved deserved to be slaves because they were unprepared to resist. The relative paucity of slave rebellions in eighteenth-century British America was not just important for reasons of security. It was important ideologically. When slaves did not resist their condition, they implicitly accepted it, according to slave owners. Slave owners were sure that if they were in the same position as their slaves, they would prefer to be killed rather than accept enslavement. Of course, such thinking elided the reality of slave lives and the near certainty that rebellious slaves would face a much worse fate when a rebellion failed than was ever likely to befall a planter protesting against British ministerial wickedness. But southern willingness to attribute agency to humans allowed them to blame their slaves for slaves' predicament. The moral burden of slavery could be easily passed under such thinking from the slaveholder, who had shown his virtue in the American Revolution by standing up to tyranny, to the slave: the abject accepter of his or her fate and someone unwilling to die for freedom.[124]

Slave owners in the new republic found it easy to incorporate slavery within republican forms of government. Their understanding of liberty strengthened the institution's ideological underpinnings by providing an argument for the protection of property.[125] Few slaveholders thought slaves were anything other than property. Colonists opposed Lord Mansfield's rulings in the *Somerset* case of 1772, which they saw as an infringement of settler rights over property, by asserting that Africans did not belong to the realm of free-born Britons. Thus, slaves had no rights that needed to be recognized. African slaves, who, it was often argued, were not made slaves in America but had also been slaves in Africa, had "no natural right of their own country [to] Liberty."[126] Independence from Britain allowed American slaveholders to put this racially exclusive idea of liberty into practice. Slave owners joined the new republic in order to protect slavery: the general recognition of property rights in humans was the sine non qua of union. Their racist understanding of who was and who was not entitled to liberty allowed them to simultaneously expand white liberties while ensuring that the powers of the state would be used to raise formidable barriers to outside interference with slavery. Revolutionary ideology was thus easily exploited to support the continued racial exploitation of people of African descent in the new American South.[127]

An Atlantic Event

Seeing the American Revolution in an Atlantic rather than an American way allows us to take the perspective that Samuel Johnson did on planter pretensions in 1775. The American Revolution was a war fought by planters in part to protect, defend, and expand slavery. One of the fundamental rights that southern planters insisted upon was their right not only to own slaves, but also to be able to determine within their own legislatures the laws and customs under which their investment in slave property could be protected. They largely succeeded in their aims to fence slavery off from interference from outside forces, whether British imperial rulers or northern abolitionists. Some of the most important people in America were deeply invested in slavery and its continuation. Not all of those people were slaveholders, but those who were insisted on protections for slavery, especially the right of slaveholders to internally police their slaves and the right to have runaway slaves returned to them from any part of the United States. As events turned out, slaveholders in the American South made the correct decision to rebel against Britain in order to protect their investment in slave property. William Lloyd Garrison was also correct to see the new United States government as founded on a proslavery constitution. The small gains that abolitionists made in the American North were more than matched by the gains slaveholders achieved in limiting the ability of a powerful centralized government to insist on the amelioration of slavery, as France and Britain did in the late 1780s and to end slavery by imperial decree, as did France 1794 and Britain 1833. Southern slaveholders were able to control the discourse over slavery and stop a powerful centralized state from interfering in their affairs. That worked until they decided to embark upon a path of self-destruction by rebelling against the United States of America in 1861.[128]

The greatest threat to slavery proved to be an assertive, self-confident imperial state with centralizing tendencies, as Britain became in the years after 1788 when it aggressively tried to reshape empire in its own image. West Indian planters found out to their cost how this new tendency

FIGURE 12. Abolitionists faced vigorous opposition from Britons convinced that their propaganda was destroying an institution that was not as bad as abolitionists depicted it and that, moreover, provided economic gain to Britain and its Empire. Robert Cruickshank, *John Bull Taking a Clear View of the Negro Slavery Question!* (G. Humphrey, 1826). © Courtesy Wilberforce House, Hull City Museums and Art Galleries.

toward imperial interference with matters colonials thought their own business, notably their power to treat slaves as they wanted, became increasingly important after the American Revolution. They were caught in a bind not of their own making. America's republican tendencies appalled them; they could not join in the American republican experiment. But they became increasingly aware of how the American Revolution encouraged Britons to traduce planter character in ways that diminished planters' importance in an empire those planters no longer controlled. They lamented also how little influence white West Indian planters had in a radically reformed British empire in which everyone was a subject, and where most subjects were not white. Wilberforce and other abolitionists seemed madmen and abolition a mindless policy designed to destroy British prosperity. As Robert Cruickshank's cartoon, entitled *John Bull Taking a Clear View of the Negro Slavery Question!*, suggests, some Britons came to share this negative opinion of the abolitionist tendency in British politics. But the dramatically weaker position of British slaveholders in an empire that after 1783 had relatively few slaveholders and an increasing number of Britons who thought slavery wrong and slaveholders evil made West Indian planters unable to stop Britain's "madness." That madness, as they saw it, was to wreck a great economic system in which the sufferings of Africans they did not care about brought about an advance in the standard of living of white people everywhere.[129]

The American Revolution was a political cataclysm in the history of British America that had economic consequences for the future of all British American plantation societies. That the break in British America between those colonies that rebelled and those that remained loyal occurred where it did not only shaped how the American Revolution began, but also affected the conduct of the war and the actions of Britons, Americans, and West Indians once the fighting had concluded. The economic consequences were not minimal—plantation areas suffered economic decline during the War of Independence, to a greater or lesser degree—but the major impact of the American Revolution was political and to an extent cultural. In the new United States of America, the lessons that the American Revolution taught an increasingly ascendant planter class was that resistance to authority in the name of settler rights worked, and that preemptive action against political power hostile to slavery was effective. The result of breaking away from Britain in the 1780s was that planters in the United States not only had a proslavery constitution that protected their right to enslaved property, but also were insulated from abolitionist humanitarian currents. The result of planters' taking preemptive action in support of their supposed liberties in 1776 was that southern planters had political clout that matched their economic success for the first half of the nineteenth century. It meant that slavery lasted for another generation longer in the United States than in the British empire and was destroyed only when planters' determination to take preemptive action to preserve their authority over enslaved people came up against a greater force: a political party that had determined that America's agreement to create a nation in which slavery was recognized was a covenant with evil.[130]

The American Revolution was less directly important in the West Indies than in British North America, although the West Indian context to the war was extremely important in determining the outcome in favor of American rebellion.[131] Economically, the American Revolution was a small blip in the strong economic performance of the West Indian plantation system, an economic performance that was increasingly successful after the next major war in the aftermath of the French Revolution opened up new plantation opportunities in mainland South America. It did not presage the start of the end of West Indian prosperity, and in dampening enthusiasm for abolitionism in Britain in the early 1780s it may have delayed metropolitan interference in the colonial West Indian management of slavery and the slave trade. But white West Indians came to regret not joining their American cousins in rebellion. Unlike the planters of the American South, who largely controlled antebellum American federal slave legislation and politics, West Indian planters' ability to influence imperial policy over slavery was greatly reduced in the aftermath of the American Revolution—in part because the British state increasingly flexed its humanitarian muscles, and in part because metropolitan exposure to the reality of planter life during the American Revolution made many Britons hostile to white West Indians. Thus, white West Indians found their loyalty during the American Revolution backfiring. By the early nineteenth century they were neither properly British nor American. They were increasingly isolated and beleaguered, no match for an intrusive British state who envisaged other forms of colonization besides slave-based plantation agriculture.

Epilogue: Slaves and Planters

Introduction

The eighteenth-century plantation system in British America was a stunning success. It made the British empire in the Americas economically worthwhile and justified the seventeenth century's investment in colonization. It contributed great wealth to the mother country, even if by the last decades of the eighteenth century such contributions were increasingly discounted by assertive abolitionists. We should be careful, of course, not to overemphasize its importance. Despite their outstanding productivity and per capita value, the wealthiest of Britain's slave colonies had gross product equal to that of a small English county in 1700 (Cumberland, perhaps) and still only a larger county (Sussex, perhaps) in 1800. That made them important but not essential to Britain's economic health. The industrialization of Britain and its imperial wealth, mostly derived from India and from investments in the United States, would have made Britain the wealthiest nation in the world in the nineteenth century even without any contribution from the plantation colonies.[1] But the slave colonies were rich enough to make a difference. The wealth they brought to the empire made Britain richer and allowed many British migrants who left Britain for the colonies to have a comfortable existence. Most important, the plantation system was very good at distributing wealth to those members of the British establishment who most counted, and who made the rules about how the empire was to be run. Thus, a lot of people had reason to think plantations a good thing.[2]

Although it is possible to argue from a purely economic cost-analysis basis that Adam Smith was right to claim that British investment in empire and slavery was a considerable misallocation of resources, this argument misses the point. Britain wanted an empire for all sorts of reasons, and the people who most wanted an empire obtained sizable benefits from their involvement in empire and slavery. It may be, as John Stuart Mill sniffed, that the empire was just a form of outdoor relief for the aristocracy, but these were the people who made decisions.[3]

Both landed and nonlanded British families sought to acquire wealth and social respectability through participation in imperial trade. Some of these were new families, but many more were well established. Their eager involvement in imperial commerce lent legitimacy to this sort of activity.[4] How the rich and powerful benefited from slavery has echoed down the centuries, as is clear in the Legacies of Slavery project being conducted at University College, London. Using records of compensation given to ex–slave owners after the end of slavery in the British empire in 1838, the organizers of this major project have traced numerous examples of money derived from compensation given to slave owners that was used to bankroll major British cultural and economic institutions and that formed the basis of socially and politically important British fortunes. The reach of slavery into a large numbers of areas of the British establishment, from the church to business to politics and to culture, of compensation monies paid to rich Britons for having had their enslaved property freed was widespread and important.[5]

Nevertheless, the plantation system was not just a useful way of redistributing money to the rich and powerful. The plantation system created real money that was used to deliver actual improvements to the quality of life for white residents in American plantation societies. Planters were fervent capitalists, able to cope with all sorts of disruptions and disasters, with ingenuity if not with equanimity. Throughout the eighteenth century their efforts produced great wealth for themselves and for their societies. The money that planters made resulted in an increase in overall product in British America and led to a stronger empire. Enough wealth trickled down to the general populace to raise living standards for white people substantially over time. Of course, little money trickled down to black people. That is something we should care about, and it was something that many Britons and Americans in the nineteenth century cared about. But in British America between 1650 and 1820, relatively few white people thought the interests of black people were something that should concern them.

This book has concentrated on the role of ordinary white people within plantation systems, because the plantation system would not have worked if they had not given it their support. Ordinary whites supported a system in which great planters were the principal beneficiaries for hardheaded reasons based on economic advantage. The growth of the plantation society occurred as a result of a bargain between ordinary whites, who found their ways into landownership and high political status blocked but whose standards of living rose as a direct result of the switch to the large integrated plantation, and great planters, who were careful to foster white support for their authority and mastership of slaves and dependents.[6]

Racism and the Plantation System

I differ from some previous accounts of this process by not assuming that whites in plantation society supported each other from a shared racism against black people. Edmund Morgan, for example argued that while racism against blacks and Native Americans was always present in colonial Virginia, it was intensified in an almost deliberate way as the plantation system emerged in order to lessen white class tensions and confrontations. Morgan argued that "racism thus absorbed in Virginia the fear and the contempt that men in England, whether Whig or Tory, monarchist or republican, felt for the inarticulate lower classes . . . By lumping Indians, mulattoes and Negroes in a single pariah class, Virginians had paved the way for a similar lumping of small and large planters in a single master class."[7]

It is hard to disagree in general with this proposition. Nevertheless, English and English American notions of who was an insider and who was an outsider were well developed before slavery was introduced into the Chesapeake. Virginians may have feared Africans, but mostly they had contempt for them.[8] Ordinary whites did not have to be inveigled into white supremacy. They supported great planters because the economic system great planters established gave ordinary white men economic benefits, access to consumer goods, and the possibility of acting as domestic patriarchs. This acquiescence to great planter rule continued after the Revolution: nine of the first twelve American presidents were connected to slave regimes. In addition, in the nineteenth-century West

Indies a truncated and diminished elite planter class was still able to gain the consent of ordinary whites for their rule after the plantation system went into terminal decline.[9]

When planters and ordinary whites behaved callously toward enslaved people and described them in the harshest language, it was not because they were displacing their fear into emotions. It was because they hated and despised blacks. In the heyday of the plantation system, between 1720 and 1770, when planters were virtually unconstrained in their behavior toward enslaved people by custom, law, abolitionist pressure, or imperial diktat, planters showed what they truly thought about Africans and slaves. It is an ugly picture. Many Britons and British Americans involved in the slave trade reveled in sadistic cruelty toward black people, as has been detailed several times in this book. Cruelty was so unexceptional as to be normal. We can see this in the rare times that contemporaries commented on particularly egregious examples of cruelty meted out to Africans. John Newton commented on Richard Jackson "jointing" rebels on a ship only because such cruelty exceeded the normal uncommented acts of brutality that slave captains dished out all the time to captives. John Taylor noted in loving detail how Colonel Ivy in late seventeenth-century Jamaica engaged in an elaborate torture of rebel slaves because what Ivy was purported to have done was an intensification of the barbarity that happened on estates every day. The pervasiveness of violence is seen in the casualness by which Robert "King" Carter recorded his request in the 1720s that two runaway slaves be dismembered by his local court, and in the laconic matter-of-fact entries in Thomas Thistlewood's diaries recording daily beatings, frequent rapes, and the humiliating excremental excess of Derby's Dose.

Blacks as Beasts

The extraordinary punishments that were picked out for exemplification by contemporaries were accompanied by a systematic demeaning of slaves in almost every aspect of their lives. Africans were renamed on arrival on the plantations, and although planters were very often careful not to give names intended to humiliate, they were fond of giving slaves names derived from classical mythology or names of grand imperial places.[10] It must have given them a sense of wry amusement to see an ordinary slave going by the moniker of a great Greek or Roman god or by the name of a famous English city like London or Bristol. The point here is that masters did not need to act with such cruelty and meanness in areas where there was no obvious correlation with work performance. It betokens an underlying contempt for Africans and an indifference to their concerns and feelings. For many planters the gap between how they viewed livestock and how they viewed human property was distressingly small. By the 1780s, for example, Jamaican planters began to list cattle and horses by name and price in their inventories in the same way as human "stock." There was considerable crossover in names. White Jamaicans went further than any other Englishmen in reducing the chasm between the animal and human realms. Planters saw slaves as property, as commodities, as bodies to be bought and sold and disposed of. That was because the money nexus was very obvious, with slaves not much different from livestock. When a traveler to Saint-Domingue in the 1780s admonished a planter for allowing his slaves to work almost naked, the colonist is reported to have replied, "Why not also ask us to put clothes on our cows, mules and dogs?"[11] In these new and highly commodified societies, no especial privilege accrued to being a human.[12]

Benjamin Franklin was not a planter, but he is such an emblematic and influential figure in eighteenth-century colonial British American life that his views on black capacity are worth examining in order to show just how deep-seated hatred of blacks as African savages was among even people who came to think that slavery was wrong. Because he was a founder of antislavery sentiment in postrevolutionary America, he is a better guide to the contempt that almost all white Americans had toward Africans than a much more obviously racist commentator such as Thomas Jefferson, whose hatred of blacks is well documented. In 1747 Franklin expostulated, "Who can, without the utmost Horror, conceive the Miseries . . . when your Persons, Fortunes, Wives and Daughters shall be subject to the wanton and unbridled Rage, Rapine and Lust of *Negroes, Mulattoes* and others the vilest and most abandoned of Mankind."[13] His words showed him as someone very fearful of blacks and what they might do if let loose, but a better reading is one that emphasizes "unbridled Rage," suggesting that he detested Africans' innate barbarity and their inability to exercise self-control.[14]

It is worth concluding this section by returning to Daniel Defoe's Jack, the overseer. Defoe felt Africans were uncontrollable except through massive applications of force. He also was mostly concerned with the effects of white brutality toward slaves on the character of white people. Defoe considers Jack's sympathy toward Africans as problematic, derived not from any fellow feeling for them as members of the same human race, but from their similar experiences of being whipped. Defoe suggests that the sympathy Jack has for slaves will not be repaid with kindness. The way to avoid such useless emotions is to make sure that no white man was ever treated as if he were a black slave. After all, his master makes Jack, but not an enslaved African, an overseer, presumably because of the shared cultural heritage and racial makeup of master and English convict servant. Jack's sympathetic identification with slaves is weakness and is repaid by slaves' becoming insolent and having "Contempt for my Authority, that we were all in Disorder." He admitted his weakness to his master, declaring that "I have such a Tenderness in my Nature, that tho' I might be fit to be your Servant; I am incapable of being an Executioner, having been an Offender myself." His master was displeased: "Well, but how then can my Business be done? And how will this terrible Obstinacy of the *Negroes*, who they tell me, can be no otherwise governed, be kept from Neglect of their Work, or even Insolence or Rebellion?" Jack learned his lesson. Whites were capable of being reformed, as he was from a criminal to a soldier, but Africans were irredeemable. The only reason to worry about disciplining African slaves was the possibility that it might lead to a hardening of white hearts. But this hardening of heart was not a sign of English savagery. It was necessary because Africans knew only violence and did not respond to kindness as whites would. These were people without feeling:

now I began indeed to see, that the Cruelty so much talk'd of, used in *Virginia* and *Barbadoes*, and other Colonies in Whipping the *Negro* Slaves, was not so much owing to the Tyranny of the English, as had been reported; the English not being accounted to be of a cruel disposition; and really are not so. But that it is owing to the Brutallity, and obstinate Temper of the *Negroes* who cannot be mannag'd by Kindness, and Courtisy; but must be rul'd with a Rod of Iron, beaten with *Scorpions*, as the Scripture calls it; and must be used as they do use them, or they would rise and murder all their Masters, which their Numbers consider'd, would not be hard for them to do, if they had Arms and Ammunition suitable to the Rage and Cruelty of their Nature.[15]

The Anxious Planter

What can we say about the men and women who held these attitudes? Should they have been concerned that they hated Africans so much? Did they worry that this hatred might be reciprocated and lead slaves to attack them? That slave owners were consumed by anxiety is a constant trope within the historiography of the planter classes in America, especially that of eighteenth-century Virginia planters. Kathleen M. Brown's lapidary comparison of the planter psyche to a poorly built building gives a flavor of the tone of historical writings on the typical planter as an unduly and deservedly anxious man. She argues that "for colonial gentlemen, authority was a delicate project, much like a home built upon an unstable foundation. To keep such a structure standing, the owner had to be extremely sensitive to fine cracks and imperfection, shoring up the edifice to prevent the entire home from tumbling down." Just about everything worried them. Were they deficient in virtue? Did various scandals show they were corrupt and addicted to luxury? Were they living beyond their means? Were evangelicals, enslaved people, or British merchants conspiring against them? Did their wives and daughters laugh at them behind their backs? And, most worrying of all, did the English elite respect their claims to gentility? The Revolution showed that the latter fear—that the English thought them ungenteel—was probably justified. There were, it seems, many signs that their claims to authority were not accepted by others, either their dependents or their superiors in London, that their anxiety was natural, and that it represented the "tortured perfectionism of colonials who could never achieve enough of an English inflection."[16]

In the West Indies the problem for outside observers by the late eighteenth century was not that planters were anxious, but that they were failures. They could not produce enough white children, a moral failing in a philoprogenitive age, compounded by their tendency to prefer the charms of colored mistresses over their lawful wives. That made them failures as men. They had extremely poor self-control, manifested in their addiction to gambling, their lack of perseverance, and most of all in their habitual and almost needless cruelty to enslaved people. This made them failures as humans. White West Indians tried to counter these negative descriptions, but they were forced to admit that some of the aspersions on the West Indian planter's character were justified. Earlier in the eighteenth century metropolitan critiques of West Indian society placed the blame on women rather than men for the islands' social shortcomings. By the late eighteenth century, however, it was men and their deficiencies that were blamed for the loose morals and customary brutality of white people in the tropics. The prevalent metropolitan conception of planters shifted during the eighteenth century as abolitionist denunciations of planters became central to discursive treatments of West Indian character. But even people who praised West Indians as men of good character and ready hospitality deplored their immorality, their venality, their tendency to excess in all things, and most of all their violence to their slaves, as well as their greed for food, money, and pleasure of all kinds.[17]

The societies they created were libertine paradises that many observers thought were debauched hells. They resembled in reality what the Marquis de Sade imagined in theory. Joan (Colin) Dayan made the link clear in her provocative and penetrating critique of plantation life in neighboring Saint-Domingue. She suggests that Sade's scenarios of terror and pleasure may have been inspired by the libertinism of Saint-Domingue planters: "Sade brought the plantation hell and its excesses into enlightenment Europe . . . The debauchery and unbridled tyranny of Sade's libertines have their sources in the emblematic Creole planters, dedicated to the heady interests of pleasure, greed, and abandon." Indeed, it was hatred of the libertine planter as much as sympathy for the benighted African that inspired in 1784 one of the first and most influential abolitionists, James Ramsay, who had spent more than twenty unhappy years in Nevis as pastor of an empty church, to write a denunciation of them and their cruelty. He thought planters belonged to the "kingdom of *I*"—unrestrained, godless narcissists who allowed their desire for pleasure and excessive self-expression to overwhelm any sense of decency and order. These were men, as an opponent described them in the 1760s in Jamaica, who were "habituated by Precept and Example, to Sensuality and Despotism."[18] Ramsay and others thought they had no business running any sort of society. Indeed, abolitionist observers believed that if there was any kind of justice they would sometime soon get their comeuppance, probably from slaves pushed beyond endurance by tyranny. Abbé Raynal's apocalyptic vision of a Caribbean likely to erupt in revolt led by a black Spartacus was much quoted, both in the Caribbean and in Europe.[19]

I have problems with this analysis—that white men were too lustful, too cruel, and too full of anxiety and uncertainty about their status to be anything than fearful about their place in plantation society. White men in plantation settings were not easily scared or unusually fearful. Bravery and aggression were essential components of planter manliness. They were emphasized more in plantation societies than in societies in which other models of masculinity were favored. In Jamaica, for example, white men were expected to be willing to fight. William Dorrill told Thomas Thistlewood in 1750, when the diarist arrived in the island, that "in this Country it is highly necessary for a Man to fight once or twice, to keep Cowards from putting upon him."[20] Being able to stand up for oneself was a crucial measure of masterfulness. It was a central way in which white Jamaicans saw themselves as free people. White Jamaicans were a combative people, "liable to sudden transports of anger." Given the omnipresence of slavery, it is not surprising that almost all white men had "something of a haughty Disposition." As Charles Leslie commented in 1740, a noticeable feature of the white male character in Jamaica was that white men "required Submission" from all around them. Moreover, every man insisted on being the "absolute master of himself and his actions."[21]

White men in other parts of plantation America were equally quick to anger and ready to use violence to get what they wanted. Indeed, that planters were violent and that slaves were not, or at least were not prepared to openly display the rage that whites felt consumed them, was a marker of slaves' servile character and a justification for their enslavement. One legacy of the American Revolution was that it justified linking freedom with an obligation to resist. Planters insisted on a Hobbesian bargain for their slaves, but rejected Hobbes for themselves. If they were not free, planters in the American South argued, they should be dead, as Patrick Henry famously was supposed to have declared: "Is life so dear, or peace so sweet as to be purchased at the price of chains and slavery? I know not what course others may take but as for me, give me liberty or give me death."[22] It was not accidental that he chose death, not slavery, as the antithesis to freedom. To choose slavery was to make a cowardly choice. The blacks he owned could be said to have made that choice; he was not willing to do so.

Planters' attitude that death was preferable to slavery made them contemptuous toward the slaves they owned who were not prepared to rebel. They grudgingly respected those slaves prepared to suffer painful deaths rather than live as slaves. This attitude is clear in the historian Bryan Edwards's poem of the early 1760s imagining the laments of a slave executed in Tacky's Revolt. Edwards even tried to evoke sensitivity to the rebel's plight through a degree of sympathetic identification. Significantly, however, Edwards later publicly regretted writing the poem. In a reprinting when he was a middle-aged man, he belittled his poem as the naive expression of a teenaged innocent only recently removed to Jamaica. Echoing Defoe's Jack, he declared that he had learned the error of his ways, having realized that Africans, being savages, vile criminals, and traitors, had no feelings that he needed to empathize with.[23]

Planters' respect for executed Africans, however, was conditional on slaves' dying painfully. They had little empathetic identification otherwise with black people, despite Edwards's later recanted poem. That lack of sympathy predated the rise of the large integrated plantation. Of course, English attitudes to Africans were multifaceted and complicated and were influenced by geohumoral notions of identity in which English identity was as problematic as African identity. But there was a strand of hatred toward Africans, and especially toward African slaves, that was not replicated toward other people. As Betty Wood notes, following the pioneering work of Winthrop Jordan, "Metropolitan English people who crossed the Atlantic to establish colonies subscribed to deeply unfavorable stereotypes about West and West Central Africans that facilitated, but did not necessarily dictate, a move towards racially based systems of bondage." She notes that attitudes to Native Americans among the English were more varied and more likely to be predicated on a common humanity. The English had more experience with Africans than might have been expected, sometimes in Africa, occasionally in England, but most often in their encounters with Spaniards and Portuguese in Iberian America, where Africans were often enslaved and were seen as commodities. It meant that, as Michael Guasco argues, "to a greater degree than other peoples of the Atlantic littoral, Europeans perceived Africans in the Americas to be rootless, mobile, merchantable, and subservient." That tendency to see Africans as valuable resources, as much as humans, coincided with negative connotations associated with blackness, which was a color often associated with evil, sin, dirtiness, danger, and the Devil himself.[24] That Africans could be devils can be seen in contemporary literature. The most implacable and violent character in all of William Shakespeare's works, for example, is the Moorish slave Aron in *Titus Andronicus*. Aron is relentless in his hatred of those who enslaved him and is willing to do just about anything to gain revenge against his oppressors. Shakespeare treats him with an unremitting hostility that amounts to explicit racism. And he kills him (having him placed up to his waist in the ground and left to die of thirst and starvation) in an act of extreme cruelty. Aron, however, retains some dignity in his furious rage by being unrepentant at the end, taking his punishment without complaint, shouting defiance and hatred toward those who were torturing him. Edwards's reluctant respect for the black male rebel who accepted death and torture with equanimity was in the line of succession to how Shakespeare treated Aron in his bloody revenge tragedy.[25]

Slave Agency

The debate over whether we should stress slave agency and slaves' ability to overcome the torments of slavery or the inhumanity that enslaved people were forced to endure is an old one. We can take a Panglossian or a Hobbesian approach to slavery.[26] We can emphasize either how slaves, through their resistance to dehumanization, overcame slavery, or we can see slavery as a relentless destroyer of people. The Hobbesian rather than the Panglossian aspects of slavery are what impress me most, in part because my focus in this book is on the eighteenth-century plantation period, where the degradation of black life was most pronounced. I have also written on eighteenth-century Jamaica and nineteenth-century British Guiana, where slaves' experience was particularly dismal. Isolated, atomized, usually employed in backbreaking labor, and experiencing unprecedented degrees of violence and social flux, slaves experienced desperate and uncertain lives that were indeed Hobbesian. The plantation was for enslaved people a state of nature, a *bellum omnium contra omnes*, in which slaves' nasty, brutish, and short existence was compounded by hunger and despair. Slave owners did little to ease their pain, applying spiritual terror to the physical grief that slaves experienced in their quotidian existence.[27]

For some commentators, this unflinching preference for the destructive as opposed to the creative characteristics of slavery both privileges the perspective of planters and also pathologizes slaves. It gets perilously close, critics argue, to supporting the nihilistic notions of slaves as being socially dead, and it might be used as a governing paradigm to explain the psychological effects of slavery.[28] But we don't need to choose between the totalizing implications of the notion of slavery as social death—an option that adopts planter notions of the irrelevance of acknowledging slaves' humanity in ways too close for comfort—and the equally totalizing idea of slaves engaged in an essentially theological battle between the forces for evil (slave owners) and the forces of good (themselves). Both options raise the stakes too high. Slavery was less an existential condition than a predicament that slaves coped with in different ways, sometimes to their advantage, sometimes not.[29]

That slaves "survived" slavery and created viable slave cultures that harked back to African beginnings and persisted into freedom is undeniable. That they also were damaged by slavery in ways that are to modern people incalculable, and that those damages also persisted past the end of slavery, is also obviously true. The best way of looking at what slaves experienced during slavery is through the lens of trauma, which accepts that traumatized and brutalized people suffer psychic pain that never goes away, no matter how efficacious the therapy, but which also accepts that the effects of trauma can be managed and some sense of self salvaged after a period of introspective analysis and treatment.[30] What this book shows is how an important system worked, and how understanding how it worked and sometimes did not work is important for understanding an important part of early modern Atlantic history. The plantation system worked very well for those who wanted it to work. It was a remarkable machine for getting money and wealth in the early modern Atlantic world. It was also a monstrous system that imposed massive physical and psychic costs on the people caught up in the cogs of the machine, some of whom survived, but many of whom, to use the words of Primo Levi writing about another monstrous machine, the Holocaust of the mid-twentieth century, were the drowned.[31] In order to understand slavery and the complicated relationship of blacks and whites in the Atlantic world, some understanding of how the plantation societies of British America grew, developed, flourished, and were attacked and defended between 1650 and 1820 is useful.

An Essay on Sources

I have not burdened readers with overly elaborate explanations in the text or footnotes of primary sources. Readers do deserve, however, a brief explanation of one major source, a database of all inventories recorded in Jamaica between 1674 and 1784, contained in IB/11/3/1–65, JA. Four volumes, dating from the 1690s and 1700s, are missing, and one, from 1760, is unreadable. I have abstracted from the remaining sixty volumes 10,222 separate individual inventories, occasionally combining inventories when it is clear that the inventories concerned relate to the same individual. Each person was given a separate file and was noted by name, occupation, parish, and total estate value. For each inventory I abstracted the number and value of enslaved people, noting whether they were male or female and determining, when appraisers gave this information (which they did sometimes) whether the slaves were men, women, boys, girls, or children. I also counted cash, plate, and jewelry to get an idea of monetary assets and summed debts owed to each estate. The total value of the estate was recorded and converted into sterling values. I also determined what percentage of total estate value was made up of slaves and what percentage was of debts.[1]

An inventory was a list of belongings of the deceased as appraised by two men, usually neighbors, under the direction of the executors of the estate. It was not a simple task to appraise estates, especially large ones, since each item of personal property had to be listed and assigned a value. The very largest estates resulted in inventories running over ten pages. Because the task was burdensome and required considerable precision, men sometimes tried to avoid being an appraiser. Nevertheless, appraising one's fellow estate was a crucial civic duty. Most appraisers took their job seriously. The evaluations in estates are remarkably detailed and are very accurate about prices assigned to goods. Occasionally inventories describe auctions, where we can presume that the prices recorded were the prices actually paid. A comparison of inventory values and prices received at auctions indicates that inventory values were 2 percent higher than auction sales. Given that many auctions were probably conducted for estates in distress, such a gap in prices is trivial and suggests that inventoried prices are accurate guides to values in Jamaica.

Nevertheless, inventories have biases.[2] Some things are enumerated better than others. The coverage of enslaved people is especially good. Appraisers counted all slaves and assigned values to slaves, usually, in the eighteenth century, as individuals. The variation in prices between individual enslaved people and the close connection between slave price values in inventories and slave price values in auctions suggest that appraisers valued individual slaves accurately.[3] They were less careful about debts. One drawback of Jamaican probate records is that, unlike Maryland probate records, they do not include a calculation of debts owed by the deceased, meaning that gross but not net wealth can be calculated.[4] Not all debts were enumerated in inventories even when it is likely that many people were lending out money. There were 131 decedents, 7 of whom were Kingston merchants, who left estates worth more than £5,000 without debts listed. There were in total 4,440 decedents who did not have debts listed. The likelihood is that appraisers did not always know what debts were owed and thus omitted them. Thus, there is probably a bias toward undercounting the wealth of planters. It is also probable that merchants' wealth is overstated in other ways. Many appraisers made detailed lists of all merchants' stock in trade. While such enumeration is a godsend for the historian of consumption, it does mean that the shop goods of merchants are counted in their estate as if they were actual possessions instead of items held in shops.

Acknowledgments

I first thought about the themes of this book when visiting the Jamaica Archives in October 1987 after taking a position at the University of the West Indies at Mona. The archivists in the Jamaica Archives have helped provide access to their rich records. I have received financial assistance from the University of Canterbury, Brunel University, the University of Sussex, the University of Warwick, and the University of Melbourne. I am grateful to the Leverhulme Foundation for a grant with Kenneth Morgan of Brunel University in 2002. Sherrylynne Haggerty, now at the University of Nottingham, was a very able research assistant. Some thinking for this book was done while I was a fellow at the National Humanities Center in 2008–9.

Many people have helped in previous projects that bear on this book. At Brunel University, Kenneth Morgan was a particular inspiration, as were Inge Dornan and David Ryden. At the University of Sussex, Steve Burman, Richard Godden, and Peter Nicholls were very supportive senior colleagues. Paul Betts, Saul Dubow, and Naomi Tadmor were wonderful companions in History, while Clive Webb and especially Richard Follett, in American Studies, were attentive and critical listeners. Conversations with Saul and Richard have increased my understanding of colonialism and race relations. At the University of Warwick, Mark Knights taught me a great deal about the British context of the early modern Atlantic; and David Dabydeen, Rebecca Earle, Roger Fagge, Cecily Jones, and Tony McFarlane made me think in exciting ways about the hemispheric Americas.

Tim Lockley and Gad Heuman changed my thinking in very productive ways. And Giorgio Riello is an agreeable housemate, a talented historian, and an ideal person off of whom to bounce ideas. Deirdre Coleman, in Melbourne, has shaped in profound ways my thinking about American plantations and about how to write. At the National Humanities Center in 2008–9, Laurent Dubois, Bob Duplessis, and Kathleen Duvall all made me think that what I was doing was worthwhile. Mary Floyd-Wilson, Florence Dore, and Cassie Mansfield were not quite as convinced about the merits of what I was doing but were wonderfully entertaining lunch companions.

I am fortunate to be a member of three exemplary academic organizations—the British Group of Early American Historians, the European Early American Association, and the Australia New Zealand American Studies Association. David Goodman, Emma Hart, Susanne Lachenicht, Ben Marsh, Simon Middleton, Simon Newman, Allan Potofsky, Marie-Jeanne Rossignol, Steve Sarson, Shane White, Natalie Zacek, Nuala Zaheidah, and the late Rhys Isaac, John Salmond, and Naomi Wulf were among the many people in these organizations who listened to and commented on papers on this topic. Mike McDonnell read a whole draft of this manuscript and gave excellent comments, as did Andrew O'Shaughnessy. In the United States, I benefited from the friendship and patronage of Peter Mancall and Lisa Bitel and have learned a great deal from John McNeill and Ann Plane. Andrew O'Shaughnessy helped me secure a fellowship at the Robert H. Smith International Center for Jefferson Studies at Monticello, Virginia, in July 2009. Nicholas Canny, Jonathan Dalby, Richard Dunn, Jack Greene, Jerry Handler, Barry Higman, Rod McDonald, James Robertson, Verene Shepherd, and Swithin Wilmot—all great Caribbean scholars—were very helpful. Mark Peterson and Ed Gray's support for this project, as part of their American Beginnings series, is greatly appreciated.

Finally, I wish to acknowledge close friends and family. Tommaso Astarita has been a great and supportive friend. John Garrigus, with whom I am collaborating on a book on Jamaica and Saint-Domingue, is another graduate school friend whose intelligence and grace continuously impress me. Greg Hess is an economist and now a university president, but he has always taken the time to offer me encouragement. He even wrote a quixotic paper with me on topics connected with this book. Tracy Bennett, Christie Billings, Mark Bolland, Aubrey Botsford, Phillippa Revell, Jane Richards, and Bryan Symons provided lodging and entertainment in Britain, as Jonathan Dalby, Juliet Williams, and Mary Sloper did in Jamaica. Caroline Repchuk provided Jamaican prints that have been used for illustrations. Glenn Burgess and Mandy Capern have listened to me talk about the West Indies for twenty-three years at Canterbury and Hull. My dear wife, Deborah Morgan, has joined me in peripatetic moves across continents, in supporting my travels to archives and conferences, and in much else besides. My son, Nick Burnard, and my daughter, Eleanor Burnard, are interested in history. I hope they find this book intriguing. I dedicate it to them.

Notes

INTRODUCTION

1. Russell R. Menard, *Sweet Negotiations: Sugar, Slavery, and Plantation Agriculture in Early Barbados* (Charlottesville: University of Virginia Press, 2006), 91.
2. For the larger context see Brendan Simms, *Three Victories and a Defeat: The Rise and Fall of the First British Empire, 1714–1783* (London: Allen Lane, 2007); P. J. Marshall, *The Making and Unmaking of Empire: Britain, India, and America, c. 1750–1783* (Oxford: Oxford University Press, 2005); and Trevor Burnard, "Placing British Settlement in the Americas in Comparative Perspective," in *British Asia and the British Atlantic, 1500–1820: Two Worlds or One?*, ed. H. V. Bowen, Elizabeth Mancke, and John G. Reid (Cambridge: Cambridge University Press, 2012), 407–32.
3. Barbara L. Solow, "Slavery and Colonisation," in *Slavery and the Rise of the Atlantic System*, ed. Barbara L. Solow (Cambridge: Cambridge University Press, 1991), 21–42.
4. James Otis, *The Rights of the British Colonies Asserted and Proved* (Boston: Edes & Gill, 1764) in *Pamphlets of the American Revolution, 1750–1776*, ed. Bernard Bailyn (Cambridge, MA: Harvard University Press, 1965), 1:435–36.
5. Giorgio Riello, *Cotton: The Fabric That Made the Modern World* (Cambridge: Cambridge University Press, 2013); and J. H. Galloway, *Sugar Cane Industry: An Historical Geography from Its Origins to 1914* (New York: Cambridge University Press, 1989), 198–208.
6. John J. McCusker and Russell R. Menard, "The Sugar Industry in the Seventeenth Century: A New Perspective on the Barbadian Sugar Revolution," in *Tropical Babylons: Sugar and the Making of the Atlantic World, 1450–1680*, ed. Stuart B.

Schwartz (Chapel Hill: University of North Carolina Press, 2004), 289–330; David Eltis, "The Total Product of Barbados, 1661–1701," *Journal of Economic History* 55 (1995): 321–36; and Philip D. Curtin, *The Rise and Fall of the Plantation Complex* (New York: Cambridge University Press, 1998).

7. Classic works are Edmund Morgan, *American Slavery, American Freedom: The Ordeal of Colonial Virginia* (New York: Norton, 1975); Richard S. Dunn, *Sugar and Slaves: The Rise of the Planter Class in the English West Indies* (Chapel Hill: University of North Carolina Press, 1972); and Philip D. Curtin, *The Rise and Fall of the Plantation Complex* (New York: Cambridge University Press, 1998).

8. Trevor Burnard, *Mastery, Tyranny, and Desire: Thomas Thistlewood and His Slaves in the Anglo-Jamaican World* (Chapel Hill: University of North Carolina Press, 2004).

9. On Hobbes and slavery see Mary Nyquist, "Hobbes, Slavery, and Despotical Rule," *Representations* 106 (2009): 1–33; and Nyquist, *Arbitrary Rule: Slavery, Tyranny, and the Power of Life and Death* (Chicago: University of Chicago Press, 2013), chapters 8–10.

10. Trevor Burnard, "Slavery and the Causes of the American Revolution in Plantation British America," in *The World of the Revolutionary American Republic: Expansion, Conflict, and the Struggle for a Continent*, ed. Andrew Shankman (New York: Routledge, 2014), 81–111.

11. David W. Galenson, "The Settlement and Growth of the Colonies: Population, Labor, and Economic development," in Stanley L. Engerman and Robert E. Gallman, *The Cambridge Economic History of the United States*, vol. 1, *The Colonial Era* (New York: Cambridge University Press, 1996), 135–41. The most recent books on the settlement of early Virginia include Alexander B. Haskell, *For God, King, and People: Forging Commonwealth Bonds in Renaissance Virginia* (Chapel Hill: University of North Carolina Press, 2015); and Douglas Bradburn and John C. Coombs, eds., *Early Modern Virginia: Reconsidering the Old Dominion* (Charlottesville: University of Virginia Press, 2013).

12. Cited in Lorena S. Walsh, *Motives of Honor, Pleasure, and Profit: Plantation Management in the Colonial Chesapeake, 1607–1763* (Chapel Hill: University of North Carolina Press, 2010), 3.

13. Philip D. Morgan, *Slave Counterpoint: Black Culture in the Eighteenth-Century Chesapeake and Lowcountry* (Chapel Hill: University of North Carolina Press, 1998), 1, 41, 58–59.

14. Lorena S. Walsh, *From Calabar to Carter's Grove: The History of a Virginia Slave Community* (Charlottesville: University of Virginia Press, 1997); and Allan Kulikoff, "A 'Prolifick' People: Black Population Growth in the Chesapeake Colonies, 1700–1790," *Southern Studies* 16 (1977): 391–428; and Morgan, *Slave Counterpoint*, 58–62, 80–95.

15. Walsh, *Motives of Honor*, 403; and Morgan, *Slave Counterpoint*, 85. Demographic changes are summarized in Allan Kulikoff, *Tobacco and Slaves: The*

Development of Southern Cultures in the Chesapeake, 1680–1800 (Chapel Hill: University of North Carolina Press, 1986), chapter 2.

16. Steven Deyle, *Carry Me Back: The Domestic Slave Trade in American Life* (New York: Oxford University Press, 2005).

17. Trevor Burnard, *Creole Gentlemen: The Maryland Elite, 1691–1776* (New York: Routledge, 2002), 39–41.

18. Mariana L. R. Dantas, *Black Townsmen: Urban Slavery and Freedom in the Eighteenth-Century Americas* (New York: Palgrave Macmillan, 2008); Charles G. Steffen, *The Mechanics of Baltimore: Workers and Politics in the Age of Revolution, 1763–1812* (Urbana: University of Illinois Press, 1984); and Seth Rockman, *Scraping By: Wage Labor, Slavery, and Survival in Early Baltimore* (Baltimore, MD: Johns Hopkins University Press, 2009). On the decline of the great Virginia planters see Emory G. Evans, *A "Topping People": The Rise and Decline of Virginia's Old Political Elite, 1680–1790* (Charlottesville: University of Virginia, 2009); and Bruce Ragsdale, *A Planter's Republic: The Search for Economic Independence in Revolutionary Virginia* (Madison: University of Wisconsin Press, 1996).

19. Steven Sarson, *The Tobacco-Plantation South in the Early American Plantation World* (London: Palgrave Macmillan, 2013).

20. For a contrasting view see James R. Irwin, "Wealth Accumulation in Virginia in the Century before the Civil War," in *Slavery in the Development of the Americas*, ed. David Eltis, Frank D. Lewis and Kenneth Sokoloff (Cambridge: Cambridge University Press, 2005), 275.

21. Kulikoff, *Tobacco and Slaves*, 298–99.

22. Ibid., 133–34, 298–99; Lois Green Carr and Lorena S. Walsh, "The Standard of Living in the Colonial Chesapeake," *WMQ*, 3rd ser., 45 (1988): 135–59; Paul G. E. Clemens, "The Consumer Culture of the Middle Atlantic, 1760–1840," *WMQ*, 3rd ser., 61 (2005): 577–624; and Walsh, *Motives of Honor*, 620–21.

23. Lois Green Carr and Russell R. Menard, "Wealth and Welfare in Early Maryland: Evidence from St. Mary's County," *WMQ*, 3rd ser., 56 (1999): 95–120; Lorena S. Walsh, "Land, Landlord, and Leaseholder: Estate Management and Tenant Fortunes in Southern Maryland, 1641–1820," *Agricultural History* 59 (1985): 373–96; and Gregory A. Stiverson, *Poverty in a Land of Plenty: Tenancy in Eighteenth-Century Maryland* (Baltimore, MD: Johns Hopkins University Press, 1977).

24. Morgan, *Slave Counterpoint*, 1; S. Max Edelson, *Plantation Enterprise in Colonial South Carolina* (Cambridge, MA: Harvard University Press, 2006), chapter 1; Russell R. Menard, "Economic and Social Development of the South," in Engerman and Gallman, *The Cambridge Economic History: The Colonial Era*, 273–75; Alan Gallay, *The Indian Slave Trade: The Rise of the English Empire in the American South, 1670–1717* (New Haven, CT: Yale University Press, 2002), chapter 2; Richard S. Dunn, "The English Sugar Islands and the Founding of South Carolina," *South Carolina Historical*

Magazine 72 (1971): 81–93; and L. H. Roper, *Conceiving Carolina: Proprietors, Planters, and Plots, 1662–1729* (New York: Palgrave Macmillan, 2004).

25. For wider contexts see Peter A. Coclanis, "Bitter Harvest: The South Carolina Low Country in Historical Perspective," *Journal of Economic History* 45 (1985): 251–59; and Coclanis, "Distant Thunder: The Creation of a World Market in Rice and the Transformations It Wrought," *AHR* 98 (1993): 1050–78. On African contributions to the origins of rice culture in the Americas, see the differing perspectives of Judith A. Carney, *Black Rice: The African Origins of Rice Cultivation in the Americas* (Cambridge, MA: Harvard University Press, 2001); David Eltis, Philip Morgan, and David Richardson, "Agency and Diaspora in Atlantic History: Reassessing the African Contribution to Rice Cultivation in the Americas," *AHR* 112 (2007): 1329–58; and S. Max Edelson, "Beyond 'Black Rice': Reconstructing Material and Cultural Contexts for Early Plantation Agriculture," *AHR* 115 (2010): 125–35.

26. Morgan, *Slave Counterpoint*, 59.

27. Alice Hanson Jones, *Wealth of a Nation to Be: The American Colonies on the Eve of the Revolution* (New York: Columbia University Press, 1980), 98, 379; and Jones, *American Colonial Wealth: Documents and Methods* (New York: Arbo Press, 1977), 2:1239–94, 2:1443–71, 3:1473–1619.

28. Morgan, *Slave Counterpoint*, 50.

29. Marc Egnal, *New World Economies: The Growth of the Thirteen Colonies and Early Canada* (New York: Oxford University Press, 1998), 102; and Menard, "Economic and Social Development of the South," 276.

30. Menard, *Sweet Negotiations*, 129–36; and Menard, "Financing the Lowcountry Export Boom: Capital and Growth in Early Carolina," *WMQ*, 3rd ser., 51 (1994): 663–64.

31. Morgan, *Slave Counterpoint*, 39–44; Morgan, "A Profile of a Mid-Eighteenth Century South Carolina: The Tax Return of Saint James Goose Creek," *South Carolina Historical Magazine* 81 (1980): 51–65; Peter A. Coclanis, *The Shadow of a Dream: Economic Life and Death in the South Carolina Low Country, 1670–1920* (New York: Oxford University Press, 1989), 97; and R. C. Nash, "South Carolina and the Atlantic Economy in the Late Seventeenth and Eighteenth Centuries," *Economic History Review* 45 (1992): 677–702.

32. Keith Wrightson, *English Society, 1580–1680* (Cambridge: Cambridge University Press, 1981), 31–32; and Philip J. Greven, Jr., *Four Generations: Population, Land, and Family in Colonial Andover, Massachusetts* (Ithaca, NY: Cornell University Press, 1970), 223–24.

33. Joyce E. Chaplin, *An Anxious Pursuit: Agricultural Innovation and Modernity in the Lower South, 1730–1865* (Chapel Hill: University of North Carolina Press, 1993).

34. S. Max Edelson, "The Nature of Slavery: Environmental Disorder and Slave Agency in Colonial South Carolina," in *Cultures and Identities in Colonial British America*, ed. Robert Olwell and Alan Tully (Baltimore, MD: Johns Hopkins University Press, 2005), 21–44.

NOTES TO PAGES 15–21

35. Edelson, *Plantation Enterprise in Colonial South Carolina*, 119; and Kenneth Morgan, "The Organization of the Colonial American Rice Trade," *WMQ*, 3rd ser., 52 (1995): 433–52.

36. Russell R. Menard, "Slavery, Economic Growth, and Revolutionary Ideology in the South Carolina Lowcountry," in *The Economy of Early America: The Revolutionary Period, 1763–1790*, ed. Ronald Hoffman, John J. McCusker, Russell R. Menard, and Peter J. Albert (Charlottesville: University of Virginia Press, 1988), 256, 268–69; and Edelson, *Plantation Enterprise*, chapter 6.

37. David Ramsay, *The History of the Revolution of South-Carolina, from a British Province to an Independent State*, 2nd ed. (Trenton, NJ: Isaac Collins, 1785), 2:206; and Joyce E. Chaplin, *An Anxious Pursuit: Agricultural Innovation and Modernity in the Lower South, 1730–1865* (Chapel Hill: University of North Carolina Press, 1993).

38. Menard, "Economic and Social Development of the South," 283–86; and Morgan, *Slave Counterpoint*, 61, 84.

39. Edelson, *Plantation Enterprise in Colonial South Carolina*, 251, 253 (quotes), 265. On John Laurens, see Gregory D. Massey, *John Laurens and the American Revolution* (Columbia: University of South Carolina Press, 2000).

40. B. W. Higman, *Slave Populations of the British Caribbean, 1807–1834* (Baltimore, MD: Johns Hopkins University Press, 1984).

41. Ibid., 46–71.

42. By comparison, the wealthiest Philadelphian dying in 1774 had wealth of £8,336 and the wealthiest New Englander had wealth, excluding financial assets, of £4,188—insufficient to make him the among the twenty-five wealthiest Jamaicans dying in this year. The total wealth of the ten wealthiest decedents dying in New Jersey, Pennsylvania, and Delaware in 1774 was £30,848, and the total wealth of the ten wealthiest men dying in 1774 in New England was £23,969. Jones, *Wealth of a Nation to Be*, 177–80.

43. Ibid., 51.

44. David Eltis, Frank D. Lewis, and David Richardson, "Slave Prices, the African Slave Trade, and Productivity in the Caribbean, 1674–1807," *Economic History Review* 4 (2005): 673–700; Higman, *Slave Populations of the British Caribbean*, 417–18; Michael Tadman, "The Demographic Cost of Sugar: Debates on Slave Societies and Natural Increase in the Americas," *AHR* 105 (2000): 1534–75; Kenneth Morgan, "Slave Women and Reproduction in Jamaica, c. 1776–1834," *History* (2006): 231–53; and Katherine Paugh, "The Politics of Childbearing in the British Caribbean and the Atlantic World during the Age of Abolition," *Past & Present* 221(2013): 119–60. On amelioration see J. R. Ward, *British West Indian Slavery, 1750–1834: The Process of Amelioration* (Oxford: Oxford University Press, 1988).

45. See B. W. Higman, *Montpelier: A Plantation Community in Slavery and Freedom, 1739–1812* (Kingston: University of the West Indies Press, 1998); and Higman, *Plantation Jamaica, 1750–1850: Capital and Control in a Colonial Economy* (Kingston: University of the West Indies Press, 2005). See also

Veront Satchell, *Hope Transformed: A Historical Sketch of the Hope Landscape, St Andrew, Jamaica, 1660–1960* (Kingston: University of the West Indies Press, 2012); Verene A. Shepherd, *Livestock, Sugar and Slavery: Contested Terrain in Colonial Jamaica* (Kingston: Ian Randle, 2009); David W. Ryden, *West Indian Slavery and British Abolition, 1783–1807* (New York: Cambridge University Press, 2009); Galloway, *Sugar Cane Industry*; and Richard B. Sheridan, *Sugar and Slavery: An Economic History of the British West Indies, 1623–1775* (Bridgetown: University of the West Indies Press, 1974).

CHAPTER ONE

1. Daniel Defoe, *Colonel Jack*, ed. Samuel Holt Monk (1722; New York: Oxford University Press, 1989), 119–52. On Defoe and slavery see Patrick Keane, "Slavery and the Slave Trade: Crusoe as Defoe's Representative," in *Critical Essays on Daniel Defoe*, ed. Roger D. Lund (New York: G. K. Hall, 1997), 97–120.

2. Jack P. Greene, *The Intellectual Construction of America: Exceptionalism and Identity from 1492 to 1800* (Chapel Hill: University of North Carolina Press, 1997), 63–94.

3. Ira Berlin, *Many Thousands Gone: The First Two Centuries of Slavery in North America* (Cambridge, MA: Harvard University Press, 1998), 95–98.

4. John J. McCusker and Russell R. Menard, "The Sugar Industry in the Seventeenth Century: A New Perspective on the Barbadian Sugar Revolution," in *Tropical Babylons: Sugar and the Making of the Atlantic World, 1450–1680*, ed. Stuart B. Schwartz (Chapel Hill: University of North Carolina, 2004), 289–330.

5. B. W. Higman, "The Making of the Sugar Revolution," in *In the Shadow of the Plantation: Caribbean History and Legacy*, ed. Alvin O. Thompson (Kingston: Ian Randle, 2002), 40–71. For a refutation of the claim that Barbados was in a depression when sugar was introduced, see Robert C. Batie, "Why Sugar? Economic Cycles and the Changing of Staples in the English and French Antilles," *Journal of Caribbean History* 8–9 (1976): 1–41.

6. Russell R. Menard, *Sweet Negotiations: Sugar, Slavery, and Plantation Agriculture in Early Barbados* (Charlottesville: University of Virginia Press, 2006); and David Eltis, "The Total Product of Barbados, 1661–1701," *Journal of Economic History* 55 (1995): 321–36.

7. William Bullock, *Virginia Impartially examined . . .* (London: John Hammond, 1649), 31–32. See Peter Thompson, "William Bullock's 'Strange Adventure': A Plan to Transform Seventeenth-Century Virginia," *WMQ*, 3rd ser., 61 (2004): 107–28.

8. Lois Green Carr, Russell R. Menard, and Lorena S. Walsh, *Robert Cole's World: Agriculture and Society in Early Maryland* (Chapel Hill: University of North Carolina Press, 1991).

9. Richard Ligon, *A True and Exact History of the Island of Barbados* (London: Humphrey Mosely, 1657). On early Barbados see Susan Dwyer Amussen, *Caribbean Exchanges: Slavery and the Transformation of English Society, 1640–1700* (Chapel Hill: University of North Carolina Press, 2007); Larry Gragg, *Englishmen Transplanted: The English Colonization of Barbados, 1627–1660* (New York: Cambridge University Press, 2003); Menard, *Sweet Negotiations*; and Simon D. Newman, *Free and Bound Labor in the British Atlantic World: Black and White Workers and the Development of Plantation Slavery* (Philadelphia: University of Pennsylvania Press, 2013), chapters 3 and 4.

10. James Horn, *Adapting to a New World: English Society in the Seventeenth-Century Chesapeake* (Chapel Hill: University of North Carolina Press, 1994); and S. Max Edelson, *Plantation Enterprise in Colonial South Carolina* (Cambridge, MA: Harvard University Press, 2006).

11. Jonathan Atkins to Committee on Trade and Plantations, 4 July 1676, W. Noel Sainsbury et al., *CSP*.

12. Richard S. Dunn, *Sugar and Slaves: The Rise of the Planter Class in the English West Indies* (Chapel Hill: University of North Carolina Press, 1972). On the settlement of early Jamaica see S. A. G. Taylor, *The Western Design: An Account of Cromwell's Expedition in the Caribbean* (Kingston: Institute of Jamaica Press, 1965); Carla Gardina Pestana, *The English Atlantic in an Age of Revolution* (Cambridge, MA: Harvard University Press, 2004); Pestana, "Early English Jamaica without Pirates," *WMQ*, 3rd ser., 71 (2014): 321–60; Amussen, *Caribbean Exchanges*, 33–39; and James Robertson, *Gone Is the Ancient Glory: Spanish Town, Jamaica, 1534–2000* (Kingston: Ian Randle, 2005).

13. David Eltis, *The Rise of African Slavery in the Americas* (New York: Cambridge University Press, 2000), 205–6; David Eltis and David Richardson, "Prices of African Slaves Newly Arrived in the Americas, 1673–1865: New Evidence on Long-Run Trends and Regional Differentials," in *Slavery in the Development of the Americas*, ed. David Eltis, Frank D. Lewis, and Kenneth L. Sokoloff (New York: Cambridge University Press, 2004), 200–202; David W. Galenson, *Traders, Planters, and Slaves: Market Behavior in Early English America* (New York: Cambridge University Press, 1986); Lorena S. Walsh, *Motives of Honor, Pleasure, and Profit: Plantation Management in the Colonial Chesapeake, 1607–1763* (Chapel Hill: University of North Carolina Press, 2010), 140; Philip D. Morgan, *Slave Counterpoint: Black Culture in the Eighteenth-Century Chesapeake and Lowcountry* (Chapel Hill: University of North Carolina Press, 1998), 58–64; and Demitri D. Debe and Russell R. Menard, "The Transition to Slavery in Maryland: A Note on the Barbados Connection," *Slavery and Abolition* 32 (2011): 129–41.

14. Eltis and Richardson, "Prices of African Slaves," 200–202.

15. Trevor Burnard, "Who Bought Slaves in Early America? Purchasers of Slaves from the Royal African Company in Jamaica, 1674–1708," *Slavery and*

Abolition 17 (1996): 68–92; and J. R. McNeill, *Mosquito Empires: Ecology and War in the Greater Caribbean, 1620–1914* (New York: Cambridge University Press, 2010), 144–48.

16. Nuala Zahedieh, "Trade, Plunder and Economic Development in Early Modern Jamaica," *Economic History Review* 39 (1986): 205–22; and Alan D. Meyers, "Ethnic Distinctions and Wealth among Colonial Jamaican Merchants, 1685–1716," *Social Science History* 22 (1998): 47–81. Eltis is right that the profits from piracy did not jump-start the plantation economy, but Zahedieh shows that profits from the nonplantation sector were sufficient to fund more planting if people had wanted to use them in this way. Eltis, *The Rise of African Slavery*, 206–7. On Jamaican politics and the central place of Spain see Leslie Theibert, "The Making of an English Caribbean, 1650–1688" (Ph.D. diss., Yale University, 2013).

17. Laura Sandy, "Supervisors of Small Worlds: The Role of Overseers on Colonial South Carolina Slave Plantations," *Journal of Early American History* 2 (2012): 178–210.

18. Defoe, *Colonel Jack*, 127–28.

19. William H. McBurney, "*Colonel Jacque*: Defoe's Definition of the Complete English Gentleman," *SEL* 2 (1962): 321–36; and Katherine Armstrong, "'I Was a Kind of an Historian': The Production of History on Defoe's *Colonel Jack*," in *Tradition in Transition: Women Writers, Marginal Texts, and the Eighteenth-Century Canon*, ed. Alvaro Ribiero and James G. Basker (Oxford: Clarendon Press, 1996), 97–110.

20. Defoe, *Colonel Jack*, 128.

21. Trevor Burnard, "Et in Arcadia Ego: West Indian Planters in Glory, 1674–1784," *Atlantic Studies* 9 (2012): 65–83; and Morgan, *Slave Counterpoint*, 41.

22. A. Roger Ekirch, *Bound for America: The Transportation of British Convicts to the Colonies, 1718–1775* (Oxford: Oxford University Press, 1987); and Bernard Bailyn, *Voyagers to the West: A Passage in the Peopling of America on the Eve of Revolution* (New York: Alfred A. Knopf, 1986), 292–95.

23. Russell R. Menard, "From Servants to Slaves: The Transformation of the Chesapeake Labor System," *Southern Studies* 16 (1977): 355–90. In Barbados, even as larger planters began buying African slaves, smaller planters continued to prefer white servants: see Mark Quintanilla, "Late Seventeenth-Century Indentured Servants in Barbados," *Journal of Caribbean History* 27 (1993): 114–28. On the switch from servants to slaves see Hilary McD. Beckles, *White Servitude and Black Slavery in Barbados, 1627–1715* (Knoxville: University of Tennessee Press, 1989).

24. Defoe, *Colonel Jack*, 128.

25. George Boulukos, *The Grateful Slave: The Emergence of Race in Eighteenth-Century British and American Culture* (Cambridge: Cambridge University Press, 2011), 82.

26. Defoe, *Colonel Jack*, 128.

27. Mary Floyd-Wilson, *English Ethnicity and Race in Early Modern Drama* (Cambridge: Cambridge University Press, 2003).
28. Defoe, *Colonel Jack*, 128.
29. Edmund Hickeringill, *Jamaica Viewed* (London: John Williams, 1661); [Charles Leslie], *A New and Exact Account of Jamaica* (Edinburgh: R. Fleming, [ca. 1740]), 38, 336–38; and James Knight, "The Natural, Moral, and Political History of Jamaica and the Territories thereon depending," Long Mss., Add. Mss., 12, 418, ff. 79–87, BL.
30. Peter Thompson, "The Thief, the Householder, and the Commons: Languages of Class in Seventeenth-Century Virginia," *WMQ*, 3rd ser., 63 (2002): 263.
31. Galenson, *Traders, Planters, and Slaves*.
32. Morgan, *Slave Counterpoint*.
33. Kenneth Morgan, *Slavery and the British Empire: From Africa to America* (Oxford: Oxford University Press, 2007).
34. David Barry Gaspar, "'Rigid and Inclement': The Origin of the Jamaican Slave Laws of the Seventeenth-Century," in *The Many Legalities of Early Modern America*, ed. Christopher L. Tomlins and Bruce H. Mann (Chapel Hill: University of North Carolina Press, 2001), 78–96.
35. Peter H. Wood, *Black Majority; Negroes in South Carolina from 1670 through the Stono Rebellion* (New York: W. W. Norton, 1974).
36. Alejandro de la Fuente, "Sugar and Slavery in Early Colonial Cuba," in Schwartz, ed., *Tropical Babylons*, 115–57. On nineteenth-century Cuba see Laird W. Bergad, *Cuban Rural Society in the Nineteenth Century: The Social and Economic History of Monoculture in Matanzas* (Princeton, NJ: Princeton University Press, 1990).
37. Gaspar, "'Rigid and Inclement.'"
38. Adam Smith, *An Inquiry into the Nature and Causes of the Wealth of Nations*, 2 vols., ed. R. H. Campbell and A. S. Skinner (Indianapolis, IN: Liberty Fund, 1999).
39. Ligon, *True and Exact History*; and Gragg, *Englishmen Transplanted*; Amussen, *Caribbean Exchanges*.
40. Richard S. Dunn, "The Barbados Census of 1680: Profile of the Richest Colony in English America." *WMQ*, 3rd ser., 26 (1969): 3–30.
41. Jack P. Greene, *Pursuits of Happiness: The Social Development of Early Modern British Colonies and the Formation of American Culture* (Chapel Hill: University of North Carolina Press, 1988).
42. Menard, *Sweet Negotiations*; Eltis, *The Rise of African Slavery*; and Newman, *Free and Bound Labor*.
43. Menard, *Sweet Negotiations*, 33.
44. Henry A. Gemery, "Emigration from the British Isles to the New World: Inferences from Colonial Populations," *Research in Economic History* 5 (1980): 179–231.

45. Newman, *Free and Bound Labor.*
46. Ligon, *True and Exact History*, 45.
47. Ann Kussmaul, *Servants in Husbandry in Early Modern England* (Cambridge: Cambridge University Press, 1981).
48. Ligon, *True and Exact History*, 43–44.
49. Ibid., 44–45, 51.
50. Newman, *Free and Bound Labor*; Alison Games, "Opportunity and Mobility in Early Barbados," in *The Lesser Antilles in the Age of European Expansion*, ed. Robert L. Paquette and Stanley L. Engerman (Gainesville: University of Florida Press, 1996), 165–81; Beckles, *White Servitude and Black Slavery*, 156; and Games, "Land Distribution and Class Formation in Barbados, 1630–1700: The Rise of a Wage Proletariat," *Journal of the Barbados Museum and Historical Society* 36 (1998): 136–43.
51. Menard, *Sweet Negotiations*, 39.
52. David W. Galenson, *White Servitude in Colonial America: An Economic Analysis* (Cambridge: Cambridge University Press, 1981); Christopher Tomlins, *Freedom Bound: Law, Labor, and Civic Identity in Colonizing English America, 1550–1865* (New York: Cambridge University Press, 2010), 8, 13, 17, 2–27; and Hilary Mc.D Beckles, "Rebels and Reactionaries: The Political Response of White Labourers to Planter-Class Hegemony in Seventeenth Century Barbados," *Journal of Caribbean History* 15 (1981): 8, 10. On the Irish see Beckles, "A 'Riotous and Unruly Lot': Irish Indentured Servants and Freemen in the English West Indies, 1644–1713," *WMQ*, 3rd ser. 47 (1990): 503–22; and Kristen Block and Jenny Shaw, "Subjects without an Empire: The Irish in the Early Modern Caribbean," *Past & Present* 210 (2011): 33–60.
53. Dunn, "Barbados Census 1680": Carla Gardina Pestana. *The English Atlantic in an Age of Revolution, 1640–1661* (Cambridge, MA: Harvard University Press, 1991).
54. For a much higher figure see Alfred D. Chandler, "The Expansion of Barbados," *Journal of the Barbados Historical and Museum Society* 1 (1946): 106–36. For more realistic figures see Dunn, *Sugar and Slaves*, 111–16. On the role of Barbadians in jump-starting plantation agriculture, see John C. Coombs, "The Phases of Conversion: A New Chronology for the Rise of Slavery in Early Virginia," *WMQ*, 3rd ser., 68 (2001): 343; Walsh, *Motives of Honor*; April Lee Hatfield, *Atlantic Virginia: Intercolonial Relations in the Seventeenth Century* (Philadelphia: University of Pennsylvania Press, 2004); Richard S. Dunn, "The English Sugar Islands and the Founding of South Carolina," *South Carolina Historical Magazine* 62 (1971): 81–93; and Menard, *Sweet Negotiations*, chapter 6. On the role of Barbados in supplying slaves to the Americas, see Greg O'Malley, "Beyond the Middle Passage: Slave Migration from the Caribbean to North America, 1619–1807," *WMQ*, 3rd ser., 66 (2009): 125–68.
55. For indicative population figures see John J. McCusker and Russell R.

Menard, *The Economy of British America, 1607–1789* (Chapel Hill: University of North Carolina Press, 1985), 15. For mortality rates see Dunn, *Sugar and Slaves*, 76–77; and Gary A. Puckrein, *Little England: Plantation Society and Anglo-Barbadian Politics, 1627–1700* (New York: New York University Press, 1984), 187–94. On yellow fever see McNeill, *Mosquito Empires*, 64; and Ligon, *True and Exact History*, 25.

56. Hilary McD. Beckles, "Black Men in White Skins: The Formation of a White Proletariat in West Indian Slave Society," *Journal of Imperial and Commonwealth History* 15 (1986): 12.

57. Governor Francis Russell to Lords of Trade and Plantations, Barbados, 23 March 1695, *CSP*, 14: 1693–96, ed. J. W. Fortescue (London: Mackie and Company for H.M. Stationary Office, 1903), 446.

58. Ibid., 447.

59. Patricia Molen, "Population and Social Patterns in Barbados in the early Eighteenth Century," *WMQ*, 3rd ser., 28 (1971): 287–300.

60. John Williamson, *Medical and Miscellaneous Observations Relative to the West India Islands* (Edinburgh: A. Smellie, 1817), 1:27; H. N. Coleridge (1834) and Sir Andrew Halliday (1834), quoted in Edward T. Price, "The Redlegs of Barbados," *Journal of the Barbados Museum and Historical Society* 29 (1962): 48; Newman, *Free and Bound Labor*, 71–107; and Hilary McD. Beckles, "Class Formation in Slave Society: The Rise of a Black Labour Elite and the Development of a White Lumpen Proletariat in Seventeenth Century Barbados," *Journal of the Barbados Museum and Historical Society* 37 (1983): 20–34. See also Jill Sheppard, *The "Redlegs" of Barbados: Their Origins and History* (Millwood, NY: KTO Press, 1977).

61. S. D. Smith. "The Account Book of Richard Poor, Quaker Merchant of Barbados," *WMQ*, 3rd ser., 66 (2009): 605–28; Smith, "Paying the Levy: Taxable Wealth in Bridgetown, Barbados, 1680–1715," *History of the Family* 12 (2007): 116–29; Pedro Welch, *Slave Society in the City: Bridgetown, Barbados, 1680–1834* (Kingston: Ian Randle, 2004); and Martyn J. Bowden, "The Three Centuries of Bridgetown: An Historical Geography," *Journal of the Barbados Museum and Historical Society* 49 (2003): 3–137.

62. Eltis, *The Rise of African Slavery*, 202–3.

63. Heather Cateau, "Conservatism and Change Implementation in the British West Indies Sugar Industry 1750–1810," *Journal of Caribbean History* 29 (1995): 1–36; Selwyn H. H. Carrington, "Management of Sugar Estates in the British West Indies at the End of the Eighteenth Century," *Journal of Caribbean History* 33 (1999): 27–53; and Morgan, *Slave Counterpoint*, 218–25.

64. Michael Craton, *Testing the Chains: Resistance to Slavery in the British West Indies* (Ithaca, NY: Cornell University Press, 1982), 109–10.

65. Willoughby to Clarendon, 5 March 1664, cited in Menard, *Sweet Negotiations*, 116; and "An Account of the English Sugar Plantacons," ca. 1660–85, Stowe Mss. 324/6, BL; Dunn, "The Barbados Census of 1680."

66. Dunn, *Sugar and Slaves*, 98–99, 280; and Gragg, *Englishmen Transplanted*, 152–53.

67. Marcellus Rivers and Oxenbridge Foyle, *England's slavery, or Barbados merchandize; represented in a petition to the high court of Parliament, by Marcellus Rivers and Oxenbridge Foyle gentlemen, on behalf of themselves and three-score and ten more free-born Englishmen sold (uncondemned) into slavery: together with letters written to some honourable members of Parliament* (London, 1659).

68. Mark S. Quintanilla, "Late Seventeenth-Century Indentured Servants in Barbados," *Journal of Caribbean History* 27 (1993): 114–28.

69. Karl Watson, *The Civilised Island, Barbados: A Social History, 1750–1816* (Bridgetown: University of the West Indies Press, 1983); and Jack P. Greene, "Changing Identity in the British West Indies in the Early Modern Era: Barbados as a Case Study," in *Imperatives, Behaviors, and Identities: Essays in Early American Cultural History* (Charlottesville: University of Virginia Press, 1992), 13–67.

70. Hilary McD. Beckles, *A History of Barbados: From Amerindian Settlement to Caribbean Single Market* (Cambridge: Cambridge University Press, 2006); Molen, "Population and Social Patterns in Barbados"; Richard Waterhouse, "England, the Caribbean, and the Settlement of Carolina," *Journal of American Studies* 9 (1975): 259–81; and Jack P. Greene, "Colonial South Carolina and the Caribbean Connection," *South Carolina Historical Magazine* 88 (1987): 192–210.

71. Philip D. Morgan, "The Poor: Slaves in Early America," in Eltis, Lewis, and Sokoloff, eds., *Slavery in the Development of the Americas*, 288–323.

72. John Poyer, *The History of Barbadoes from the first discovery of the island, 1605 . . .* (London: J. Mawman, 1808), 61, 242, 286; Karl Watson, "Salmugundis vs. Pumpkins: White Politics and Creole Consciousness in Barbadian Slave Society, 1800–1834," in *The White Minority in the Caribbean*, ed. Howard Johnson and Karl Watson (Kingston: Ian Randle, 1998), 17–31; Cecily Jones, "Mapping Racial Boundaries: Gender, Race, and Poor Relief in Barbadian Plantation Society," *Journal of Women's History* 10 (1998): 9–31; and David Lambert, *White Creole Culture, Politics and Identity during the Age of Abolition* (Cambridge: Cambridge University Press, 2005), chapter 3, 170–71, 210–11.

73. John Oldmixon, *The British Empire in America . . .* (London: John Nicholson, 1708), 2:126.

74. Defoe, *Colonel Jack*, 128.

75. Dunn, *Sugar and Slaves*, 215.

76. J. Harry Bennett, "Cary Helyar: Merchant and Planter of Seventeenth-Century Jamaica," *WMQ*, 3rd ser., 21 (1964): 53–76.

77. John C. Coombs makes a compelling case that assumptions that planters preferred to buy servants rather than slaves as long as servants were available does not apply to the richest planters in Virginia. Coombs, "The Phases of Conversion: A New Chronology for the Rise of Slavery in Early

Virginia," *WMQ*, 3rd ser., 68 (2001): 347–49. Virginia planters received small numbers of slaves from the Caribbean. O'Malley, "Beyond the Middle Passage."

78. Walsh, *Motives of Honor*, chapter 2; and Lois Green Carr and Russell R. Menard, "Land, Labor, and Economies of Scale in Early Maryland: Some Limits to Growth in the Chesapeake System of Husbandry," *Journal of Economic History* 49 (1989): 407–18.

79. Lois Green Carr, Russell R. Menard, and Lorena S. Walsh, *Robert Cole's World: Agriculture and Society in Early Maryland* (Chapel Hill: University of North Carolina Press, 1991).

80. William Dampier, *The voyages and adventures of Capt. William Dampier. Wherein are described the inhabitants, manners, customs, . . . &c. of Asia, Africa, and America* (London: W. Nevett, 1776), 6–11.

81. John Taylor, "Multum in Parvo," MSS. 105, 2:491–507, National Library of Jamaica, Kingston; and David Buisseret, *Jamaica in 1687: The Taylor Manuscript at the National Library of Jamaica* (Kingston: University of the West Indies Press, 2008), 238–42, 247.

82. Wills (1683) 3/24; (1700) 11/38; (1728) 16/24, IRO; T70/936–45, NA; Survey of landholders, Jamaica, 23 April, 1670, *CSP* 7, 1669–70, #270, 99–104; and AC/WO/16 (27) 105 (a), Spring Plantation Papers, Ashton Court Papers, Woolnough Papers, Bristol, Archives Office, Bristol. On landholding patterns in St. Andrew by 1754 see David Ryden, "'One of the Fertilest Pleasantest Spotts': An Analysis of the Slave Economy in Jamaica's St. Andrew Parish," *Slavery and Abolition* 21 (2000): 32–55.

83. Richard Blome, *A Description of the Island of Jamaica . . .* (London: T. Milbourn, 1672) 9, 16–21; Buisseret, *Jamaica in 1687*; and Eltis, "The Total Product of Barbados," 331–32.

84. John Norris, *Profitable Advice for Rich and Poor* (London: J. How, 1712); and Thomas Nairne, *A Letter from South Carolina* (London: A. Baldwin, 1710), as reprinted in Jack P. Greene, ed., *Selling a New World: Two Colonial South Carolina Promotional Pamphlets* (Columbia: University of South Carolina Press, 1989).

85. Greene, *Selling a New World*.

86. Walsh, *Motives of Honor*, 131–37, 179.

87. William Claypole, "The Merchants of Port Royal" (Ph.D. diss., University of the West Indies, 1974).

88. Dunn, *Sugar and Slaves*; Michael Craton and James Walvin, *A Jamaican Plantation: The History of Worthy Park, 1670–1970* (London: W. H. Allen, 1970); Michael Pawson and David Buisseret, *Port Royal, Jamaica* (Oxford: Clarendon Press, 1975); and James Robertson, *Gone Is the Ancient Glory: Spanish Town, Jamaica, 1534–2000* (Kingston: Ian Randle, 2005).

89. Dunn, *Sugar and Slaves*, 88–96.

90. Ibid., 170–78.

91. Eltis, "Total Product of Barbados," 331–32; and Eltis, "New Estimates

of Exports from Jamaica and Barbados, 1665–1701," *WMQ*, 3rd ser., 52 (1995): 631–48.

92. Nuala Zahedieh, "Trade, Plunder, and Economic Development in Early English Jamaica, 1655–1689," *Economic History Review* 39 (1986): 211.

93. Dunn, *Sugar and Slaves*, 180–81.

94. "Muster Roll, May 1680," "Inhabitants both Masters and Servants of Port Royal, 12 May, 1680," C.O. 1/45/2–4, 11, 97–109; and Dunn, *Sugar and Slaves*, 179–80.

95. William Beeston to the Board of Trade, 20 May 1700, C.O. 138/10/152, NA; and Nuala Zahedieh, *The Capital and the Colonies: London and the Atlantic Economy, 1660–1700* (Cambridge: Cambridge University Press, 2010), 259–60, 268.

96. Zahedieh, *The Capital and the Colonies*, 200, 230–31, 260; Zahedieh, "The Merchants of Port Royal, Jamaica and Spanish Contraband Trade," *WMQ*, 3rd ser., 43 (1986): 570–93; Zahedieh, "'A Frugal, Prudential and Hopeful Trade': Privateering in Jamaica, 1655–89," *Journal of Imperial and Commonwealth History* 18 (1990): 145–68; F. J. Osborne, "James Castillo, Asiento Agent," *Jamaican Historical Review* 8 (1971): 9–18; and Burnard, "Who Bought Slaves in Early America?"

97. Russell R. Menard, "Making a 'Popular Slave Society' in Colonial British America," *Journal of Interdisciplinary History* 43 (2013): 394–95.

CHAPTER TWO

1. Edmund Morgan, *American Slavery, American Freedom: The Ordeal of Colonial Virginia* (New York: Norton, 1975). On the fiscal-military state see John Brewer, *The Sinews of War: War, Money and the English State, 1688–1763* (London: Unwin Hyman, 1989).

2. Gabriel Debien, "Sur les plantations Mauger à l'Artibonite (Saint-Domingue, 1763–1803)," in Debien, *Enquêtes et documents: Nantes, Afrique, Amérique* (Nantes: Centre de Recherches sur l'Histoire de la France Atlantique, 1981), 300; and Robin Blackburn, *The Making of New World Slavery: From the Baroque to the Modern, 1492–1800* (London: Verso, 1997).

3. Peter Thompson, "Henry Drax's Instructions on the Management of a Seventeenth-Century Barbadian Plantation," *WMQ*, 3rd ser., 86 (2009): 565–604; and Larry Gragg, *Englishmen Transplanted: The English Colonization of Barbados, 1627–1660* (New York: Cambridge University Press, 2003), 99–100, 123–24, 140.

4. Menard thinks that gang labor was not a regular feature of Barbados plantations until after 1740 and discounts Richard Ligon's early references to slaves working in gangs. He is unduly cautious. In Virginia, Robert "King" Carter (1663–1732) made frequent reference to gang labor in the 1720s. Russell R. Menard, *Sweet Negotiations: Sugar, Slavery, and Plantation Agriculture in Early Barbados* (Charlottesville: University of Virginia Press,

2006), 91–97; Lorena S. Walsh, *Motives of Honor, Pleasure, and Profit: Plantation Management in the Colonial Chesapeake, 1607–1763* (Chapel Hill: University of North Carolina Press, 2010), 261–62; and Jerome S. Handler and Frederick W. Lange, *Plantation Slavery in Barbados: Archaeological and Historical Investigation* (Cambridge, MA: Harvard University Press, 1978), 72.

5. Philip D. Morgan, "Work and Culture: The Task System and the World of Lowcountry Blacks, 1700–1880," *WMQ*, 3rd ser., 39 (1982): 563–99. See also Justin Roberts, *Slavery and the Enlightenment in the British Atlantic, 1750–1807* (New York: Cambridge University Press, 2013).

6. Anon., *Great Newes from the Barbadoes* (London: L. Curtis, 1676), 6–7.

7. Richard Ligon, *A True and Exact History of the Island of Barbados* (London: Humphrey Mosely, 1657), 44–45, 53, 93; Carla Gardina Pestana, *The English Atlantic in an Age of Revolution, 1640–1661* (Cambridge, MA: Harvard University Press, 2004), 191; and Susan Scott Parrish, "Richard Ligon and the Atlantic Science of Commonwealth," *WMQ* 67 (2010): 211, 215, 223–27, 245, 247.

8. For differing views, see David Eltis, *The Rise of African Slavery in the Americas* (New York: Cambridge University Press, 2000); and Hilary McD. Beckles, *White Servitude and Black Slavery in Barbados, 1627–1715* (Knoxville: University of Tennessee Press, 1989).

9. Jennifer Morgan, *Laboring Women: Reproduction and Gender in New World Slavery* (Philadelphia: University of Pennsylvania Press, 2004), 42–46.

10. Hilary McD. Beckles and Andrew Downes, "The Economics and Transition to the Black Labour System in Barbados, 1630–1680," *Journal of Interdisciplinary History* 18 (1987): 236.

11. Thompson, "Henry Drax's Instructions"; and John C. Coombs, "The Phases of Conversion: A New Chronology for the Rise of Slavery in Early Virginia," *WMQ*, 3rd ser., 68 (2001): 347–49.

12. Jerome S. Handler, ed., "Father Antoine Biet's Visit to Barbados in 1654," *Journal of the Barbados Museum and Historical Society* 32 (1967): 66; Gragg, *Englishmen Transplanted*, 129; and Beckles, *White Servitude*, 135.

13. Ira Berlin, *Many Thousands Gone: The First Two Centuries of Slavery in America* (Cambridge, MA: Harvard University Press, 1998), 115–16.

14. Michael Craton, *Testing the Chains: Resistance to Slavery in the British West Indies* (Ithaca, NY: Cornell University Press, 1982).

15. Richard S. Dunn, *Sugar and Slaves: The Rise of the Planter Class in the English West Indies* (Chapel Hill: University of North Carolina Press, 1972), 260. For medieval punishments see Robert Bartlett, *England under the Normans and Angevin Kings, 1075–1225* (Oxford: Oxford University Press, 2000).

16. B. W. Higman, *Plantation Jamaica, 1750–1850: A Plantation Community in Slavery and Freedom, 1739–1812* (Kingston: University Press of the West Indies, 2005). On the American South see William Kaufman Scarborough, *The Overseer: Plantation Management in the Old South* (Baton Rouge: Louisiana State University Press, 1966).

17. Laura Sandy, "Supervisors of Small Worlds: The Role of Overseers on Colonial South Carolina Slave Plantations," *Journal of Early American History* 2 (2012): 178–210.

18. Philippe R. Girard and Jean-Louis Donnedieu, "Toussaint before Louverture: New Archival Findings on the Early Life of Toussaint Louverture," *WMQ*, 3rd ser., 70 (2013): 41–78.

19. Robert Robertson, *A Letter to the Right Reverend the Lord Bishop of London from an Inhabitant of His Majesty's Leeward-Caribbee Islands* . . . (London: J. Wilford, 1730), 94.

20. Daniel Parke to Council of Trade and Plantations, 31 October 1706, *CSP*, 23:284; and Natalie A. Zacek, *Settler Society in the English Leeward Islands, 1670–1776* (Cambridge: Cambridge University Press, 2010), 57.

21. Keith Mason, "The World an Absentee Planter and His Slaves Made: Sir William Stapleton and His Nevis Sugar Estate, 1722–1740," *Bulletin of the John Rylands Library* 75 (1993): 103–31.

22. Keith Mason, "The Absentee Planter and the Key Slave: Privilege, Patriarchalism, and Exploitation in the Early Eighteenth-Century Caribbean," *WMQ*, 3rd ser., 70 (2013): 87, 89–90, 93–96.

23. Ibid., 89–96.

24. Ibid., 93–96.

25. Thompson, "Henry Drax's Instructions."

26. David Eltis, "The Total Product of Barbados, 1661–1701," *Journal of Economic History* 55 (1995): 321–36; Trevor Burnard, " 'The Countrie Continues Sicklie': White Mortality in Jamaica, 1655–1780," *Social History of Medicine* 12 (1999): 45–72; and John J. McCusker and Russell R. Menard, *The Economy of British America, 1607–1789* (Chapel Hill: University of North Carolina Press, 1985), 135–36.

27. Patricia A. Molen, "Population and Social Patterns in Barbados in the early Eighteenth Century," *WMQ*, 3rd ser., 28 (1971): 287–300; and S. D. Smith, "Paying the Levy: Taxable Wealth in Bridgetown, Barbados, 1680–1715," *History of the Family* 12 (2007): 119–22.

28. Trevor Burnard, "A Failed Settler Society: Marriage and Demographic Failure in Early Jamaica," *Journal of Social History* 28 (1994): 63–82; Burnard, " 'The Countrie Continues Sicklie'"; Richard S. Dunn, "The Barbados Census of 1680: Profile of the Richest Colony in English America," *WMQ*, 3rd. ser., 26 (1969): 3–30; and Zacek, *Settler Society*, 46–64.

29. David W. Galenson, "The Settlement and Growth of the Colonies: Population, Labor, and Economic development," in *The Cambridge Economic History of the United States*, vol. 1, *The Colonial Era*, ed. Stanley L. Engerman and Robert E. Gallman (New York: Cambridge University Press, 1996), 171, 178; and Henry A. Gemery, "Emigration from the British Isles to the New World, 1630–1700," *Research in Economic History* 5 (1980): 215.

30. Burnard, " 'The Countrie Continues Sicklie,' " 48–52; Smith, "Paying the Levy," 120; M. J. Dobson, "Mortality Gradients and Disease Exchanges: Com-

parisons from Old England and Colonial America," *Social History of Medicine* 2 (1989): 264, 268, 271; and Peter A. Coclanis, "Death in Early Charleston: An Estimate for the Crude Death Rate for the White Population of Charleston, 1722–1732," *South Carolina Historical Magazine* 85 (1984): 280–91.

31. F. G. Spurdle, *Early West Indian Government* (privately printed, [1950?]): 143–46.

32. *Act to oblige the several inhabitants of the island to provide themselves with a sufficient number of white people . . .* (1716), in *Acts of Assembly passed in the Island of Jamaica, 1681–1737* (London: J. Baskett, 1738–39); Michael Craton and James Walvin, *A Jamaican Plantation: The History of Worthy Park, 1670–1970* (London: W. H. Allen, 1970), 52, 68; and Frank Wesley Pitman, *The Development of the British West Indies, 1700–1763* (New Haven, CT: Yale University Press, 1917), 35–36, 50–54. The monies obtained from public taxation, including the Deficiency Act, were substantial, amounting to £50,000 per annum in the early 1750s and £200,000 per annum by the early 1780s. Spurdle, *Early West Indian Government*, 120.

33. C.O. 137/4/97; 137/7/23137/10; 137/15; 140/2, NA; Burnard, " 'The Countrie Continues Sicklie' "; and J. R. McNeill, *Mosquito Empires: Ecology and War in the Greater Caribbean, 1620–1914* (New York: Cambridge University Press, 2010).

34. John Helyar to William Helyar, 27 March 1686, Helyar Mss., Somerset Record Office.

35. The revolt at Duck's plantation actually occurred in 1678. David Buisseret, *Jamaica in 1687: The Taylor Manuscript at the National Library of Jamaica* (Kingston: University of the West Indies Press, 2008), 276; and Dunn, *Sugar and Slaves*, 260.

36. Buisseret, *Jamaica in 1687*, 276.

37. Susan Dwyer Amussen, *Caribbean Exchanges: Slavery and the Transformation of English Society, 1640–1700* (Chapel Hill: University of North Carolina Press, 2007), 164–74.

38. Taylor got the details of the Duck revolt wrong: the husband survived, but the wife was murdered. Buisseret, *Jamaica in 1687*, 274–78. Planters often used the term "family" to refer to their white servants.

39. Ibid., 274–78.

40. Ibid.

41. Ibid., 266–70.

42. Trevor Burnard, *Mastery, Tyranny, and Desire: Thomas Thistlewood and His Slaves in the Anglo-Jamaican World* (Chapel Hill: University of North Carolina Press, 2004), 16.

43. "Henry Barham's Account of Jamaica [1722]," Sloane Mss., 3918, BL.

44. Marcus Rediker, *Villains of All Nations: Atlantic Pirates in the Golden Age* (Boston: Beacon Press, 2004).

45. Matthew Mulcahy, *Hurricanes and Society in the British Greater Caribbean, 1624–1783* (Baltimore, MD: Johns Hopkins University Press, 2006).

46. Burnard, "'The Countrie Continues Sicklie,'" 56–57; and McNeill, *Mosquito Empires*.

47. Burnard, "Who Bought Slaves in Early America? Purchasers of Slaves from the Royal African Company in Jamaica, 1674–1708," *Slavery and Abolition* 17 (1996): 68–92.

48. *TSTD*.

49. Inventories, IB1/11/1–6, JA.

50. Inventories, IB1/11/1–65, JA.

51. Russell R. Menard, "From Servants to Slaves: The Transformation of the Chesapeake Labor System," *Southern Studies* 26 (1977): 355–90; Menard, *Sweet Negotiations*, 32–35; and Menard, "Transitions to African Slavery in British America, 1630–1730: Barbados, Virginia, and South Carolina," *Indian Historical Review* 15 (1988–89): 53–49.

52. Paul Musselwhite, "Annapolis Aflame: Richard Clarke's Conspiracy and the Imperial Urban Vision in Maryland, 1704–8," *WMQ*, 3rd ser., 71 (2014): 361–99, quotes at 376–77. On economic problems in Maryland and the choices planters had to make, see Paul G. E. Clemens, *The Atlantic Economy and Maryland's Eastern Shore: From Tobacco to Grain* (Ithaca, NY: Cornell University Press, 1980).

53. Musselwhite, "Annapolis Aflame," 361, 365, 371–72; and Russell R. Menard, "Five Maryland Censuses, 1700–1712: A Note on the Quality of the Quantities," *WMQ*, 3rd ser., 37 (1980): 620, 624.

54. Musselwhite, "Annapolis Aflame," 380, 387, 393. For a lament about the parlous situation of Maryland in 1705, albeit from the lower eastern shore rather than Ann Arundel, see Francis Makemie, "A Plain and Friendly Perswasive to the Inhabitants of Virginia and Maryland for Promoting Towns and Colonization," *Virginia Magazine of History and Biography* 4 (1896–97): 252–71.

55. Musselwhite, "Annapolis Aflame," 399; and Trevor Burnard, *Creole Gentlemen: The Maryland Elite, 1691–1776* (New York: Routledge, 2002), 187–89, 195–98.

56. William Hand Browne and Jacob Hall Pleasants, eds., *Archives of Maryland* (Baltimore: Maryland Historical Society, 1899–1900), 25:237–38.

57. Nancy T. Baker, "Annapolis, Maryland, 1695–1730," *Maryland Historical Magazine* 81 (1986): 191–209; and Walsh, *Motives of Honor*, 320.

58. Menard, "From Servants to Slaves."

59. "Memoranda of Agreements to Serve in America and the West Indies," London Metropolitan Archives, London; Peter Coldham Wilson, *The Complete Book of Emigrants*, 4 vols. (Baltimore, MD: Genealogical Publishing, 1987–93); and David W. Galenson, *White Servitude in Colonial America: An Economic Analysis* (Cambridge: Cambridge University Press, 1981), chapter 4.

60. Mason, "Absentee Planter and the Key Slave," 87.

61. Marcus Rediker, *The Slave Ship: A Human History* (London: Penguin, 2007), 250, 253.

62. Matthew Mulcahy, "'That fatall spott': The Rise and Fall—and Rise and Fall Again—of Port Royal, Jamaica," in *Investing in the Early Modern Built Environment: Europeans, Asians, Settlers, and Indigenous Societies*, ed. Carole Shammas (Leiden: Brill, 2012), 191–218.

63. "List of a Company of Foot where Hon Nicholas Lawes is Captain, St. Andrew, January 1694," C.O. 137/1; "List of Foot, 1695, St. Andrew," C.). 137/3/263; "List of a Foot of Troop of Horse in St. Andrew and Kingston, 1700," C.O. 137/5/113; and "Company of Soldiers in Regiment of Colonel Nicholas Lawes, 24 June 1700," C.O. 137/5/113, NA.

64. W. A. Claypole, "Land Settlement and Agricultural Development on the Liguanea Plains, 1655–1700" (master's thesis, University of the West Indies, 1973), 170–75.

65. David Ryden, "'One of the Fertilest Pleasantest Spotts': An Analysis of the Slave Economy in Jamaica's St. Andrew Parish," *Slavery and Abolition* 21 (2000): 32–55.

66. Ibid.

67. William Wood, *A Survey of Trade etc.* (London: W. Wilkins, 1718).

68. "A List of Landholders in Jamaica together with the Quantity of Acres of Land each one Possesses, & the Quantity Supposed to be Occupied & Planted," C.O. 142/31, NA and Long Mss., Add. Mss. 12,436, BL; and Richard B. Sheridan, *Sugar and Slavery: An Economic History of the British West Indies, 1623–1775* (Bridgetown: University of the West Indies Press, 1974), 218–19.

69. Robin Blackburn, *The Making of New World Slavery: From the Baroque to the Modern, 1492–1800* (London: Verso, 1997).

70. Michael Roberts, *The Military Revolution, 1560–1660* (Belfast: Boyd, 1956); Geoffrey Parker, *The Military Revolution: Military Innovations and the Rise of the West, 1500–1800*, 2nd ed. (Cambridge: Cambridge University Press, 1996); Jeremy Black, *A Military Revolution: Military Change and European Society, 1550–1800* (London: Macmillan, 1991); and Azar Gat, "What Constituted the Military Revolution of the Early Modern Period," in *War in an Age of Revolutions, 1775–1815*, ed. Roger Chickering and Stig Förster (Cambridge: Cambridge University Press, 2010), 21–48.

71. Stephen Saunders Webb, *The Governor-General: The English Army and the Definition of Empire, 1569–1681* (Chapel Hill: University of North Carolina Press, 1979). The French invasion of 1694 and counterattack of 1695 can be followed in C.O. 138/7/192–404, NA. See also Dunn, *Sugar and Slaves*, 163–64.

72. Stephen Saunders Webb, "Army and Empire: English Garrison Government in Britain and America, 1569 to 1763," *WMQ*, 3rd ser., 34 (1977): 1–31; Webb, *Marlborough's America* (New Haven, CT: Yale University Press, 2013);

and John Childs, *The British Army of William III, 1689–1702* (Manchester: Manchester University Press, 1987), 103.

73. W. H. McNeill, *The Pursuit of Power: Technology, Armed Force, and Society since A.D. 1000* (Oxford: Basil Blackwell, 1983), 131–33; and McNeill, *Keeping Together in Time: Dance and Drill in Human History* (Cambridge, MA: Harvard University Press, 1995).

74. J. R. Dinwiddy, "The Early Nineteenth-Century Campaign against Flogging in the Army, *English Historical Review* 97 (1982): 310.

75. John Childs, *Armies and Warfare in Europe, 1648–1789* (New York: Holmes & Meier, 1982), 67–78.

76. Roger B. Manning, *An Apprenticeship in Arms: The Origins of the British Army, 1585–1702* (Oxford: Oxford University Press, 2006), chapter 4; and Manning, *Swordsmen: The Martial Ethos in the Three Kingdoms* (Oxford: Oxford University Press, 2003).

77. Michael Braddick, *God's Fury, England's Fire: A New History of the English Civil Wars* (London: Allen Lane, 2008), 389.

78. Charles Carlton, *Going to the Wars: The Experience of the English Civil Wars, 1638–1651* (London: Routledge, 1992); and Barbara Donagan, "Atrocity, War Crime, and Treason in the English Civil War," *AHR* 99 (1994): 1137–66. See also Pestana, *The English Atlantic in an Age of Revolution*; and Jonathan Scott, *England's Troubles: Seventeenth-Century English Political Instability in European Context* (Cambridge and New York: Cambridge University Press, 2000).

79. Manning, *An Apprenticeship in Arms*, 220, 226–27.

80. Ibid., 209.

81. Tony Claydon, *Europe and the Making of England, 1660–1760* (Cambridge: Cambridge University Press, 2007), 129.

82. J. R. Western, *The English Militia in the Eighteenth Century: The Story of a Political Issue, 1660–1802* (London: Routledge & Kegan Paul, 1965); and Manning, *An Apprenticeship in Arms*, 298–305.

83. Thompson, "Henry Drax's Instructions," 570.

84. Wayne E. Lee, "The Military Revolution of Native North America: Firearms, Forts, and Polities," in *Empires and Indigenes: Intercultural Alliance, Imperial Expansion, and Warfare in the Early Modern World* (New York: New York University Press, 2011), 49–80; and Kris Lane, *Pillaging the Empire: Piracy in the Americas, 1500–1700* (Armonk, NY: M. E. Sharpe, 1998), 96–150.

85. Manning, *An Apprenticeship in Arms*, chapters 16 and 17; Childs, *The British Army of William III*, 124–25; and Manning, "War, Crime Waves and the English Army in the Late Seventeenth Century," *War and Society* 15 (1997): 10–16.

86. Stephanie E. Smallwood, *Saltwater Slavery: A Middle Passage from Africa to American Diaspora* (Cambridge, MA: Harvard University Press, 2007); Emma Christopher, *Slave Ship Sailors and Their Captive Cargoes, 1730–1807* (New York: Cambridge University Press, 2006); Alexander X. Byrd, *Captives and*

Voyagers: Black Migrants across the Eighteenth-Century British Atlantic World (Baton Rouge: Louisiana University Press, 2008); and Robert Harms, *The "Diligent": A Voyage through the Worlds of the Slave Trade* (New York: Basic Books, 2006).

87. Stephen D. Behrendt, "Markets, Transaction Cycles, and Profits: Merchant Decision Making in the British Slave Trade," *WMQ*, 3rd ser., 58 (2001): 171–204.

88. Jerome S. Handler, "The Middle Passage and the Material Culture of Captive Africans," *Slavery and Abolition* 30 (2009): 2–4.

89. Harms, *The "Diligent,"* 267; Rediker, *The Slave Ship*, 9, 43–44, 57–58, 68–71; David Richardson, "Shipboard Revolts, African Authority, and the Atlantic Slave Trade," *WMQ*, 3rd ser., 58 (2001): 69–92; Eric Robert Taylor, *If We Must Die: Shipboard Insurrection in the Era of the Atlantic Slave Trade* (Baton Rouge: Louisiana State University Press, 2006); and W. S. [William Snelgrave], "Instructions for a First Mate When in the Road att Whydah," Humphrey Morice Papers, Bank of England Archive, London.

90. Malachy Postlethwayt, *The African Trade, the Great Pillar and Support of the British Plantation Trade in America* (London: J. Robinson, 1745); Rediker, *The Slave Ship*, 9, 227, 237; and James Field Stanfield, *Observations on a Guinea Voyage . . .* (London: James Phillips, 1788).

91. Rediker, *The Slave Ship*, 218–20; Christopher, *Slave Ship Sailors*, 169–73; and Smallwood, *Saltwater Slavery*.

92. Henry Smeathman, "Copy of Two Letters, addressed to Dr Knowles, on the Rice Trade of Africa," in *The New-Jerusalem Magazine . . .* (London: London Universal Society, 1790), 289–90, cited in Deirdre Coleman, *Romantic Colonization and British Anti-Slavery* (Cambridge: Cambridge University Press, 2005), 50–52.

93. For militia lists see n205. For lists of seamen see ships' ledgers for 1688–96 in T. 70/1218, NA.

94. *TSDB*; and Naval Officer Lists, 1744–53, C.O. 142/15, NA.

95. Stephen D. Behrendt, "Crew Mortality in the Transatlantic Slave Trade in the Eighteenth Century," *Slavery and Abolition* 18 (1997): 49–71.

96. Christopher, *Slave Ship Sailors*, 206–14; William Butterworth, *Three Years Adventures of a Minor, in England, Africa and the West Indies, South Carolina and Georgia* (Leeds: Edward Barnes, 1822), 137.

97. John Thornton, "War, the State, and Religious Norms in Coromantee Thought," in *Possible Pasts: Becoming Colonial in America*, ed. Robert Blair St. George (Ithaca, NY: Cornell University Press, 2000), 181–200; Thornton, *Warfare in Atlantic Africa, 1500–1800* (London: University College London Press, 1999); Boubacar Barry, *Senegambia and the Atlantic Slave Trade* (Cambridge: Cambridge University Press, 2002); and Robin Law, *The Slave Coast of West Africa, 1550–1750* (Oxford: Clarendon Press, 1992).

98. Morgan, *American Slavery, American Freedom*; Peter Thompson, "The Thief, the Householder, and the Commons: Languages of Class in

Seventeenth-Century Virginia," *WMQ*, 3rd ser., 63 (2006): 263; and Jack P. Greene, ed., *Selling a New World: Two Colonial South Carolina Promotional Pamphlets* (Columbia: University of South Carolina Press, 1989).

99. Burnard, *Mastery, Tyranny, and Desire*, 45–48.

100. See Trevor Burnard and John Garrigus, *The Plantation Machine: Wealth and Belonging in British Jamaica and French Saint-Domingue, 1748–1788* (New York: Oxford University Press, forthcoming).

101. J. H. Plumb, *The Growth of Political Stability in England, 1675–1725* (Oxford: Oxford University Press, 1967), xvi.

102. Trevor Burnard, *Creole Gentlemen: The Maryland Elite, 1691–1776* (New York: Routledge, 2002), chapter 8.

103. Burnard, *Mastery, Tyranny, and Desire*.

104. Winthrop D. Jordan, *White over Black: American Attitudes towards the Negro, 1550–1812* (Chapel Hill: University of North Carolina Press, 1968). Literary scholars have disputed some of Jordan's key claims. See also Roxann Wheeler, *The Complexion of Race: Categories of Difference in Eighteenth-Century British Culture* (Philadelphia: University of Pennsylvania Press, 2000); Mary Floyd-Wilson, *English Ethnicity and Race in Early Modern Drama* (Cambridge: Cambridge University Press, 2003); and Kim F. Hall, *Things of Darkness: Economies of Race and Gender in Early Modern England* (Ithaca, NY: Cornell University Press, 1995). See also Joyce B. Chaplin, *Subject Matter: Technology, the Body, and Science on the Anglo-American Frontier, 1500–1676* (Cambridge, MA: Harvard University Press, 2001).

105. David Eltis, "Europeans and the Rise and Fall of African Slavery in the Americas: An Interpretation," *AHR* 98 (1993): 139–1423. See also James L. Watson, "Slavery as an Institution: Open and Closed Systems," in *Asian and African Systems of Slavery* (Berkeley and Los Angeles: University of California Press, 1980), 1–15.

106. Colin Kidd, *The Forging of Races: Race and Scripture in the Protestant Atlantic World, 1600–2000* (Cambridge: Cambridge University Press, 2006).

107. Morgan, *Laboring Women*, 45–49.

108. For contrasting views see Simon Newman, *Free and Bound Labor in the British Atlantic World: Black and White Workers and the Development of Plantation Slavery* (Philadelphia: University of Pennsylvania Press, 2013); and Christopher Tomlins, *Freedom Bound: Law, Labor, and Civic Identity in Colonizing English America, 1580–1865* (New York: Cambridge University Press, 2010).

109. Carlton, *Going to the War*, 253; Michael J. Rozbicki, " 'To Save them from Themselves': Proposals to Enslave the British Poor, 1698–1755," *Slavery and Abolition* 22 (2001): 29–50; N. A. M. Rodger, *The Safeguard of the Sea: A Naval History of Britain, 660–1649* (London: Harper Collins, 1997), 384; C. S. L. Davies, "Slavery and Protector Somerset: The Vagrancy Act of 1547," *Economic History Review* 19 (1966): 533–49; and Tomlins, *Freedom Bound*, 36, 273, 291.

110. B. S. Capp, *Cromwell's Navy: The Fleet and the English Revolution, 1648–1660* (Oxford and New York: Clarendon Press, 1989), chapter 8; Seymour Drescher, "White Atlantic? The Choice for African Slave Labor in the Plantation Americas," in *Slavery in the Development of the Americas*, ed. David Eltis, Frank D. Lewis, and Kenneth L. Sokoloff (Cambridge: Cambridge University Press, 2004), 60; Miranda Spieler, *Empire and Underworld: Captivity in French Guiana* (Cambridge, MA: Harvard University Press, 2012); Christopher R. Browning, *Nazi Policy, Jewish Workers, German Killers* (Cambridge: Cambridge University Press, 2000); and Edwin Bacon, *The Gulag at War: Stalin's Forced Labor System in the Light of the Archives* (Basingstoke: Macmillan, 1994).

111. On the voluntary nature of public allegiance in early modern England, see Michael J. Braddick and John Walter, eds., *Negotiating Power in Early Modern Society: Order, Hierarchy and Subordination in Britain and Ireland* (Cambridge: Cambridge University Press, 2001); and Steve Hindle, *The State and Social Change in Early Modern England, c. 1550–1640* (Basingstoke: Macmillan, 2000). On English opposition to all forms of slavery see Seymour Drescher, *Capitalism and Antislavery: British Mobilization in Comparative Perspective* (New York: Oxford University Press, 1987), chapter 2.

112. Drescher, "White Atlantic?," 50–53; and Arthur L. Stinchcombe, *Sugar Island Slavery in an Age of Enlightenment: The Political Economy of the Caribbean World* (Princeton, NJ: Princeton University Press, 1995), chapter 2.

113. Alan Gallay, *The Indian Slave Trade: The Rise of the English Empire in the American South, 1670–1717* (New Haven, CT: Yale University Press, 2002), 3.

114. On the rise of a planter elite in Virginia, see, among others, Bernard Bailyn, "Politics and Social Structure in Virginia," in *Seventeenth-Century America: Essays in Colonial History*, ed. James Morton Smith (Chapel Hill: University of North Carolina Press, 1959), 90–115; Emory G. Evans, *A "Topping People": The Rise and Decline of Virginia's Old Political Elite, 1680–1790* (Charlottesville: University of Virginia Press, 2009); 5–22; Walsh, *Motives of Honor*; and Anthony Parent, Jr., *Foul Means: The Formation of a Slave Society in Virginia, 1660–1740* (Chapel Hill: University of North Carolina Press, 2003). On the Leewards, see Zacek, *Settler Society in the English Leeward Islands*, 15–65. On the continuing vitality of the planter class into the nineteenth century, see Christer Petley, *Slaveholders in Jamaica: Colonial Society and Culture during the Era of Abolition* (London: Pickering & Chatto, 2009); and Thomas C. Holt, *The Problem of Freedom: Race, Labor, and Politics in Jamaica and Britain, 1832–1938* (Baltimore, MD: Johns Hopkins University Press, 1992), 115–42.

115. For an especially acerbic commentary on the dubious social origins of the mid-seventeenth-century Jamaican elite, see John Style to Secretary of State, 4 January 1670, C.O. 1/25/1, NA.

116. Mathew Gregory Lewis Lewis, *Journal of a West India Proprietor* (London: John Murray, 1834); and B. W. Higman, *Montpelier: A Plantation Community*

in Slavery and Freedom, 1739–1812 (Kingston: Press University of the West Indies, 1998), 19–25, 29–32.

117. Higman, *Montpelier*, 20.

118. Trevor Burnard, *Creole Gentlemen: The Maryland Elite, 1691–1776* (New York: Routledge, 2002).

119. David Hancock, *Citizens of the World: London Merchants and the Integration of the British Atlantic Community, 1735–1785* (New York: Cambridge University Press, 1995), 50–51, 148, 410.

120. Trevor Burnard, "The Planter Class," in *The Routledge History of Slavery*, ed. Gad Heuman and Trevor Burnard (London: Routledge, 2010), 193–94.

121. Burnard, *Creole Gentlemen*, 240.

122. Ibid., chapter 8; Burnard, "The Planter Class," 188, 193–94, 200; Morgan, *Slave Counterpoint*, 258–59; and Parent, *Foul Means*, 200–201.

CHAPTER THREE

1. Barbara L. Solow, "Slavery and Colonisation," in *Slavery and the Rise of the Atlantic System*, ed. Barbara L. Solow (Cambridge: Cambridge University Press, 1991), 21–42; and Trevor Burnard, "Plantation Societies," in *The Cambridge World History*, ed. Jerry H. Bentley and Sanjay Subrahmanyam, vol. 6, *The Construction of a Global World, 1400–1800 CE* (Cambridge: Cambridge University Press, 2014).

2. Benjamin Franklin, *Observations on the Increase of Mankind*, in *The Papers of Benjamin Franklin*, ed. Leonard W. Labaree Whitfield J. Bell, Helen C. Boatfield, Helene H. Fineman, et al. (New Haven, CT, 1961), 4:225–34.

3. Adam Smith, *An Inquiry into the Nature and Causes of the Wealth of Nations*, 2 vols., ed. R. H. Campbell and A. S. Skinner (Indianapolis: Liberty Fund, 1999), 387–88.

4. Richard Whatmore, *Republicanism and the French Revolution: An Intellectual History of Jean-Baptiste Say's Political Economy* (New York: Oxford University Press, 2000).

5. Jean-Baptiste Say, *Traité d'économie politique, ou, simple exposition de la manière dont se forment . . .* (Paris: Déterville, 1803), 224–25.

6. Smith, *Wealth of Nations*, book 4, chapter 7, part 2.

7. Richard Pares, *Merchants and Planters*, suppl. 4 of *Economic History Review* (1960): 47; Jacob M. Price, "Credit in the Slave Trade and Plantation Economies," in *Slavery and the Rise of the Atlantic System*, ed. Barbara L. Solow (Cambridge: Cambridge University Press, 1991), 293–339; Russell R. Menard, "Financing the Lowcountry Export Boom: Capital and Growth in Early Carolina," *WMQ*, 3rd ser., 51 (1994): 660–61; David Hancock, *Citizens of the World: London Merchants and the Integration of the British Atlantic Community, 1735–1785* (New York: Cambridge University Press, 1995), 241–47; and S. D. Smith, *Slavery, Family and Gentry Capitalism in the British Atlantic: The*

World of the Lascelles, 1648–1834 (Cambridge: Cambridge University Press, 2006), chapter 6.

8. Kenneth Pomeranz, *The Great Divergence: China, Europe, and the Making of the Modern World Economy* (Princeton, NJ: Princeton University Press, 2000), 113; and Nuala Zahedieh, *The Capital and the Colonies: London and the Atlantic Economy 1660–1700* (Cambridge: Cambridge University Press, 2010), 226.

9. Christer Petley, ed., "Special Issue: Rethinking the Fall of the Planter Class," *Atlantic Studies* 9 (2012).

10. Franklin Knight, "The Haitian Revolution: AHR Forum: Revolution in the Americas," *AHR* 105 (2000): 107.

11. Joel Mokyr, *The Enlightened Economy: Britain and the Industrial Revolution, 1700–1850* (New York: Yale University Press, 2009), 161.

12. Chris Evans, "The Plantation Hoe: The Rise and Fall of an Atlantic Commodity, 1650–1850," *WMQ*, 3rd ser., 69 (2012): 71–100.

13. Avery Odelle Craven, *Soil Exhaustion as a Factor in the Agricultural History of Virginia and Maryland, 1606–1860* (Gloucester, MA: P. Smith, 1965 [1926]).

14. Rhys Isaac, *The Transformation of Virginia, 1740–1790* (Chapel Hill: University of North Carolina Press, 1982).

15. Lorena S. Walsh, *Motives of Honor, Pleasure, and Profit: Plantation Management in the Colonial Chesapeake, 1607–1763* (Chapel Hill: University of North Carolina Press, 2010), 12, 228–32; and B. W. Higman, *Plantation Jamaica, 1750–1850: Capital and Control in a Colonial Economy* (Kingston: Press of the University of the West Indies, 2005), chapter 4.

16. T. H. Breen, *Tobacco Culture: The Mentality of the Great Tidewater Planters on the Eve of Revolution* (Princeton, NJ: Princeton University Press, 1985). On plantation management see Walsh, *Motives of Honor*; and Justin Roberts, "Working between the Lines: Labor and Agriculture on Two Barbadian Sugar Plantations, 1796–1797," *WMQ*, 3rd. ser., 63 (2006): 551–86.

17. Joyce E. Chaplin, *An Anxious Pursuit: Agricultural Innovation and Modernity in the Lower South, 1730–1865* (Chapel Hill: University of North Carolina Press, 1993), chapter 5; Londa Schiebinger, *Plants and Empire: Colonial Bioprospecting in the Atlantic World* (Cambridge, MA: Harvard University Press, 2004); and S. Max Edelson, *Plantation Enterprise in Colonial South Carolina* (Cambridge, MA: Harvard University Press, 2006). For a skeptical take on the effects of the application of agricultural theory to actual practice, see Walsh, *Motives of Honor*, 24, 628.

18. Walsh, *Motives of Honor*, 24.

19. Robin Blackburn, *American Crucible: Slavery, Emancipation and Human Rights* (London: Verso, 2011); and Nicholas Draper, "The Rise of a New Planter Class? Some Countercurrents from British Guiana and Trinidad, 1807–33," *Atlantic Studies* 9 (2012): 65–83.

20. Robert W. Fogel, *The Slavery Debates, 1952–1990: A Retrospective* (Baton Rouge: Louisiana University Press, 2003), 30.

21. Robert W. Fogel and Stanley L. Engerman, *Time on the Cross: The Economics of American Negro Slavery*, 2 vols. (Boston: Beacon Press, 1974); and Fogel, *Without Consent or Contract: The Rise and Fall of American Slavery* (New York: W. W. Norton, 1989). See also Gavin Wright, "Slavery and American Agricultural History," *Agricultural History* 77 (2003): 527–52. For objections see Herbert G. Gutman, *Slavery and the Numbers Game: A Critique of "Time on the Cross"* (Urbana: University of Illinois Press, 1975).

22. Elizabeth B. Field-Hendrey and Lee A. Craig, "The Relative Efficiency of Free and Slave Agriculture in the Antebellum United States: A Stochastic Production Frontier Approach," in *Slavery in the Development of the Americas*, ed. David Eltis, Frank D. Lewis, and Kenneth L. Sokoloff (Cambridge: Cambridge University Press, 2004), 236–57.

23. Trevor Burnard, ""Who Deceived Whom? Eugene Genovese and Planter Self-Deception," *Slavery and Abolition* 34 (2013): 508–14.

24. On slavery as original sin see B. W. Higman, *Writing West Indian Histories* (Basingstoke: Macmillan, 1999). Abolitionists' equation of slavery with sin is canvassed in Roger Anstey, *The Atlantic Slave Trade and British Abolition, 1760–1810* (London: Macmillan, 1975). On the inadequacies of the resistance paradigm as an interpretive strategy, see Smith, *Slavery, Family, and Gentry Capitalism*, 344–47.

25. Simon D. Newman, *Free and Bound Labor in the British Atlantic World: Black and White Workers and the Development of Plantation Slavery* (Philadelphia: University of Pennsylvania Press, 2013); and Justin Roberts, *Slavery and the Enlightenment in the British Atlantic, 1750–1807* (New York: Cambridge University Press, 2013).

26. Philip D. Morgan, *Slave Counterpoint: Black Culture in the Eighteenth-Century Chesapeake and Lowcountry* (Chapel Hill: University of North Carolina Press, 1998).

27. Rhys Isaac, *Landon Carter's Uneasy Kingdom: Revolution and Rebellion on a Virginia Plantation* (New York: Oxford University Press, 2004); and Trevor Burnard, *Mastery, Tyranny, and Desire: Thomas Thistlewood and His Slaves in the Anglo-Jamaican World* (Chapel Hill: University of North Carolina Press, 2004).

28. Jeremy Popkin, *You Are All Free: The Haitian Revolution and the Abolition of Slavery* (New York: Cambridge University Press, 2010), 12. The literature on slave revolts is enormous. An excellent overview is Gad Heuman, "Slave Rebellions," in *The Routledge History of Slavery*, ed. Gad Heuman and Trevor Burnard (London: Routledge, 2010), 220–33.

29. Michael A. McDonnell, *The Politics of War: Race, Class and Conflict in Revolutionary Virginia* (Chapel Hill: University of North Carolina Press, 2007); Woody Holton, *Forced Founders: Indians, Debtors, Slaves, and the Making of the American Revolution in Virginia* (Chapel Hill: University of North

Carolina Press, 1999); and Steven Sarson, *The Tobacco-Plantation South in the Early American Plantation World* (London: Palgrave Macmillan, 2013).

30. David Hancock, *Oceans of Wine: Madeira and the Emergence of American Trade and Taste* (New Haven, CT: Yale University Press, 2009), xvi–xvii; and Hancock, "A World of Business to Do: William Freeman and the Foundations of England's Commercial Empire, 1645–1707," *WMQ*, 3rd ser., 57 (2000): 1–34.

31. Richard S. Dunn, *Sugar and Slaves: The Rise of the Planter Class in the English West Indies* (Chapel Hill: University of North Carolina Press, 1972).

32. Lois Green Carr and Russell R. Menard, "Wealth and Welfare in Early Maryland: Evidence from St. Mary's County," *WMQ*, 3rd ser., 56 (1999): 106–11; and Carr, "Emigration and the Standard of Living: The Eighteenth Century Chesapeake," John J. McCusker and Kenneth Morgan, eds., *The Early Modern Atlantic Economy* (Cambridge: Cambridge University Press, 2001), 338. A good overview is Russell R. Menard, "Economic and Social Development of the South," in *The Cambridge Economic History of the United States*, vol. 1, *The Colonial Era*, ed. Stanley L. Engerman and Robert E. Gallman (New York: Cambridge University Press, 1996), 249–95.

33. On rising slave prices see Peter C. Mancall, Joshua L. Rosenbloom, and Thomas Weiss, "Slave Prices and the South Carolina Economy, 1722–1809," *Journal of Economic History* 61 (2001): 616–39. On rising land prices see Ahmed Reid and David Ryden, "Sugar, Land Markets, and the Williams Thesis: Evidence from Jamaica's Property Sales, 1750–1810," *Slavery and Abolition* 34 (2013): 401–24.

34. Robert C. Ritchie, *Captain Kidd and the War against the Pirates* (Cambridge, MA: Harvard University Press, 1986); Adrian Finucane, *The Temptations of Trade: British Agents in Eighteenth-Century Spanish America* (Philadelphia: University of Pennsylvania, forthcoming); Isaac, *The Transformation of Virginia*; McDonnell, *The Politics of War*; Jim Piecuch, *Three Peoples, One King: Loyalists, Indians, and Slaves in the Revolutionary South, 1775–1782* (Columbia: University of South Carolina Press, 2007); and David Lambert, *White Creole Culture, Politics and Identity during the Age of Abolition* (Cambridge: Cambridge University Press, 2005).

35. Michael Craton, *Testing the Chains: Resistance to Slavery in the British West Indies* (Ithaca, NY: Cornell University Press, 1982), 61–98.

36. Jeremy Popkin, *You Are All Free: The Haitian Revolution and the Abolition of Slavery* (New York: Cambridge University Press, 2010), 20, 43, 62.

37. Isaac, *The Transformation of Virginia*; and T. H. Breen, *Tobacco Culture: The Mentality of the Great Tidewater Planters on the Eve of the Revolution* (Princeton, NJ: Princeton University Press, 1985). Particularly good summaries of colonial political culture are Michal Jan Rozbicki, *Culture and Liberty in the Age of the American Revolution* (Charlottesville: University of Virginia Press, 2011); and Richard R. Beeman, *The Varieties of Political Experience in Eighteenth-Century America* (Philadelphia: University of Pennsylvania Press, 2004).

38. Staple production, of course, was important. Marc Egnal notes that "the value added by the individuals who harvested the grain, fish, furs, tobacco, rice, indigo, and other exports was far greater than the wealth produced by merchants and artisans." Egnal's thesis that the regional economies of colonial British America "grew in a series of long swings that were shaped primarily by changes in the terms of trade and capital flows" and that "also reflected additions to the capital stock, gains in productivity, and patterns of culture" makes sense. I differ from Egnal on the limited role of improvements in the quality of the labor force and better management practices in leading to advances in productivity. Marc Egnal, *New World Economies: The Growth of the Thirteen Colonies and Early Canada* (New York: Oxford University Press, 1998), 4–7, 17–20; and Higman, *Plantation Jamaica*.

39. Nuala Zahedieh, *The Capital and the Colonies: London and the Atlantic Economy, 1660–1700* (Cambridge: Cambridge University Press, 2010), 189–200. Eltis has constructed higher rates for the islands, suggesting commodity exports around 1700 were £838,200. David Eltis, *The Rise of African Slavery in the Americas* (New York: Cambridge University Press, 2000), 196, 199, 211.

40. David Eltis, "The Total Product of Barbados, 1661–1701," *Journal of Economic History* 55 (1995): 321–36.

41. David W. Galenson, "The Settlement and Growth of the Colonies: Population, Labor, and Economic Development," in Engerman and Gallman, *The Cambridge Economic History: The Colonial Era*, 198; and Richard Pares, *Yankees and Creoles: The Trade between North America and the West Indies before the American Revolution* (London: Longmans, 1956).

42. Kenneth Morgan, "Robert Dinwiddie's Reports on the British American Colonies," *WMQ*, 3rd ser., 65 (2008): 305–46, quote at 305.

43. Dinwiddie's 1740 report coincided with a request from Britain for all mainland colonies to contribute soldiers to the Cartagena expedition. Thomas C. Barrow, *Trade and Empire: The British Customs Service in Colonial America, 1660–1775* (Cambridge, MA: Harvard University Press, 1967), 137; and Fred Anderson, *A People's Army: Massachusetts Soldiers and Society in the Seven Years' War* (Chapel Hill: University of North Carolina Press, 1984).

44. Dinwiddie's analysis was drawn on by Scottish-born settler James Abercromby for an updated report on the twenty-three British American colonies from Newfoundland to Barbados. Jack P. Greene, Charles F. Mullett, and Edward C. Papenfuse, Jr., eds., *Magna Charta for America: James Abercromby's "An Examination of the Acts of Parliament Relative to the Trade and the Government of our American Colonies" (1752) and "De Jure et Gubernatione Coloniarum, or An Inquiry into the Nature, and the Rights of Colonies, Ancient and Modern"* (Philadelphia: American Philosophical Society, 1986), 14–15. Britain was very concerned about competition from the French. John Ashley, *Memoirs and Considerations concerning the Trade and Revenues of*

the British Colonies in America with Proposals for rendering those Colonies more Beneficial to Great Britain (London: C. Corbett, 1740), 75–95.

45. Thomas M. Truxes, *Irish-American Trade, 1660–1783* (Cambridge: Cambridge University Press, 1988).

46. Jamaica was able to import large amounts of bullion into the island, thus considerably enhancing the wealth and power of Kingston merchants. Trevor Burnard, "'The Grand Mart of the Island': Kingston, Jamaica in the Mid-Eighteenth Century and the Question of Urbanisation in Plantation Societies," in *A History of Jamaica, from Indigenous Settlement to the Present,* ed. Kathleen Monteith and Glen Richards (Kingston: University of West Indies Press, 2002), 225–41; and Finucane, *Temptations of Trade.* Governor Charles Knowles estimated that annual imports of bullion from Spanish America amounted to £71,000 per annum between 1735 and 1752. John J. McCusker and Russell R. Menard, *The Economy of British America, 1607–1789* (Chapel Hill: University of North Carolina Press, 1985), 84. See also Allan Christelow, "Contraband Trade between Jamaica and the Spanish Main and the Free Port Act of 1766," *Hispanic American Historical Review* 22 (1942): 309–43; and George H. Nelson, "Contraband Trade under the Asiento," *AHR* 51 (1945): 55–67.

47. Morgan, "Dinwiddie."

48. For the traditional view that the plantation contributed little to modern management methods, see Alfred D. Chandler, *The Visible Hand: The Managerial Revolution in American Business* (Cambridge, MA: Harvard University Press, 1977), 64–66. For a contrary view see Bill Cooke, "The Denial of Slavery in Management Studies," *Journal of Management Studies* 40 (2003): 1895–1918. See also Higman, *Plantation Jamaica, 1750–1850*, 1–6, quote at 5; and R. Keith Aufhauser, "Slavery and Scientific Management," *Journal of Economic History* 33 (1973): 811–24.

49. Bernard Bailyn, *Voyagers to the West: A Passage in the Peopling of America on the Eve of Revolution* (New York: Alfred A. Knopf, 1986).

50. Aaron Fogelman, "Migrations to the Thirteen British North American Colonies, 1700–1775: New Estimates," *Journal of Interdisciplinary History* 22 (1992): 691–709; Trevor Burnard, "European Migration to Jamaica, 1655–1780," *WMQ*, 3rd ser., 53 (1996): 769–94; and James Horn and Philip D. Morgan, "Settlers and Slaves: European and African Migrations to Early Modern British America," in *The Creation of the British Atlantic World*, ed. Elizabeth Mancke and Carole Shammas (Baltimore, MD: Johns Hopkins University Press, 2005), 19–44. Fogelman's low estimate and Horn and Morgan's medium estimate are below the high estimate proffered by Russell R. Menard, "Migration, Ethnicity, and the Rise of an Atlantic Economy: The Repeopling of British America," in *A Century of European Migrations*, ed. Rudolph J. Vecoli and Suzanne M. Sinke (Urbana: University of Illinois Press, 1991), 58–77.

51. Bailyn, *Voyagers to the West*, 209; Trevor Burnard, "European Migration to Jamaica," *WMQ*, 3rd ser., 53 (1996): 728–30, 793; and Horn and Morgan, "Settlers and Slaves," 32–33.

52. Peter McCandless, *Slavery, Disease, and Suffering in the Southern Lowcountry* (New York: Cambridge University Press, 2011).

53. Jamaican wealth is accounted to be 52 percent of total British West Indian wealth throughout Sheridan, *Sugar and Slavery*.

54. Bernard Bailyn and Philip D. Morgan, eds., *Strangers in the Realm: Cultural Margins of the British Empire* (Chapel Hill: University of North Carolina Press, 1991).

55. Stephen Conway, *War, State, and Society in Mid-Eighteenth-Century Britain and Ireland* (Oxford: Oxford University Press, 2006), chapter 9; and Andrew O'Shaughnessy, *The Men Who Lost America: British Leadership, the American Revolution, and the Fate of Empire* (New Haven, CT: Yale University Press, 2013).

56. Franklin, *Observations*, 374; and Anthony Stokes, *A View of the Constitution of the British Colonies in North America and the West Indies at the Time the Civil War Broke Out on the Continent of America* (London: B. White, 1783), 140.

57. Bailyn, *Voyagers to the West*, 32.

58. Julie Flavell, *When London Was Capital of America* (New Haven, CT: Yale University Press, 2010). On absenteeism see Trevor Burnard, "'Passengers Only': The Extent and Significance of Absenteeism in Eighteenth-Century Jamaica," *Atlantic Studies* 1 (2004): 178–195. On Britons' negative opinions of Massachusetts see Flavell, "British Perceptions of New England and the Decision for a Coercive Colonial Policy, 1774–1775," in *Britain and America Go to War: The Impact of War and Warfare in Anglo-America, 1754–1815*, ed. Julie Flavell and Stephen Conway (Gainesville: University Press of Florida, 2004), 95–115.

59. Herman Merivale, *Lectures on Colonization and Colonies* (London: Longman, 1861).

60. P. J. Marshall, *The Making and Unmaking of Empire: Britain, India, and America, c. 1750–1783* (Oxford: Oxford University Press, 2005); James Belich, *Replenishing the Earth: The Settler Revolution and the Rise of the Anglo-World, 1783–1939* (New York: Oxford University Press, 2009); and John Darwin, *Unfinished Empire: The Global Expansion of Britain* (London: Allen Lane, 2012).

61. Sophus A. Reinert, *Translating Empire: Emulation and the Origins of Political Economy* (Cambridge, MA: Harvard University Press, 2011), chapters 1 and 2; Stephen Pincus, "Rethinking Mercantilism: Political Economy, the British Empire, and the Atlantic World in the Seventeenth and Eighteenth Centuries," *WMQ*, 3rd ser., 69 (2012): 3–34; and Brendan Simms, *Three Victories and a Defeat: The Rise and Fall of the First British Empire, 1714–1783* (London: Allen Lane, 2007).

62. J. H. Elliott, *Empires of the Atlantic World: Britain and Spain in America, 1492–1830* (New Haven, CT: Yale University Press, 2007).

63. S. Max Edelson, *Plantation Enterprise in Colonial South Carolina* (Cambridge, MA: Harvard University Press, 2006), 2–3.

64. Franklin was not alone in his predictions. In Maryland, the center of British immigration to the colonies in the years immediately before the American Revolution, Charles Carroll of Carrollton exclaimed that "the growing population of the colonies, increased by such a considerable annual influx of newcomers, bids fair to render British America in a century or two the most populous and of course the most potent part of the world. I fancy many in England begin to entertain the same opinion." Charles Carroll to William Graves, 7 September 1773, reproduced in *Maryland Historical Magazine* 32 (1937): 219.

65. Emma Rothschild, "Adam Smith in the British Empire," in *Empire and Modern Political Thought*, ed. Sankar Muthu (Cambridge: Cambridge University Press, 2012), 184–98.

66. Burnard, "European Migration to Jamaica"; and Fogelman, "Migrations to the Thirteen British North American Colonies."

67. Bailyn, *Voyagers to the West*, 206–7.

68. Zahedieh, *The Capital and the Colonies*; and Hancock, *Citizens of the World*.

69. David Hancock, "'Domestic Bubbling': Eighteenth-Century London Merchants and Individual Investment in the Funds," *Economic History Review* 57 (1994): 691. See also H. V. Bowen, *Revenue and Reform: The Indian Problem in British Politics, 1757–1773* (Cambridge: Cambridge University Press, 1991).

70. Smith, *Slavery, Family and Gentry Capitalism*.

71. S. D. Smith, "Gedney Clarke of Salem and Barbados: Transatlantic Super Merchant," *New England Quarterly* 76 (2003): 499–549.

72. Pieter C. Emmer, "The Dutch and the Slave Americas," in Eltis, Lewis, and Sokoloff, *Slavery in the Development of the Americas*, 74–76; and Marjoleine Kars, "'Cleansing the Land'": Dutch-Amerindian Co-operation in the Suppression of the 1763 Slave Rebellion in Dutch Guiana," in *Empires and Indigenes: Intercultural Alliance, Imperial Expansion, and Warfare in the Early Modern World*, ed. Wayne E. Lee (New York: New York University Press, 2011), 251–76.

73. John Fowler, *A Summary Account of the Present Flourishing State of the Respectable Colony of Tobago* (London: A. Grant, 1774).

74. Smith, *Slavery, Family and Gentry Capitalism*, 132–33; Richard B. Sheridan, "The British Credit Crisis of 1772 and the American Colonies," *Journal of Economic History* 20 (1960): 172–73; S. D. Smith, "Sugar's Poor Relation: Coffee Planting in the British West Indies, 1720–1833," *Slavery and Abolition* 19 (1988): 76–84; Johannes Postma, "The Fruits of Slave Labor: Tropical Commodities from Surinam to Holland, 1683–1794," in *Oceanic Trade, Colonial Wares, and Industrial Development, 1600–1800*, ed. Maxine

Berg, Eleventh International History Congress (Milan, 1994); and Gert Oostindie, "The Economics of Surinam Slavery," *Economic and Social History in the Netherlands* 5 (1993): 8.

75. D. V. Glass, "The Population Controversy in Eighteenth-Century England," *Population Studies* 6 (1952): 69–91. See also Alison Bashford, *Life on Earth: Geopolitics and the World Population Problem* (New York: Columbia University Press, 2013).

76. Amanda Vickery, *Behind Closed Doors: At Home in Georgian England* (New Haven, CT: Yale University Press, 2009); and E. A. Wrigley and R. S. Schofield, *The Population History of England, 1541–1871: A Reconstruction* (Cambridge: Cambridge University Press, 1989).

77. Seymour Drescher, *The Mighty Experiment: Free Labor versus Slavery in British Emancipation* (New York: Oxford University Press, 2002), 48.

78. Mark Harrison, *Medicine in an Age of Commerce and Empire: Britain and Its Tropical Colonies, 1660–1830* (Oxford: Oxford University Press, 2010); and Trevor Burnard and Richard Follett, "Caribbean Slavery, British Anti-slavery and the Cultural Politics of Venereal Disease," *Historical Journal* 55 (2012): 427–51.

79. P. J. Cain and A. G. Hopkins, "Gentlemanly Capitalism and British Expansion Overseas—I: The Old Colonial System, 1688–1850," *Economic History Review* 39 (1986): 501–25.

80. *Philosophical and Political History of the Settlements and Trade of the Europeans in the East and West Indies . . . by the Abbé Raynal*, trans. J. O. Justamond, six vols. (London: T. Cadell Jr. & W. Davies, 1798; reprint, New York: Negro Universities Press, 1969), 485–86.

81. Merivale, *Lectures on Colonization and Colonies*, 314–41.

82. B. W. Higman, *Slave Populations of the British Caribbean, 1807–1834* (Baltimore, MD: Johns Hopkins University Press, 1984), 51, 59–64. We lack a decent history of slavery and the plantation system in British Guiana before emancipation. The best treatment is Emilia Viotti da Costa, *Crowns of Glory, Tears of Blood: The Demerara Slave Rebellion of 1823* (New York: Oxford University Press, 1994); but see also Trevor Burnard, *Hearing Slaves Speak* (Georgetown, Guyana: Caribbean Press, 2010); Randy Browne, "The 'Bad Business' of Obeah: Power, Authority, and the Politics of Slave Culture in the British Caribbean," *WMQ*, 3rd ser., 68 (2011): 451–80; and Kit Candlin, *The Last Caribbean Frontier, 1795–1815* (London: Palgrave Macmillan, 2012), chapter 2.

83. Higman, *Slave Populations*, 41, 45, 48, 51, 63; and Nicholas Draper, *The Price of Emancipation: Slave-ownership, Compensation, and British Society at the End of Slavery* (Cambridge: Cambridge University Press, 2010), 101, 118, 139, 150–51, 267–73; Draper, "The Rise of a New Planter Class? Some Countercurrents from British Guiana and Trinidad, 1807–1833," *Atlantic Studies* 9 (2012): 65–83; and da Costa, *Crowns of Glory*, chapters 1 and 2.

84. Higman, *Slave Populations*, 308–10; Michael Tadman, "The Demographic Cost of Sugar: Debates on Slave Societies and Natural Increase in the Americas," *AHR* 105 (2000): 1534–1575; and A. Meredith John, *The Plantation Slaves of Trinidad, 1783–1816: A Mathematical and Demographic Enquiry* (Cambridge: Cambridge University Press, 1988).

85. Ira Berlin, *Generations in Captivity: A History of African American Slaves* (Cambridge, MA: Harvard University Press, 2003), chapter 4; and Michael Tadman, *Speculators and Slaves: Masters, Traders, and Slaves in the Old South* (Madison: University of Wisconsin Press, 1989).

86. Gregory Smithers, "American Abolitionism and Slave-Breeding Discourse: A Re-evaluation," *Slavery and Abolition* 33 (2012): 551–70; and Richard Follett, "Heat, Sex, and Sugar: Pregnancy and Childbearing in the Slave Quarters," *Journal of Family History* 28 (2003): 510–39.

87. Adam Rothman, *Slave Country: American Expansion and the Origins of the Deep South* (Cambridge, MA: Harvard University Press, 2005), x–xi; and Daniel H. Usner, Jr., *Indians, Settlers, and Slaves in a Frontier Exchange Economy: The Lower Mississippi Valley before 1783* (Chapel Hill: University of North Carolina Press, 1992), 104–44.

88. Christopher Morris, *Becoming Southern: The Evolution of a Way of Life, Warren County, Vicksburg, Mississippi, 1770–1860* (New York: Oxford University Press, 1995); and Richard Follett, *The Sugar Masters: Planters and Slaves in Louisiana's Cane World, 1820–1860* (Baton Rouge: Louisiana State University Press, 2005).

89. Rothman, *Slave Country*, 51, 76, 217–18; and Follett, *Sugar Masters*. The great example of a technologically advanced and wealthy plantation society in the nineteenth century was Cuba. See Laird Bergad, *Cuban Rural Society in the Nineteenth Century: The Social and Economic History of Monoculture in Matanzas* (Princeton, NJ: Princeton University Press, 1990).

90. William Stork, *An Account of East Florida . . .* (London: G. Woodfall, 1766); and see George C. Rogers, Jr., "The East Florida Society of London, 1766–1767," *Florida Historical Quarterly* 54 (1976): 483–89.

91. J. R. McNeill, *Mosquito Empires: Ecology and War in the Greater Caribbean, 1620–1914* (New York: Cambridge University Press, 2010), 123–34; and Emma Rothschild, "A Horrible Tragedy in the French Atlantic," *Past and Present* 192 (2006): 67–108.

92. Bailyn, *Voyagers to the West*, 451–60, (quote at 460); and E. P. Panagopoulus, *New Smyrna: An Eighteenth Century Greek Odyssey* (Gainesville: University of Florida Press, 1966).

93. Bailyn, *Voyagers to the West*, 430–74; and Daniel L. Schafer, "Plantation Development in British East Florida: A Case Study of the Earl of Egmont," *Florida Historical Quarterly* 63 (1984): 172–83.

94. Hancock, *Citizens of the World*, 153–70, quotes at 153 and 170; and Henry Laurens to Richard Oswald, 28 May 1771, *Papers of Henry Laurens*, 7:501.

95. Daniel L. Schafer, " 'Settling a Colony over a Bottle of Claret: Early Planta-tion Development in British East Florida," *El Escribano* 19 (1982): 47–50; and Jane Landers, *Black Society in Spanish Florida* (Urbana: University of Illinois Press, 1999), 66–67, 158–59.

96. Stanley L. Engerman and Robert E. Gallman, eds., *The Cambridge Economic History of the United States*, vol. 1, *The Colonial Era* (New York: Cambridge University Press, 1996); John J. McCusker and Russell R. Menard, *The Economy of British America, 1607–1789* (Chapel Hill: University of North Carolina Press, 1985); and Marc Egnal, *New World Economies: The Growth of the Thirteen Colonies and Early Canada* (New York: Oxford University Press, 1998). On different plantation regions see the primacy of regional divi-sions in Walsh, *Motives of Honor*, and Higman, *Slave Populations*. See also David Eltis, *The Rise of African Slavery in the Americas* (New York: Cambridge University Press, 2000).

97. Lorena S. Walsh, "Summing the Parts: Implications for Estimating Chesa-peake Output and Income Subregionally," *WMQ*, 3rd ser., 56 (1999): 53–94.

98. Walsh, *Motives of Honor*; Sheridan, *Sugar and Slavery*, 398–401; Dunn, *Sugar and Slaves*; Eltis, *The Rise of African Slavery*, 197–202; Menard, *Sweet Negotiations*, 81–82; Zahedieh, *The Capital and the Colonies*; and Douglas Bradburn, "The Visible Fist: The Chesapeake Tobacco Trade in War and the Purpose of Empire, 1690–1715," *WMQ*, 3rd ser., 68 (2011): 361–86.

99. Russell R. Menard, "The Tobacco Industry in the Chesapeake Colonies, 1617–1730: An Interpretation," *Research in Economic History* 5 (1980): 109–77; Douglas M. Bradburn and John M. Coombs, "Smoke and Mirrors: Reinterpreting the Society and Economy of the Seventeenth-Century Chesapeake," *Atlantic Studies* 3 (2006): 131–57; Peter A. Coclanis, *The Shadow of a Dream: Economic Life and Death in the South Carolina Low Country, 1670–1920* (New York: Oxford University Press, 1989); and Sheridan, *Sugar and Slavery*, 426–32.

100. Walsh, *Motives of Honor*, 409.

101. Pennant, Custis, and Tilghman were all fortunate inheritors who did not need to buy slaves or land to start their enterprises. They were also careful accountants and skilled planters. These figures should be thought of as high estimates. Trevor Burnard, "From Periphery to Periphery: The Pennants' Jamaican Plantations, 1771–1812 and Industrialization in North Wales," in *Wales and Empire, 1607–1820*, ed. H. V. Bowen (Manchester: Manchester University Press, 2011), 114–42; Menard, "Economic and Social Development of the South," 274; Paul Langford, *A Polite and Commercial People: England, 1727–1783* (Oxford: Oxford University Press, 1989), 594; and Walsh, *Motives of Honor*, 442, 446, 564–71.

102. Samuel Martin, *An Essay Upon Plantership* (Antigua: T. Smith, 1750); and Burnard, *Mastery, Tyranny, and Desire*, 24, 52–53.

103. Burnard, *Mastery, Tyranny, and Desire*, 46–47, 50–51, 64.

104. Perry Gauci, *William Beckford: First Prime Minister of the London Empire* (New

Haven, CT: Yale University Press, 2013); and Evans, *A "Topping People,"* 113–14, 193.

105. Evans, *A "Topping People"*; Breen, *Tobacco Culture*; Walsh, *Motives of Honor,* chapter 8; Trevor Burnard, *Creole Gentlemen: The Maryland Elite, 1691–1776* (New York: Routledge, 2002), 22–24, 241–43; and Thomas M. Doerflinger, *A Vigorous Spirit of Enterprise: Merchants and Economic Development in Revolutionary Philadelphia* (Chapel Hill: University of North Carolina Press, 1986), 344–64.

106. Edward Long, *History of Jamaica . . .* , 3 vols. (London: T. Lowndes, 1774).

107. Higman, *Plantation Jamaica*, 200.

108. Ibid., 201.

109. Ibid., 203–4, 216–17.

110. Simon Taylor to Chaloner Arcedeckne, 30 January, 11 June, 29 October 1782, Vanneck Mss., Bundle 2/10, Cambridge University Library.

111. Smith, *Slavery, Family and Gentry Capitalism*, 133, 211–13; Mark Quintanilla, "The World of Alexander Campbell: An Eighteenth-Century Grenadian Planter," *Albion* 35 (2003): 1–29; and Sheridan, "The British Credit Crisis of 1772," 172–73.

112. Russell R. Menard, "Economic and Social Development of the South," in Engerman and Gallman, *The Cambridge Economic History: The Colonial Era,* 278.

113. Allan Kulikoff, "The Economic Growth of the Eighteenth Century Chesapeake Colonies," *Journal of Economic History* 39 (1978): 275–88; Lois Green Carr and Russell R. Menard, "Wealth and Welfare in Early Maryland: Evidence from St. Mary's County," *WMQ*, 3rd ser., 56 (1999): 95–120; Walsh, *Motives of Honor*, chapters 3–5; and Burnard, *Creole Gentlemen*, 7–10.

114. Kenneth Morgan, "The Organization of the Colonial American Rice Trade," *WMQ*, 3rd ser., 52 (1995): 433–53. See also James F. Shepherd and Gary M. Walton, *Shipping, Maritime Trade, and the Economic Development of Colonial North America* (Cambridge: Cambridge University Press, 1972).

115. Robin Blackburn, *The Making of New World Slavery: From the Baroque to the Modern, 1492–1800* (London: Verso, 1997), 558–73.

116. Paul M. Pressly emphasizes that the first jump in rice production came in the 1760s. Apart from a few early large plungers, such as Jonathan Bryan, the entry of men with substantial capital and other resources came after smaller planters had started rice production in the 1750s. Paul M. Pressly, *On the Rim of the Caribbean: Colonial Georgia and the British Atlantic World* (Athens: University of Georgia Press, 2013), 138; and Allan Gallay, "Jonathan Bryan's Plantation Empire: Land, Politics, and the Formation of a Ruling Class in Colonial Georgia," *WMQ*, 3rd ser., 45 (1988): 253–79.

117. Jack P. Greene, "Travails of an Infant Colony: The Search for Viability, Coherence, and Identity in Colonial Georgia," in *Imperatives, Behaviors, and Identities: Essays in Early American Cultural History* (Charlottesville: University of Virginia Press, 1992), 113–42; Philip D. Morgan, "Lowcountry

Georgia and the Early Modern Atlantic World, 1733–ca. 1820," in *African American Life in the Georgian Lowcountry: The Atlantic World and the Gullah Geecher*, ed. Philip D. Morgan (Athens: University of Georgia Press, 2010), 13–47; and Betty Wood, "James Edward Oglethorpe, Race and Slavery: A Reassessment," in *Oglethorpe in Perspective: Georgia's Founder after Two Hundred Years*, ed. Phinizy Spalding and Harvey H. Jackson (Tuscaloosa: University of Alabama Press, 1989), 66–79. See also Ben Marsh, *Georgia's Frontier Women: Female Fortunes in a Southern Colony* (Athens: University of Georgia Press, 2007).

118. Joyce E. Chaplin, *An Anxious Pursuit: Agricultural Innovation and Modernity in the Lower South, 1730–1815* (Chapel Hill: University of North Carolina Press, 1993); and Pressly, *On the Rim of the Caribbean*, 19, 216.

119. Pressly, *On the Rim of the Caribbean*, 165.

120. Gallay, "Jonathan Bryan's Plantation Empire."

121. Pressly, *On the Rim of the Caribbean*, 141–42.

122. Ibid., 142.

123. Betty Wood, *Slavery in Colonial Georgia, 1730–1775* (Athens: University of Georgia Press, 1984), 115, 129.

124. James F. Shepherd, "Commodity Exports from the British North American Colonies to Overseas Areas, 1768–1772," *Explorations in Economic History* 8 (1971): 5–76.

125. "Private information on the present State of the Island of Grenada, to Lords Commissioners for Trade and Plantations" [ca. 1770–79], Beinecke Collection, M237, Hamilton College, NY; D. H. Murdoch, "Land Policy in the Eighteenth-Century British Empire: The Sale of Crown Lands in the Ceded Islands," *Historical Journal* 27 (1984): 549–75; and Smith, *Slavery, Family and Gentry Capitalism*, 211–13. For a case study see Mark Quintanilla, "The World of Alexander Campbell: An Eighteenth Century Grenadian Planter," *Albion* 35 (2003): 229–56. See also Aron Willis, "The Standing of New Subjects: Grenada and the Protestant Constitution after the Treaty of Paris (1763)," *Journal of Imperial and Commonwealth History* 42 (2014): 1–21.

126. Higman, *Slave Populations of the British Caribbean*, 50, 55–58.

127. David Beck Ryden, "'One of the Finest and Most Fruitful Spots in America': An Analysis of Eighteenth-Century Carriacou," *Journal of Interdisciplinary History* 43 (2013): 539–70.

128. The two plantation worlds are summarized in Higman, *Slave Populations of the British Caribbean*; and Ira Berlin and Ronald Hoffman, eds., *Slavery and Freedom in the Age of the American Revolution* (Charlottesville: University of Virginia Press, 1983). For detailed comparisons of two slave systems see Morgan, *Slave Counterpoint*, and especially Richard S. Dunn, *A Tale of Two Plantations: Slave Life and Labor in Jamaica and Virginia* (Cambridge, MA: Harvard University Press, 2014).

129. Holton, *Forced Founders*, 70–71. The proposed ban on the Atlantic slave trade did not mean that Virginia would not be able to get African captives. There was an extensive intercolonial trade between the West Indies and the Chesapeake. Gregory O'Malley, *Final Passages: The Intercolonial Slave Trade of British America, 1619–1807* (Chapel Hill: University of North Carolina Press, 2014), 66–72.

130. Holton, *Forced Founders*, 70; and Bruce Ragsdale, *A Planter's Republic: The Search for Economic Independence in Revolutionary Virginia* (Madison: University of Wisconsin Press, 1996), 126–27.

131. Morgan, *Slave Counterpoint*; Lorena S. Walsh, "The Chesapeake Slave Trade, Regional Patterns, African Origins, and Some Implications," *WMQ*, 3rd ser., 58 (2001): 166–67; Higman, *Slave Populations of the British Caribbean*, 304–7, 375–77; and Higman, *The Jamaican Censuses of 1844 and 1861* (Mona, Jamaica: Department of History, University of the West Indies, 1980), 2–3, 16.

132. Hugh Jones, *The Present State of Virginia . . .* , ed. Richard L. Morton (Chapel Hill: University of North Carolina Press, 1956), 75; and Morgan, *Slave Counterpoint*, 81.

133. Ann Maury, ed. and trans., *Memoirs of a Huguenot Family . . .* (Baltimore: Genealogical Publishing, 1967), 347–48.

134. Ward, *British West Indian Slavery*; Roberts, *Slavery and the Enlightenment*, chapter 1; and Mary Turner, "Planter Profits and Slave Rewards: Amelioration Reconsidered," in *West Indies Accounts: Essays on the History of the British Caribbean and the Atlantic Economy in Honour of Richard Sheridan*, ed. Roderick A. McDonald (Kingston: University of the West Indies Press, 1996), 232–52. But see Alvin O. Thompson, *Unprofitable Servants: Crown Slaves in Berbice, Guyana, 1803–1831* (Kingston: University of the West Indies Press, 2002), 36–44.

135. Roberts, *Slavery and the Enlightenment*, chapter 1.

136. Edwin Morris Betts, *Thomas Jefferson's Farm Book, with Commentary and Relevant Extracts from Other Writings* (Princeton: Princeton University Press, 1953), 46.

137. Lorena S. Walsh, *From Calabar to Carter's Grove: The History of a Virginia Slave Community* (Charlottesville: University of Virginia Press, 1997); and Allan Kulikoff, "A 'Prolifick' People: Black Population Growth in the Chesapeake Colonies, 1700–1790," *Southern Studies* 16 (1977): 391–428.

138. Kenneth Morgan, "Slave Women and Reproduction in Jamaica, c. 1776–1834," *History* (2006): 231–53.

139. Dunn, *A Tale of Two Plantations*, chapter 1.

140. Richard S. Dunn, "The Story of Two Jamaican Slaves: Sarah Affir and Richard McAlpine of Mesopotamia Estate," in McDonald, *West Indies Accounts*, 188–210.

141. Richard S. Dunn, "Winney Grimshaw, a Virginia Slave, and Her Family," *Early American Studies* 9 (2011): 497–509.

142. Richard S. Dunn, "A Tale of Two Plantations: Slave Life at Mesopotamia in Jamaica and Mount Airy in Virginia, 1799 to 1828," *WMQ*, 3rd ser., 34 (1977): 32–65.

143. Tadman, "Demographic Costs of Sugar."

144. Jan de Vries, "The Industrial Revolution and the Industrious Revolution," *Journal of Economic History* 54 (1994): 249–70.

145. Roberts, *Slavery and the Enlightenment*, 12–18.

146. McCandless, *Slavery, Disease, and Suffering in the Southern Lowcountry*.

147. McCusker and Menard, *The Economy of British America*, 136, 154, 172; Horn and Morgan, "Settlers and Slaves"; Higman, *Slave Populations of the British Caribbean*; Bailyn, *Voyagers to the West*, 208, 263; and Roger Ekirch, "Bound for America: A Profile of British Convicts Transported to the Colonies, 1718–1775," *WMQ*, 3rd ser., 42 (1985): 188.

148. Morgan, "Lowcountry Georgia," 20.

149. A good guide to the historiographical literature is David Brown, "A Vagabond's Tale: Poor Whites, Herrenvolk Democracy, and the Value of Whiteness in the Late Antebellum South," *Journal of Southern History* 79 (2013): 800–807. On the centrality of household relations see Stephanie McCurry, *Masters of Small Worlds: Yeoman Households, Gender Relations, and the Political Culture of the Antebellum South Carolina Low Country* (New York: Oxford University Press, 1995).

150. Burnard, *Creole Gentlemen*; and Michael A. McDonnell, "A World Turned 'Topsy-Turvy': Robert Munford, *The Patriots*, and the Crisis of the Revolution in Virginia," *WMQ*, 3rd ser., 61 (2004): 235–70.

151. Brown, "A Vagabond's Tale," 806.

152. William Byrd, *The History of the Dividing Line Betwixt Virginia and North Carolina* . . . (Petersburg, VA: Edmund & Julian Ruffin, 1841), 27–28.

153. George Pinckard, *Notes on the West Indies* . . . , 2nd ed. (London: Baldwin, Cradock, & Joy, 1816), 1:309; and Frederic William Naylor Bayley, *Four Months Residence in the West Indies* . . . (London: William Kidd, 1833), 62. On the term "redleg" see Edward T. Price, "The Redlegs of Barbados," *Journal of the Barbados Museum and Historical Society* 29 (1962): 48.

154. John Garrigus, "Free Coloureds," in Burnard and Heuman, *The Routledge History of Slavery*, 234–47.

155. Higman, *Slave Populations of the British Caribbean*, 433; Ira Berlin, *Generations of Captivity: A History of African-American Slaves* (Cambridge, MA: Harvard University Press, 2003), 272–79; Gad J. Heuman, *Between Black and White: Race, Politics, and the Free Coloreds in Jamaica, 1792–1865* (Westport, CT: Greenwood Press, 1981), 7–8; and Jerome S. Handler, *The Unappropriated People: Freedmen in the Slave Society of Barbados* (Kingston: University of the West Indies Press, 2009).

156. Heuman, *Between Black and White*, 3–20.

157. Ira Berlin, *Slaves without Masters: The Free Negro in the Antebellum South* (New York: Oxford University Press, 1974). But see Michael P. Johnson and James L.

Roark, *Black Masters: A Free Family of Color in the Old South* (New York: Oxford University Press, 1984).

158. Walsh, "Land, Landlord, and Leaseholder"; and Steven Sarson, "Landlessness and Tenancy in Early National Prince George's County, Maryland," *WMQ*, 3rd ser., 57 (2000): 569–98.

159. Christine Daniels, "Gresham's Laws: Labor Management on an Early-Eighteenth Century Chesapeake Plantation," *Journal of Southern History* 62 (1996): 205–38; and Daniels, "'Getting His [or Her] Livelyhood': Free Workers in Slave Anglo-America," *Agricultural History* 71 (1997): 143–44.

160. Aaron S. Fogleman, "From Slaves, Convicts, and Servants to Free Passengers: The Transformation of Immigration in the Era of the American Revolution," *Journal of American History* 85 (1998): 43–76.

161. Philip D. Morgan, "The Poor: Slaves in Early America," in Eltis, Lewis, and Sokoloff, *Slavery in the Development of the Americas*, 289.

162. B. W. Higman, "Economic and Social Development of the British West Indies, from Settlement to ca. 1850," in Engerman and Gallman, *The Cambridge Economic History: The Colonial Era*, 323–24.

CHAPTER FOUR

1. Patrick Browne, *The Civil and Natural History of Jamaica* (London: T. Osborne, 1756), 9.

2. Andrew O'Shaughnessy, *An Empire Divided: The American Revolution and the British Caribbean* (Philadelphia: University of Pennsylvania Press, 2000), 15; and Perry Gauci, *William Beckford: First Prime Minister of the London Empire* (New Haven, CT: Yale University Press, 2013).

3. Ahmed Reid and David Ryden, "Sugar, Land Markets, and the Williams Thesis: Evidence from Jamaica's Property Sales, 1750–1810," *Slavery and Abolition* 34 (2013): 404.

4. Inventories, 1778, IB/11/3/60/168; 1805, IB/11/3/104/33, JA; and 23 October 1765, Thomas Thistlewood's Diaries, Beinecke Library, Yale University.

5. Richard B. Sheridan, "Simon Taylor, Sugar Tycoon of Jamaica, 1740–1813," *Agricultural History* 45 (1971): 285–96, quotes at 286, 296.

6. My calculations of wealth are explained in Trevor Burnard, "'Prodigious Riches': The Wealth of Jamaica before the American Revolution," *Economic History Review* 54 (2001): 506–24, especially 517.

7. [Charles Leslie], *A New and Exact Account of Jamaica* [Edinburgh: R. Fleming, ca. 1740], 353.

8. Stanley L. Engerman, "The Atlantic Economy of the Eighteenth Century: Some Speculations on Economic Development in Britain, America, Africa and Elsewhere," *Journal of European Economic History* 24 (1995): 145–75.

9. Trevor Burnard and Emma Hart, "Kingston, Jamaica and Charleston, South Carolina: A New Look at Comparative Urbanization in Plantation Colonial British America," *Journal of Urban History* 39 (2013): 214–34; Burnard, "'Gay

and Agreeable Ladies': White Women in Mid-Eighteenth-Century Kingston, Jamaica," *Wadabagei* 9 (2006): 27–49; Burnard, "Kingston, Jamaica: A Crucible of Modernity," in *The Black Urban Atlantic in the Age of the Slave Trade*, ed. Jorge Canizares-Esguerra, Matt D. Childs, and James Sidbury (Philadelphia: University of Pennsylvania Press, 2013), 123–46; and Trevor Burnard, "'The Grand Mart of the Island': Kingston, Jamaica in the Mid-Eighteenth Century and the Question of Urbanisation in Plantation Societies," in *A History of Jamaica, from Indigenous Settlement to the Present*, ed. Kathleen Monteith and Glen Richards (Kingston: University of West Indies Press, 2002), 225–41.

10. Keith Mason, "The Absentee Planter and the Key Slave: Privilege, Patriarchalism, and Exploitation in the Early Eighteenth-Century Caribbean," *WMQ*, 3rd ser., 70 (2013): 80.

11. See Jack P. Greene, *Settler Jamaica in the 1750s: A Social Portrait* (Charlottesville: University of Virginia Press, 2015); and David Ryden, "'One of the Fertilest Pleasantest Spotts': An Analysis of the Slave Economy in Jamaica's St. Andrew Parish," *Slavery and Abolition* 21 (2000): 32–55.

12. Leslie, *New and exact account*; and James Knight, "The Natural, Moral and Political History of Jamaica and the Territories thereon depending," Long Papers, Add. Mss. 12,418–19, BL.

13. Bryan Edwards, *The History, Civil and Commercial, of the British Colonies in the West Indies*, 2nd ed., 3 vols. (London: J. Stockdale, 1793).

14. Winthrop D. Jordan, *White over Black: Attitudes toward the Negro, 1550–1812* (Chapel Hill: University of North Carolina Press, 1968); and David Brion Davis, *The Problem of Slavery in Western Culture* (Ithaca, NY: Cornell University Press, 1969). For Long's views on race see Roxann Wheeler, *The Complexion of Race: Categories of Difference in Eighteenth-Century British Culture* (Philadelphia: University of Pennsylvania Press, 2000), 260–87.

15. Robert Mowbray Howard, ed., *Records and Letters of the Family of Longs of Longville, Jamaica and Hampton Lodge, Surrey* (London: Simpkin, Marshall, Hamilton, Kent, 1925).

16. Edward Long, *History of Jamaica . . .* , 3 vols. (London: T. Lowndes, 1774). See also Elizabeth A. Bohls, "The Gentleman Planter and the Metropole: Long's *History of Jamaica*," in *The Country and the City Revisited: England and the Politics of Culture, 1550–1850*, ed. Gerald Maclean, Donna Landry, and Joseph P. Ward (Cambridge: Cambridge University Press, 1999), 180–96.

17. Long, *History of Jamaica*, 1:433–34.

18. Ibid., 1:40, 1:380, 2:595.

19. Ibid., 1:377–78, 1:386–87. Trevor Burnard, "'The Countrie Continues Sicklie': White Mortality in Jamaica, 1655–1780," *Social History of Medicine* 12 (1999): 45–72; and Burnard, "'Passengers Only': The Extent and Significance of Absenteeism in Eighteenth-Century Jamaica," *Atlantic Studies* 1 (2004): 178–95.

20. Long, *History of Jamaica*, 1:379–80, 462.

21. His figure for 1768 is probably about right, but that for 1751 is an underestimate: in 1744 exports of sugar, rum, and molasses alone were £703,798. Yu Wu, "Jamaican Trade, 1688–1769: A Quantitative Study" (Ph.D. diss., Johns Hopkins University, 1995), 521–24.

22. Long, *History of Jamaica*, 1:495–508, quote at 508.

23. Ibid.; and Browne, *The Civil and Natural History of Jamaica*, 9.

24. Figures derived from Long, *History of Jamaica*, vol. 2, and Edwards, *History, Civil and Commercial*, vol. 2. Data for 1788 includes the parish of Trelawney, which was created in 1770 out of St. James and St. Mary.

25. Ibid.

26. Reid and Ryden, "Sugar, Land Markets, and the Williams Thesis."

27. Sidney W. Mintz and Douglas Hall, "The Origins of the Jamaican Internal Marketing System," *Yale University Publications in Anthropology* 57 (1960): 3–26. See also B. W. Higman, *Slave Population and Economy in Jamaica, 1807–1834* (Cambridge: Cambridge University Press, 1976); Higman, *Jamaica Surveyed: Plantation Maps and Plans of the Eighteenth and Nineteenth Centuries* (Kingston: Institute of Jamaica Publications, 1988); Higman, *Montpelier: A Plantation Community in Slavery and Freedom, 1739–1912* (Kingston: University of the West Indies Press, 1998).

28. Burnard, "Prodigious Riches," 517.

29. "Essay towards an Estimate of the Riches and Value of Jamaica," in [Anon.], *An Inquiry concerning the Trade, Commerce, and Policy of Jamaica* (London: G. Woodfall, 1759).

30. Wu, "Jamaican Trade," 521–24.

31. Alan L. Karras, *Sojourners in the Sun: Scottish Migrants in Jamaica and the Chesapeake, 1740–1800* (Ithaca, NY: Cornell University Press, 1992); and Douglas Hamilton, *Scotland, the Caribbean and the Atlantic World, 1750–1820* (Manchester: Manchester University Press, 2005).

32. Trevor Burnard, "European Migration to Jamaica, 1655–1780," *WMQ*, 3rd ser., 53 (1996): 784.

33. Long, *History of Jamaica*, 2:295; and Thomas August, "Jewish Assimilation and the Plural Society in Jamaica," *Social and Economic Studies* 36 (1987): 109–22.

34. Burnard, "European Migration," 784.

35. Ibid., 772; Higman, *Slave Populations of the British Caribbean*, 61; and *TSTDB*.

36. Michael Craton, *Searching for the Invisible Man: Slaves and Plantation Life in Jamaica* (Cambridge, MA: Harvard University Press, 1978), chapters 2 and 3; and "History of Slaves on York Estate, 1 January 1778," Gale-Morant Papers, 3/c, University of Exeter Library, Devon, England.

37. David Eltis, "The Volume and Structure of the Transatlantic Slave Trade: A Reassessment," *WMQ*, 3rd ser., 58 (2001): 45; and Trevor Burnard and Kenneth Morgan, "The Dynamics of the Slave Market and Slave Purchasing Patterns in Jamaica, 1655–1788," *WMQ*, 3rd ser., 58 (2001): 207–8.

38. Trevor Burnard, "E Pluribus Plures: Ethnicities in Early Jamaica," *Jamaican Historical Review* 21 (2001): 8–22, 56–59.

39. Trevor Burnard, "The Atlantic Slave Trade and African Ethnicities in Seventeenth Century Jamaica," in *Liverpool and Transatlantic Slavery*, ed. David Richardson, Suzanne Schwarz, and Anthony J. Tibbles (Liverpool: Liverpool University Press, 2007), 139–64.

40. "The Account of the Families both whites and Negroes in the Parish of St. John's, Jamaica [ca. 1680]," NA, CO 1/45/109; and T 70/937–942, NA.

41. Burnard and Morgan, "Dynamics of the Slave Market."

42. Burnard, "European Migration to Early Jamaica," 784.

43. Census of 1730—C.0.137/19 (pt.2)/48, NA; Long, *History of Jamaica*, 2:337; Census of 1774—C.0.137/70/88; Census of 1788—C.0.137/87, NA; "Mulattoes, Quads, Negroes able to bear arms," Add. Mss. 12,435, BL, London; St. Andrew Parish Register, 1666–1780, St. Catherine Parish Register, 1667–1764, Manumissions, vols. 5 & 7, JA; Wills, vols. 1–60, IRO; and Kingston Parish Register, 1722–1774, Island Record Office Armoury, Spanish Town, Jamaica.

44. Hans Sloane, *A Voyage to the Islands of Madera, Barbados, Nieves, St. Christopher and Jamaica . . .* , 2 vols. (London: B.M. for the author, 1707), 1:xlvii–lvii; Alison Games, "Migration," in *The British Atlantic World, 1500–1800*, ed. David Armitage and Michael J. Braddick (London: Palgrave Macmillan, 2002), 12; and Richard D. E. Burton, *Afro-Creole: Power, Opposition, and Play in the Caribbean* (Ithaca, NY: Cornell University Press, 1997), 14–15.

45. Higman, *Slave Population*, 70, 144, 274–75.

46. Trevor Burnard, "Et in Arcadia Ego: West Indian Planters in Glory, 1674–1784," *Atlantic Studies* 9 (2012): 24–25.

47. David Eltis, Frank D. Lewis, and David Richardson, "Slave Prices, the African Slave Trade, and Productivity in the Caribbean, 1674–1807," *Economic History Review* 4 (2005): 679. Because the profit per laborer includes children and superannuated slaves, the average purchased laborer probably paid for himself or herself in considerably less than three years. The average cost to maintain a slave was about £5 per annum. Extrapolated from Sheridan, *Doctors and Slaves*, 127–84.

48. Trevor Burnard, "From Periphery to Periphery: The Pennants' Jamaican Plantations, 1771–1812 and Industrialization in North Wales," in *Wales and Empire, 1607–1820*, ed. H. V. Bowen (Manchester: Manchester University Press, 2011), 114–42.

49. AC/WO/16 (7) and (8), Spring Plantation Papers, Ashton Court Papers, Woolnough Papers, Bristol, Archives Office, Bristol. Specific quotes are from Mary Elbridge to Henry Woolnough, 29 June 1739; Elbridge to Woolnough, 22 November 1739; Elbridge to John Elbridge, 29 January 1740; Hibbert and Co. to Sir James Hugh Smyth, 7 March 1788, AC/WO/16 (17) 3, g; and AC/WO/16 (22) a, AC/WO 16 (27) 131 (b).

50. "Quantity of Land Cultivated and in What kind of Manufacture, with

the Number of White Servants, Negroes and Cattle Employed in Each Settlement, Anno 1753," C.O. 137/28/192–96, NA.

51. "A List of Landholders in Jamaica together with the Quantity of Acres of Land each one Possesses, & the Quantity Supposed to be Occupied & Planted," C.O. 142/31, NA, and Long Mss., Add. Mss. 12,436, BL; Thomas Craskell and James Simpson, *The Map of the County of Cornwall in the Island of Jamaica* (London, 1763); Craskell and Simpson, *Map of the County of Middlesex in the Island of Jamaica* (London, 1763); and Craskell and Simpson, *Map of the County of Surry in the Island of Jamaica* (London, 1763).

52. Greene, *Settler Jamaica*, chapter 4; and Ryden, "'One of the Fertilest Pleasantest Spotts.'"

53. David Beck Ryden and Russell R. Menard, "South Carolina's Colonial Land Market: An Analysis of Rural Property Sales, 1720–1775," *Social Science History* 29 (2005): 599–623; and Veront Satchell, *From Plots to Plantation: Land Transactions in Jamaica, 1866–1900* (Kingston: Institute of Social and Economic Research, University of the West Indies, 1990).

54. For technical issues see Robert Margo, "The Rental Price of Housing in New York City, 1830–1860," *Journal of Economic History* 56 (1996): 605–25.

55. W. A. Claypole, "Land Settlement and Agricultural Development on the Liguanea Plains, 1655–1700" (master's thesis, University of the West Indies, Mona, 1973).

56. Trevor Burnard, "A Failed Settler Society: Marriage and Demographic Failure in Early Jamaica," *Journal of Social History* 28 (1994): 63–82.

57. Ryden and Reid, "Sugar, Land Markets, and the Williams Thesis"; Ryden and Menard, "South Carolina's Colonial Land Market"; and H. R. French and R. W. Hoyle, "English Individualism Refuted—and Reasserted: The Land Market of Earls Colne (Essex), 1550–1750" *Economic History Review* 56 (2003): 595–622.

58. Thomas Coke, *A History of the West Indies*, 2 vols. (Liverpool: Nuttall, Fisher & Dixon, 1808), 1:356. On the intensification of commerce between Britain and tropical Latin America, see Jeremy Adelman, *Sovereignty and Revolution in the Iberian Atlantic* (Princeton, NJ: Princeton University Press, 2006). See also Dorothy Burne Goebel, "British Trade to the Spanish Colonies, 1796–1823," *AHR* 43 (1938): 289–94; and Gilbert Farquhar Mathison, *Notices Respecting Jamaica, 1808–1809–1810* (London: J. Stockdale, 1811), 6.

59. Long, *History of Jamaica*, 1:458–62.

60. Ibid.

61. Reid and Ryden, "Sugar, Land Markets, and the Williams Thesis," 405.

62. Trevor Burnard, *Mastery, Tyranny, and Desire: Thomas Thistlewood and His Slaves in the Anglo-Jamaican World* (Chapel Hill: University of North Carolina Press, 2004).

63. Reid and Ryden, "Sugar, Land Markets, and the Williams Thesis," 419.

64. Michael Craton and James Walvin, *A Jamaican Plantation: The History of Worthy Park, 1670–1970* (London: W. H. Allen, 1970).

65. For the 1670s land census see Richard S. Dunn, *Sugar and Slaves: The Rise of the Planter Class in the English West Indies* (Chapel Hill: University of North Carolina Press, 1972). By far the best summary of this intense constitutional battle between Governor Knowles, Kingston merchants, and the Jamaica Assembly is Jack P. Greene, " 'Of Liberty and the Colonies': A Case Study of Constitutional Conflict in the Mid-Eighteenth-Century British American Empire," in *Creating the British Atlantic: Essays on Transplantation, Adaptation, and Continuity* (Charlottesville: University of Virginia Press, 2013), 140–207.

66. "List of Landholders"; Burnard, "Passengers Only"; Greene, *Settler Jamaica*; Long, *History of Jamaica*, 1:459–61; and Ryden, " 'One of the Fertilest, Pleasantest Spotts,' " 41, 44, 48.

67. Burnard and Hart, "Kingston, Jamaica and Charleston, South Carolina."

68. Eltis, Lewis, and Richardson, "Slave Prices, the African Slave Trade, and Productivity in the Caribbean." For a full description of the slave price data see Eltis and Richardson, "Prices of African Slaves Newly Arrived in the Americas, 1673–1865: New Evidence on Long-Run Trends and Regional Differentials," in *Slavery in the Development of the Americas*, ed. David Eltis, Frank D. Lewis, and David Richardson (Cambridge: Cambridge University Press, 2005), 181–218.

69. Eltis, Lewis, and Richardson, "Slave Prices, the African Slave Trade, and Productivity in the Caribbean," 690.

70. Craton, *Searching for the Invisible Man*, chapters 2 and 3.

71. The percentage of children in slave forces between 1715 and 1724 was 28 percent compared to 22 percent between 1775 and 1784.

72. Craton, *Searching for the Invisible Man*, 697–98; J. R. Ward, *British West Indian Slavery, 1750–1834: The Process of Amelioration* (New York: Oxford University Press, 1988), 61–118; David W. Ryden, *West Indian Slavery and British Abolition, 1783–1807* (New York: Cambridge University Press, 2009), 84–92; and Justin Roberts, *Slavery and the Enlightenment in the British Atlantic, 1750–1807* (New York: Cambridge University Press, 2013).

73. Ryden, *West Indian Slavery*, 235.

74. P. J. Mills to John Clark, 1 February 1803, Tharp Papers, R.55.7.128 9 (c) 6 and 7, Cambridge County Record Office. For how slaves were described in inventories see Trevor Burnard, "Collecting and Accounting: Representing Slaves as Commodities in Jamaica, 1674–1784," in *Collecting across Cultures: Material Exchanges in the Early Modern World*, ed. Daniela Bleichmar and Peter C. Mancall (Philadelphia: University of Pennsylvania Press, 2011), 177–91.

75. 17 March 1761, Thomas Thistlewood Diaries, Beinecke Library, Yale University.

76. Trevor Burnard, "Who Bought Slaves in Early America? Purchasers of Slaves from the Royal African Company in Jamaica, 1674–1708," *Slavery and Abolition* 17 (1996): 68–92; Burnard and Morgan, "Dynamics of the Slave Market"; Stephen D. Behrendt, "Ecology, Seasonality, and the Transatlantic

Slaver Trade," in *Soundings in Atlantic History: Latent Structures and Intellectual Currents, 1500–1830,* ed. Bernard Bailyn and Patricia Denault (Cambridge, MA: Harvard University Press, 2009), 44–85; and Will Pettigrew, *Freedom's Debt: Politics and the Escalation of Britain's Transatlantic Slave Trade, 1672–1752* (Chapel Hill: University of North Carolina Press, 2013).

77. Frank Wesley Pitman, *The Development of the British West Indies, 1700–1763* (New Haven, CT: Yale University Press, 1917), 135–36; K. G. Davies, *The Royal African Company* (London: Longmans, 1957), 51, 76; and Eltis, Lewis, and Richardson, "Slave Prices, the African Slave Trade, and Productivity in the Caribbean," 671.

78. J. R. Ward, "The Profitability of Sugar Planting in the British West Indies, 1650–1834," *Economic History Review* 31 (1978): 206; and Ryden, *West Indian Slavery and British Abolition,* 226.

79. Beckfords; History of Slaves on York Estate, 1 January 1778, Gale-Morant Papers; and Inventory of John McLeod, Inventories 1B/11/ 55 /72–76, JA.

80. Philip D. Morgan, *Slave Counterpoint: Black Culture in the Eighteenth-Century Chesapeake and Lowcountry* (Chapel Hill: University of North Carolina Press, 1998), 85–90; Gregory Smithers, "American Abolitionism and Slave-Breeding Discourse: A Re-evaluation," *Slavery and Abolition* 33 (2012): 551–70; and Steven Deyle, *Carry Me Back: The Domestic Slave Trade in American Life* (New York: Oxford University Press, 2005).

81. Kenneth Morgan, "Slave Women and Reproduction in Jamaica, c. 1776–1834," *History* 91 (2006): 231–53.

82. Higman, *Plantation Jamaica,* 238.

83. Ryden, *West Indian Slavery*; J. R. Ward, *British West Indian Slavery, 1750–1834: The Process of Amelioration* (Oxford: Clarendon Press, 1988).

84. Higman, *Plantation Jamaica,* 2.

85. Kenneth Morgan, *The Bright-Meyler Papers: A Bristol–West India Connection, 1732–1837* (Oxford: Oxford University Press, 2007), 99–102, 105–7; S. D. Smith, *Slavery, Family and Gentry Capitalism in the British Atlantic: The World of the Lascelles, 1648–1834* (Cambridge: Cambridge University Press, 2006); and Jacob M. Price, "Credit in the Slave Trade and Plantation Economies," in *Slavery and the Atlantic System,* ed. Barbara L. Solow (Cambridge: Cambridge University Press, 1991), 309.

86. Richard Pares, *War and Trade in the West Indies, 1739–1763* (Oxford, 1936), 84.

87. On the importance of country stores in the Chesapeake see, for example, Ann Smart Martin, *Buying into the World of Goods: Early Consumers in Backcountry Virginia* (Baltimore, MD: Johns Hopkins University Press, 2008).

88. Long, *History of Jamaica,* 2:105.

89. Burnard and Morgan, "Dynamics of the Slave Market."

90. Henry Bright, Kingston, to Richard Meyler II, Bristol, 25 July 1750, in Morgan, *Bright-Meyler Papers,* 226.

91. Daniel Defoe, *Mercator,* nos. 171–3, 24 June-1 July 1714; [Robert Allen],

"An Essay on the Nature and methods of Carrying on a Trade to the South Seas," [1712], Add. Mss. 28,140, f. 24v, BL; and Colin A. Palmer, *Human Cargoes: The British Slave Trade to Spanish America, 1700–1739* (Urbana: University of Illinois Press, 1981), 97–98.

92. Georges Marie Butel-Dumont, *Histoire et commerce des Antilles Angloises* (Paris, 1758), 17.

93. Allan Christelow, "Contraband Trade between Jamaica and the Spanish Main, and the Freeport Act of 1766," *Hispanic American Historical Review* 22 (1942): 309–43; Curtis Nettels, "England and the Spanish-American Trade, 1680–1715," *Journal of Modern History* 3 (1931): 1–32; George H. Nelson, "Contraband Trade under the Asiento, 1730–1739," *AHR* 51 (1945): 55–67; Vera Lee Brown, "South Sea Company and Illicit Trade," *AHR* 31 (1926): 662–78; and Adrian Finucane, *The Temptations of Trade: British Agents in Eighteenth-Century Spanish America* (Philadelphia: University of Pennsylvania, forthcoming). On Gresham's law in Jamaica see Sidney W. Mintz, "Currency Problems in Eighteenth-Century Jamaica and Gresham's Law," in *Process and Pattern in Culture*, ed. Robert A. Manners (Chicago: University of Chicago Press, 1964): 248–65.

94. Testimony of Kender Mason, 14 November 1786, B.T. 5/4/37–8, NA as cited in Adrian J. Pearce, *British Trade with Spanish America, 1763–1808* (Liverpool: Liverpool University Press, 2007): 83.

95. Pearce, *British Trade with Spanish America*, chapter 3.

96. Pearce provides the following estimates for Spanish American trade undertaken from Jamaica: 1679—£20,000; 1690—£100,000; 1707—£275,000; 1713–39—£300,000; 1739–63—£200,000; 1766—£70,000; 1780—£340,000; 1795—£1,000,000; and 1808—£1,576,000. All British trade with Spanish America was between £3,000,000 and £4,000,000 in 1807, or 6 percent of all British exports in that year. Pearce, *British Trade with Spanish America*, chapter 7.

97. Burnard and Hart, "Kingston, Jamaica and Charleston, South Carolina."

98. Naval Officers' Shipping Lists, 1744–46, C.O. 142/15, NA.

99. Noel Deerr, *The History of Sugar* (London: Chapman & Hall, 1949–50), 1:498; and Mario Samper and Radin Fernando, "Historical Statistics of Coffee Production and Trade from 1700 to 1960," in *The Global Coffee Economy in Africa, Asia, and Latin America, 1500–1989*, ed. William Gervase Clarence-Smith and Steven Topik (Cambridge: Cambridge University Press, 2003), 412.

100. Stephen Conway, "'A Joy Unknown for Year's Past': The American War, Britishness and the Celebration of Rodney's Victory at the Saints," *History* 86 (2001): 180–99; and O'Shaughnessy, *An Empire Divided*, 235–37.

CHAPTER FIVE

1. Andrew O'Shaughnessy, *The Men Who Lost America: British Leadership, the American Revolution, and the Fate of Empire* (New Haven, CT: Yale University Press, 2013).

2. Brendan Simms, *Three Victories and a Defeat: The Rise and Fall of the First British Empire, 1714–1783* (London: Penguin, 2007).

3. Emory G. Evans, *A "Topping People": The Rise and Decline of Virginia's Old Political Elite, 1680–1790* (Charlottesville: University of Virginia Press, 2009).

4. Rhys Isaac, *Landon Carter's Uneasy Kingdom: Revolution and Rebellion on a Virginia Plantation* (New York: Oxford University Press, 2004), 299.

5. The extent to which the American Revolution unleashed new democratic forces or was a continuation of patterns already established in the colonies is a perennial issue. For two opposing views see Gordon Wood, *The Radicalism of the American Revolution* (New York: Alfred A. Knopf, 1992); and Michael Zuckerman, "Authority in Early America: The Decay of Deference on the Provincial Periphery," *Early American Studies* 1 (2003): 1–29. On emotion see Sarah Knott, *Sensibility and the American Revolution* (Chapel Hill: University of North Carolina Press, 2009); and Nicole Eustace, *Passion Is the Gale: Emotion, Power, and the Coming of the American Revolution* (Chapel Hill: University of North Carolina Press, 2008).

6. Trevor Burnard, "Freedom, Migration and the Negative Example of the American Revolution: The Changing Status of Unfree Labor in the Second British Empire and the New American Republic," in *Empire and Nation: The American Revolution*, ed. Eliga H. Gould and Peter Onuf (Baltimore, MD: Johns Hopkins University Press, 2005), 295–314. For similar speculations see David Brion Davis, *Inhuman Bondage: The Rise and Fall of Slavery in the New World* (New York: Oxford University Press, 2006), 155.

7. Stephen Conway, " 'A Joy Unknown for Year's Past': The American War, Britishness and the Celebration of Rodney's Victory at the Saints," *History* 86 (2001): 180–99; J. G. A. Pocock, "British History: A Plea for a New Subject: A Reply," *Journal of Modern History* 47 (1975): 627; and P. J. Marshall, *Remaking the British Atlantic: The United States and the British Empire after American Independence* (Oxford: Oxford University Press, 2012), chapter 1.

8. Marshall, *Remaking the British Atlantic*, 16–17; and H. V. Bowen, "British Conceptions of Global Empire, 1756–1783," *Journal of Imperial and Commonwealth History* 26 (1998): 1–27.

9. Bowen, "British Conceptions of Global Empire"; Marshall, *Remaking the British Atlantic*; Nicholas B. Dirks, *The Scandal of Empire: India and the Creation of Imperial Britain* (Cambridge, MA: Harvard University Press, 2009); and Maya Jasanoff, *Liberty's Exiles: American Loyalists in the Revolutionary World* (New York: Alfred A. Knopf, 2011).

10. H. M. Scott, *British Foreign Policy in the Age of the American Revolution* (Oxford: Oxford University Press, 1990); John Sainsbury, *Disaffected Patriots: London Supporters of Revolutionary America, 1769–1782* (Kingston: McGill–Queen's University Press, 1987), 156–60; and Stephen Conway, *The British Isles and the War of American Independence* (Oxford: Oxford University Press, 2000), 252–59.

11. Sam W. Haynes, *The Early Republic in a British World* (Charlottesville:

University of Virginia Press, 2010); Stephen Conway, "From Fellow-Nationals to Foreigners: British Perceptions of the Americans circa 1739–1783," *WMQ*, 3rd ser., 59 (2002): 65–100; Troy Bickham, *Making Headlines: The American Revolution as Seen through the British Press* (DeKalb: Northern Illinois University Press, 2009); and John E. Crowley, *The Privileges of Independence: Neomercantilism and the American Revolution* (Baltimore, MD: Johns Hopkins University Press, 1993).

12. Trevor Burnard, "Powerless Masters: The Curious Decline of Jamaican Sugar Planters in the Foundational Period of British Abolitionism," *Slavery and Abolition* 32 (2011): 185–98; Marshall, *Remaking the British Atlantic*; and C.A. Bayly, *Imperial Meridian: The British Empire and the World, 1780–1830* (London: Longman, 1989). On West Indian protests about the ban on American shipping, see "Memorial and Petition of the Assembly of Jamaica to the King," 4 December 1784, *Journals of the Assembly of Jamaica* (Kingston: Jamaica Assembly, 1805), 8:40–41; and Andrew O'Shaughnessy, *An Empire Divided: The American Revolution and the British Caribbean* (Philadelphia: University of Pennsylvania Press, 2000), 239–40.

13. Deirdre Coleman, *Romantic Colonization and British Anti-Slavery* (Cambridge: Cambridge University Press, 2005), chapter 1; and Alan Frost, *The Global Reach of Empire: Britain's Maritime Expansion in the Indian and Pacific Oceans, 1764–1815* (Melbourne: Miegunyah Press, 2003).

14. [Maurice Morgann], *Plan for the Abolition of Slavery in the West Indies* (London: William Griffin, 1772).

15. Planter [Edward Long], *Candid Reflections Upon the Judgement lately awarded by The Court of King's Bench in Westminster-Hall, on what is commonly called The Negroe-Cause* (London: T. Lowndes, 1772); Samuel Estwick, *Considerations on the Negroe Cause Commonly So Called, Addressed to the Right Honourable Lord Mansfield . . .* , 2nd ed. (London: J. Dodsley, 1773), 4–5; Christopher Brown, "Empire without Slaves: British Concepts of Emancipation in the Age of the American Revolution," *WMQ*, 3rd. ser., 56 (1999) 273–306; Elsa Goveia, *The West Indian Slave Laws of the Eighteenth Century* (Barbados: University of the West Indies Press, 1970), 20–21; and P. J. Marshall, "Empire and Authority in the Later Eighteenth Century," *Journal of Imperial and Commonwealth History* 15 (1987): 105–22.

16. Eliga H. Gould, *Among the Powers of the Earth: The American Revolution and the Making of a New World Empire* (Cambridge, MA: Harvard University Press, 2012); and Christopher Leslie Brown, *Moral Capital: Foundations of British Abolitionism* (Chapel Hill: University of North Carolina Press, 2006).

17. David Brion Davis, *The Problem of Slavery in the Age of Revolution, 1770–1823* (Ithaca, NY: Cornell University Press, 1975); and Christopher Leslie Brown, "The Problems of Slavery," in *The Oxford Handbook of the American Revolution*, ed. Edward G. Gray and Jane Kamensky (New York: Oxford University Press, 2013), 427–46.

18. Sylvia Frey, *Water from the Rock: Black Resistance in a Revolutionary Age* (Princeton, NJ: Princeton University Press, 1991), 45–142; Cassandra Pybus, "Jefferson's Faulty Maths: The Question of Slave Defections in the American Revolution," *WMQ*, 3rd ser., 62 (2005): 243–64; and Philip D. Morgan, "Low Country Georgia and the Early Modern Atlantic," in *African American Life in the Georgia Lowcountry: The Atlantic World and the Gullah Geechee* (Athens: University of Georgia Press, 2010), 36. On the military consequences arising from Lincoln and the Republican Party's commitment to antislavery in the early years of the American Civil War, see James Oakes, *Freedom National: The Destruction of Slavery in the United States, 1861–1865* (New York: W. W. Norton, 2013). See also Alan Taylor, *The Internal Enemy: Slavery and War in Virginia, 1772–1832* (New York: W. W. Norton, 2013).

19. Brown, "The Problems of Slavery," 430–31; Frey, *Water from the Rock*, 89–96, 125–32; O'Shaughnessy, *An Empire Divided*; and James Piecuch, *Three Peoples, One King: Loyalists, Indians, and Slaves in the Revolutionary South, 1775–1782* (Columbia: University of South Carolina Press, 2008), 39–44.

20. Brown, *Moral Capital*, 334–89; Margaret M. R. Kellow, "'We Are No Less Friendly to Liberty than They': British Antislavery Activists Respond to the Crisis in the American Colonies," in *English Atlantics Revisited*, ed. Nancy L. Rhoden (Montreal: McGill–Queens University Press, 2007), 450–73; and Eva Sheppard Wolf, "Manumission and the Two-Race System in Early National Virginia," in *Paths to Freedom: Manumission in the Atlantic World*, ed. Rosemary Brana-Shute and Randy J. Sparks (Columbia: University of South Carolina Press, 2009), 309–37.

21. Bickham, *Making Headlines*, 164–67; Brown, *Moral Capital*, 391–433; James Walvin, *The Zong: A Massacre, the Law and the End of Slavery* (New Haven, CT: Yale University Press, 2011), 153; J. R. Oldfield, *Popular Politics and British Anti-slavery: The Mobilization of Popular Opinion, 1787–1807* (Manchester: Manchester University Press, 1995); Srividhya Swaminathan, "Reporting Atrocities: A Comparison of the *Zong* and the Trial of Captain John Kimber," *Slavery and Abolition* 31 (2010): 483–99; and Seymour Drescher, "The Shocking Birth of British Abolitionism," *Slavery and Abolition* 33 (2012): 572–74, 577–78, 588–89.

22. Gould, *Among the Powers of the Earth*, chapter 2.

23. George Van Cleve, *A Slaveholder's Republic: Slavery, Politics, and the Constitution in Early America* (Chicago: University of Chicago Press, 2010), 57–151; Burnard, "Freedom, Migration, and the Negative Example of the American Revolution"; Ira Berlin, *Many Thousands Gone: The First Two Centuries of Slavery in North America* (Cambridge, MA: Harvard University Press, 1998), 230–39; Richard Follett, *The Sugar Masters: Planters and Slaves in Louisiana's Cane World, 1820–1860* (Baton Rouge: Louisiana State University Press, 2005); and Walter Johnson, *River of Dark Dreams: Slavery and Empire in the Cotton Kingdom* (Cambridge, MA: Harvard University Press, 2013).

24. Michael A. McDonnell, *The Politics of War: Race, Class, and Conflict in Revolutionary Virginia* (Chapel Hill: University of North Carolina Press, 2007).

25. Allan Kulikoff, "Revolutionary Violence and the Origins of American Democracy," *Journal of the Historical Society* 2 (2002): 229–60.

26. O'Shaughnessy, *An Empire Divided*, 137–212; and Piers Mackesy, *The War for America, 1775–1783* (1964; reprint, Lincoln: University of Nebraska Press, 1993), 225–36, 301–37, 446–59. For an argument that the American Revolution was economically disastrous, see Selwyn H. H. Carrington, *The British West Indies during the American Revolution* (Dordrecht: Foris, 1988). For a view that the American Revolution saw temporary economic bliss, not the start of permanent decline, see John J. McCusker, "The Economy of the British West Indies, 1763–1790: Growth, Stagnation, or Decline?" in *Essays on the Economic History of the Atlantic World* (London: Routledge, 1997), 330.

27. Michael Mulcahy, *Hurricanes and Society in the British Greater Caribbean, 1624–1783* (Baltimore, MD: Johns Hopkins University Press, 2006), 165–74.

28. The attempted invasion of Jamaica is not noted in standard accounts of the war, even though the French losses of men to disease were at least as great as their total losses in North America. It is not mentioned, for example, in Kamensky and Gray, *Oxford Handbook of the American Revolution*.

29. Christer Petley, *Slaveholders in Jamaica: Colonial Society and Culture during the Era of Abolition* (London: Pickering & Chatto, 2009); and Nicholas Draper, "The Rise of a New Planter Class? Some Counter-currents from British Guiana and Trinidad, 1807–1834," *Atlantic Studies* 9 (2012): 65–83. See also Herman Merivale, *Lectures on Colonization and Colonies* (London: Longman, 1861).

30. *Morning Chronicle*, 28 May 1787, 11; *London Chronicle*, 20–22 September 1787, cited in Drescher, "The Shocking Birth of British Abolitionism," 583; *TSTDB*; and Richard B. Sheridan, "The Crisis of Slave Subsistence in the British West Indies during and after the American Revolution," *WMQ*, 3rd ser., 33 (1976): 615–41.

31. Walvin, *The Zong*.

32. Ottabah Cuguano, *Thoughts and Sentiments on the Evil and Wicked Traffic of the Commerce of the Human Species* (London, 1787), 111–12.

33. The *Zong* case did not resonate with the general public immediately. It became notorious only after the mobilization of abolitionism, in 1787–88. Drescher, "The Shocking Birth of British Abolitionism," 575–76.

34. In 1788 Clarkson wrote of the *Zong* that it was an event "unparalleled in the memory of man . . . and of so black and complicated a nature, that were it to be perpetuated to future generations . . . it could not possibly be believed." Thomas Clarkson, *Essay on the Slavery and Commerce of the Human Species* (London: J. Philips, 1788), 99. See also John Newton,

Thoughts upon the African Slave Trade (London: J. Buckland and J. Johnson, 1788), 11.

35. Linda Colley, *Britons: Forging the Nation*, 3rd ed (New Haven, CT: Yale University Press, 2009), 350–60; Bayly, *Imperial Meridian*; Conway, *The British Isles and the War for American Independence*; and Dror Wahrman, *The Making of the Modern Self: Identity and Culture in Eighteenth-Century England* (New Haven, CT: Yale University Press, 2004).

36. Dirks, *The Scandal of Empire*, 32–34; and Tillman W. Nechtman, *Nabobs: Empire and Identity in Eighteenth-Century Britain* (Cambridge: Cambridge University Press, 2010).

37. See Emma Christopher, *A Merciless Place: The Lost Story of Britain's Convict Disaster in Africa and How It Led to the Settlement of Australia* (Sydney: Allen & Unwin, 2010); Simon Schama, *Rough Crossings: Britain, the Slaves and the American Revolution* (London: BBC Books, 2006); and Cassandra Pybus, *Epic Journeys of Freedom: Runaway Slaves of the American Revolution and their Global Quest for Liberty* (Boston: Beacon Press, 2006); Jasanoff, *Liberty's Exiles*.

38. Richard Bourke, "Pocock and the Presuppositions of the New British History," *Historical Journal* 53 (2010): 750; and Jasanoff, *Liberty's Exiles*. See also Dane Kennedy, *Islands of White: Settler Society and Culture in Kenya and Southern Rhodesia, 1890–1939* (Durham, NC: Duke University Press, 1987).

39. Mimi Sheller, *Consuming the Caribbean: From Arawaks to Zombies* (London: Routledge, 2003), 114; and Christer Petley, "Gluttony, Excess and the Fall of the Planter Class in the British Caribbean," *Atlantic Studies* 9 (2012): 85–106.

40. P. J. Marshall, "Britain and the World in the Eighteenth Century—II: Britons and Americans," *Transactions of the Royal Historical Society*, 6th ser., 9 (1999): 12.

41. Jeremy Bentham, "The Nonsense upon Stilts" (1792), in *Rights, Representation, and Reform: Nonsense upon Stilts and Other Writings in the French Revolution*, ed. Philip Schofield, Catherine Pease-Watkin, and Cyprian Blamires (Oxford: Oxford University Press, 2002), 330; and [John Lind and Jeremy Bentham], *Answer to the Declaration of the American Congress*, 120.

42. Marshall, *Remaking the British Atlantic*, 70–72; and Linda Colley, "The Apotheosis of George III: Loyalty, Royalty and the British Nation, 1760–1820," *Past & Present* 102 (1984): 94–129.

43. Franklin, *Observations*, 374; and Franklin, "American Discontents," *London Chronicle*, 5–7 January 1768, in *The Papers of Benjamin Franklin*, ed. William B. Willcox, Dorothy W. Bridgwater, Mary L. Hart, Claude A. Lopez, and G. B. Warden (New Haven, CT: Yale University Press, 1972–), 15:12.

44. James Oldham, "New Light on Mansfield and Slavery," *Journal of British Studies* 27 (1988): 45–68.

45. Cited in Eliga H. Gould, "Zones of Law, Zones of Violence: The Legal Geography of the British Atlantic, circa 1772," *WMQ*, 3rd ser., 60 (2003): 506.

46. *London Evening Post*, 23 May 1772.
47. Benjamin Franklin to Anthony Benezet, 22 August 1772, in Labaree, *The Papers of Benjamin Franklin*, 19:269.
48. Daniel J. Hulsebosch, "Nothing but Liberty: *Somerset's* Case and the British Empire," *Law and History Review* 24 (2006): 451.
49. Oldham, "New Light on Mansfield and Slavery;" Oldham, *English Common Law in the Age of Mansfield* (Chapel Hill: University of North Carolina Press, 1992), 305–23; George Van Cleve, "*Somerset's Case* and Its Antecedents in Imperial Perspective," *Law and History Review* 24 (2006): 601–45; David Waldstreicher, *Slavery's Constitution: From Revolution to Ratification* (New York: Hill & Wang, 2009), chapter 1; and Ruth Paley, "Mansfield, Slavery, and the Law in England, 1772–1830," in *Law, Crime and English Society, 1660–1830*, ed. Norma Landau (Cambridge: Cambridge University Press, 2002), 165–84.
50. *Virginia Gazette*, 30 September 1773; Vincent Carretta, *Equiano*, 208–12; Walvin, *The Zong*; and Emma Rothschild, *The Inner Life of Empires: An Eighteenth-Century History* (Princeton, NJ: Princeton University Press, 2011), 91–96.
51. Long, *Candid Reflections*; Estwick, *Considerations on the Negroe Cause*; and Samuel Martin, Sr., *A Short Treatise on the Slavery of Negroes in the British Colonies* (Antigua: Robert Mearns, 1775).
52. Srividhya Swaminathan, "Developing the West Indian Proslavery Position after the Somerset Decision," *Slavery and Abolition* 24 (2003): 40–60; and Swaminathan, *Debating the Slave Trade: Rhetoric of British National Identity, 1759–1815* (Burlington, VT: Ashgate, 2009).
53. Peter S. Onuf, "Federalism, Democracy, and Liberty in the New American Nation," in *Exclusionary Empire: English Liberty Overseas, 1600–1900*, ed. Jack P. Greene (New York: Cambridge University Press, 2010), 155.
54. O'Shaughnessy, *An Empire Divided*, 131–32.
55. Van Cleve, "*Somerset's* Case and Its Antecedents," 627; and Hulsebosch, "Nothing but Liberty," 656.
56. Brown, *Moral Capital*, 93–97; and F. O. Shyllon, *Black Slaves in Britain* (London and New York: Oxford University Press for the Institute of Race Relations, 1974), 82–164. Sharp was not being unduly fearful: proposals to enslave the poor had been reasonably popular in early eighteenth-century Britain. Michael J. Rozbicki, "'To Save Them from Themselves': Proposals to Enslave the British Poor, 1698–1755," *Slavery and Abolition* 22 (2001): 29–50.
57. Alan Taylor, *The Civil War of 1812: American Citizens, American Subjects, Irish Rebels, and Indian Allies* (New York: Alfred A. Knopf, 2010). Historians tend to see the mid-nineteenth-century Civil War less as America's second or third civil war than as the second American Revolution. Eric Foner, *Reconstruction: America's Unfinished Revolution* (New York: Harper & Row, 1988).

58. R. R. Palmer, *The Age of Democratic Revolution: A Political History of Europe and America, 1760–1800* (Princeton, NJ: Princeton University Press, 1959), 1:188; Jerry Bannister and Liam Riordan, eds., *The Loyal Atlantic: Remaking the British Atlantic in the Revolutionary Era* (Toronto: University of Toronto Press, 2012).

59. Thomas Iredell to James Iredell, [ca. 1770]; and Thomas Iredell to James Iredell, 8 January 1775, St. Dorothy, Jamaica, in *The Papers of James Iredell,* vol. 1, 1767–77, ed. Don Higginbotham (Raleigh: North Carolina Division of Archives and History, 1976), 54, 280.

60. Maya Jasanoff, "The Other Side of Revolution: Loyalists in the British Empire," *WMQ*, 3rd ser., 65 (2008): 205–32.

61. Douglas H. Ubelaker, "North American Indian Population Size: Changing Perspectives," in *Disease and Demography in the Americas*, ed. John W. Verara and Ubelaker (Washington, DC: Smithsonian Institution Press, 1992), 173.

62. Samuel Johnson believed both that American republicanism was cant and that American slavery was morally reprehensible. James G. Basker, " 'To the Next Insurrection of the Negroes': Johnson, Race, and Rebellion," *Age of Johnson* 11 (2000): 43–49.

63. The literature on the causes of the revolution in the Chesapeake and the Lower South is vast. Few historians, however, have addressed whether these regions might have stayed loyal. For representative works see Woody Holton, *Forced Founders: Indians, Debtors, Slaves, and the Making of the American Revolution in Virginia* (Chapel Hill: University of North Carolina Press, 1999); John E. Selby, *The Revolution in Virginia, 1775–1783* (Charlottesville: University of Virginia Press, 1988); Rhys Isaac, *The Transformation of Virginia, 1740–1790* (Chapel Hill: University of North Carolina Press, 1982); and Michael A. McDonnell, "A World Turned 'Topsy-Turvy': Robert Munford, *The Patriots*, and the Crisis of the Revolution in Virginia," *WMQ*, 3rd ser., 61 (2004): 235–70. For works on South Carolina and Georgia see Robert Olwell, *Masters, Slaves, and Subjects; The Culture of Power in the South Carolina Low Country, 1740–1790* (Ithaca, NY: Cornell University Press, 1998); Edward Cashin, *Governor Henry Ellis and the Transformation of British North America* (Athens: University of Georgia Press, 1994); Pauline Maier, "The Charleston Mob and the Evolution of Popular Politics in Revolutionary South Carolina, 1765–1784," *Perspectives in American History* 4 (1970): 173–96; and Piecuch, *Three Peoples, One King*.

64. T. R. Clayton, "Sophistry, Security, and Socio-political Structures in the American Revolution; or, Why Jamaica Did Not Rebel," *Historical Journal* 29 (1986): 319–44; and O'Shaughnessy, *An Empire Divided*.

65. Burnard, "Freedom, Migration and the Negative Example of the American Revolution."

66. Ira Berlin, *Generations of Captivity: A History of African-American Slaves* (Cambridge, MA: Harvard University Press, 2003), 97–158; and Douglas R.

Egerton, *Death of Liberty: African Americans and Revolutionary America* (New York: Oxford University Press, 2009).

67. Besides Tacky's, there was a well-developed plot in Antigua in 1736 that was discovered before it was put into action; rebellions in the later 1760s initiated by some of the Jamaican slaves transported after Tacky's Revolt in British Honduras; and several rebellions in Tobago in the 1770s and 1780s. In addition, Black Caribs (free Maroons, closer to Amerindian than to African culture) in St. Vincent engaged in fierce resistance to imperial authority in the ten years after the end of the Seven Years' War. Michael Craton, *Testing the Chains: Resistance to Slavery in the British West Indies* (Ithaca, NY: Cornell University Press, 1982), chapters 10 and 12; David Barry Gaspar, *Bondmen and Rebels: A Study of Master-Slave Relations in Antigua with Implications for Colonial British America* (Baltimore, MD: Johns Hopkins University Press, 1985); and Jack P. Greene, *Evaluating Empire and Confronting Colonialism in Eighteenth-Century Britain* (Cambridge: Cambridge University Press, 2013), 1–19.

68. Philip D. Morgan, *Slave Counterpoint: Black Culture in the Eighteenth-Century Chesapeake and Lowcountry* (Chapel Hill: University of North Carolina Press, 1998), 58–101.

69. Lyttleton's plan echoed the famous "Join or Die" woodcut made by Benjamin Franklin and published in the *Pennsylvania Gazette* on 9 May 1754 in response to the Albany Congress of 1754, where Pennsylvania's Joseph Galloway proposed a plan of union uniting all the colonies of British North America into one body. Franklin depicted eight regions of British North America as a snake cut into segments, making a point about how a unified set of colonies would be stronger than they were at present. Recycled in the lead-up to the Revolution, the cartoon proved a powerful visual commentary on the need for organized action against British ministerial excesses. Gordon S. Wood, *The Americanization of Benjamin Franklin* (New York: Penguin, 2004), 105–52.

70. British ministers saw New England as an exceptional colony characterized by poverty, religious fanaticism, and martial spirit. These prejudices played a significant role in shaping the disastrous implementation of the Coercive Acts in Boston. Julie Flavell, "British Perceptions of New England and the Decision for a Coercive Colonial Policy, 1774–1775," in Julie Flavell and Stephen Conway, *Britain and America Go to War: The Impact of War and Warfare in Anglo-America, 1754–1815* (Gainesville: University Press of Florida, 2004). On the Coercive Acts see David Ammerman, *In the Common Cause: The American Responses to the Coercive Acts of 1774* (Charlottesville: University Press of Virginia, 1974).

71. Richard Walsh, ed., *The Writings of Christopher Gadsen, 1746–1805* (Columbia: University of South Carolina Press, 1966), 93; and William Lyttleton's Speech to the House of Commons, 26 October 1775, in *Proceedings and Debates of the British Parliaments Respecting North America, 1754–1783*, ed.

R. C. Simmons and P. D. G. Thomas (White Plains, NY: Kraus International, 1986), 6:96.

72. Ralph Izard to "A friend in Bath," 27 October 1775, in *Correspondence of Mr. Ralph Izard of South Carolina . . .* , ed. Anne Izard Deas (New York: Charles S. Francis, 1844), 1:135.

73. Lyttleton's motion lost 278 to 108. Frey, *Water from the Rock*, 67.

74. McDonnell, *The Politics of War*, 133–66; and Pybus, "Jefferson's Faulty Math."

75. J. William Harris, *The Hanging of Thomas Jeremiah: A Free Black Man's Encounter with Liberty* (New Haven, CT: Yale University Press, 2009); and William R. Ryan, *The World of Thomas Jeremiah: Charles Town on the Eve of the American Revolution* (New York: Oxford University Press, 2010).

76. Holton, *Forced Founders*; Robert Olwell, " 'Domestick Enemies': Slavery and Political Independence in South Carolina, May 1775-March 1776," *Journal of Southern History* 55 (1989): 21–48. A powerful counterargument that suggests that "excessive emphasis on the racial motive could lead to the erroneous notion that the southern parts of America would not have joined their northern neighbors had the southern peoples been as predominantly white as those in the middle or New England provinces" is found in Higginbotham, "Some Reflections on the South in the American Revolution," 662.

77. Berlin, *Generations of Captivity*, 99.

78. Laurent Dubois, *Avengers of the New World: The Story of the Haitian Revolution* (Cambridge, MA: Harvard University Press, 2004), 3.

79. David Geggus, "The Enigma of Jamaica in the 1790s: New Light on the Causes of Slave Rebellions, *WMQ*, 3rd ser., 44 (1987): 274–99; Egerton, *Death or Liberty*, 60–61, 79–80; Mathew Mulcahy, *Hurricanes and Society in the British Greater Caribbean, 1624–1783* (Baltimore, MD: Johns Hopkins University Press, 2006), 110–19; and Berlin, *Generations of Captivity*, 111–40.

80. William Dickson, *Letters on Slavery* (London: J. Phillips, 1789), 93, 107.

81. *The Humble Petition and Memorial of the Assembly of Jamaica to the King's Most Excellent Majesty in Council* (Philadelphia: William and Thomas Bradford, 1774).

82. 7–9 October 1762, *JAJ*, 5:352–53; and Nicholas Bourke, *The Privileges of the Island of Jamaica Vindicated* (Kingston: A. Aikman, 1765).

83. Amanda Thornton, "Coerced Care: Thomas Thistlewood's Account of Medical Practice on Enslaved Populations in Colonial Jamaica, 1751–1786," *Slavery and Abolition* 32 (2011): 543, 550, 553, 557n67.

84. Bryan Edwards, *The History, Civil and Commercial, of the British West Indies*, 5 vols. (London: Stockdale, 1794), 2:169–70.

85. Claudius Fergus, " 'Dread of Insecurity': Abolitionism, Labor, and Security in Britain's West Indian Colonies, 1760–1823," *WMQ*, 3rd ser., 66 (2009): 757–80.

86. Craton, *Testing the Chains*, 81–98.
87. J. R. McNeill, *Mosquito Empires: Ecology and War in the Greater Caribbean, 1620–1914* (New York: Cambridge University Press, 2010).
88. Burnard, *Mastery, Tyranny, and Desire*, 94.
89. Isaac de Pinto, *Letters on the American Troubles*, trans. from the French (London: John Boosey & John Forbes Hackney, 1776), 35–46, 72, 83.
90. Emory G. Evans, *A "Topping People": The Rise and Decline of Virginia's Old Political Elite, 1680–1780* (Charlottesville: University of Virginia Press, 2009), 111–16.
91. George Metcalf, *Royal Government and Political Conflict in Jamaica, 1729–1783* (London: Longman, 1965), 167.
92. T. G. Burnard, "'Prodigious Riches': The Wealth of Jamaica before the American Revolution," *Economic History Review* 54 (2001): 506–24; and B. W. Higman, *Plantation Jamaica, 1750–1850: Capital and Control in a Colonial Economy* (Kingston: University of the West Indies Press, 2005), 1–6.
93. Julie Flavell, *When London Was Capital of America* (New Haven, CT: Yale University Press, 2010), 21–23, 249–50; and Andrew O'Shaughnessy, "The West India Interest and the Crisis of American Independence," in *West Indies Accounts: Essays on the History of the British Caribbean and the Atlantic Economy in Honour of Richard Sheridan*, ed. Roderick A. McDonald (Kingston: University of the West Indies Press, 1996), 126.
94. S. Max Edelson, *Plantation Enterprise in Colonial South Carolina* (Cambridge, MA: Harvard University Press, 2006); and Joyce B. Chaplin, *An Anxious Pursuit: Agricultural Innovation and Modernity in the Lower South, 1730–1815* (Chapel Hill: University of North Carolina Press, 1993).
95. Russell R. Menard, "Financing the Lowcountry Export Boom: Capital and Growth in Early South Carolina," *WMQ*, 3rd ser., 51 (1994): 659–76.
96. The interior tended toward Loyalism, making the relatively large number of whites in South Carolina on the eve of the Revolution more a barrier to independence than a source of strength. In this way ordinary whites in South Carolina were different from ordinary whites in Virginia, where support for independence was more widespread. Holton, *Forced Founders*. Historians tend to think that the British southern strategy of cultivating the support of southern Loyalists was a sound one. Piecuch, *Three Peoples, One King*; Robert Stansbury Lambert, *Southern Loyalists in the American Revolution* (Columbia: University of South Carolina Press, 1987).
97. McNeill, *Mosquito Empires*, 209–19.
98. In 1769 the South Carolina Assembly gave a large monetary gift to the radical British politician John Wilkes. By voting money to support a radical opponent of the Crown in Britain, the Assembly showed its support for such actions in the colonies. It was also stating that it was not only New England that could engage in radical action. Jack P. Greene, "Bridge to Revolution: The Wilkes Fund Controversy in South Carolina, 1769–75," *Journal of Southern History* 29 (1963): 19–52.

99. Ibid., 51.
100. O'Shaughnessy, *An Empire Divided*, 131.
101. Richard R. Beeman, *The Varieties of Political Experience in Eighteenth-Century America* (Philadelphia: University of Pennsylvania Press, 2004), 127–56.
102. Paul M. Pressly, *On the Rim of the Caribbean: Colonial Georgia and the British Atlantic World* (Athens: University of Georgia Press, 2013), 215–27; Kenneth Coleman, *American Revolution in Georgia, 1763–1789* (Athens: University of Georgia Press, 1958; Chaplin, *An Anxious Pursuit*, 277–80; and Jack P. Greene, "Early Modern Southeastern North America and the Broader Atlantic," *Journal of Southern History* 73 (2007): 536.
103. Rebecca Starr, *A School for Politics: Commercial Lobbying and Political Culture in Early South Carolina* (Baltimore, MD: Johns Hopkins University Press, 1998), 73–80, 148–58.
104. South Carolina was different from Jamaica in that by the 1760s it had a naturally increasing slave population. It was no longer dependent on the Atlantic slave trade and thus had more freedom of action than did Jamaica, where the slave trade was vital to its economy. Morgan, *Slave Counterpoint*, 82–84. Nevertheless, even though South Carolina and Georgia were able to cope (just) without access to fresh slaves from Africa in the War for Independence, they remained as devoted to the institution as Jamaicans. The Revolution merely interrupted, rather than stopped, a veritable orgy of African slave trading. See Ira Berlin and Ronald Hoffman, eds., *Slavery and Freedom in the Age of the American Revolution* (Charlottesville: University of Virginia Press, 1983), 49–171.
105. Harris, *The Hanging of Thomas Jeremiah*; Olwell, "'Domestick Enemies;' and Burnard, "Freedom, Migration and the Negative Example of the American Revolution."
106. On the central role of colonial elites in developing revolutionary ideology and practice, see Gordon S. Wood, *The Radicalism of the American Revolution* (New York: Alfred A. Knopf, 1992); and Bernard Bailyn, *The Ideological Origins of the American Revolution* (Cambridge, MA: Harvard University Press, 1967). On stimulating explications of the assumptions behind eighteenth-century colonial American politics and the role that ordinary white men played, see Barbara Clark Smith, *The Freedoms We Lost: Consent and Resistance in Revolutionary America* (New York: The New Press, 2010); and Michal Jan Rozbicki, *Culture and Liberty in the Age of the American Revolution* (Charlottesville: University Press of Virginia, 2011).
107. Smith, *The Freedoms We Lost*, ix–x, xii, 18–46.
108. Edwards, *History, Civil and Commercial*, 3:7; Trevor Burnard, *Mastery, Tyranny, and Desire: Thomas Thistlewood and His Slaves in the Anglo-Jamaican World* (Chapel Hill: University of North Carolina Press, 2004), 70; Charles Andrews and Evangeline Walker Andrews, *Journal of a Lady of Quality, Being the Narrative of a Journey from Scotland to the West Indies, North Carolina, and Portugal in the years 1774 to 1776* (New Haven, CT: Yale University

Press, 1923), 53–54; Benjamin Carp, *Rebels Rising: Cities and the American Revolution* (New York: Oxford University Press, 2007), 168.

109. Michael Zuckerman, "Authority in Early America: The Decay of Deference on the Provincial Periphery," *Early American Studies* 1 (2003): 1–29; Richard R. Beeman, "Deference, Republicanism, and the Emergence of Popular Politics in Eighteenth-Century America," *WMQ*, 3rd ser., 49 (1992): 401–30; McDonnell, *The Politics of War*, chapter 4; and Smith, *The Freedoms We Lost*, chapter 5.

110. Richard Walsh, *Charleston's Sons of Liberty: A Study of the Artisans, 1763–1789* (Columbia: University of South Carolina Press, 1959).

111. Allan Kulikoff, *From British Peasants to Colonial American Farmers* (Chapel Hill: University of North Carolina Press, 2000), 290; Michael A. McDonnell, "The Struggle Within: Class Politics on the Eve of Independence," in Kamensky and Gray, *Oxford Handbook of the American Revolution*, 103–20; and Marjoleine Kars, *Breaking Loose; The Regulator Rebellion in Pre-revolutionary North Carolina* (Chapel Hill: University of North Carolina Press, 2002).

112. Allan Kulikoff, "'Such Things Ought Not to Be': The American Revolution and the First National Great Depression," in *The World of the Revolutionary American Republic: Expansion, Conflict, and the Struggle for a Continent*, ed. Andrew Shankman (Routledge: New York, 2014), 134–64.

113. Trevor Burnard and John Garrigus, *The Plantation Machine: Wealth and Belonging in British Jamaica and French Saint-Domingue, 1748–1788* (New York: Oxford University Press, forthcoming); David Lambert, *White Creole Culture, Politics and Identity during the Age of Abolition* (Cambridge: Cambridge University Press, 2005); and Piecuch, *Three Peoples, One King*.

114. Piecuch, *Three Peoples, One King*, 2–24, 331; and Rachel N. Klein, *Unification of a Slave State: The Rise of the Planter Class in the South Carolina Backcountry, 1760–1808* (Chapel Hill: University of North Carolina Press, 1990), 107. The narrative about Loyalists was established first in David Ramsay, *The History of the Revolution of South-Carolina, from a British Province to an Independent State* (Trenton, NJ: Isaac Collins, 1785). Modern treatments of Loyalists that repeat Ramsay's claims include Paul David Nelson, "British Conduct of the Revolutionary War: A Review of Interpretations," *Journal of American History* 65 (1976): 628; and Mackesy, *War for America*, 36.

115. Cited in Piecuch, *Three Peoples, One King*, 330.

116. Cited in Holton, *Forced Founders*, 149, 158–59.

117. McDonnell, *The Politics of War*, chapter 5, quotation at 153.

118. Philip D. Morgan and Andrew O'Shaughnessy, "The Arming of Slaves During the American Revolution," in *The Arming of Slaves: Classical Times to the Modern Age*, ed. Philip D. Morgan and Christopher Leslie Brown (New Haven, CT: Yale University Press, 2007), 180–208.

119. Brown, "The Problems of Slavery," in Kamensky and Gray, *Oxford Handbook of the American Revolution*, 423–30; Philip D. Morgan, "Lowcountry Georgia and the Early Modern Atlantic World, 1733–ca. 1820," in *African American*

Life in the Georgian Lowcountry: The Atlantic World and the Gullah Geecher, ed. Philip D. Morgan (Athens: University of Georgia Press, 2010), 13–47; and Klein, *Unification of a Slave State,* 104–8.

120. Kathleen DuVal, *The Dangers of Independence: The American Revolution in the Gulf Coast* (New York: Random House, 2014).

121. Duval, "Independence for Whom? Expansion and Conflict in the South and Southwest," in Shankman, *The World of the Revolutionary American Republic,* 98, 104–5.

122. James Sidbury, *Ploughshares into Swords: Race, Rebellion, and Identity in Gabriel's Virginia, 1730–1810* (Cambridge: Cambridge University Press, 1997); Henry Wiencek, *An Imperfect God: George Washington, His Slaves and the Creation of America* (New York: Farrar, Strauss & Giroux, 2003).

123. Gary B. Nash, "Sparks from the Altar of '76: International Repercussions and Reconsiderations of the American Revolution," in Armitage and Subrahmanyam, *The Age of Revolutions in Global Context,* 1–19.

124. François Furstenberg, "Beyond Freedom and Slavery: Autonomy, Virtue and Resistance in Early American Political Discourse," *Journal of American History* 89 (2003): 1295–1330. For a West Indian example of sympathy for a tortured slave see Bryan Edwards, "Stanzas, Occasioned by the Death of Alico, an African Slave, Condemned for Rebellion in Jamaica, 1760," *Poems Written Chiefly in the West Indies* (Kingston: Alexander Aikman, 1792), 38.

125. Rozbicki, *Culture and Liberty.*

126. Estwick, *Considerations on the Negroe Cause,* 82.

127. Peter Onuf, "Federalism, Democracy, and Liberty in the New American Nation," in Greene, *Exclusionary Empire,* 153–59; Matthew Mason, *Slavery and Politics in the Early American Republic* (Chapel Hill: University of North Carolina Press, 2006); and Van Cleve, *A Slaveholders' Union.*

128. David Brion Davis, "American Slavery and the American Revolution ," in *Slavery and Freedom in the Age of the American Revolution,* ed. Ira Berlin and Ronald Hoffman (Urbana: University of Illinois Press, 1983), 283–301; Van Cleve, *A Slaveholder's Union*; and Christopher Tomlins, *Freedom Bound: Law, Labor, and Civic Identity in Colonizing America, 1580–1865* (New York: Cambridge University Press, 2010), chapter 10.

129. Christer Petley, "'Home' and 'This Country': Britishness and Creole Identity in the Letters of a Transatlantic Slaveholder," *Atlantic Studies* 6 (2009): 43–61.

130. Mark A. Grabner, *Dred Scott and the Problem of Constitutional Evil* (Cambridge: Cambridge University Press, 2006).

131. Piers Mackesy, *The War for America, 1775–1783* (Lincoln: University of Nebraska Press, 1964).

EPILOGUE

1. Joel Mokyr, *The Enlightened Economy: Britain and the Industrial Revolution, 1700–1850* (New Haven, CT: Yale University Press, 2009); John Darwin,

Unfinished Empire: The Global Expansion of Britain (London: Penguin, 2012), 158–78; and Darwin, *The Empire Project: The Rise and Fall of the British World-System, 1830–1970* (Cambridge: Cambridge University Press, 2009), chapter 3.

2. For a stimulating essay that looks at the value of empire from the view of the British political nation, see Jacob M. Price, "Who Cared about the Colonies? The Impact of the Thirteen Colonies on British Politics and Society," in *Strangers in the Realm: Cultural Margins of the British Empire*, ed. Bernard Bailyn and Philip D. Morgan (Chapel Hill: University of North Carolina Press, 1991), 395–436.

3. Richard Sheridan, "The Wealth of Jamaica in the Eighteenth Century," *Economic History Review* 18 (1965): 292–311; and Robert Paul Thomas, "The Sugar Colonies of the Old Empire: Profit or Loss for Great Britain," *Economic History Review* 21 (1968): 30–45.

4. P. J. Cain and A. G. Hopkins, "Gentlemanly Capitalism and British Expansion Overseas I: The Old Colonial System, 1688–1850," *Economic History Review* 39 (1986): 501–25; Patrick K. O'Brien, "Central Government and the Economy, 1688–1815," in *The Economic History of Britain since 1700*, ed. Roderick Floud and Donald McCloskey, 2nd ed., 3 vols. (Cambridge: Cambridge University Press, 1994), 1:205–41; S. D. Smith, *Slavery, Family and Gentry Capitalism in the British Atlantic: The World of the Lascelles, 1648–1834* (Cambridge: Cambridge University Press, 2006), 9; and H. V. Bowen, *The Business of Empire: The East India Company and Imperial Britain, 1756–1833* (Cambridge: Cambridge University Press, 2006).

5. Nicholas Draper, *The Price of Emancipation: Slave-ownership, Compensation, and British Society at the End of Slavery* (Cambridge: Cambridge University Press, 2010), 275; and Legacies of British Slaveownership, http://www.ucl.ac.uk/lbs.

6. Draper, *The Price of Emancipation*.

7. Ibid., 386.

8. Ibid.

9. Thomas C. Holt, *The Problem of Freedom: Race, Labor, and Politics in Jamaica and Britain, 1832–1938* (Baltimore, MD: Johns Hopkins University Press, 1992).

10. Trevor Burnard, "Slave Naming Patterns: Onomastics and the Taxonomy of Race in Eighteenth-Century Jamaica," *Journal of Interdisciplinary History* 31 (2001): 325–46.

11. Jean Fouchard, *The Haitian Maroons: Liberty or Death* (New York: Edward W. Blyden Press, 1981), 41.

12. Philip D. Morgan, "Slaves and Livestock in Eighteenth-Century Jamaica: Vineyard Pen, 1750–1751," *WMQ* 52 (1995): 47–76.

13. [Benjamin Franklin], *Plain Truth, or Serious Considerations on the Present State of the City of Philadelphia and Province of Pennsylvania* (Philadelphia: B. Franklin, 1747), 13–14.

14. Ibid. On the relationship between the growth of democratic institutions in the English-speaking world, see Jack P. Greene, ed., *Exclusionary Empire: English Liberty Overseas, 1600–1900* (New York: Cambridge University Press, 2010).

15. Daniel Defoe, *Colonel Jack*, ed. Samuel Holt Monk (1722; New York: Oxford University Press, 1989), 128, 133.

16. Kathleen M. Brown, *Good Wives, Nasty Wenches, and Anxious Patriarchs: Gender, Race, and Power in Colonial Virginia* (Chapel Hill: University of North Carolina Press, 2006), 319, 321, 323.

17. Natalie A. Zacek, " 'Banes of Society' and "Gentlemen of Strong Natural Parts': Attacking and Defending West Indian Creole Masculinity," in *New Men: Manliness in Early America*, ed. Thomas A. Foster (New York: New York University Press, 2011), 116–33; Christer Petley, "Gluttony, Excess and the Fall of the Planter Class in the British Caribbean," *Atlantic Studies* 9 (2012): 85–106; and Trevor Burnard, "Powerless Masters: The Curious Decline of Jamaican Sugar Planters in the Foundational Period of British Abolitionism," *Slavery and Abolition* 32 (2011): 185–98.

18. Joan Dayan, *Haiti, History, and the Gods* (Berkeley and Los Angeles: University of California Press, 1995), 213–14; and James Ramsay, "Motives for the Improvement of the Sugar Colonies," Add. Mss. 27261, BL, ff. 44, 69.

19. Guillaume Thomas Raynal, *Histoire philosophique et politique des éstablisse-ments et du commerce des Européens dans les Deux Indes* (Geneva: J. Pellet, 1780), 3:204–5.

20. Trevor Burnard, *Mastery, Tyranny, and Desire: Thomas Thistlewood and His Slaves in the Anglo-Jamaican World* (Chapel Hill: University of North Carolina Press, 2004), 21.

21. Edward Long, *History of Jamaica . . .* , 3 vols. (London: T. Lowndes, 1774), 2:262–65; and Charles Leslie, *A New and Exact Account of Jamaica* (Edinburgh: R. Fleming, [ca. 1740]), 319.

22. William Wirt, *Sketches of the Life and Character of Patrick Henry* (Philadelphia: James Webster, 1818), 123.

23. Bryan Edwards, *Poems, Written Chiefly in the West Indies* (Kingston: Alexander Aikman, 1792), 37.

24. Betty Wood, "The Origins of Slavery," in Burnard and Heuman, *The Routledge History of Slavery*, 69; Winthrop D. Jordan, *White over Black: American Attitudes towards the Negro, 1550–1812* (Chapel Hill: University of North Carolina Press, 1968); and Michael Guasco, *Slaves and Englishmen: Human Bondage in the Early Modern World* (Philadelphia: University of Pennsylvania Press, 2014), 119.

25. Christopher Tomlins, "Law's Wilderness: The Discourse of English Coloniz-ing, the Violence of Intrusion, and the Failures of American History," in *New World Orders: Violence, Sanction, and Authority in the Colonial Americas*, ed. John Smolenski and Thomas J. Humphrey (Philadelphia: University of Pennsylvania Press, 2005), 37–40.

26. Michael Craton, "Hobbesian or Panglossian? The Two Extremes of Slave Conditions in the British Caribbean, 1783–1834," *WMQ*, 3rd ser., 35 (1978): 324–56.

27. Trevor Burnard, "British West Indies and Bermuda," in *The Oxford Handbook of Slavery in the Americas*, ed. Robert L. Paquette and Mark M. Smith (New York: Oxford University Press, 2010), 143; Burnard, *Mastery, Tyranny, and Desire*, 178–79; and Vincent Brown, "Spiritual Terror and Sacred Authority in Jamaican Slave Society," *Slavery and Abolition* 24 (2003): 27–29.

28. Orlando Patterson, *Slavery and Social Death: A Comparative Study* (Cambridge, MA: Harvard University Press, 1982). See Herman Bennett, "Genealogies to a Past: Africa, Ethnicity, and Marriage in Seventeenth-Century Mexico," in *New Studies in the History of American Slavery*, ed. Edward E. Baptist and Stephanie M. H. Camp (Athens: University of Georgia Press, 2006), 127–47; and Vincent Brown, "Social Death and Political Life in the Study of Slavery," *AHR* 114 (2009): 1231–49.

29. Brown, "Social Death and Political Life," 1248.

30. Judith Lewis Herman, *Trauma and Recovery: The Aftermath of Violence, from Domestic Abuse to Political Terror* (New York: Basic Books, 1992). Nell Painter describes the process memorably as soul-murder. Nell Irvin Painter, *Southern History across the Color Line* (Chapel Hill: University of North Carolina Press, 2002), chapter 1.

31. Primo Levi, *The Drowned and the Saved*, trans. Raymond Rosenthal (London: Abacus, 1988).

APPENDIX

1. John J. McCusker, *How Much Is That in Real Money? A Historical Commodity Price Index for Use as a Deflator of Money Values in the Economy of the United States*, 2nd ed. (Worcester, MA: American Antiquarian Society, 2001), 246–54.

2. Gloria L. Main, "Probate Records as a Source for Early American History," *WMQ*, 3rd ser., 32 (1975): 85–99.

3. Trevor Burnard, "Collecting and Accounting: Representing Slaves as Commodities in Jamaica, 1674–1784," in *Collecting across Cultures: Material Exchanges in the Early Modern World*, ed. Daniela Bleichmar and Peter C. Mancall (Philadelphia: University of Pennsylvania Press, 2011), 177–91.

4. Trevor Burnard, *Creole Gentlemen: The Maryland Elite, 1691–1776* (New York: Routledge, 2002).

Index

Page numbers in italics refer to illustrations.

Lightning Source UK Ltd.
Milton Keynes UK
UKHW010712170219
337440UK00001B/2/P